TERRORISM ON TRIAL

T0386061

TERRORISM
Political Violence and
ON TRIAL
Abolitionist Futures

NICOLE NGUYEN

University of Minnesota Press | Minneapolis | London

Published by the University of Minnesota Press
111 Third Avenue South, Suite 290
Minneapolis, MN 55401–2520
http://www.upress.umn.edu

ISBN 978-1-5179-1438-7 (hc)
ISBN 978-1-5179-1439-4 (pb)

A Cataloging-in-Publication record for this book is available from the Library of Congress.

Printed in the United States of America on acid-free paper

The University of Minnesota is an equal-opportunity educator and employer.

CONTENTS

ACKNOWLEDGMENTS

The idea for this book has been years in the making; I am grateful to all those who supported its development by showing me that another world is possible. Although this book examines terrorism trials, it also tells the stories of those charged, prosecuted, and often convicted of terrorism-related crimes. I hope I have told these stories with the care they deserve, knowing that they capture only one dimension of people's lives: their experiences with the criminal-legal system. Their families, and the love they share, inspired this book and informed my thinking on bringing abolition to the global war on terror.

Coconspirators across the globe offered intellectual engagement and encouragement. I especially thank Andy Clarno, Dan Cohen, Christy Darcangelo, Julia Dratel, Beyhan Farhadi, Alice Huff, Nausheen Husain, Olivia Ildefonso, Emily Kaufman, Amrit Kaur, Elizabeth Kubis, Pauline Lipman, Nadine Naber, Eric Nguyen, Marlynne Nishimura, A. Naomi Paik, Cecily Relucio, Aja Reynolds, Atef Said, Megan Scanlon, Debbie Southorn, and David Stovall. Lisa Hajjar and Sherene Razack offered constructive feedback that sharpened my thinking. L. Boyd Bellinger's masterful editing made this book possible. Nico Darcangelo and Jennifer Reynolds provided substantial research support. My students continue to share their joy, brilliance, and wisdom, all of which have shaped this book. I am appreciative of the Vigilant Love community for the constant support, sharp analysis, and incisive jokes, including Mehak Anwar, traci ishigo, Sahar Pirzada, Celine Qussiny, and Yazan Zahzah.

I wrote this book at the same time I began volunteering with the Forest Preserve District of Cook County, and I owe a debt of gratitude to Ren Dean, Dona Denson, Mat Goertel, Gloria Orozco, Alex Peimer, June Webb, and all those whose lifelong learning, curiosity, and personal growth have brought me such pleasure and fulfillment.

At the University of Minnesota Press, I thank editorial director Jason Weidemann for continuing to believe in me as a writer and thinker. I am grateful for editorial assistant Zenyse Miller and the many others who worked hard to finish this book.

I am appreciative of the administrative staff at the University of Illinois Chicago, especially Maria De La Paz, whose invisible labor made this book possible.

And finally, many thanks to Azalea and Eleanor, who keep my heart full.

Introduction

CONVICTING DETAINEE #001
LOCATING THE COURTS IN THE GLOBAL WAR ON TERROR

In May 2019, John Walker Lindh was released from federal prison after serving seventeen years for terrorism-related crimes. Nicknamed the "American Taliban" and officially listed as Detainee #001 in the global war on terror, Lindh was captured in November 2001 by Northern Alliance forces soon after the United States invaded Afghanistan. In July 2002, Lindh pleaded guilty to charges brought by the U.S. government, including "supplying services to the Taliban" and "carrying an explosive during the commission of a felony."[1] United States Attorney Paul McNulty described Lindh's conviction as a global war on terror victory, explaining, "Today's sentence proves that the American criminal justice system is a powerful and effective tool in America's struggle against terrorism" (qtd. in Candiotti 2002). For McNulty and others, domestic courts have played a vital role in the global war on terror.

Citing national security concerns, political leaders expressed fierce opposition to Lindh's 2019 release. Secretary of State Mike Pompeo described the release of Lindh as an "unexplainable and unconscionable decision" (qtd. in Montanaro 2019). Congressman Bradley Byrne (R-Ala.) similarly challenged Lindh's release, stating, "If you're convicted of a crime of terrorism, you don't get out of jail. You're there forever because terrorism strikes at the very basis of civilized society. We can't let these people continue to do what they're doing. We need to take them out of society altogether and not let them back in" (qtd. in Kraychik 2019).

Byrne's provocative assertion aligns with the legal finding that "even terrorists with no prior criminal behavior are unique among criminals in the likelihood of recidivism, the difficulty of rehabilitation, and the need for incapacitation."[2] Integrating both criminological thinking and military doctrine, this incapacitation strategy assumes that certain defendants are "beyond rehabilitation and redemption," thereby necessitating long, if not indefinite, prison sentences to prevent future crimes or acts of war (Kaiser and Hagan 2018, 314).

In the years leading up to Lindh's release, national security agencies speculated that individuals convicted of terrorism-related crimes "will probably reengage in terrorist activity," giving rise to the specter of "terrorist recidivism" (National Counterterrorism Center 2017, 1). Given the lack of scientific evidence to support such a claim, security professionals have inferred that the "high rate of recidivism among those who are incarcerated for non–terrorism related criminal activity" means "the likelihood of violent extremism recidivism is also high" (1). Such inferences have reinvigorated incapacitation practices through prolonged or indefinite detention in federal prisons and military facilities. Despite these predictions, none of the 465 post–September 11 terrorism defendants released before Lindh ever reoffended (McKelvey 2019). Such statistics "suggest that convicted terrorists can be rehabilitated completely after relatively brief sentences or that many of these people weren't particularly dangerous in the first place" (Aaronson qtd. in McKelvey 2019). Reflecting on his own clients, one defense attorney explained that terrorist recidivism "is not a thing because the conduct was not part of a criminal lifestyle. It was more of a politically motivated offense" (interview, November 2020). Even though terrorist recidivism remains negligible, the impetus to control, incapacitate, or eliminate perceived enemies of the state persists, such that many legal thinkers and military strategists support long prison terms to inhibit the return of soldiers to the front lines of the endless global war on terror or to communities across the United States.

Consonant with military and police strategists, some scholars and practitioners support expanding the legal tools used to fight the global war on terror. Legal scholar Brian Comerford (2005), for example, contends that for the rule of law "to be successful in fighting the war on terror," federal prosecutors "must be equipped with adequate tools to *prevent* acts of terrorism and respond to *all* terrorist threats" (724). Attorneys Richard B. Zabel and James J. Benjamin Jr. (2008) similarly argue that "prosecuting terrorism defendants in the court system appears as a general matter to lead to just, reliable results and not cause serious security breaches or other problems that threaten the nation's security," making the criminal-legal system an "effective means of convicting and incapacitating terrorists" (2). Despite these endorsements, others object to converting the rule of law and its enforcement in domestic courtrooms into effective weapons of war. For example, one criminal defense attorney explained that adjudicating armed struggles is "*well* outside the scope of the judicial system in the United States," yet since the September 11 attacks, the judicial system has "found itself swept up in the geopolitical direction and strategy of the U.S. government." For this attorney, terrorism-related cases "are all about politics," meaning the U.S. security state has sought to align its judicial system with its geopolitical agenda as armed groups engage in violent struggles for alternative forms of governance after "a lifetime of politics, of pain, of passion" (interview, March 2021). Although the role of the criminal-legal system and its status as a legitimate weapon of war have evolved over time, the courts consistently have adjudicated terrorism-related cases and regulated executive wartime powers, even if in sometimes contradictory and conflicted ways.

Despite the centrality of the courts in the global war on terror, social scientists have yet to more extensively examine the judicial system as a "counterterrorism tool" that can incapacitate terrorists, reinforce the perceived necessity of national security operations, and circulate particular interpretations of prevailing geopolitical conflicts (Office of Public Affairs 2010). Put differently, social scientists have not yet investigated how the courts' getting "swept up" in the global war on terror has shaped the daily work of legal actors and the lives of their clients. Most research studies on the prosecution of terrorism-related crimes have focused on the legal issues these cases have raised, the criminal-legal system's accommodation of national security priorities, and the use of the law as a weapon of war (Said 2015; Ahmed 2017; Engle 2004; Szpunar 2017). The judge presiding over Lindh's case, for example, examines how "national security cases present challenging problems for federal courts," such as the use of classified information in discovery, the inclusion of evidence obtained through torture conducted outside of the United States, and the defendant's entitlement to lawful combatant immunity (Ellis 2013, 1607). Law professor Wadie E. Said (2015) explores how terrorism prosecutions have an "outsize influence and effect on criminal law and procedure, despite the relatively small number of such prosecutions" (46). These "distorting effects" on the criminal-legal system include the use of preventative tactics that criminalize and prosecute "highly inchoate activity that may never result in illegality, as well as construct political activism as suspicious and potentially subversive" (4). These academic interventions provide important insight into the legal challenges raised in national security cases and how terrorism prosecutions have shaped the broader criminal-legal system. Although critical to understanding the role of the judicial system in the global war on terror, these legal approaches often forgo sociological, geographical, and anthropological analyses of terrorism prosecutions and deeper explorations of the form and content of these proceedings.

To understand the relationship between law and violence, we must consider "not only the ways in which laws are made, used, enforced, and violated but also the ways in which ideas and discourses of legality and justice inform people's consciousness and activities and pursuit of their rights, however those rights are constructed" (Hajjar 2005, 248). Understanding the role of the judicial system in the global war on terror requires investigating the daily practices of legal actors and the discourses, narratives, and logics they reach for to argue, defend, and make sense of the cases before them. Attorney Agatha Koprowski (2011), for example, identifies how judicial opinions often reinforce "negative stereotypes about Muslims" and sustain "a monolithic image of Islam that is generally fanatical, foreign, and intolerant," forms of race thinking that lead to unfavorable outcomes for Muslim litigants (184–85). Given the significant role of judges in adjudicating terrorism-related cases, as well as the "popular misconceptions about Islam" that inform judicial opinions, one terrorism lawyer described how criminal defense attorneys must confront "the Muslim bias" in terrorism cases through strategies like educating judges on the politics surrounding each case (personal communication, September 2021). Another terrorism lawyer reported that locating a defendant's actions in the broader "political context," such as the Syrian war or anti-Muslim aggression, could lead to "better" outcomes at sentencing and militate against the "monolithic concept of terrorism" that lumps all defendants into a single category: evildoers (interview, October 2020). Another terrorism lawyer, however, explained that while judges fluent in contemporary geopolitics might "be receptive" to a reduced sentence given the social contexts in which a defendant acted, "most judges don't have a clue about what's going on," making it difficult to mount a successful defense (interview, March 2021). These divergences in legal strategy highlight the deeply embodied nature of the criminal-legal system, as legal actors differentially negotiate the politics and power that organize the courts and generate uneven outcomes for terrorism defendants. The sociological study of the courts can provide insight into how the judicial system has "found itself swept up in the geopolitical direction and strategy of the U.S. government," especially because U.S. laws and policies historically "have been founded on the assumption that Arab and Muslim noncitizens are potential terrorists and have targeted them for special treatment under the law" (Akram and Johnson 2002, 302).[3]

Like other scholars who view immigration judges as the "linchpin of U.S. asylum policy," which necessitates an analysis of the case-level decision-making processes of these legal actors, this book explores the broader social contexts that inform judicial decision-making and shape legal outcomes in terrorism-related cases (Miller, Keith, and Holmes 2015, 1). Judges presiding over terrorism-related cases, after all, admit or exclude evidence, permit or deny expert testimony, rule on motions, review plea bargains, and sentence defendants. In fact, "very few terrorism cases go to jury trials," meaning that most cases are determined through bench trials—trials by judge rather than by jury—or are resolved through plea deals (interview, March 2021). As national security scholar Karen J. Greenberg (2016) explains, "It is the quiet decisions, the individual judicial rulings and laws and executive orders—generally fashioned by well-meaning people, often in the plain light of day but overlooked for their homeliness, their implications lost in the weeds of their small details—that make possible the fiascoes, the follies, and the excesses that turn governments into the enemies of their constituents" (3). In this analysis, "in no part of the government has that betrayal by accretion, the death of liberty by a thousand cuts, been more momentous, or more disturbing, than in the institutions of justice—the courts, the laws, and the Justice Department" (3).

By recognizing how terrorism trials irrevocably affect defendants and their families, this book explores how legal actors and institutions are bound up in the uneven and sometimes chaotic production, circulation, and adaptation of dominant narratives and practices that treat Muslims as incipient terrorists. Such an approach appreciates emerging summaries that detail the aggregate trends in terrorism prosecutions across time (Center on National Security 2017) while engaging in a more embodied analysis of the global war on terror by considering the individual decision-making of judges, jurors, attorneys, and defendants (Mountz 2010; Secor 2007; Painter 2006). This book also locates the adjudication of terrorism-related cases in broader U.S. efforts to use the criminal-legal system to authorize and advance illiberal global war on terror practices, such as the indefinite detention and torture of suspected terrorists, the criminalization of nonstate actors challenging despotic regimes, and the all-pervasive surveillance of Muslim diasporas, whose transnational connections themselves arouse suspicion and punishment in the name of national security.

Given this complex geolegal terrain, *Terrorism on Trial* offers a window into how the courts serve as important sites where legal actors work to litigate the global war on terror. To do so, this book explores how dominant academic discourses, geographical imaginations, and social processes shape the adjudication of terrorism-related cases and the invocation of the law as a weapon of war. Rather than identify a causal relationship between an epistemic framework and a legal outcome, this book investigates the conflicted and uneven ways legal actors have engaged the courtroom as a global war on terror site and mobilized strategic understandings of terrorism, war, and national security. In doing so, this book considers how the judicial system "is a site of competing discourses of legal legitimacy and wide variations of legal agency and legal consciousness" (Hajjar 2005, 4). The sociological study of the judicial system's role in the global war on terror can facilitate a more robust analysis of globalized punishment and its articulation with war-making and empire-building enterprises. Such an approach also provides insight into the material conditions that incite armed resistance, thereby illustrating the criminal-legal system's limited capacity to address the social contexts in which violence circulates. In other words, studying the adjudication of terrorism-related cases and locating the courts in the global war on terror can create openings to further nourish social movement work that infuses abolitionist campaigns with anti-imperialist demands to create a less violent and more liberatory world.

Bestowing Symbolic Victories? The Role of the Judicial System in the Global War on Terror

Across the United States, law enforcement agencies continuously have redefined "terrorism," an elastic term mobilized to reinforce racial hierarchies, repress political organizing, and support the global war on terror. As the courts adjudicate terrorism-related cases, they engage in epistemic, political, and legal struggles over what constitutes terrorism and terrorists. Lindh's lawyer, for example, refused to classify his client as a terrorist, arguing, "John is not a terrorist, he's a certified, court-approved, non-terrorist" (qtd. in Candiotti 2002). Lindh's conviction, however, reaffirmed the popular conclusion that the "American Taliban" is "the most famous jihadist America has ever produced," a symbolic reminder of the perceived rise of homegrown terrorists and the urgent need to incapacitate such threats (Wood 2019). Given these struggles, the courts can affirm, challenge, and/or oppose the global war on terror efforts led by other entities within the criminal-legal system, such as federal, state, local, and private law enforcement agencies.

The criminal-legal system maintains its own internal incoherence, particularly given its bureaucratic composition of individual institutional actors "with distinct objectives and perspectives, often struggling amongst themselves over state projects" (Mountz 2004, 328). One terrorism researcher, for example, explained, "Not surprisingly, DHS and FBI are huge bureaucracies and the people who work in them don't see things all the same way. So, depending on who you talk to, you get very different outlooks and perspectives. . . . Even the same person isn't necessarily consistent with what they're saying" (interview, February 2017). To better understand the conflicted role of the courts in the global war on terror, I investigate how socially embedded legal actors exercised discretion within the criminal-legal system, which they unevenly engaged depending on their own intellectual understandings of terrorism, security, and the laws of armed conflict.

The tensions that define all institutions surfaced in court transcripts as judges differentially interpreted, negotiated, and acted on prevailing understandings of terrorism, leading to a range of outcomes for the defendants before them. Some judges challenged commonsense understandings of terrorism by refusing to apply the Sentencing Commission's terrorism enhancement, a legal guidance that encourages harsher sentences for individuals convicted of a federal crime of terrorism. In declining to apply the terrorism enhancement in *United States v. Asher Abid Khan*, Judge Lynn Hughes reasoned that there are "degrees of terrorism," with some acts "more reprehensible" than others.[4] For Judge Hughes, the terrorism enhancement imposed unilateral sentencing guidelines that failed to account for these "degrees of terrorism." Other judges, however, sentenced terrorism defendants to long prison terms, communicating "a message that terrorism is especially heinous, and those convicted of terrorist crimes are particularly dangerous to the point of being irredeemably incapable of deterrence" (Said 2014, 478). Such an approach ignores the fact that "not *all* terrorism cases are alike, not all terrorism *defendants* are alike, and the difference in treatment would reflect a difference in threat level presented by the defendant, as well as the individual's capacity for rehabilitation" (Dratel 2011, 58). These epistemic struggles necessarily shaped jury verdicts, judicial opinions, sentencing decisions, and public understandings of these cases.

As these disparate judicial practices demonstrate, the embodied nature of the criminal-legal system generates competing logics, knowledges, practices, and outcomes in the courtroom. In some instances, federal prosecutors pursued terrorism cases by charging individuals with ordinary criminal activities like tax fraud, as in *United States v. Muhamed Mubayyid*. While judges sometimes limited the use of the term terrorism in these types of cases and refused to align their courts with "American law enforcement priorities" or to "bestow symbolic 'victories'" through their verdicts, security professionals publicly celebrated these convictions as global war on terror triumphs.[5] Defense attorneys specializing in terrorism-related cases, however, refused to see these convictions as wartime victories, arguing that "criminal courts aren't designed to fight wars."[6]

In other cases, judges used their authority from the bench to reaffirm fears of an imminent terrorist threat. In the sentencing hearing for Mohamed Farah, who expressed interest in traveling to Syria to fight President Bashar al-Assad's brutal regime, Judge Michael J. Davis concluded, "I think today makes clear that the Court is correct, that there is a terrorist cell in Minneapolis."[7] Prosecutor John Docherty affirmed this view, arguing that with Farah, "it has been impossible, short of putting him in handcuffs and putting him in custody, to stop him from trying to go and join ISIL [Islamic State of Iraq and the Levant]," thereby justifying the government's request for a thirty-year prison term.[8] In other words, judges differentially understood the role of their courts in the global war on terror, with some seeking to "keep references of terrorism out" of their courtrooms and others directly engaging this political discourse.[9] These discrepancies illustrate how the security state "does not contain or enact a unified series of agendas, objectives, or actors" as "state practices encompass . . . a series of diverse interests and bodies that are often themselves in conflict" (Mountz 2004, 325). Furthermore, understanding the use of the law as a weapon of war—that is, lawfare—requires locating legal actors and their practices in the broader social contexts, geographical imaginaries, and power relations in which they operate. Given these analytical demands, *Terrorism on Trial* explores how these competing interests, agendas, and imaginations have shaped the uneven prosecution, conviction, and sentencing of individuals charged with terrorism-related crimes.

In addition to the internal incoherence within the courts, agencies across the criminal-legal system have engaged in competing and contradictory practices such that one entity can thwart another. In 2016, Energy Transfer Partners contracted a private mercenary company, Tiger-Swan, to disrupt and discredit Indigenous water protectors contesting the company's Dakota Access Pipeline (#NoDAPL). With support from federal, state, and local law enforcement agencies, TigerSwan classified the water protectors as "jihadists" with a "strong female Shia following" and described the overall movement as an "ideologically-driven insurgency with a strong religious component" (Porter 2017, 4). By framing the water protectors as "jihadists," TigerSwan argued that "aggressive intelligence preparation of the battlefield and active coordination between intelligence and security elements are now a proven method of defeating pipeline insurgencies" (Porter 2017, 5). As the protests dwindled, TigerSwan anticipated a "jihadist bleedout model" similar to the "anti-Soviet Afghanistan jihad" where "many, especially external supporters (foreign fighters), went back out into the world looking to start or join new jihadist insurgencies," a phenomenon expected with "the ideologically driven pipeline fighters from Standing Rock" (Porter 2017, 4–5).

Drawing on anti-Muslim discourses, TigerSwan mobilized the "jihad-ist" label to justify a series of brutal policing campaigns to suppress the movement and advance the settler-colonial project (Barker 2021).

To support its on-the-ground activities, TigerSwan met with the North Dakota Bureau of Criminal Investigation "regarding video and still photo evidence collected for prosecution" and detailed plans to "con-tinue building Person of Interest (POI) folders and coordination with [law enforcement] intelligence" (Porter 2016, 3). Although TigerSwan and law enforcement agencies portrayed the water protectors as a terror-ist threat, North Dakota courts dismissed or settled many of the cases, ultimately refusing to endorse TigerSwan's aggressive tactics.[10] A federal judge later dismissed an Energy Transfer Partners lawsuit that alleged that the water protectors "incited, funded, and facilitated crimes and acts of terrorism" (Energy Transfer 2017). In January 2021, however, climate activists Ruby Montoya and Jessica Reznicek pleaded guilty to charges related to their sabotage of machinery at Dakota Access Pipe-line sites in Iowa and South Dakota.[11] In July 2021, Judge Rebecca Goodgame Ebinger found that Reznicek's conduct constituted a federal crime of terrorism, applied the terrorism enhancement, and sentenced Reznicek to eight years in federal prison. After Reznicek's sentencing hearing, the FBI special agent in charge, Eugene Kowel, declared, "Pro-tecting the American people from terrorism—both international and domestic—remains the FBI's number one priority. We will continue to work with our law enforcement partners to bring domestic terrorists like Jessica Reznicek to justice. Her sentence today should be a deterrent to anyone who intends to commit violence through an act of domes-tic terrorism" (qtd. in U.S. Attorney's Office, Southern District of Iowa 2021). These uneven legal decisions reveal the complicated role the courts play in affirming, challenging, and/or rejecting prevailing narratives about national security threats in the United States, including the refusal to reinforce an ever-expanding domestic war on terror.

Similar to the classification of Indigenous water protectors as ter-rorists, the FBI established the Black Identity Extremist (BIE) category in 2017 by identifying a new terrorist threat. The FBI (2017) argued that "incidents of alleged police abuse against African Americans" will con-tinue to "feed the resurgence in ideologically-motivated, violent criminal activity within the BIE movement," including "premediated, retaliatory lethal violence against law enforcement" (2). The BIE category classified Black political organizers contesting police brutality as potential terrorists driven by dangerous ideologies. Drawing from the FBI's Counterintelligence Program (COINTELPRO), which was used to "expose, disrupt, misdirect, discredit, or otherwise neutralize" the Black freedom struggle in the 1960s (Hoover 1967), the BIE designation justified the launch of the FBI's threat mitigation strategy, Iron Fist, to surveil, infiltrate, and disrupt Black political groups (FBI 2018). FBI director Christopher Wray later admitted that white supremacists posed a "persistent, pervasive threat" whereas Black Identity Extremists did not—a concession that signaled disagreement even among FBI officials enacting the agency's own antiterrorism agenda (qtd. in Scott 2019).

After a federal judge dismissed the first—and only—formal BIE case in 2018, the FBI abandoned the term "Black Identity Extremist" in favor of a broader but equally murky designation: "racially motivated violent extremism." While the FBI alleged that this category reflected a commitment to addressing the threat posed by white supremacist groups, others warned that the reclassification would intentionally "obscure data that could be used to compare the FBI resources devoted to white supremacists versus Black Identity Extremists" and target political dissidents of color disproportionately (German 2021, 8). Federal prosecutors, for example, largely refrained from charging participants in the January 6 attempted armed takeover of the U.S. Capitol with federal crimes of terrorism or invoking the terrorism enhancement at sentencing (Gerstein 2022). As with Indigenous water protectors, the U.S. criminal-legal system has pursued Black dissidents and their coconspirators as terrorists, ultimately justifying an even wider array of punitive force to repress these perceived insurgencies.

Mapped onto racialized bodies, these security classifications have material effects: criminalization, stigmatization, and alienation felt in people's everyday lives. Court proceedings actively participate in the making of the legal, social, and cultural category of the terrorist—unworthy of the law's protection but subject to its punishment. As Colin Dayan (2011) reminds us, "It is through law that persons, variously figured, gain or lose definition, become victims of prejudice or inheritors of privilege" (xi). In this context, domestic courtrooms have served as important sites of struggle over interpreting, applying, and responding to the pseudo-legal categories of "terrorism" and "terrorists" and over their role in the global war on terror, especially as judges "are not immune to social prejudices" and "reinforce widespread American stereotypes about Muslims" (Koprowski 2011, 189).

Terrorism on Trial examines these tensions and what they meant for defendants and their attorneys who engaged this system with the limited legal tools and strategies available to them. This book also considers how judges negotiated the competing roles imposed on their courtrooms as they observed that "the struggle against religious and political extremism in general, and terrorism in particular, is likely to be the principal challenge facing this nation, and the rest of the world, for many years to come," while reaffirming that the "proper place of the trial court in the American constitutional system" is to "make a relatively narrow and focused inquiry" as to whether the evidence presented before the court supports the conviction of each defendant.[12] Judges thus have been acutely aware of how the U.S. security state has mobilized the courts in the service of its geopolitical agenda, which impinges on the perceived impartiality and neutrality of the judicial system in the global war on terror.

Defense attorneys evaluated, negotiated, and navigated these judicial variations, often reaching for frameworks that could confirm and/or challenge dominant understandings of political violence and the role of the courts in the global war on terror. Although some defense attorneys argued that "trying to explain to a district court judge what *Syria* is about is a waste of time," others viewed contextualizing their defendants' actions as important to "telling your client's story" and negotiating a more favorable sentence (interview, March 2021; interview, October 2020). Even when defense attorneys contextualized their clients' stories, culture—namely Islam—often has been "teleologized in courts of law, transformed from a conceptual tool of anthropological analysis into 'objective evidence,' or asserted as the direct cause of persecution or delinquency" (Good 2008, s47). In fact, the courts have allowed "expert testimony that confirmed widespread fears about Islamic fanaticism in furtherance of the government's prosecution" while excluding "testimony intended to challenge these stereotypes in support of the defense" (Koprowski 2011, 194). Tinged by anti-Muslim racism, such judicial decisions and cultural understandings have shaped the adjudication of terrorism-related cases.

Given these complex tensions and how they come to bear on the lives of defendants and their communities, this book offers a window into the inner workings of terrorism trials to better understand how these legal processes unevenly have criminalized, stigmatized, and disempowered communities of color. In examining the different types of terrorism-related cases, this book recognizes that the U.S. security state continues to mobilize the judicial system as a counterterrorism tool and therefore views understanding these legal processes as politically useful for broader abolitionist campaigns to end war, empire, and globalized punishment.[13] As Alison Mountz (2010) writes, "When people believe that the state is all-powerful and mysterious, existing somewhere 'out there,' they do not participate in protest or dialogue" (178n7). Deconstructing the monolithic security state—and more specifically the judicial system—can provide openings to challenge state practices related to the criminalization, prosecution, and incarceration of Muslim communities, which are already fraught with contention and contradiction.

Starting at the Missing End Point: The Aftermath of Terrorism Trials

As an education researcher, I often have referred to prisons as the final stop in the school-to-prison pipeline. This abstracted approach, however, misses what happens in domestic courtrooms and what happens after defendants are convicted, sentenced, and incarcerated. Given these absences in my own work, my political and intellectual interest in the judicial system emerged through my observation of it. Initially, I witnessed the aftermath of these court cases, observing the fear, outrage, and devastation terrorism convictions produced in Muslim communities across the country. Sitting in courtrooms to offer court support, however, changed my orientation to these legal proceedings as the palpable grief, sorrow, and anguish of parents punctuated my observations. On reflection, I realized that parents needed to navigate a complex criminal-legal system, absorb the enormous costs of defense attorneys, endure stigma and social exclusion, and, most significantly, bear the loss of their children to long prison terms. In losing their children, many parents also lost their businesses, their friends, their communities, their health, and their homes. Loss was a constant fixture in these court proceedings, almost sutured to the terrorist label, but so often missing from academic, public, and professional discussions. As a prison abolitionist and social scientist, I realized I had never considered how we might think about and develop abolitionist alternatives to terrorism prosecutions in ways responsive to the complexity of these cases and the geopolitical contexts in which they are embedded.

These parents, their children, and their struggles with the criminal-legal system served as the starting point for this project and were a constant presence in my work. I wanted to understand how an affable young man who never committed an act of violence could be sentenced to thirty-five years in federal prison, marked by the court as "extraordinarily dangerous," and described by federal prosecutors as "unfixable." I wanted to understand how the courts reduced such young people to disposable enemies of the state, undeserving of living and loving in society.

Rather than view the adjudication of terrorism-related crimes as the final stop in the criminalization of youth, I came to understand these court proceedings as an explanatory moment in their own right. Such proceedings reveal how the law can serve as a weapon of war, but only in halting and uncertain ways, as dominant geographical imaginations, epistemic frameworks, legal demands, and national security imperatives unevenly cohere in the courtroom. Furthermore, legal actors differentially have engaged the criminal-legal system according to their own personal and professional understandings of the law and its relationship to national security; their knowledge of the governing geopolitical contexts that define the global war on terror; and the demands placed on them by their supervisors, the general public, and the families involved in these cases. This book lives and breathes in these epistemic uncertainties, legal hesitancies, and "rough interior ridges of governance," exploring their contours to better understand these legal processes and the social forces shaping them (Stoler 2009, 2).

Through my immersion in terrorism trials, I came to locate the judicial system in transnational carceral regimes that articulate with racialized systems of war and empire. Laleh Khalili (2013) argues that as "direct coercion and wartime violence" have become politically, economically, and morally untenable, liberal counterinsurgencies have come to "depend on law and administration for their continuation"; constant contestations over the use of lethal force by state militaries have led to "the rise of confinement and incarceration as central tactics of counterinsurgency warfare" (3–5). By mapping the relationship between imperial regimes, military operations, and confinement techniques, the study of terrorism prosecutions offers insight into one node of this transnational web of globalized punishment (Platt and Shank 2004, 1). Harsha Walia (2021) similarly documents how the "entanglements of border formation in imperial expansion, anti-Black enslavement, and Indigenous elimination are mirrored in our contemporary moment with border agents patrolling alongside the military in Iraq and Afghanistan, policing Black neighborhoods in the aftermath of Hurricane Katrina, repressing Indigenous water protectors at Standing Rock, and using counterinsurgency tactics" to suppress Black political dissidence (36). Erica Edwards (2021) refers to these interrelated imperial logics, discourses, and practices of invasion, occupation, and perpetual detainment as "military-carceral modalities of counterterrorism" whereby U.S. empire's "inward modes of containment" articulate with "outward modes of expansion and resource extraction" to formulate a racial gendered regime of state protection (22, 31). In recognizing the transnational force of U.S. empire, these analyses challenge the distinction between domestic and foreign security regimes and therefore identify the urgent need to nourish transnational social movement work aimed at ending the global, regional, and local circulations of war, empire, and confinement.

Given these entanglements, I center the figure of the terrorist—the migrant, the Indigenous water protector, the Black Lives Matter protestor, the al-Qaeda soldier, the suicide bomber—to think through an abolitionist approach capacious enough to take seriously armed resistance—violence—and therefore reckon with war-making and empire-building enterprises that depend on confinement, detention, and incarceration for their continuation. Doing so can militate against more liberal reforms that accommodate state power, sidestep the question of political violence, and do little to disrupt the violent regimes of governance that incite armed struggles. This includes refusing calls to "bring abolition to national security" (Jamshidi 2020) or to "abolish the concept and infrastructure of counterterrorism" (Husain 2020) by eliminating agencies like the Department of Homeland Security or relocating Guantánamo detainees to federal prisons, without attending to the imperial logics, policies, and practices that give rise to armed resistance.

Abolitionist approaches to the global war on terror primarily have focused on ending the criminalization of "otherwise law-abiding Muslim communities" and arresting the expansion of police powers in the name of national security (McGhee 2008, 26), but without a "grounded and reflexive approach to violence" waged by nonstate actors (Li 2020, 26). If anti-Muslim racism "obscures the fact that so much of what security measures claim to address would be much better dealt with through ending the conditions of racism, imperialism, and capitalism that give rise to violence," how might we repeal antiterrorism policies and practices while also "creatively and collectively imagining new ways to create eco-systems of well-being" and "envisioning an entirely different framework for thinking about justice" (Manzoor-Khan 2022, 60–61)? What abolitionist futures can we conjure for the political militant who enacts, or desires to enact, lethal force to effect social change?

Centering the figure of the terrorist necessitates reckoning with the politics that animates violence and the power asymmetries that create the conditions for "the violent exercise of freedom outside the frame of law" (Asad 2007, 91). In this book, I use the case of criminal prosecution in the global war on terror to explore the transnational intersections of war, empire, and prisons and enunciate an emergent abolitionist imaginary that takes seriously politics, violence, and the inextricable relationship between the two. In doing so, this intervention draws on and contributes to broader discussions on the social practices that "evict" Muslims from Western law and politics (Razack 2008); the extraordinary rendition and indefinite detention of alleged terrorists (Begg 2007); the extradition of terrorism suspects from Britain to the United States (Kapoor 2018); the racial representations that reify the image of the "terrifying" Muslim (Rana 2011); the coercive state practices that produce a "sense of internal incarceration" in Arab and Muslim communities pivoting on the fear that "at any moment, one may be picked up, locked up, or disappeared" (Naber 2006, 240); the anticolonial revolutions and antiblack struggles led by Muslims (Daulatzai 2012; Li 2020; Qureshi 2017); and the community policing regimes that further criminalize Muslim communities and infringe on their civil rights and civil liberties (Kundnani 2014; Meer 2007; Alsultany 2008; Jamal 2008; Selod 2018; Alimahomed-Wilson 2019; Cainkar 2019; Walker 2021; Manzoor-Khan 2022; Sabir 2022; Kazi 2019). These empirical, conceptual, and theoretical contributions serve as the foundation for this book's abolitionist analysis of terrorism prosecutions, which recognizes how "race thinking" organizes the judicial system and shapes the role of law in the global war on terror (Arendt 1951; Razack 2008; Silverblatt 2005).

Such abolitionist visioning not only requires an understanding of how war, empire, and prisons cohere; it also necessitates rejecting dominant conceptual frameworks that reduce political violence to the mere expression of an individual defendant's perverse pathologies, such as "religious fanaticism" or "psychological disturbance," irrespective of the social contexts in which such violence circulates (Kruglanski and Fishman 2006). Indicting Muslim culture, ideology, or religiosity mobilizes a logic that "is eventually genocidal since it means the cause of terrorism is not a political issue to be resolved; it is Muslimness which can only be resolved through elimination" (Manzoor-Khan 2022, 27). By abstracting political violence from its formative conditions, these reductive analyses draw on decades of social science research allegedly documenting the racial roots of violence, from eugenicist Francis Galton's (1909) formulation of "race science" to anthropologist Raphael Patai's (1973) psychological exploration of the "Arab mind" to political scientist John J. DiIulio's (1995) theorization of the "coming of the super-predators" to historian Walter Laqueur's (1999) taxonomy of the "new terrorist." Such scientific studies typically locate violence in the psychological, cultural, and/or theological pathologies of individual actors, without considering the social, economic, and political contexts in which people live or the use of the law to criminalize political dissidence and revolutionary violence (Benjamin 1978; Munif 2020; Husain 2020a). For example, in the mid-1990s, DiIulio (1996) blamed a "correctable moral defect" festering in "angry young Black males" for the rising "Black crime problem" in the United States. To solve this alleged moral crisis, DiIulio (1995) argued that "a growing body of scientific evidence from a variety of academic disciplines indicates that churches can help cure or curtail many severe socioeconomic ills" and encouraged government officials to "strengthen the community-rebuilding and child-protection capacities of local churches." Rather than reinvesting in Black communities, however, most cities responded to the coming superpredator by intensifying their coercive policing practices in Black communities. President Bill Clinton's Violent Crime Control and Law Enforcement Act of 1994 increased funding for prisons, established new capital offenses, and rendered incarcerated individuals ineligible for federal financial aid for college. The manufactured specter of the coming superpredator authorized new policing tools to enclose, capture, and punish Black youth while reinforcing antiblack research on the alleged "Black crime problem" and putative "moral defects" in Black communities.

Like DiIulio's (1995) warning that "Americans are sitting atop a demographic crime bomb," Laqueur (1999) similarly cautioned that terrorism "has become one of the gravest dangers facing mankind," necessitating new strategies to respond to the changing character of terrorists (4). Laqueur predicted that the future will see terrorism assume a "more pathological complexion" as "fanaticism, whether sectarian, ethnic, or just personal, moves into the foreground" and political motivations recede (226). These two rising moral panics demonstrate the distinct yet co-constitutive social processes of racialized policing, war, and empire. Yet the prominence of social science research like DiIulio's has encouraged the public to view such national security threats as the violent expression of an individual's theological, psychological, and/or cultural pathologies, such as the claim that "moral poverty begets juvenile super-predators whose behavior is driven by . . . developmental defects" (DiIulio 1995).

The twin specters of the terrorist and the superpredator feed on racialized narratives that position Black and Muslim youth as national security threats and accelerate through federally funded research on such "apocalyptic groups" (Laqueur 1996, 33). Samuel P. Huntington's (1996) "clash of civilizations" thesis facilitated the making of these dual pillars of U.S. state formation by arguing that "culture and cultural identities . . . are shaping the patterns of cohesion, disintegration, and conflict in the post–Cold War world" (20). The concept of the clash of civilizations "brought the cultural pathology thesis into foreign affairs, with faulty social reproduction being the link between the 1960s social movements [in the United States] and the 'warfare between Arabs and the West' that Huntington (1993, 32) predicted would become more virulent" (Edwards 2021, 42). Focused on the psychological perversions of individual actors, these analyses have authorized regimes of war and policing to fortify national security, such that "carceral technologies of racial control in the United States" articulate with "practices of foreign counterinsurgency," as in the 1960s-era policing of the Black freedom struggle simultaneous to the repression of Arab liberation movements that intensified after the 1967 Arab-Israeli war (45).

In 1968, psychiatrists Walter Bromberg and Frank Simon detailed the relationship between "political events of national or international import" and "psychotic reactions" (155). To do so, they identified a psychological profile that mirrored many of the "primary signs of schizophrenia": a "protest psychosis" that "is influenced by social pressures (the Civil Rights Movement), dips into religious doctrine (the Black Muslim Group), is guided in content by African subcultural ideologies, and is colored by a denial of Caucasian values and hostility thereto" (155). Triggered by "socio-political events," this "reactive psychosis" led to Black men developing "antiwhite aggressive feelings," espousing "African subcultural ideologies," and adopting "Islamic names" (155). Rooted in a struggle to "reverse the 'white supremacy' tradition or at least state objection to the accepted superiority of 'white' values in terms of African ideology," such behaviors reflected the "paranoid projections of racial antagonism of the Negroes to the Caucasian group" (155–56). Much like the invention of "drapetomania"—the alleged disease that caused enslaved people to flee plantations—the concept of "protest psychosis" located political protest in the psychological, cultural, and theological pathologies of individual actors engaged in militant freedom struggles; such conceptual work ultimately "blackened" the line between "lawful citizen and unlawful terrorist" while depoliticizing and delegitimizing armed resistance, from the Black Panther Party for Self-Defense to the Palestine Liberation Organization. The repression of Black, Muslim, and Arab liberation movements "drew together the domestic terrorist and the foreign terrorist in ways that continue to inform and provoke U.S. counterinsurgency" (Edwards 2021, 56).

As racist counterinsurgency tools, these psychological profiles reappear in contemporary national security policies as social scientists have sought to taxonomize the "terrorist mind" and map "what makes terrorists tick" (Post 2009, xi). In this view, to "optimally counter terrorists, it is imperative to have a clear understanding of their psychology," with an emphasis on the "generational transmission of hatred—a hatred 'bred in the bone'" (xi). This orthodox approach to the study of terrorism hinges on the racialization of Muslims as enemies of the state whose shared psychological, cultural, and theological pathologies drive them to indiscriminate violence, even if they invoke different religious idioms and identify divergent political aspirations (Rana 2011, 54). For example, in one court case, the presiding judge viewed al-Shabaab, the Islamic State of Iraq and Syria (ISIS), and al-Qaeda as analogous, even interchangeable, organizations given their allegedly shared "strict interpretation of the Sharia law" and commitment to violence in the name of "jihadi religion."[14] The image of a menacing Islam collapses different armed militias into a single frame that refuses to consider the politics animating the use of violence: terrorists.

Despite the influence of these studies on security policies, other scholars have challenged the orthodoxy inherent in this "terrorology" paradigm, which applies positivist discourses to the study of violent political conflict while ignoring the deeper geopolitical, economic, and social contexts in which such violence occurs (McEvoy and Gormally 1997). Critics argue that terrorism "is useful as a scientific category only if—beyond all semantic positional warfare—it successfully locates what is specific to certain economies and strategies of political violence and not to others" (Ould Mohamedou 2007, 76). Such *differentia specifica* indicates that political terrorism has been pursued by al-Qaeda as a strategic reaction to the absence of military reciprocity in its war with the United States, as well as the asymmetrical evolution of methods of warfighting" (77). Al-Qaeda is distinct from other armed political groups like ISIS, especially given the vastly different geopolitical contexts in which these organizations operate and their conflicting political aspirations. In this view, armed militias cannot ahistorically and acontextually be reduced to terrorist organizations driven by the "generational transmission of hatred" or the sedimentation of religious fanaticism.

Even if we disagree with the politics animating their use of violence, these armed militias must be understood as political organizations that recognize, negotiate, and challenge globalized power asymmetries and repressive governance regimes by using lethal force to "overcome the violence of the law and counter the power of the sovereign" in despotic societies, colonialized territories, and/or liberal democracies that themselves use violence to maintain territorial control and sovereign power (Munif 2020, 19). *Terrorism on Trial* assesses how legal actors unevenly mobilize dominant understandings of terrorism in the courtroom, how these interpretations shape judicial decision-making and legal outcomes, and how these proceedings often reduce political violence to the work of individual actors and therefore absolve the structurally powerful in creating the material conditions that incite violence, whether that violence takes the form of a slave insurrection, an anticolonial rebellion, or another kind of armed resistance (Jackson 2019; Abraham 2014; Ghosh 2017; Benjamin 1978; Asad 2007).

Despite the continued critiques of terrorism studies, the courts often have admitted terrorologists as expert witnesses whose testimony arguably could be useful in interpreting the factual evidence in terrorism-related cases. Such expert witnesses typically have focused their testimony on the perceived theological, cultural, and psychological features of terrorism and terrorist recruitment. One expert witness testified that "pop jihadism" is the "youth subculture circling around the Jihad identity of becoming a mujahideen or warrior"—a recruitment tactic that exploits the perceived psychological vulnerabilities that make young people especially susceptible to "indoctrination."[15] In this view, pop jihadism reflects a "very vibrant youth movement that basically uses that instant identity of becoming an elite warrior to build up a new identity and refill these political ideals and values."[16] By locating political violence in the psychological profiles of individual actors, terrorologists have severed politics from violence, erasing the formative contexts giving rise to violent political action. By denying the political dimensions of terrorism—often racially stylized as jihad—terrorologists and political leaders have insisted that the criminal-legal system can support the global war on terror by preemptively incapacitating individual actors whose theological, psychological, and cultural pathologies drive their turn to violence. This understanding of terrorism absolves the United States of its role in creating the conditions that armed groups challenge through their death dealing.

Imagining alternatives to policing and prisons requires rethinking how we understand political violence. In the context of the global war on terror, social scientists and legal actors have sensationalized political violence as "Islamic holy war," "Islamic extremism," or "terrorism." These interpretive maneuvers effectively render such violence as an apolitical expression of theological perversions, ignoring the ways soldiers of all stripes kill and die for politics, especially within liberal democracies (Euben 2002). Given its moralizing intonations in Western discourse, the term terrorism collapses the many ways armed actors have pursued violent political projects in a world order defined by U.S. empire. For example, in a sentencing hearing for a young man who discussed his desire to travel to Syria to fight President Bashar al-Assad's brutal regime, Judge Davis observed, "We had a number of individuals . . . that were involved in a Jihadist ideology to provide material support, their bodies, to be foot soldiers in the Islamic State. . . . And part of that ideology was that you were going to fight for Allah, you were going to be a soldier for Allah, whether or not you lived or died, you're making sacrifices for Allah."[17] By indicting "Jihadist ideology," this judicial logic blamed theological perversions for the creation of "foot soldiers in the Islamic State," irrespective of the broader social contexts organizing such violence; it also collapsed different types of actors—from young people ensnared in elaborate sting operations to fighters seeking to depose the Assad regime to individuals donating money to Islamic relief organizations in besieged places to boys expressing outrage over anti-Muslim violence—into a single frame: jihadists driven by jihadist ideology. As the courts have circulated, endorsed, and adapted these commonsense understandings of terrorism, the criminal-legal system has celebrated such convictions as key global war on terror victories.

Given the prominence of terrorism experts "ideologically committed [to] and practically engaged in supporting Western state power" (Miller and Mills 2009, 414), academic scholars have challenged such orthodoxy by offering more nuanced conceptual frameworks that refuse to essentialize Islam, reduce political actors to the "manipulated tools of Western powers," or define political violence as the "epiphenomenal 'blowback'" of destructive Western policies (Li 2020, 25). In his exploration of suicide bombers, cultural anthropologist Talal Asad (2007) argues "against thinking of terrorism simply as an illegal and immoral form of violence" and encourages "an examination of what the discourse of terror—and the perpetration of terror—does in the world of power" (26). Noting how jihad often is abstracted from "the ethico-political context in terms of which the actors themselves understand it," political theorist Roxanne L. Euben (2002) contends that "jihad is neither simply a blind and bloody-minded scrabble for temporal power nor solely a door through which to pass into the hereafter. Rather, it is a form of political action in which, to use Hannah Arendt's language, the pursuit of immortality is inextricably linked to a profoundly this-worldly endeavor—the founding or recreating of a just community on earth" (7). These analyses foreground the explicitly political dimensions of jihad, refuting dominant antiterrorism frameworks that abstract political violence from its formative conditions and that individualize such violence by indicting psychological, theological, and/or cultural pathologies as the primary drivers of violent political action. Such analyses do not seek to endorse or even condone political violence; rather, they seek to consider "the import of death on the premises of politics," including the making of liberal democracies that invoke the right to kill in the name of national security, political freedom, and humanitarian intervention (11).

By insisting that we consider the political dimensions of violence, *Terrorism on Trial* contributes to the growing body of literature reconceptualizing "contemporary groups invoking jihad" by taking seriously "the social forces driving them, the worldly goals they pursue, and the antagonisms that they face" (Li 2015, 16). To do so, social scientists and abolitionist organizers cannot treat violence and politics as occupying separate spheres. We must situate violence in the historical, social, and geographic contexts in which it circulates, rather than employ a "simple agentive model" that locates the problem of violence in the theological, psychological, and/or cultural pathologies of alleged terrorists and that ignores how violence is a continuous feature of liberal democracies (Asad 2007, 15; Euben 2002).

Considering how the courts unevenly interpret and act on unstable and shifting concepts like terrorism, jihad, and political violence, *Terrorism on Trial* examines the role of the judicial system in reinforcing global, regional, and local regimes of war, empire, and confinement through the adjudication of terrorism-related cases. This approach offers community organizers, political activists, and civil rights advocates alternative ways of understanding political violence—vital conceptual work to build an anti-imperial abolitionist approach that recognizes that "abolition requires decolonization and an end to imperialism" (Naber and Rojas 2021).

Terrorism prosecutions make plain how policing regimes, imperial incursions, and military interventions in the context of globalized power asymmetries are mutually constitutive. Furthermore, the figure of the terrorist expands the organizing principle that abolition "is about presence not absence"—what Ruth Wilson Gilmore (2022) defines as the building of life-affirming institutions to reduce community-based violence by creating accountability practices for community members who do harm—as the use of lethal force by political actors necessitates attending to the geopolitical contexts and material conditions that incite armed resistance (qtd. in Clark 2021). In other words, the figure of the terrorist demands that we think more clearly about the use of lethal force—violence—in political struggles waged by nonstate actors in an unequal world of sovereigns. Abolitionist demands to end anti-Muslim policing practices lose shape when considering violent political actors like Khalid Sheikh Mohammed—the alleged 9/11 mastermind held and tortured at Guantánamo Bay—or the five thousand Taliban prisoners released months before the Taliban regained control of Afghanistan in 2021. How might we craft an abolitionist imaginary capacious enough to consider the range of individuals criminalized, hunted, and prosecuted under U.S. terrorism laws, including vulnerable people ensnared in elaborate sting operations, young people outraged over anti-Muslim aggression enacted by despotic regimes, longtime al-Qaeda leaders, and Indigenous water protectors classified as jihadists? Less of a blueprint and more of a starting point, *Terrorism on Trial* is an invitation to engage in these unfinished conversations, develop new conceptual tools, and craft emergent political strategies to support ongoing social movement work that seeks to dismantle policing and security regimes in a world order defined by U.S. empire.

With an explicit commitment to anti-imperial abolitionist organizing, *Terrorism on Trial* draws contour lines to connect seemingly disparate sites by their shared relations to specific social processes, such as U.S.-led indefinite detention and military intervention. While topographies detail the social and historical relations through which places are made, countertopographies follow expansive social processes and relations of force that link far-flung places and struggles together. Such an approach "offers a multifaceted way of theorizing the connectedness of vastly different places and in so doing enables the inference of connection in uncharted places in between" (Katz 2001a, 1229). Attuned to the specificity of location and differentiated experiences, countertopographies analytically link distant and distinct places, such as the Salt Pit, the Central Intelligence Agency's black site prison; Camp Delta, the permanent detention facility at Guantánamo Bay; and "Guantánamo North" prison units in the United States. Countertopographical contour lines also draw connections between racialized policing practices that differentially but interrelatedly infiltrate Asian, Arab, Black, Indigenous, Latinx, and Muslim communities; border enforcement tactics that enclose migrants; and counterinsurgency techniques that confine and kill Iraqis and Afghans, all in the name of national security. By nourishing a geographical imagination with a more associative politics, countertopographies analytically link disparate places to reconfigure alternative geographic landscapes and to supplant dominant, imperial topographies. Such countertopographical analyses can "undermine the apparent fixity of current geometries of power" by examining the distinct yet interconnected ways Western societies render racialized bodies terrorist threats and plot openings ripe with political possibility (Belcher et al. 2008, 503). Producing such countertopographies "can be a way, not only to reimagine a politics that redresses the toll" of U.S. empire, "but also to actually begin to build a practical response that is at once translocal and strategically focused" (Katz 2001b, 720).

Mapping these contour lines can strengthen social movement work by charting the lines of flight forged by differently situated individuals marked as terrorists to evade ever-expanding imperial regimes and by building coalitions across communities subjected to such co-constitutive excesses of state power. Such an approach can nurture an oppositional politics that both appreciates and transcends the specificity of place to develop effective strategies that challenge state violence. Like women of color organizing in the early 2000s, *Terrorism on Trial* analyzes the adjudication of terrorism-related crimes to forge (forgotten) translocal links between abolitionist struggles to end racialized policing, imperialism, colonialism, and other forms of violence globally. In doing so, *Terrorism on Trial* insists that abolitionist organizing, and social movement work more generally, must (re)center the voices of those targeted as terrorists and be "more consistent in [our] alliances with struggles against imperialism, colonialism, and racism" (Naber, Desouky, and Baroudi 2016, 100). To do so, this book documents how terrorism trials unevenly criminalize, stigmatize, and alienate communities of color, staging an analysis that seeks to support broader campaigns to end globalized punishment, domestic war on terror operations, and imperial formations. Doing so guards against deceptive solutions, such as viewing criminal prosecution in federal courts as a liberal alternative to trials held in military commissions, and renews the possibility for solidarity work across contexts and struggles (Rovner and Theoharis 2012).

On Violence: Retheorizing Terrorism as Political Violence

If my training in educational policy studies focused my attention on the criminalization of youth in schools while neglecting the prosecution of youth in criminal courts, it also primed me to question the concept of terrorism. As criminologist Stuart Henry (2017) notes, conventional approaches to school violence assume that students, especially minoritized youth, "constitute the scope of the problem" and therefore ignore "the wider context of violence in shaping the more visible forms of physical violence manifested by students" (18). Rather than simply locate the problem of school violence in individual students who engage in violent acts, Henry encourages us to consider the institutional harm and interpersonal violence children experience in schools to develop a fuller account of school violence. In this view, "what may appear as an outburst in school is merely one manifestation of more systemic societal problems" that "may begin, or be modified by, activities in other locations," such as local neighborhoods, national political arenas, and the wider political economy (21). Understanding school violence requires an assessment of the "hidden crimes of the structurally powerful in society" (18). These "hidden crimes" include "harms committed by teachers against students and by administrators against both students and teachers"; "the organization of schooling where it creates harm to both student creativity and education processes"; and "harmful institutionalized social and educational practices" like "processes of institutionalized racism or sexism, other discrimination, labeling and tracking, authoritarian discipline, militaristic approaches to school security, sexual harassment, and predation" (18). For Henry, it is "just such harm perpetrated by the structurally powerful in schools that is correlated with a high incidence of violence by students" (24). By indicting the "hidden crimes of the structurally powerful," Henry compels us to consider the formative contexts in which violence circulates, including the confluence of social forces, education policies, and power relations that contributes to the harmful conditions youth sometimes resist, or solidify, through the use of violence. By considering these formative conditions, this approach insists that preventing school violence cannot be reduced to teaching children conflict resolution skills alone; we must address the "hidden crimes of the structurally powerful" and the institutional violence children endure, or reproduce, daily.

Henry's (2017) discussion of school violence is instructive to the study of other forms of political violence. Rather than simply attribute violence to individual actors, we must consider the "real initiator" of violence, which could be repressive states, oppressive institutions, or regressive policies that harm constituents (Teltumbde 2017, 54). By challenging the normative and moral distinction between "routinized violence" enacted by structures and policies and the "episodic/organized violence" of nonstate actors, this approach views violence as a "necessary mode of political mobilization to counter the invisibilized violence of the current political system" (Gudavarthy 2017, 13–14). Episodic violence often "is germinated in" structural violence as "revolutionaries are inspired to change the structures of exploitation, oppression, dispossession of people to usher in a society," making it impossible to separate violence from the governing political contexts (Teltumbde 2017, 53–54). "Entrenched in social relations," violence "does not arise in a vacuum" but rather in the prevailing geopolitical contexts that have incited such militant struggles (Ray 2011, 12–13). Despite ongoing efforts to classify, typologize, and taxonomize terrorists—noted in the uptick in "domestic violent extremist" categories, from "racially or ethnically motivated violent extremists" to "abortion-related violent extremists" to "animal rights violent extremists"—political violence is rooted in specific historical, social, economic, and geopolitical contexts that must be accounted for in our analyses and responses (Office of the Director of National Intelligence 2021).

Despite these findings, mainstream terrorism scholars have tried to "create a framework within which all acts of terrorism carried out across a range of historical geographical settings can be made legible as belonging to a singular—though multifaceted—category of analysis," although to no avail (McQuade 2021, 12). No single framework has the explanatory power to account for a wide range of political conditions and actors who use lethal force to effect social change. Rather than fit disparate violent acts into a single frame, this book theorizes violence by refusing "to root current geopolitical crises" like the rise of the Islamic State in "primordial traditions of religiously sanctioned violence" and by beginning with the historical, social, and economic contexts in which particular forms of violence circulate (McQuade 2021, 10).

Political philosopher Verena Erlenbusch-Anderson (2018) writes that "an adequate and fruitful account of terrorism must begin with a consideration of the contexts within which terrorism is embedded and becomes meaningful," such as colonialism, nationalism, and racial capitalism (3). Scholars have excavated the genealogies of terrorism to show how empires historically have marked anticolonial violence as terrorism and to identify how parliamentary democracies have engaged in similar acts of indiscriminate violence, as in Dresden, Hiroshima, and Nagasaki (Hyams 1975, 184). Historian Stephen Frederic Dale (1988) warns against "present-minded bias" that fails to "take into account long-term conflicts that give rise to terrorist attacks" (37). In his study of terrorism, Dale explores how "suicidal jihads" were "one of the few means by which" the Muslim merchants exploited and harassed by European colonialists and traders "could injure and intimidate those who had usurped trade and otherwise assaulted their community," particularly during the Spanish occupation of the Philippines (sixteenth to nineteenth centuries), the Portuguese maritime trade dominance in the region (sixteenth century), and the British occupation of India (nineteenth and twentieth centuries) (49, 37). With this historical understanding, Dale (1980) rejects the classification of eighteenth-century attacks against the British East India Company's factories as "random, fanatical attacks" but rather as "directly or indirectly related to the continuing struggle for the spice trade" (51). Confrontations between European powers and Muslims in the "south Asian frontier" sparked violent anticolonial attacks organized by "the specific idiom of Islam" (5). In this approach, understanding violence requires an assessment of the historical and contemporary conditions that give rise to anticolonial attacks.[18]

Despite Dale's (1988) diligent documentation of the shifting political conditions under different colonial regimes and his rejection of "present-minded bias," he ultimately concludes that each wave of Muslim resistance "shared a common feature": the Mappilas launched these attacks "as jihads, as wars for the faith," such that these militants "intentionally martyred themselves at the conclusion of each assault" (1). It is this historicization of modern Muslim resistance as a mere continuation of the violent rebellions that began in 1498 that Dilip Menon (1999) rejects as he identifies the need to take seriously the contemporary politics organizing violent struggles for justice. Menon (1999) contends that Dale's analysis views anticolonial violence as "tinged by Islam" and "assiduously traces the growth of a beleaguered Muslim identity back to 1498 and sees its culmination in an apocalyptic expression in the rebellion of 1921" (2001). K. N. Panikkar (1989) similarly critiques Dale's analysis, arguing that although he "notices agrarian exploitation and rural poverty," Dale (1988) defines the Mappila uprisings as "religious acts inspired by a small faction of the *ulama,*" rather than as political militancy incited by the "interplay" between economic discontent and religious ideology (Panikkar 1989, 192–93). For Menon (1999), "While there is certainly some virtue in a history over the long term, there is always the danger of ignoring short-term conjunctures and more contingent factors" (2001). Menon's critique of Dale and other similar scholars insists on a reading of the current, not just historical, contexts in which violent struggles emerge, such that simplistic explanations, like Islamicization or nationalist ambitions, do little to explain the relationship between politics and violence. These interventions insist on taking seriously the historical contexts and contemporary conditions that give rise to political violence, without reducing such armed struggles to wars of faith.

Instead of framing anticolonial resistance as a militant expression of Islam in the context of colonial occupation as in Dale's analysis, Santhosh Abraham (2014) shows how "the [anti-British] resistance by Mappila chieftains [in India] was carried out well within the region as the inheritors of the authority of those they had displaced and hence there was no attempt to expand beyond the frontiers of the area of authority" (380–81). Rather than conceptualize this violence as "wars for the faith" defined by "religious militancy" (Dale 1980, 1), Abraham (2014) argues that Muslims used violence, petitions, and other forms of resistance to challenge colonial incursions that eroded their territorial sovereignty, trade routes, and political autonomy. Even British colonialists later recognized the anticolonial politics of similar twentieth-century attacks by referring to "the wide-ranging acts of political violence that were directed at the government and its officials" in the 1920s and 1930s as *dacoity* (terrorism) enacted by *bhadralok dacoity* (gentlemanly terrorists)—anticolonial Indian elites who took up arms to expel the British from India (Ghosh 2017, 2). Edward Hyams (1975) similarly redefines terrorism as social warfare, finding it impossible to "pay the usual lip-service to the convention of treating terrorism as irredeemably wicked and cruel" because "it is a waste of words, ink, space, and spirit in the waste of shame created by the high explosive and fire bombs, the H-bombs and napalm, the political police terrorism, the crafty economic manipulations of the established parties in the Capitalist and Communist imperialist empires" (175). By taking seriously the formative conditions that give rise to political violence waged by "militant minorities" seeking to "weaken both the hold and will of the tenants of political power" (11), these studies challenge terrorism discourse that "singles out and removes from the larger historical and political context a psychological trait (terror), an organizational structure (the terrorist network), and a category (terrorism) in order to invent an autonomous and aberrant realm of gratuitous evil that defies any understanding" (Zulaika and Douglass 1996, 22).

In attending to the power relations that organize political violence, Gopal Singh (1976) draws on the Marxist approach to power to distinguish "establishment violence" from "mass violence." In this view, "establishment violence is an activity that flows from the dominant socio-economic groups of society," whereas mass violence "represents counter-violence" (65). This distinction accounts for how power organizes the constitution of lawful and legitimate violence and unlawful and illegitimate violence; both forms of force constitute "political violence," which "is the by-product of interaction between dominant socio-economic groups having a monopoly of control over the political apparatus of the society and the subsequent exploitation of the under-privileged and alienated masses" (65). For Singh, "politics, formal power structures, and violence are closely related to each other" (65). Samira Kawash (1999) draws on Frantz Fanon's 1959 book *A Dying Colonialism* and its analysis of Algerian resistance to French rule to similarly reframe terrorist violence as "a necessary counterforce to the more pervasive and ongoing terror instilled in the Algerian populace by the colonizing French" (237). In this reading of Fanon, "the revolutionary fighter's use of terrorist tactics is contextualized by insisting that these tactics be understood as a strategic response to the far more violent and ubiquitous terrorism of the colonial regime" (237). In this reframing, "this terror of decolonization is equally the terror that reappears today in the form of the 'terrorist' who confronts Western hegemony with the threat of a total destruction that—because it has been produced in and by Western hegemony—can never be contained or controlled" (242). While the terrorism discourse depoliticizes, dehistoricizes, and delegitimizes political violence, Kawash's analysis reframes such resistance as anticolonial:

> Terrorism in its contemporary incarnation appears uniquely linked to antagonisms formed in the aftermath of colonialism; the particular acts of violence labeled "terrorist" are typically the violence of formerly colonized groups against neocolonial or state oppressors. From the perspective of anticolonial sympathizers, such terrorism is a guerrilla tactic, one element in a larger struggle for liberation. But if a particular style of terrorism became a familiar revolutionary tactic in the anticolonial wars of the 1950s and 1960s, the "terrorist threat" as it appears in terrorism discourse today is no longer geographically localizable, nor does it any longer seem to be an expression of particular or local struggles. In its postcolonial incarnation in the 1980s and 1990s, "terrorism" stands as the violence of decolonization gone global. (240)

By considering the historical, social, and economic conditions that give rise to political violence, such as colonial occupation and military intervention, these theorizations of counterviolence and counterforce challenge how orthodox terrorism studies define terrorism as an irrational, amoral, and apolitical expression of religious fanaticism. Retheorizing political violence can help identify and address the root causes of armed struggles, even if we disagree with the political aspirations of armed groups or their use of lethal force.

Drawing on these anticolonial analyses, Joseph McQuade (2021) offers a more historical understanding of political violence, noting that "the first English-language use of the term 'terrorism' or 'terrorist' dates back to conservative philosopher Edmund Burke's analysis of the French Revolution at the end of the eighteenth century" to capture the political violence used to liberate oppressed peoples and establish a new government (12). McQuade (2021) draws on the work of historian Mikkel Thorup, who writes that while tyrannicide "is the slaying of a tyrant for the common good and its legitimation is contingent upon an idea of a natural and just order violated by the tyrant," terrorism "attacks the system or society which has already corrupted everybody, including the 'tyrant' and his helpers" (Thorup 2010, 9). In other words, "even though actual persons are being targeted, and perhaps their killing is being legitimated by specific actions they have committed, the real target of the attack is not the person but the abstraction of the system" (9–10). In this way, the political violence enacted after the French Revolution "concerns predominantly either the creation or the prevention of a new order. Revolution takes the place of tyrannicide as the premier legitimating reference of oppositional violence" (10). The rise of terrorist violence reflects the changing power relations "from throne to office, from king to minister, from sovereign to executive," making targeted assassinations not retributive justice against a specific ruler but a political effort to effect systemic change, as in the execution of King Louis XVI (10). Thorup therefore theorizes terrorism as "one expression of violence among many others, characterized not by a specific quality of the violence perpetrated, but rather by the structural position of the perpetrator and to investigate the ongoing interaction, the 'hostile dialectics' or 'violent dialogue' between state and nonstate actors" (2). Rather than exceptionalize terrorism as a modern trend instantiated by religious fanaticism, Thorup locates terrorism "within the much broader phenomenon of political violence" and examines "the structural constraints of convincing arguments for legitimate violence" (4–5). This approach to the study of terrorism focuses on the concrete conditions that give rise to violence, the political demands of armed militants, and the "structural constraints" that delegitimize nonstate violence challenging state power.

In his analysis of the Syrian revolution, sociologist Yasser Munif (2020, 19) draws on Walter Benjamin's theorization of violence to distinguish law-preserving violence exercised by constituted power from revolutionary violence enacted by disempowered constituents. Benjamin

(1978) identifies two types of violence: mythic "power-making" violence that establishes and preserves the law, and divine violence that ruptures the cycle maintained by mythic forms of the (violent) law and abolishes state power to institute "a new historical epoch" (252). As Benjamin writes, "If mythic violence is lawmaking, divine violence is law destroying; if the former sets boundaries, the latter boundlessly destroys them; if mythic violence brings at once guilt and retribution, divine power only expiates; if the former threatens, the latter strikes; if the former is bloody, the latter is lethal without spilling blood" (249–50). In this formulation, anticolonial violence seeking to institute a new world order can never be lawful, as it, by its very nature, challenges the law and its power-making functions. In Kawash's (1999) reading of Benjamin, anticolonial violence "oscillates" between mythic violence aimed at instituting "a new arrangement of rule within the flow of history" and divine violence that "would herald the blasting open of history to an order not after but on the other side of colonialism" (243). For Munif (2020), "the only violence that can oppose the violence of the sovereign is pure or revolutionary violence," as this type of violence "operates outside the law and revolves around the lives of the subaltern" (19). In each of these readings, understanding armed struggles requires an analysis of the social contexts, material conditions, and power relations that give rise to violence without reducing such violence to expressions of religious fanaticism or perverse ideologies.

While these studies amply demonstrate how "terrorism emerged as a category of exceptional criminality within the context of broader global forces such as colonialism, nationalism, and international law," the legal demand to adjudicate terrorism-related cases narrows the court's inquiry to the individual defendant, often at the exclusion of an analysis of the material conditions implicated in the making of political violence (McQuade 2021, 248). Given both the role of the criminal-legal system in the global war on terror and the narrowed inquiry criminal courts undertake in their proceedings, understanding this category of "exceptional criminality" is especially critical for abolitionists. Ending antiterrorism regimes that criminalize Muslim, Arab, and other nondominant communities requires an approach that advocates not just for those wrongly incarcerated, subjected to warrantless surveillance, or victimized through sting operations; it also must consider the perspectives of those who engage, or seek to engage, in violence to change intolerable conditions, affect public policy, or challenge despotic regimes. Unfortunately, orthodox approaches to terrorism "hide the root causes of violence by focusing on a cultural/religious explanation" and therefore ignore how "a genuine concern about violence" would "lead to ending imperialist foreign policy that terrorizes people across the global, and that is the initial violence 'terrorism' responds to" (Manzoor-Khan 2022, 28). Locating such armed struggles in the context of broader social forces illustrates that antiterrorism tactics to deter young people from the perceived pathway to violent extremism or to encourage nonviolent political engagement do little to change the inherent violence in certain modes of governance, including liberal democracies, which political actors challenge through their use of lethal force. Instead, as abolitionists, we must integrate an organizing approach that contests imperial regimes and military interventions while decriminalizing and destigmatizing violent political actors. Doing so refuses to condone nonstate violence while understanding that creating a less violent world requires attending to the "hidden crimes of the structurally powerful" (Henry 2017, 18) and to the structural violence that "shows up as unequal power and consequently as unequal life chances" (Galtung 1969, 171), both of which "can be far deadlier than direct violence" (Teltumbde 2017, 53).

By examining the legal making and remaking of the terrorist category, *Terrorism on Trial* offers insight into how the criminal court generally privileges state security over human security and reinforces the criminal-legal system's role as a counterterrorism tool, albeit it in halting and contested ways. This means that the criminal court is an insufficient if not outright harmful site to arrest cycles of political violence waged in the context of U.S. empire. My immersion in terrorism-related court proceedings taught me that how we understand—or perhaps, more accurately, misunderstand—political violence has enormous consequences for those marked, investigated, and tried as terrorists and for their families and communities. Shifting our understandings of terrorism is a vital step in creating a less violent world by better accounting for the broader social forces implicated in and shaped by the making of political violence and for the perspectives and politics of those driven to violence by intolerable conditions. In this way, *Terrorism on Trial* considers political violence by the disempowered to unfold on an entirely different plane than the kind of political violence enacted by the structurally powerful.

Making the Case: Exploring Terrorism Trials

Given the ample research documenting the trends in trying terrorism defendants (Center on Law and Security 2011; Center on National Security 2017; Greenberg et al. 2012; Said 2015; Norris and Grol-Prokopczyk 2017, 2018), this book does not offer a comprehensive analysis of every terrorism-related case in the United States. Instead, it investigates the messy contradictions, complexities, and contestations that define these court proceedings. Although security professionals treat the role of the criminal-legal system in the global war on terror as a settled matter, court records communicate legal anxieties and epistemic uncertainties often elided in public celebrations of terrorism convictions and academic analyses of terrorism prosecutions. This book therefore offers a more embodied analysis of global war on terror lawfare by exploring the microlevel practices of legal actors, the dynamic social contexts in which they conducted their work, and the geographical imaginations they incited. Far from the spectacular, and controversial, use of indefinite detention and torture at Guantánamo Bay, trying terrorism defendants in domestic courts registers a more mundane set of global war on terror practices that similarly degrade and confine suspected terrorists. Such legal pronouncements reflect broader social, political, and imperial logics that continue to dwell in the law, making domestic courtrooms not just expressions of legal thought but also of the deeper values, beliefs, and commitments that sustain U.S. empire. As Laleh Khalili (2013) explains, "The incarceration of civilians and combatants in warfare most clearly illuminates the inner workings of asymmetric neo-imperial warfare and its incorporation of law, administration, and knowledge production" (239). In this managerial approach to warfare, the law justifies, enables, and legitimizes illiberal practices of coercion, confinement, and lethal force to defeat insurgencies. In other words, the U.S. security state invokes the law to detain, confine, and incapacitate perceived enemies of the state—policing practices "rooted in colonialism and therefore racial violence" (Manzoor-Khan 2022, 77). This book therefore explores how legal actors negotiated the complex and conflicted role of the judicial system in the global war on terror and examines the law's relationship to violence.

To set the stage for this embodied analysis, chapter 1 introduces readers to the concept of offensive lawfare, which refers to the aggressive use of the law as a weapon of war. To do so, this chapter examines the history of legal codes that both constrained and enabled warfare to understand the contemporary invocation of the law to legitimize, justify, and execute controversial global war on terror practices, such as the indefinite detention of enemy combatants at Guantánamo Bay and the use of military commissions to try alleged global war on terror fighters. Rather than situate contemporary law as a progression of legal innovations over time, this chapter affirms how social scientists have rehistoricized the law by taking seriously how "the tactics of instantiating difference and forging an 'internal enemy' are colonial reverberations with a difference—and with more than a distant semblance to earlier racial logics, engendered fears, and counterinsurgent tactics from which they gained support" (Stoler 2016, 28).

Drawing on interviews with terrorism lawyers and security professionals, observation of court proceedings, and document analysis of court filings, chapters 2 and 3 examine how the courts have functioned as critical sites where certain understandings of geopolitical contexts, world affairs, and political violence shaped the decision-making of judges and the legal strategies of lawyers. To do so, I explore how legal actors asserted competing constellations of geographic knowledge and racial logics that judges and jurors drew on to understand the factual evidence in terrorism-related cases and interpret defendants' actions. For example, several cases debated the role of rebel groups in the Syrian war, whereby joining such armed forces could constitute a crime or a lawful military engagement authorized by the United States. Other cases questioned if the international community recognized ISIS as a legitimate state, meaning its soldiers met the legal definition of lawful combatants immune to criminal prosecution. Although security professionals often asserted coherent narratives celebrating terrorism prosecutions as global war on terror victories, a deeper exploration of court proceedings reveals a more embodied judicial system composed of legal actors with their own distinct perspectives, objectives, and geopolitical understandings.

By taking seriously how certain constellations of geographic knowledge have shaped the adjudication of terrorism-related cases, chapter 4 explores how domestic courts have legitimized, circulated, and consumed "orthodox terrorism expertise," particularly by admitting terrorologists as expert witnesses (Miller and Mills 2009). Because orthodox approaches to the study of terrorism abstract political violence from its formative conditions, the use of such expertise has narrowed how terrorism is made knowable in domestic courtrooms and strategically shaped how judges and jurors understood the defendants before them. By endorsing these scholars as terrorism experts and conferring legitimacy onto their testimony, the courts often denied defendants their credibility and capacity as knowers of their own lives and the political contexts in which they operated.

In chapter 5, I examine what I refer to as the legal life of radicalization research. This excavation reveals the different ways the courts have relied on federally funded scholarship to interpret the factual evidence in terrorism-related cases and then evaluate the dangerousness of the defendants before them. Unfortunately, this research typically reduces terrorism to the cultural, psychological, and/or theological pathologies of individual actors and abstracts violence from its formative conditions. By locating the problem of terrorism within individual actors rather than broader geopolitical contexts like war and empire, radicalization research reaffirms the role of the judicial system in incapacitating individual terrorists while obfuscating the very conditions that shape the making of political violence prosecutable under domestic law, such as the Syrian war.

In the Conclusion, I revisit how domestic courts serve as a counterterrorism tool and as a site of political contestation. To do so, I outline a radical imaginary that applies an abolitionist framework to the perceived problem of terrorism and that takes seriously how war, empire, and prisons are mutually constitutive in the context of the global war on terror. Despite calls to #AbolishICE and #AbolishDHS, terrorism trials demonstrate the urgent need to further develop emergent anti-imperial abolitionist imaginaries to reconceptualize the concept of terrorism, implicate U.S. empire in the making of political violence, and consider how to build a less violent and more liberatory world without relying on state security regimes.

Beginning with the situated experiences of terrorism defendants and their families, this book explores the social relations, academic discourses, and legal processes that have structured the uneven prosecution of terrorism-related cases in the United States. Given the continued (and contested) role of the judicial system as a counterterrorism tool, terrorism trials are important sites to understand the global war on terror and its manifold manifestations domestically. Through this analysis, *Terrorism on Trial* affirms the humanity of terrorism defendants and recognizes the state's invocation of the law to advance its military aims. In doing so, I argue that criminal prosecution expands the criminalization of communities of color without making the United States safer. Integrating an anti-imperialist framework into abolitionist organizing provides openings to craft new conceptual tools to develop radical alternatives to terrorism prosecutions, such as ending military interventions and colonial incursions that incite armed resistance, without accommodating state power.

1

OFFENSIVE LAWFARE
THE JURIDIFICATION OF THE GLOBAL WAR ON TERROR

On January 11, 2002, the first global war on terror captives arrived at the Guantánamo Bay naval base, located on a small strip of Cuban territory leased to the United States. Just two days earlier, legal advisors determined that "international treaties and federal laws on the treatment of detainees by the U.S. Armed Forces during the conflict in Afghanistan . . . do not protect members of the al-Qaeda organization, which as a non-State actor cannot be a party to the international agreements governing war. We further conclude that these treaties do not apply to Taliban militia" (Yoo and Delahunty 2002, 1). Described by Defense Secretary Donald Rumsfeld as "the hardest of the hardcore," these suspected al-Qaeda, Taliban, and other nonstate fighters faced an uncertain future as captives without legal rights in an endless war (qtd. in Gillan 2002).

Given these interpretations of the limited applicability of international law to the global war on terror, human rights advocates forewarned possible abuses at Guantánamo. In fact, Rumsfeld (2002) quietly authorized the use of "counter-resistance techniques" designed to "yield critical intelligence support" during military interrogations at Guantánamo, such as the "use of a wet towel and dripping water to induce the misperception of suffocation," also known as waterboarding (2, 6). As reports of prisoner abuse surfaced, journalist James Meek (2003) described Guantánamo as a "full-grown mongrel of international law, where all the harshness of the punitive U.S. legal system is visited on foreigners, unmitigated by any of the legal rights U.S. prisoners enjoy." In this offshore prison, Guantánamo detainees have been subjected to the law's punishment without the law's protection (Brännström 2008; Cacho 2012; Esmeir 2012; Dayan 2011).

Before the military transferred its detainees to Guantánamo, the Bush administration initiated a series of legislative changes that made illiberal practices like indefinite detention and counterresistance techniques lawful. For example, President Bush issued a November 2001 military order on the "Detention, Treatment, and Trial of Certain Non-citizens in the War against Terrorism."[1] This military order authorized the indefinite detention of suspected terrorists and their prosecution in special military tribunals "to protect the United States and its citizens, and for the effective conduct of military operations and prevention of terrorist attacks."[2] Given the "danger to the safety of the United States and the nature of international terrorism," the order further provisioned that "it is not practicable to apply in military commissions under this order the principles of law and the rules of evidence generally recognized in the trial of criminal cases in the United States district courts." Under this order, military tribunals could bypass constitutional obligations and procedural protections, such as the Sixth Amendment right to a speedy and public trial by an impartial jury and the Federal Rules of Evidence that govern the use of evidence at trial. Instead, the presiding officer could close trial proceedings to the public and order the "deletion" of classified materials without disclosure to the civilian defense counsel.[3] Through this military order, President Bush also imbued these military tribunals with "exclusive jurisdiction," meaning defendants "shall not be privileged to seek any remedy or maintain any proceeding . . . in (i) any court of the United States, or any State thereof, (ii) any court of any foreign nation, or (iii) any international tribunal." By giving military tribunals "exclusive jurisdiction," the Bush administration stripped federal courts of their power to provide judicial review of convictions and nullified the influence of international law on such proceedings. Unlike its rapid prosecution of Lindh in federal court, the Bush administration created the legal foundation to indefinitely detain noncitizens in offshore prisons and try them in military tribunals, even as it struggled to discern if its captives were enemy fighters or "innocent farmers scooped up in Afghanistan" (Goldsmith 2009, 118).

In addition to this military order, the Bush administration declared that the Republic of Cuba held "ultimate sovereignty" over Guantánamo, meaning "neither the Constitution nor U.S. obligations to international treaties apply" (Kaplan 2005, 834). By affirming Cuba's "ultimate sovereignty," the Bush administration claimed that Guantánamo was outside of the jurisdiction of the United States and thus beyond the reach of its laws. The naval base and its detention camps could not be regulated by domestic courts and detainees could not access the rights afforded to traditional criminal defendants held in the United States.

Although many human rights activists have described Guantánamo as a lawless place where U.S. soldiers can subject detainees to torture, abuse, and cruel treatment with impunity, social scientists have shown how the global war on terror "is *both* a war on law *and* a war fought through the law" (Gregory 2006, 420). Far from a legal "limbo" (Butler 2002), "legal black hole" (Steyn 2004, 1), or "prison beyond the law" (Margulies 2006, 100), Guantánamo reflects the "abundance of [law] that allows the government to engage seemingly illegal practices" (Dayan 2011, 61). Rather than a "lawless enclave" (Gibbons, qtd. in "Lawless Enclave?," 2004), Guantánamo operates through a kind of *hyper*-legality as the aggressive use of the law authorizes otherwise unlawful warfare, such as the indefinite detention of captured "enemy combatants" (Hussain 2007, 744). This means that "law becomes the site of political struggle not only in its suspension *but also in its formulation, interpretation, and application*" (Gregory 2006, 420). Legal innovations, not the law's absence, have facilitated the global war on terror (Johns 2005). Recognizing the law as a strategic weapon of war, the United States has used the law creatively to legitimize illiberal practices in its global war on terror, such as affirming Cuba's "ultimate sovereignty" over Guantánamo, and to sidestep the legal rights usually afforded to prisoners of war and other detainees held in U.S. custody.

President Bush's legal innovations demonstrate how political leaders have used the law to justify, defend, and expand U.S.-led military operations and other illiberal practices. As Laleh Khalili (2013) writes, "Liberal empires and conquering powers create *ostensibly* lawless places through a conscious and deliberate legal process of temporarily and functionally setting aside one body of law and adopting another, or in rarer and more extreme instances, replacing legal procedures with administrative procedures" (67). Given this influence, this chapter examines the dynamic relationship between law and violence by excavating the historical use of the law to symbiotically constrain and enable war. In doing so, I consider how presidential administrations and political leaders differentially have deployed these legal tools to achieve their military goals, often in contested ways. In fact, one legal advisor working to make U.S. military operations lawful reports that "one of the underappreciated stories in the war on terrorism" was "the daily clash inside the Bush administration between fear of another attack, which drives officials into doing whatever they can to prevent it, and the countervailing fear of violating the law, which checks their urge toward prevention" (Goldsmith 2009, 90). I also focus specifically on the changing, and sometimes contradictory, role of the judicial system in the global war on terror. These governing legal practices have criminalized armed struggles responsive to despotic regimes and foreign interventions while authorizing unrestrained state violence waged in the name of self-defense. Rather than objective tools to restrain war making, international laws and domestic criminal-legal systems have participated in the legitimation and expansion of state violence as well as the delegitimation and repression of nonstate violence.

This exploration takes seriously how "the legal system, always and everywhere, seeks to delegitimize and criminalize violence by actors other than those authorized to use violence (normally, the agents of the State—the police, the paramilitary forces, and the armed forces) and provides a normative language which camouflages the core coercion underlying the law" (Baxi 1993, 19). Examining the creative use of the law is central to understanding the U.S. security state's reliance on legal innovations to expand its military operations and the role of the judicial system in incapacitating nonstate fighters. As the global war on terror ravages on, the judicial system continues to play an important, albeit halting and contested, role in pursuing the U.S. security state's geopolitical goals, making it a key site to study. As globalized punishment continues to articulate with empire-building and war-making enterprises at Guantánamo, this analysis contributes to abolitionist struggles by offering a conceptual framework to understand and challenge these interlocking military–carceral modalities—one that does not rely on state intervention.

Lawfare: A Genealogy of the Relationship between Law and Violence

President Bush's use of the law as a global war on terror tool draws on a longer legacy of legal warfare, often referred to as "lawfare" (Dunlap 2001, 5). Colonel Mark W. Holzer (2012) defines lawfare as the "legal activities within the context of armed conflict." In theorizing lawfare, military strategists contend that state and nonstate actors alike can use and misuse the law to protect besieged populations, degrade their enemies, amplify violence, and/or mitigate hostilities in armed conflicts. For example, "defensive lawfare" constrains military strategy by ensuring such hostilities conform to the laws of armed conflict, as enemies can exploit the violation of these laws to "undermine the legitimacy of military operations" (Rousseau 2017, 19). "Offensive lawfare," however, actively contributes to armed hostilities by protecting certain fighters from facing prosecution in international criminal court while using the courts to incapacitate enemy soldiers. In both cases, the law actively participates in the making of war (Holzer 2012).

The distinction between offensive and defensive lawfare challenges popular portrayals of the law as a regulatory tool to restrain war making. Political geographer Craig A. Jones (2016) explains that "war, violence, and law are not separate or oppositional spheres, but rather animate one another in all kinds of ways" (222). For example, when the United States invaded Iraq in 2003, sanctions had "crippled the Iraqi air force to the point where fewer than one-third of its aircraft were flyable," making such legal arrangements as effective as shooting down enemy planes (Dunlap 2017, 10). In August 2002, Assistant Attorney General Jay Bybee signed a memo that formed the legal basis for President Bush's use of "enhanced interrogation techniques."[4] In the memo, Bybee determined that under the United Nations Convention against Torture, interrogators' conduct only qualified as torture if they inflicted physical pain "equivalent in intensity to the pain accompanying serious physical injury, such as organ failure, impairment of bodily function, or even death" (6). Furthermore, interrogators must "specifically intend" to "cause severe mental pain or suffering" for their actions to constitute torture (8). As these examples of offensive warfare illustrate, the United States government has mobilized the law to legitimize, commit, and protect illiberal practices that advance its global war on terror agenda.

Evident in the uneven juridification of the global war on terror, governing geopolitical contexts shape how the law is weaponized. This means that lawfare can be put to work by differently situated actors, such as powerful politicians who use state institutions to advance their military agendas or disempowered constituents who strategically engage the criminal-legal system to make reparative claims for justice. Such an approach recognizes the various ways lawfare "is performed by social actors acting in a milieu of power relations" such that some forms of lawfare are viewed as permissible and others as abusive (Jones 2016, 232). Understanding the Bush administration's initiation of lawfare in the global war on terror requires a historical exploration of the evolution of the laws governing war and their uses, particularly by state-sponsored military strategists.

Law professor Michal Belknap (2002) reports that the "first use of something comparable to what President Bush has authorized following the adoption and ratification of the Constitution occurred during the [1846–48] Mexican War" when General Winfield Scott declared martial law (448). General Orders Number 20 noted the "silence" in written codes on "offenses committed by individuals of the enemy country against individuals in the [U.S.] army or their properties" (Scott 1847). The orders therefore established military commissions to try "any Mexican inhabitant, denizen, or traveler" who committed certain crimes against U.S. soldiers, such as murder, malicious beatings, robbery, and theft (Scott 1847). The orders stipulated that all armies needed to observe the "rules and articles of war" while in "enemy countries" and that violators of these war doctrines would be tried in military commissions (Scott 1847). These early "councils of war" and military commissions sought to regulate warfare, a principled practice that would continue to guide U.S. military engagements. Over time, the federal government developed and mobilized additional laws of war to constrain military conduct (Chomsky 1990; Skinner 2013).

Although laws of war and their attendant military tribunals sought to regulate permissible behavior and normalize conduct during armed conflicts, such laws always developed in tension with the desire to win wars, sustain the gains achieved through such military victories, and punish opposing soldiers and their supporters. For example, after the Dakota

War of 1862, U.S. Army field commander Colonel Henry Sibley tried, convicted, and sentenced to death more than three hundred Dakota men in Minnesota for "murders or other outrages upon the Whites." Sibley used these military commissions to punish Dakota men for "killings committed in warfare" (Chomsky 1990, 14). Although Indigenous soldiers fought on behalf of a sovereign nation at war with the United States, these military commissions denied Indigenous soldiers their legal right to wartime protections, such as immunity from prosecution for lawful acts of war. Legal historian Carol Chomsky explains the unfair conduct and genocidal logic that organized these trials:

> The evidence was sparse, the tribunal biased, the defendants were unrepresented in unfamiliar proceedings conducted in a foreign language, and authority for convening the tribunal was lacking. More fundamentally, neither the Military Commission nor the reviewing authorities recognized that they were dealing with the aftermath of a war fought with a sovereign nation and that the men who surrendered were entitled to treatment in accordance with that status. (qtd. in Charles 2017)

These military proceedings reflect how laws of war historically and presently have sought to constrain warfare while strategically supporting the military operations of powerful states. Such tensions enabled President Lincoln to authorize the execution of thirty-eight Indigenous soldiers, condone settler violence, and sanction the expulsion of Dakotans from Minnesota and the abolishment of their reservations. In this legal context, "Enlightenment rules [could] stand alongside wars of extermination on the [Indigenous] frontier" (Witt 2012, 5). Ensuing U.S.-led military operations generated similar laws of armed conflict that symbiotically constrained and enabled warfare. In fact, the United States' "long history of leadership in creating the laws of war stands cheek by jowl with a destructive style of warfare that has become known among military historians as the 'American way of war'" (Witt 2012, 5). The United States has waged war by mobilizing the law as a strategic tool to expand its powers and to punish its enemies.

In the midst of federal aggression against Indigenous resistance, President Lincoln both intensified the Union army's participation in the Civil War and sought to develop rules of warfare to normalize military conduct. Drafted by Francis Lieber in 1863, General Orders 100 identified 157 provisions regulating the methods and means of warfare in the United States.[5] Through his work, Lieber crafted a framework that integrated humanitarian principles into the regulation of warfare.

Although President Lincoln sought to constrain the conduct of war through this Lieber Code, these provisions also expanded the legal tools available to advance the Union's interests. For example, the Lieber Code outlined that it is "against the usage of modern war to resolve, in hatred and revenge, to give no quarter" while also authorizing that "deserters from the American Army, having entered the service of the enemy, suffer death if they fall again into the hands of the United States, whether by capture, or being delivered up to the American Army." The Lieber Code also asserted that "military necessity" justified "all direct destruction of life or limb of armed enemies, and of other persons whose destruction is incidentally unavoidable in the time of armed contests of the war," in addition to the destruction of property and the withholding of the means to life from the enemy. Over time, the Lieber Code would influence the organizing principle that under *jus in bello*—the law governing warfare—a state has "the authority to employ *all* measures not otherwise prohibited by international law to bring about prompt submission of the enemy" (Corn 2012, 68). The Lieber Code legalized the Union's expansive wartime activities, a legacy that would inform future laws of armed conflict.

To support these methods of warfighting, the Lieber Code also replaced civilian criminal courts with military commissions, which were seen as "the best option for unconventional combatants" not formally enlisted in the Confederate army (Skinner 2013, 315). Such military commissions could try unconventional combatants for their participation in armed hostilities, such as attacking Union supply lines, railways, and military forces. By classifying these wartime participants as unlawful combatants, the Lieber Code facilitated their prosecution for activities that supported the Confederate army, ultimately denying their status as lawful soldiers and thus their immunity from prosecution. Like General Orders 20, the Lieber Code distinguished lawful combatants from illegitimate belligerents unentitled to legal protections. As we will see, the legacy of the Lieber Code continues to bear on late modern warfare by categorically denying nonstate actors like Taliban fighters the protections typically afforded to lawful combatants.

The Lieber Code demonstrates how laws of armed conflict can both constrain and enable violence. Despite prohibiting torture, assassination, the use of poison, and acts of perfidy, "the law of war Lincoln approved in early 1863 was not merely a constraint on the tactics of the Union. It was also a weapon for the achievement of Union war aims, like the Springfield rifle, the minie ball, and the ironclad ship"—military tools "for vindicating the destiny of the nation" (Witt 2012, 4). As a weapon of war, the Lieber Code would later inform the development of international laws of armed conflict that similarly constrained and enabled brutal warfare.

Informed by the Lieber Code, the international community developed new laws of armed conflict in the late nineteenth century. This led to the 1864 adoption of the First Geneva Convention for the Amelioration of the Condition of the Wounded and Sick in Armed Forces in the Field.[6] Subsequently revised in 1906, 1929, and 1949, the First Geneva Convention detailed the "basis on which rest the rules of international law for the protection of the victims of armed conflicts." The First Geneva Convention provides a set of laws to govern war and the corresponding treatment of civilians and combatants. For example, the convention mandates the humane treatment of wounded and sick military personnel entitled to prisoner of war status. The First Geneva Convention also codified the laws of armed conflict, with subsequent revisions expanding and clarifying such rules of war to sixty-four articles.

Responding to the "terrorism-like offenses" utilized by Nazi Germany during World War II, the international community convened military tribunals that charged, convicted, and sentenced Nazi officials for war crimes (Chomsky 1990, 316). For its part, the United States convicted 142 members of the Third Reich in its Nuremberg military tribunals, twenty-four of whom were sentenced to death (Skinner 2013). The Nuremberg trials, however, conformed to few legal standards, offering little systemized guidance on how these proceedings reached sentencing decisions that could inform future military tribunals. The trials also reinforced the idea that "justice" following war means punishing "crimes" through confinement and death. These understandable desires for punishment, if not outright revenge, reflect the practical and imaginative limitations of how we conceptualize what constitutes justice in the wake of war and genocide. In this understanding of justice, wartime violations must be punished through sanctions, confinement, and even death.

In 1948, the International Red Cross convened an international conference to expand wartime protections in response to Nazi atrocities and to establish protocols to enforce these protections. The convening led to a final revision of the First Geneva Convention and the adoption of three additional international protocols to regulate warfare: the Convention for the Amelioration of the Condition of the Wounded, Sick, and Shipwrecked Members of Armed Forces at Sea; the Convention Relative to the Treatment of Prisoners of War; and the Convention Relative to the Protection of Civilian Persons in Time of War. Today, the international community refers to these collective agreements as the Geneva Conventions.

Because these conventions refused to use the term genocide, the United Nations General Assembly drafted and adopted the Convention on the Prevention and Punishment of the Crime of Genocide in 1948, explicitly condemning genocidal acts and providing provisions to punish "persons guilty of genocide."[7] In 1977, the United Nations General Assembly called on member states to ratify two additional protocols to improve the legal protections during unconventional international conflicts and civil wars. Protocol I grants protections to irregular guerrilla forces engaged in unconventional international conflicts "in which peoples are fighting against colonial domination, alien occupation, or racist regimes."[8] By outlawing the use of indiscriminate attacks and the destruction of food and water sources in these unconventional conflicts, Protocol I expands wartime protections to women, children, civilian medical workers, and journalists, and prohibits attacks on critical infrastructures, cultural artifacts, and places of worship. As the only provision applicable to noninternational armed conflicts, Protocol II "elaborates on protections for victims caught up in high-intensity internal conflicts such as civil wars" by prohibiting "violence to the life, health, and physical or mental well-being of people" (American Red Cross 2011, 6). Informed by the Lieber Code, these conventions have sought to constrain the conduct of war and regulate military aggression while ensuring the protection of civilians, combatants, and captured, wounded, or sick soldiers. In doing so, these agreements codify what is now known as international humanitarian law, which integrates humanitarian principles into the regulation of armed conflicts.

Criminalizing Armed Resistance: International Law and the State's Monopoly on Violence

Despite the global affirmation of these legal developments to regulate armed conflicts, critical scholars have documented how Western powers established these conventions in the midst of brutal colonial wars. For example, historian Mohammad-Mahmoud Ould Mohamedou (2011) notes:

> Explicitly, at the very same time that diplomatic conferences were held in Europe—Geneva (1963), Brussels (1874), The Hague (1899 and 1907), and London (1909)—to agree [on] humane, professional, and civilized ways to conduct warfare and avoid unnecessary suffering in the prosecution of international armed conflict, a significant number of the states gathered therein were involved in conflicts in Africa, the Middle East, and Asia in which targeting of civilian populations was tolerated and often planned for as a part of "necessary" security measures. (21–22)

Political scientist Mahmood Mamdani (2004) similarly writes that at the onset of the twentieth century, "it was a European habit to distinguish between civilized wars and colonial wars. The laws of war applied to wars among the civilized nation-states, but the laws of nature were said to apply to colonial wars, and the extermination of the lower races was seen as a biological necessity" (7). This means that the "standard-setting efforts that were under way during the nineteenth century mostly concerned powerful European nations" such that "colonized civilians (and their assets) subject to European rule would continue to be attacked indiscriminately well into the twentieth century" (Ould Mohamedou 2011, 21). In this view, international law regulated wars between European states, not European states engaged in colonial warfare in Algeria, Kenya, Congo, and elsewhere. In this way, the "construction and universalization of international law were essential to the imperial expansion that subordinated non-European peoples and societies to European conquest and domination" (Mutua 2000, 31). These critiques identify how power relations, racial formations, and colonial regimes shape the uneven development and enforcement of laws of armed conflict, such that powerful state militaries sometimes can kill civilians, torture prisoners of war, and destroy villages with impunity.

Critical analyses of the judicialization of international politics and the juridification of war illustrate how the law mediates violence in ways that protect sovereign power and repress popular uprisings. This means that international law both absolves Western states of their excessive violence in their colonies and criminalizes violence waged by nonstate actors challenging sovereign power. In a state-centric world order, the state is defined by its monopoly on the legitimate use of force, meaning that "the state is considered the sole source of the 'right' to use violence" (Weber 1946, 77). In this formulation, nonstate armed conflicts are by definition illegal and illegitimate. International law reinforces what cultural critic Walter Benjamin (1978) refers to as the distinction between law-preserving violence and revolutionary violence. For Benjamin, law-preserving violence "pertains to the order of the 'constituted power' and consists in legal, para- or extra-legal measures that sustain the existing law and order of things" (Prozorov 2014, 116). Revolutionary violence, however, "pertains to the dimension of 'constituent power' and serves to institute a new form of order, which makes it *ipso facto* impossible to subsume under the existing laws and norms" (116). Here, "the law's defense of its monopoly on violence stems from the fact that violence outside the law threatens the law itself" (Erlenbusch 2010, 168). In this way, "power is revealed as the true end of law, and violence takes the character of a performative that guarantees and reinforces power" (169). Put simply, the law enacts and protects sovereign power. By criminalizing revolutionary violence and legitimizing law-preserving violence, international law safeguards the state's monopoly on violence.

Benjamin's (1978) concept of revolutionary violence challenges the authority of international law in defining what constitutes legitimate warfare by recognizing the formative conditions that give rise to nonstate armed groups and their political aspirations while also acknowledging how states use law-preserving violence to reinforce sovereign power. As sociologist Yasser Munif (2020) assesses, "International law does not recognize non-state actors or subaltern violence outside the state. In short, it delegitimizes Benjamin's revolutionary violence" (19).

By criminalizing popular uprisings and legitimizing state violence, international law reaffirms state sovereignty and ignores the lived realities of subaltern actors engaged in armed struggles. In doing so, international law declares nonstate violence, by its very definition, illegal, irrespective of the everyday conditions that give rise to such armed conflicts, including colonial warfare and military occupation.

Regulating a New Grammar of War: Asymmetric Warfare and International Law

Legal strategists developed state-centric international law in the context of a specific grammar of war, largely defined by "simultaneous and orderly, symmetrical interstate conflict" (Ould Mohamedou 2011, 20). In this archetypal war between or within states, battles occur at a specific time and place between identified soldiers, without harming civilians. Conflict, however, evolves, with a new type of warfare emerging at the end of the twentieth century. Unlike previous generations of warfare "focused respectively on gathered manpower, assembled firepower, and decisive maneuvering, this latest generation is concerned centrally with the destruction of the enemy's political will to fight and is, thus, characterized by the notion of network warfare" (Ould Mohamedou 2011, 25). Defined as asymmetric warfare, these conflicts occur between groups with unbalanced military capabilities, where "asymmetries of strength are based on a capacity for acceleration which outstrips that of the enemy, whereas asymmetries of weakness are based on a readiness and ability to slow down the pace of war" (Munkler 2003, 9). For example, al-Qaeda has recognized its limited military capabilities by decelerating armed conflicts, ultimately attacking "when it is ready while keeping its enemy constantly in a protracted state of defensive anticipation" (Ould Mohamedou 2011, 28). Outmatched technologically, al-Qaeda revolutionized war according to its own strategic strengths, abandoning the speed and force that define more conventional armed conflicts. International law, however, was not designed to regulate asymmetric warfare waged by transnational fighters who engage state militaries at different velocities and at unidentified times and places. As Toni Pfanner (2005) writes, "It is debatable whether the challenges of asymmetrical war can be met with the current law of war. If wars between States are on the way out, perhaps the norms of international law that were devised for them are becoming obsolete as well" (158). In the absence of alternative laws that recognize both transnational conflicts and revolutionary violence, powerful states can weaponize international law in ways unavailable to nonstate fighters.

Because state-centric international law regulates symmetric inter- and intra-state war, it categorically defines many of the strategies used by nonstate armed groups as illegal and illegitimate violence. For example, as transnational armed groups strategize in the context of asymmetric warfare, they often target civilians. Although some scholars blame Islamic perversions for this civilian targeting (Laqueur 1999), nonstate actors often identify civilians as complicit participants in the violent making of the current world order. In this political view, civilians bear some responsibility for the conditions that give rise to armed conflicts as they pay taxes and elect political leaders who wage war, impose sanctions, and kill civilians on their behalf. For example, in a 1999 interview, Osama bin Laden explained that "Muslim scholars have issued a fatwa against any American who pays taxes to his government. He is our target because he is helping the American war machine against the Muslim nation" (*Newsweek* 1999). Facing condemnation for killing civilians, bin Laden reasoned in May 1998, "Through history, America has not been known to differentiate between the military and the civilians or between men and women and children. Those who threw the atomic bombs and used the weapons of mass destruction against Nagasaki and Hiroshima were the Americans. Can the bombs differentiate between military and women and infants and children? America has no religion that can deter her from exterminating whole peoples" (qtd. in Miller 1999). Given al-Qaeda's political analysis and subsequent military strategy, "the responsibilization and resulting targeting of civilians cannot be reconciled with the central international humanitarian law tenet of discrimination [between soldiers and civilians]; the *ius in bello* principle of non-combatant immunity" (Ould Mohamedou 2011, 39).[9] Although the international community determined that al-Qaeda's conduct violates the laws of armed conflict, "holding the citizens of the state responsible individually and documenting their rationale for such conduct indicates effective control and a potential measure of respect for the rules" (39). This political analysis recognizes that al-Qaeda's indiscriminate warfare corresponds to its enemies' own tactics and strategically imputes civilians.

Yet international law categorically prohibits indiscriminate attacks, thus delegitimizing al-Qaeda's military strategy without regulating U.S. drone strikes, which mostly kill unintended targets.[10]

The uneven enforcement of international law demonstrates how power relations shape the law's mediation of violence, which means that the popular struggles waged by armed nonstate actors can never constitute legal and legitimate violence. My analysis does not intend to condone one type of violence and not another; it merely meditates on how prevailing power relations infuse international law as it marks state violence and its indiscriminate targeting as more permissible—and more moral—than nonstate violence and its indiscriminate targeting.

Given the role of international law in delegitimizing and depoliticizing popular armed struggles, critical scholars have insisted on understanding revolutionary violence by studying the governing historical, geopolitical, and social contexts that generate conflict rather than employing the state-centric principles that currently organize international law. Frantz Fanon (1963), for example, writes:

> The violence which has ruled over the ordering of the colonial world, which has ceaselessly drummed the rhythm for the destruction of native social forms and broken up without reserve the systems of reference of the economy, the customs of dress and external life, that same violence will be claimed and taken over by the native at the moment when, deciding to embody history in its own person, he surges into forbidden quarters. To wreck the colonial world is henceforward a mental picture of action which is very clear, very easy to understand, and which may be assumed by each one of the individuals which constitute the colonized people. (40–41)

For Fanon, violence is the "natural state" of colonial rule organized by the racialized dehumanization of the colonized subject such that for the colonized, "this violence represents the absolute praxis. The militant therefore is one who works. . . . The colonized man liberates himself in and through violence" (44). Fanon's analysis highlights how violence cannot be understood by narrowly assessing the psychology of individual actors; violence must be placed in its formative conditions, such as colonial rule. This approach insists on considering the material conditions that drive armed struggles and the political aspirations of armed fighters.

Like Fanon's study of violent armed resistance to violent colonial rule, Munif argues that the Syrian revolution cannot be understood without examining its formative conditions, such as the Assad family's imposition of a state of emergency under which it has intimidated, incarcerated, and assassinated its political opponents. For Munif (2020), the "international context allowed the Assad family to impose the state of emergency for almost half a century with no real consequences. International institutions such as the United Nations failed to address the issue, due to the pressure of powerful state actors" (15). These conditions led to the 2011 Syrian uprising, which challenged the despotic ideology of the Ba'ath party and its brutal violence under the Assad regime. In this view, the broader 2011 Arab revolts challenged "both post-colonial despotism and neoliberalism" and marked the emergence of popular nationalisms defined by their political pluralities and decolonial possibilities (97). Understanding popular struggles to establish livable spaces forces us to consider the *politics* inherent in revolutionary violence and the *power* in declaring such violence unlawful; such analyses require a conceptual framework that envisions a politics not bound by the state. Unfortunately, international law merely reinscribes the centrality of the state by categorically criminalizing armed nonstate groups and ignoring what transnational militias are fighting for and why.

Although the drive to regulate war making and death dealing through international law is understandable, treating international law as an apolitical mechanism to constrain armed conflicts ignores the colonial roots of such legal conventions, which legitimize brutal state violence and criminalize armed struggles challenging state power (Mutua 2000; Rousseau 2017). Put differently, "international law has never been a project that universalizes benign principles across difference, but has been a key institution in the production and management of difference, a tool of governance for the 'First World' to rule over the 'Third World'" (Jones 2016, 230). These colonial histories and legal geographies illustrate how it is not just insurgents who engage lawfare; the weaponization of the law is "at the heart of empire and colonialism" (232). It is precisely through the law that the United States could invade Afghanistan and Iraq, kill civilians, and detain and torture al-Qaeda soldiers with impunity while criminalizing armed resistance to such military operations.

The concept of revolutionary violence also militates against reductive analyses that conflate transnational armed groups like al-Qaeda and ISIS, and define their fighters as religious fanatics rather than as political actors. For example, Ould Mohamedou (2011) describes al-Qaeda as an armed political movement that "concluded that given the current configuration of Arab politics, it is not possible to realistically expect the region's long-time a-dying regimes to defend the populations' interests. The group then organized to achieve those goals and, in the process, effect a more legitimate social, political, economic, and religious rule" (42). Through its efforts, al-Qaeda "constituted in effect an alternative international community to the official one" (Rubin 2002, xv–xvi). In al-Qaeda's political perspective, the failure of Arab states to respond to U.S. military aggression constituted a casus belli, with the intention of establishing a governance regime capable of defending local populations and their interests.

Osama bin Laden identified these geopolitical goals in several public statements, including his 1996 Declaration of Jihad against the Americans Occupying the Land of the Two Holiest Sites. In this declaration, bin Laden held the United States, in its alliance with Saudi Arabia, responsible for "killing hundreds of thousands of Muslims and desecrating their sacred sites." Given this violence, bin Laden declared that the "blood of American enemy troops occupying the Muslim lands is lawful." In a 1998 statement, bin Laden similarly indicted the United States for "occupying the lands of Islam in the holiest of places, the Arabian Peninsula, plundering its riches, dictating to its rulers, humiliating its people, terrorizing its neighbors, and turning its bases in the Peninsula into a spearhead through which to fight neighboring Muslim peoples." Bin Laden concluded that these "crimes and sins committed by the Americans are a clear declaration of war on Allah, his messenger, and Muslims." Through these statements, bin Laden identified clear political grievances which he defined as justifiable conditions to initiate an armed struggle with occupying forces. Under international law, however, the United States could lawfully impose economic sanctions and inflict military aggression on al-Qaeda, but, as a nonstate militia, al-Qaeda could not engage the same tactics. The law, after all, "is the expression of a particular order, which in turn represents a power configuration. That order and that force are inseparable from their context" (Ould Mohamedou 2011, 33).

As these issues illustrate, international law remains "tautologously state-centered, state-defined, and state-controlled" even as "twenty-first century warfare is not," such that the "ritualization and regulation of war have become problematic" (Ould Mohamedou 2011, 34). As a state-centric model organized by the dynamics of the current world order, international law can intensify, rather than eliminate, power asymmetries, demonstrative of how certain rules of armed conflict apply to interstate wars but not colonial wars.[11] In this legal context, the United States could weaponize international law by authorizing illiberal practices like using counterresistant techniques, criminalizing nonstate violence, and denying nonstate actors standard legal protections.

Understanding lawfare is critical to abolitionist organizing as it clarifies the social structures, racial formations, and legal regimes that have brought military-carceral modalities like Guantánamo into existence. Although closing Guantánamo is an important struggle, social scientists and community organizers alike cannot lose sight of the legal architectures, geopolitical conditions, and military operations that have enabled this offshore prison and the brutal practices within it. Abolishing Guantánamo therefore requires dismantling the imperial paradigms and practices precipitating offshore detention, such as inward and outward U.S.-led military operations, economic sanctions, security regimes, and offensive lawfare, as well as the global racial system in which these technologies circulate. The struggle to close Guantánamo is intimately tied to eliminating these expansive forms of globalized punishment, from indiscriminate drone strikes to legalized torture to domestic terrorism prosecutions, and to addressing the conditions, like U.S.-led military intervention and colonial occupation, that give rise to armed struggles criminalized under international law.

The carceral use of Guantánamo is tied to both U.S.-led imperial warfare in the Arab region and coercive policing practices to repress political dissidence in Arab, Muslim, Black, and other nondominant communities in the United States. As Daulatzai (2007) explains, "The racialized discourse of empire" produced "a subject where the foreign and domestic collapse upon themselves, as the fears of 'terror' are conflated with 'Black criminality,' gangs, prison culture, and urban violence" such that the "carceral logic and captive power that has historically been forged around Blackness in the United States not only makes legible this new emerging threat, but it also becomes the template for the exporting of this prison regime to the colony in the 'War on Terror'" (136). Furthermore, "carceral technologies of racial control in the United States" articulate with "the practices of foreign counterinsurgency," as policing has "domesticated anti-imperial Black politics and depoliticized radicalism" (Edwards 2021, 48). In other words, antiblackness not only "has historically shortened the rhetorical distances between domestic 'criminal' and foreign Muslim 'terrorist'"; it also has forged counterinsurgency regimes of state protection that have criminalized, pathologized, and delegitimized radical political organizations as terrorist threats, like the Black Panther Party for Self-Defense and the Palestine Liberation Organization (55). Such inextricable links demand an abolitionist approach that attends to inward and outward modes of colonial containment, expansion, and occupation and that takes seriously the politics animating the use of lethal force.

The Bush Doctrine: Preemptive Self-Defense, Preventative Detention, and Military Commissions

On September 11, 2001, President Bush reassured the U.S. public that he "would take every precaution to protect our citizens at home and around the world from further attacks" (Bush 2001b). President Bush's pledge aligned with international law, which permits the anticipatory use of force in the face of an imminent attack. The Bush administration, however, also began pushing the limits of this legal standard to authorize preemptive military operations, even in the absence of evidence forecasting an imminent attack.

In 2002, President Bush issued his "National Security Strategy of the United States of America," which declared his administration's legal right to "preemptive actions to counter a sufficient threat to our national security" (15). President Bush argued, "For centuries, international law recognized that nations need not suffer an attack before they can lawfully take action to defend themselves against forces that present an imminent danger of attack" (15). Although the Bush administration recognized that "legal scholars and international jurists often conditioned the legitimacy of preemption on the existence of an imminent threat" most evident in the mobilization of enemy armed forces, it also argued that "rogue states and terrorists" engage in unconventional armed conflicts such that "the United States cannot remain idle while dangers gather" (15). Referred to as the Bush Doctrine, this approach asserted the legal right to self-defense to justify "acting preemptively against such terrorists, to prevent them from doing harm against our people and our country" (6). In this cold military calculus, "our best defense is a good offense" (6).

Under the Bush Doctrine, preemption required preventative wars that could initiate regime change by ousting political leaders and destroying insurgent networks before they could threaten U.S. national security. Using the cover of international law, the Bush administration designed a series of unilateral initiatives that advanced its imperial interventions in Afghanistan and Iraq in the name of national security. Even in the absence of an imminent threat, the Bush administration invoked the right to self-defense to justify its military invasions.

Despite the Bush administration's reinterpretation of international laws regulating the use of force, many legal scholars contend that "the doctrine of preemptive strikes formulated in the *U.S. National Security Strategy* . . . constitutes an unacceptable expansion on the right of anticipatory self-defense" (Aggelen 2009, 35). More specifically, President Bush's preemptive military campaigns violated the four principles that organize the use of anticipatory force: the immediacy of the threat, the certainty of the threat, the necessity of an armed response, and the proportionality of the armed response (Badalič 2021, 175). Both the Bush and Obama administrations redefined the concept of imminent threat in the context of the global war on terror by eliminating considerations of the immediacy and certainty of the threat. Assistant to the President for Homeland Security and Counterterrorism John O. Brennan (2011), for example, argued, "We are finding increasing recognition in the international community that a more flexible understanding of 'imminence' may be appropriate when dealing with terrorist groups, in part because threats posed by nonstate actors do not present themselves in ways that evidenced imminence in more traditional conflicts." Although the United States has been unwilling to rethink the international laws regulating armed conflicts involving nonstate actors, it also has insisted that the "threats posed by nonstate actors" necessitated a "more flexible" rubric of imminence that authorized the use of preemptive military strikes, without a clear immediate and certain threat. In other words, the law could accommodate U.S., but not insurgent, military tactics.

To support these preemptive military strikes, Attorney General John Ashcroft (2003) announced that the Department of Justice "added a new paradigm to that of prosecution—a paradigm of prevention." Ashcroft mobilized the criminal-legal system to support the global war on terror through preemptive prosecutions facilitated by preventative policing practices. Under this "paradigm of prevention," law enforcement agencies aggressively have gathered intelligence, conducted interrogations, intensified surveillance, and expanded preventative detention—strategies that have complemented the military's preemptive operations. Rather than pursue and punish individuals after they commit a crime, the Department of Justice has deployed preemptive tactics to surveil, detain, and prosecute suspected terrorists on the basis of speculative fears about future acts of violence.

Vice President Cheney's one percent doctrine organized this prevention paradigm. According to this doctrine, "if there's just a one percent chance of the unimaginable coming due, act as if it is a certainty" (qtd. in Suskind 2006, 62). In subscribing to the one percent doctrine, law enforcement agencies have pursued thousands of tips—"threats"—even as the number of al-Qaeda operatives "actually in this country has held at zero or nearly so, and the FBI's inability to find sleeper cells has persisted to the present day—the ghostly terrorists espied in the thousands by the intelligence community in 2002 either never existed or afterward obligingly vanished" (Mueller and Stewart 2016, 17). This means that law enforcement agencies have targeted individuals who appear susceptible to terrorist radicalization and recruitment, even if such individuals have not yet committed a crime. When using anticipatory logic to identify unknowable future threats, "the relation of past, present, and future is reconfigured such that future uncertainty can be acted upon in the present, even when there is little or no knowledge of past instances or probabilities" (Amoore 2013, 62). Citing the doctrine of preemptive self-defense, the Bush administration sought to legalize a new set of otherwise unconstitutional investigative and prosecutorial tools, such as broad preventive detention authority and warrantless electronic surveillance, in the name of national security. To align with international law, the Bush Doctrine muddied the distinction between preemption (imminent enemy attack) and prevention (nonimminent enemy attack).[12]

For the Bush administration, military commissions offered a forum to try suspected terrorists without being held accountable for sidestepping its constitutional obligations and stripping defendants of their legal rights under international and domestic laws. Law professor David Cole (2013) argues that "military commissions are a by-product of the 'paradigm of prevention'" as the government chose to "sweep broadly, presume guilt without substantial evidence, detain innocents, and adopt 'enhanced interrogation techniques' to coerce detainees into talking" (99). Such policing practices "have greatly complicated and compromised the task of holding terrorists accountable, because such illegal shortcuts in investigatory rules taint any evidence obtained therefrom, and make it inadmissible in a criminal trial" (99). Initially authorized by President Bush's November 2001 military order, military commissions could, by design, punish suspected fighters while protecting the coercive practices employed by U.S. armed forces, contracted mercenaries, and law enforcement agencies that could be called into question through civilian court proceedings. As former assistant attorney general Jack Goldsmith (2009) reports:

> By February 2002, the administration had developed a coherent legal strategy for incapacitating terrorists. Congress had authorized the war and triggered the President's traditional war powers, and the President possessed independent war powers as Commander in Chief. The President exercised these traditional powers to detain enemy soldiers and, possibly, to try them in military commissions. He chose Guantánamo Bay as the main detention site, a place that other presidents had used for similar purposes. And he had embraced the traditional American view that the Geneva Conventions did not give [prisoner of war] protections to combatants who fought out of uniform and failed to comply with the laws of war. Inside the administration the legal foundation for counterterrorism policies seemed strong. (114–15)

Organized by the logic of anticipatory force and self-defense, military commissions complemented the Bush administration's tactics of preemptive military strikes, preventative policing practices, and indefinite detention.

Military Commissions: From the Civil War to the Global War on Terror

The Bush administration drew part of its confidence in the legality of military commissions from case precedent, as previous presidents similarly used such forums to quickly try suspected war criminals. For example, in 1942, eight German residents surreptitiously traveled from France to the United States by submarine, with the intention of sabotaging U.S. military production capabilities on behalf of the German military. Although the eight operatives wore "complete or partial German uniforms to ensure treatment as prisoners of war rather than as spies if they were caught in the act of landing," they removed and buried their uniforms with sabotage materials once they arrived on shore, with one group landing at Ponte Verde Beach, Florida, and the other at Amagansett, New York (FBI, n.d.). President Franklin D. Roosevelt determined that, without uniforms and with the intention of sabotage, the men acted perfidiously and thus violated the laws of war. Classifying the men as unlawful combatants, President Roosevelt ordered the men to stand trial by military commission, which found all eight men guilty and sentenced them to death.[13] On appeal, the Supreme Court held that the president was authorized to order a military commission, that the military commission was lawfully constituted, and that the men were held in lawful custody for trial before the military commission and had not shown cause for being discharged by writ of habeas corpus. Through its ruling, the Supreme Court determined the men were enemy belligerents—a status that affirmed the denial of their right to be tried in civilian court and the suspension of their writs of habeas corpus, the primary legal mechanism through which defendants can challenge their detention.[14]

In October 1945, the Truman administration convened a military commission to try Japanese general Tomoyuki Yamashita for war crimes committed by troops under his command during the Japanese defense of the occupied Philippines. The United States charged Yamashita with "violations of the laws of war," arguing that he "unlawfully disregarded and failed to discharge his duty as commander to control the operations of the members of his command, permitting them to commit brutal atrocities and other high crimes against people of the United States and of its allies and dependencies, particularly the Philippines." In finding Yamashita guilty, the military commission sentenced the general to death. On appeal, the Supreme Court affirmed that the "trial and punishment of enemy combatants who have committed violations of the law of war" are "not only a part of the conduct of war operating as a preventive measure against such violations, but also [are] an exercise of the authority sanctioned by Congress to administer the system of military justice recognized by the law of war."[15] As in *Yamashita,* the Bush administration viewed military tribunals as an effective forum to incapacitate suspected fighters and support its war strategy while upholding the rule of law.

Even though *Quirin* and *Yamashita* upheld the president's power to convene military commissions to try individuals charged with war crimes, global war on terror defendants have challenged the use of military commissions by citing a Civil War case, *Ex parte Milligan.*[16] After the 1861 attack on Fort Sumter, President Lincoln ordered General Winfield Scott to "suspend the writ of *habeas corpus* for the public safety." Citing Article 1, Section 9 of the Constitution, President Lincoln reasoned that the current "insurrection against the laws of the United States" justified this suspension. In 1862, President Lincoln issued a proclamation that declared martial law, suspended the writ of habeas corpus, and authorized the use of military commissions. Using the law to advance the Union's military strategy, President Lincoln's proclamation specifically targeted "rebels and insurgents, their aiders and abettors within the United States, and all persons discouraging volunteer enlistments, resisting militia drafts, or guilty of any disloyal practice, affording aid or comfort to rebels against the authority of the United States." In 1863, Congress passed the Habeas Corpus Suspension Act, which provisioned that "during the present rebellion, the President of the United States, whenever, in his judgement, the public safety may require it, is authorized to suspend the privilege of the writ of *habeas corpus* in any case throughout the United States, or any part thereof." These legislative decisions supported the Union army and protected the Lincoln administration while laying the legal foundation to suspend the writ of habeas corpus and convene military commissions in future times of war.[17]

Under this legislation, U.S. army officials arrested Indianan Lambdin P. Milligan and other political dissidents leading antiwar efforts by discouraging military enlistments, conspiring to seize munitions, and planning to liberate Confederate soldiers held in Northern military prisons. To avoid the unpredictable sentiments of Indianan jurors, army officials tried Milligan by military commission, which found Milligan guilty and sentenced him to death. On appeal, the Supreme Court overturned Milligan's conviction, on the premise that it was unconstitutional to try civilians in military tribunals if civilian courts were available and that Congress, not the president, held the power to suspend the writ of habeas corpus. The primary holding in *Ex parte Milligan* continues to provide relief to global war on terror defendants who have challenged the suspension of the writ of habeas corpus and the use of military commissions.

Before global war on terror defendants invoked *Ex parte Milligan* to challenge their indefinite detention, the Bush administration initiated a series of legislative decisions that provided the legal standing for its use of military tribunals, indefinite detention, and torture. For example, in September 2001, President Bush signed the Authorization for Use of Military Force (AUMF). With congressional approval, the AUMF granted the president the right to use "all necessary and appropriate force against those nations, organizations, or persons he determines" were responsible for the September 11 attacks.[18] National security scholar Karen J. Greenberg (2016) explains that this law "took the place of the declaration of war required by the Constitution, but rather than simply declaring war, it granted the president broad power to act in the name of national security—even if it meant diluting the Constitution's checks on presidential authority in the name of keeping the country safe" (33). Under the AUMF, President Bush could take any action he determined would prevent future terrorist attacks against the United States.

After the passage of the AUMF, the administration took additional steps to expand the president's constitutional and executive powers (Goldsmith 2009, 102). For example, Office of Legal Counsel (OLC) assistant attorney general Jay Bybee issued a series of binding legal opinions. A 2002 memorandum detailed the OLC's "views on the laws applicable to the transfer of members of the Taliban militia, al-Qaeda, or other terrorist organizations, who have come under the control of the United States armed forces, to other countries" (Bybee 2002, 1). Bybee's memo clarified that the Geneva Convention Relative to the Treatment of Prisoners of War "does not restrict the President's discretion" to "transfer al-Qaeda and Taliban prisoners captured overseas and detained outside of the territorial jurisdiction of the United States to third countries" because "the President has determined that the al-Qaeda and Taliban detainees are not entitled to prisoner of war ('POW') status within the meaning of the Conventions" (1). Such circuitous legal logic affirmed the president's "exclusive authority" to "handle captured enemy soldiers" (5). Because customary definitions of prisoners of war exclude nonstate actors, the Bush administration could classify al-Qaeda and Taliban soldiers as "unlawful enemy combatants" unentitled to standard legal protections under international law, despite Protocol I protections afforded to nonstate actors "fighting against colonial domination, alien occupation, or racist regimes" (Mofidi and Eckert 2003, 74). Given this liminal status, the president's "exclusive authority" included not only "killing and capturing the enemies in the battlefield but also detaining and interrogating them" (Lokaneeta 2011, 75). By denying captured al-Qaeda, Taliban, and other irregular fighters prisoner of war status, Bybee's (2002) memo imbued the Bush administration with the "plenary power to dispose of the liberty of military detainees" (6).

Through the creation of new legislation and the expansion of presidential power, the Bush administration established a legal foundation for its global war on terror strategies, from preemptive combat operations to preventative detention to military commissions. Such efforts, however, met unending legal, political, and public challenges. Most significantly, a series of Supreme Court rulings began to weaken this legal foundation. Reflecting on this time, Goldsmith (2009) writes:

> Starting in the summer of 2004 . . . the [Supreme] Court handed the administration a series of defeats on terrorism policy. In its least bad ruling for the President, the Court held that he could exercise his traditional military powers to detain Yaser Hamdi [a Taliban foot soldier] until the end of the Afghanistan conflict. But the Court questioned whether the President could exercise these traditional powers indefinitely in the war against al-Qaeda, and for the first time it imposed constitutional due-process shackles on

the President during wartime. Much worse for the Bush administration, on the same day in a different opinion, the Court announced, after turning somersaults to distinguish an important World War II precedent that the government had relied on heavily, that it had the authority to scrutinize the legality of the government's actions on Guantánamo. . . . The legal culture had become very suspicious of the administration's grand assertions of executive power in the face of growing complaints. (134–35)

Goldsmith's reflections illustrate the Bush administration's fraught desire to develop legal standards to expand its wartime powers while resisting the use of the law to constrain such powers.

Challenging the Bush Doctrine: The Law's Constraint on Wartime Powers

In 2004, the United States government charged Osama bin Laden's chauffeur, Salim Ahmed Hamdan, with conspiracy to commit terrorism and sought to try him before a military commission. Hamdan filed a habeas suit to challenge the constitutionality of the military commission in federal court. The U.S. Court of Appeals for the District of Columbia Circuit determined that Hamdan could not be tried by a military commission unless he was first declared a prisoner of war. On appeal, the court reversed, arguing that Congress imbued President Bush with the power to convene military commissions when it authorized the "use of all necessary and appropriate force against those nations, organizations, or persons he determines planned, authorized, committed, or aided" the September 11, 2001, attacks.[19] With these wartime powers, President Bush could order Hamdan to stand trial before a military commission, regardless of his prisoner of war status. However, in 2006, the Supreme Court overturned this ruling, determining that military commissions used to try individuals detained at Guantánamo lacked "the power to proceed because its structures and procedures violate both the Uniform Code of Military Justice and the four Geneva Conventions signed in 1949."[20] If the Bush administration wanted to convene military commissions, it would require explicit Congressional approval.

    In 2004, another Supreme Court ruling, *Rasul v. Bush,*[21] affirmed the jurisdiction of the federal courts over Guantánamo and the right of foreign nationals to invoke the writ of habeas corpus, the legal recourse through which detainees can challenge their detention. In this case, Shafiq Rasul and other detainees filed a habeas petition challenging their incarceration, arguing that it was unlawful to hold them without a hearing to determine their status and the legitimacy of their detention. In its ruling, the Supreme Court held that the men had a right to challenge their detention and recognized the federal courts' power to review applications for habeas relief, including "a right to judicial review of the legality of Executive detention of aliens in a territory over which the United States exercises plenary and exclusive jurisdiction, but not 'ultimate sovereignty.'" In other words, Guantánamo detainees could challenge their detention in federal court, even as noncitizens held extraterritorially.

In *Hamdi v. Rumsfeld*,[22] the Supreme Court rejected the U.S. Court of Appeals for the Fourth Circuit's determination that under *Ex parte Quirin,* the president's wartime powers included the authority to detain those captured in armed service and to deport or detain enemies during the duration of hostilities. Instead, the Supreme Court held that, although the military classified Yaser Hamdi as an enemy combatant and alleged Taliban foot soldier, as a U.S. citizen, he still had the right to legal counsel and the right to file a writ of habeas corpus petition. As in *Rasul,* the Supreme Court reaffirmed detainees' constitutional rights.

Finally, in *Padilla v. Rumsfeld*,[23] the U.S. District Court for the Southern District of New York ruled that the lawfulness of U.S. citizen Jose Padilla's detention depended on "whether the President had some evidence to support his finding that Padilla was an enemy combatant." On appeal, the U.S. Court of Appeals for the Second Circuit held that the president lacked inherent authority to order Padilla's military detention, ordered Padilla's release from military custody, and authorized the government to transfer him to civilian custody. The Supreme Court held that Padilla had a right to file a habeas petition but that he had improperly filed in the Southern District of New York, rather than South Carolina, where he was being held. The Court transferred the case to the South Carolina District Court, which ruled that Padilla was entitled to a hearing before a neutral tribunal to review his status as an enemy combatant. Although the Supreme Court upheld Padilla's detention in civilian custody, it affirmed his right to file a habeas petition.

Legal scholar Steve Vladeck (2014) writes that the 2004 *Hamdi,* *Rasul,* and *Padilla* trilogy demonstrated "the Court's unbridled assertion of *judicial* power" in response to the Bush administration's "open effort" to "*exclude* the courts." In each of these decisions, the Supreme Court ruled that the president's wartime powers were not as expansive as he claimed. As Justice Sandra Day O'Connor wrote in her *Hamdi* opinion, "A state of war is not a blank check for the President when it comes to the rights of the Nation's citizens. Whatever power the United States Constitution envisions for the Executive in its exchanges with other nations or with enemy organizations in times of conflict, it most assuredly envisions a role for all three branches when individual liberties are at stake."[24] These three cases provided a judicial check on the Bush administration's efforts to expand its wartime powers. As the Bush administration tested the limits of its executive authority, the Supreme Court sought to constrain the president's wartime powers.

In response to these 2004 Supreme Court rulings, President Bush signed into law the Detainee Treatment Act of 2005. After images of prisoner abuse at Abu Ghraib (Iraq) surfaced, Senator John McCain introduced this act to prohibit the "cruel, inhuman, or degrading treatment or punishment" of any person under custody or control of the United States government, regardless of citizenship status or physical location.[25] Yet the act also reinforced the administration's global war on terror legal strategy that the Supreme Court reined in through its rulings. For example, the act formalized the Combatant Status Review Tribunals (CSRT), charged with periodically reviewing each Guantánamo case "to determine the need to continue to detain an alien who is a detainee" and assessing if any evidence "was obtained as a result of coercion."[26] These administrative hearings allowed detainees to contest their status as enemy combatants and informed them of their right to seek relief in federal court through a writ of habeas corpus petition. The Detainee Treatment Act also gave the D.C. Circuit Court of Appeals "exclusive jurisdiction" to review the CSRT's status decisions.

The court, however, could only decide if the status determination followed "the standards and procedures" of the Defense Department, offering little opportunity for independent judicial review. This means that "this limited review prevents any examination of the underlying legitimacy of CSRT procedures, despite the fact that the process denies detainees bedrock procedural guarantees at the core of the American legal system" (Arik 2009, 660). In other words, the Detainee Treatment Act institutionalized CSRTs with little judicial oversight—a strategic maneuver to reinstate executive authority after the *Hamdi, Hamdan,* and *Padilla* decisions. Furthermore, the act exempted the Central Intelligence Agency (CIA) from its mandate to follow the U.S. Army Field Manual on Intelligence Interrogation (FM 34-52) and refrain from "cruel, inhuman, or degrading" treatment. As the Supreme Court mobilized its judicial power to regulate the detention, treatment, and protection of Guantánamo detainees, the Bush administration created new legislation that reinforced the role of Guantánamo, indefinite detention, and military commissions in the global war on terror.

In addition to the Detainee Treatment Act, the Military Commissions Act of 2006 (MCA) "explicitly authorized many aspects of the military commission regime that the Supreme Court had invalidated three months earlier" in *Hamdan* and expanded the president's wartime powers (Goldsmith 2009, 138). For example, the act authorized trials by military commission for violations of the laws of war and provisioned that "no court, justice, or judge shall have jurisdiction to hear or consider an application for a writ of habeas corpus filed by or on behalf of an alien detained by the United States who has been determined by the United States to have been properly detained as an enemy combatant or is awaiting such determination."[27] Through this legislation, the Bush administration "asserted an entitlement to hold detainees indefinitely, subject them to harsh methods of interrogation, and try them, if it chose not to simply hold them, before specially constituted military commissions" (Dorf 2007, 47). The American Civil Liberties Union (2006) warned that the MCA "casts aside the Constitution and the principle of *habeas corpus* which protects against unlawful and indefinite imprisonment," "[gives] the president absolute power to designate enemy combatants and to set his own definitions for torture," and empowers the president "to declare—on his or her own—who is an enemy combatant."

The Military Commissions Act "effectively nullified the *Hamdan* decision," making it explicit that the prisoners at Guantánamo—and anyone else the government declared an enemy combatant, including (at least according to some lawyers) U.S. citizens—were not entitled to the protections of U.S. or international law. This abrogation of rights was no longer lurking in the shadows of closely held (and shoddily argued) legal memos; nor was it merely something "stumbled upon." It was now the law of the land. (Greenberg 2016, 141)

Rather than evade or suspend the law, the Bush administration mobilized the law as a global war on terror weapon, such that it could exert its sovereign power with impunity and subvert judicial oversight.

Like the judicial check on the Bush administration's wartime powers, detainees also used the courts to challenge the Military Commissions Act. Algerian-born Bosnian resident Lakhdar Boumediene filed a habeas petition to contest his detention at Guantánamo and the constitutionality of the Military Commissions Act. In 2001, Bosnian police arrested Boumediene and five others at the request of U.S. intelligence agencies on the belief that the six men were planning to attack the U.S. embassy in Sarajevo. In 2002, Bosnia's supreme court ruled that there was no evidence to hold the men and ordered their release. The U.S. military immediately seized all six men and transferred them to Guantánamo, where they were detained and interrogated without being charged. In 2008, the Supreme Court ruled that U.S. federal courts held jurisdiction over Boumediene's habeas petition. Writing for the majority, Justice Kennedy observed that "the petitioners do have the habeas corpus privilege," even as "aliens designated as enemy combatants and detained at the United States Naval Station at Guantánamo Bay, Cuba."[28] In this ruling, the Supreme Court concluded that the Military Commissions Act was unconstitutional because it barred "enemy combatants" from challenging their detention in U.S. federal courts and suspended the writ of habeas corpus. Legal scholar Jonathan Hafetz (2008) describes the Supreme Court's decision as a "dramatic blow to the President's lawless detention policies," ultimately serving as "the culmination of the quest for due process that began in 2002 when the first habeas corpus petitions were filed by Guantánamo detainees in federal court."

Despite this victory, other legal challenges proved less successful for detainees held in other offshore prisons. In 2006, for example, three detainees held at the Bagram Air Force Base in Afghanistan petitioned the D.C. District Court for habeas relief from their confinement by the United States military in *Al-Maqaleh v. Gates.*[29] Citing the *Boumediene* ruling, the defendants argued that they had a constitutional right to habeas, even as noncitizens held extraterritorially.

In *Boumediene,* Justice Kennedy detailed a functional test judges could use to determine the applicability of the Constitution in extraterritorial cases like *Al-Maqaleh.* Justice Kennedy drew from a World War II case, *Johnson v. Eisentrager,*[30] which decided that U.S. courts had no jurisdiction over German soldiers captured in China, convicted in China by a U.S. military commission, and then repatriated to Germany to serve their sentences in a U.S.-administered prison for "engaging in, permitting, or ordering continued military activity against the United States after surrender of Germany and before surrender of Japan." In this case, the Supreme Court held that enemy aliens captured and detained beyond the sovereign territory of the United States did not have a right to the writ of habeas corpus. Citing *Eisentrager* in his *Boumediene* opinion, Justice Kennedy outlined three factors judges could use to determine if the suspension of the writ of habeas corpus was constitutional in extraterritorial cases: (1) the detainees' citizenship and status and the adequacy of the process through which that status was determined; (2) the nature of the sites where apprehension and then detention took place; and (3) the practical obstacles inherent in resolving the prisoner's entitlement to the writ.[31] In *Boumediene,* Justice Kennedy reasoned that the United States had long exercised "unchallenged and indefinite control" of Guantánamo such that detainees were entitled to habeas review. Judge Bates ruled similarly in *Al-Maqaleh v. Gates,* stating that although "the United States' control over the base at Bagram Airfield was less absolute than its control over Guantánamo Bay," it was enough to "tip the balance" in favor of the detainees.[32] Using Justice Kennedy's functional test, Judge Bates ruled that the United States could not constitutionally suspend Bagram detainees' writs of habeas corpus.

On appeal, however, Chief Judge Sentelle argued that Bagram and Guantánamo were qualitatively different since "Bagram remains in a theatre of war" and that such detention "is within the sovereign territory of another nation." Given these extraterritorial conditions, Judge

Sentelle determined that the court "cannot . . . hold that the right to the writ of *habeas corpus* and the constitutional protections of the Suspension Clause extend to the Bagram detention facility in Afghanistan."[33] As the federal judiciary sought to rein in the Bush administration and restrain the president's wartime powers through their rulings in *Hamdi, Hamdan, Rasul,* and *Boumediene,* the *Al-Maqaleh* decision demonstrated the split legal interpretations of the laws of war.

Even as the Bush administration intensified the use of offshore prisons and military commissions to circumvent the legal protections afforded to prisoners of war, it still relied on the federal court system to expand and affirm its wartime powers by denying habeas petitions and classifying Taliban, al-Qaeda, and other nonstate fights as unlawful enemy combatants unentitled to prisoner of war protections guaranteed under international and common law. In this way, the U.S. government has used the law to confer and rescind personhood and to "establish boundaries that exclude, marginalize, and discipline" (Brickell and Cuomo 2019, 108; see also Esmeir 2012; Cacho 2012; Dayan 2011). In this political calculus organized by imperial logics, the law prefigures Muslims as "uncivil, inferior, and inhumane" (Patel 2017, 4). Framing Muslims as "the worst type of criminal—the fundamentalist terrorist" has facilitated the creative use of the law to justify invasion, occupation, and indefinite detention (Patel 2017, 4).

The Obama Doctrine: Remaking the Global War on Terror

When President Barack Obama assumed office in 2009, he initially worked to fulfill campaign promises to reform the Bush administration's aggressive global war on terror tactics. On his first day in office, President Obama ordered a 120-day suspension of Guantánamo military commissions. The next day, President Obama issued Executive Order 13491, which revoked all Bush-era torture guidances and reinforced the ban on the use of torture in interrogations under both military procedure and international law. President Obama also signed Executive Order 13492, directing the attorney general to immediately review every Guantánamo case, with the intention of closing the offshore prison "as soon as practicable, and no later than 1 year from the date of this order."[34] Many viewed these quick actions as key victories in reining in the global war on terror.

Yet President Obama's focus on suspending, rather than eliminating, these practices led to their eventual reinstatement. After the Guantánamo Review Task Force assessed each case, it recommended which detainees should be prosecuted in federal court, tried in military commissions, transferred to other countries for detention, released in accordance with court orders already rendered, or continued to be detained at Guantánamo without charge or trial. After reviewing the military commission process, the Obama administration introduced a series of reforms that would allow for their revitalization. Military commissions would not admit as evidence "statements that have been obtained from detainees using cruel, inhuman, and degrading interrogation methods" (Obama 2009b). The Obama administration also limited the use of hearsay evidence, granted the accused "greater latitude in selecting their counsel," provided basic protections for those who refused to testify, and allowed military commission judges to "establish the jurisdiction of their own courts" (Obama 2009b). For President Obama, military commissions were "appropriate for trying enemies who violate the laws of war, provided that they are properly structured and administered." President Obama therefore established a "legitimate legal framework" for these military commissions, which would ensure that these forums could "prosecute terrorists effectively" (Obama 2009b). Despite President Obama's campaign promises, his administration viewed Guantánamo and military commissions as indispensable to its national security pursuits. Rather than eliminate these global war on terror tools, President Obama focused on reforming them.

President Obama's failure to close Guantánamo reflects the legal and political quagmire associated with releasing alleged global war on terror fighters given the perceived exceptional status of suspected terrorists. In fact, President Obama (2009a) reassured the public that he had no plans to "release individuals who endanger the American people," including "a number of people who cannot be prosecuted for past crimes, in some cases because the evidence may be tainted, but who nonetheless pose a threat to the security of the United States." President Obama's logics illustrate how terrorism has emerged as a "distinct category of international law," one organized around the belief that "terrorists deserve exceptional treatment as enemies rather than ordinary criminals," particularly given the "exceptional danger" they allegedly pose (Moeckli 2008–9, 171, 174). Through an exploration of the social and political construction of terrorism, sociologist Atiya Husain (2021) contends that prevailing national security logics suggest that "rational means would be ineffective for managing a problem of exceptional, unimaginable violence" (208). The exceptional status of terrorism justifies extreme measures to ensure national security, including the indefinite detention of individuals who will never be charged with a crime.

Although abolitionists have argued for the closure of Guantánamo, the prohibition of torture, and the suspension of domestic counterterrorism programs, the enduring image of the irrationally, exceptionally, and unpredictably violent terrorist makes it nearly impossible to imagine a world that takes seriously violent political action, without relying on regimes of war and policing that repress armed struggles for political change in a state-centric world order. Guantánamo itself reflects the entanglement of social structures, legal mandates, and war-making enterprises that do the work of empire. Abolishing Guantánamo necessitates a reckoning with the political violence and racialized world order that brought the detention facilities into existence and that rely on military-carceral modalities for their continuation. Campaigns to abolish Guantánamo must confront urgent questions about the futures of current detainees, such as alleged al-Qaeda lieutenant Walid Mohammed Bin Attash, "9/11 mastermind" Khalid Shaikh Mohammed, and al-Qaeda public relations director Ali Hamza Ahmad Suliman al-Bahlul. While the abolitionist principle of nourishing life-affirming institutions and developing transformative justice practices to crowd out the need for police and prisons makes sense in the domestic U.S. context, it must be reconfigured to understand and respond to the material conditions, governance regimes, and power relations that incite armed resistance. If terrorism is "decolonization gone global" (Kawash 1999, 240), how can abolitionist campaigns take seriously the politics animating violence—and in turn destabilize the "globalized order of racial violence that the national security state aims to protect" (Li 2020, 26)? In this way, the figure of the terrorist demands that community organizers and social scientists alike work toward an emergent anti-imperial abolitionist imaginary to dismantle coercive security regimes and the racial logics, legal architectures, social structures, military interventions, and daily practices that bring such imperial formations into being.

With the terrorist other as an orienting figure, we can see how abolishing Guantánamo requires more than just closing the offshore prison; it demands ending the exercises of racialized imperial warfare that brought Guantánamo into (renewed) existence, eliminating coercive security regimes used to thwart the perceived terrorist threat inside the United States, and enhancing our geopolitical literacies to understand the conditions that have incited armed struggles and, in some cases, work in solidarity with such armed groups. As Fanon (1963) contends, "decolonization is always a violent phenomenon" (27). Although this analysis hardly glorifies, let alone condones, revolutionary violence, it recognizes the violent conditions in which people live and refuses the "moral dismissal of nonstate perpetrators of violence—via the label 'terrorist'" (Razak 2018). This more expansive view of the demand to close Guantánamo requires reckoning with our understandings of what constitutes "terrorism," who "terrorists" are, what they are fighting for, and why. This sociological study of the role of the judicial system in the global war on terror invites us to consider what anti-imperial abolitionist alternatives might look like for the different types of people detained at Guantánamo, from innocent men to active participants in political violence to the architects of the September 11 attacks.

Trying Terrorism: Federal Courts as an Answer to the Failures of Military Commissions

Although President Bush used his executive powers to establish military commissions to try suspected global war on terror fighters, constitutional, procedural, and practical challenges derailed this lawfare strategy. By 2018, military commissions had convicted just eight individuals charged with terrorism-related crimes, and three of the convictions were later overturned. Meanwhile, federal civilian criminal courts had convicted more than 660 individuals on terrorism-related charges, including "high-value" detainees like Faisal Shahzad, who attempted to detonate a car bomb in New York City's Times Square. Federal courts also upheld illiberal practices such as indefinite detention, deferred constitutional issues to the executive branch, and expanded presidential power. Greenberg (2016) argues that across administrations, federal courts and lawyers "have weakened" the rule of law, ultimately protecting "government excess from citizens' objections—and, in some cases, citizens' knowledge" (7). Although the preference for military commissions has fluctuated throughout the global war on terror, they, and federal courts, have continued to play a critical role in prosecuting suspected terrorists and in defending the use of indefinite detention, extraordinary rendition, and torture.

Given the legislative and public resistance to the use of military commissions, political leaders have disagreed on where to try global war on terror detainees, if at all. For example, Attorney General Eric Holder insisted that the federal court was the appropriate and constitutional forum to try suspected terrorists. Deputy Assistant Attorney General John Yoo (2010), however, lamented that "even military commissions put an unnecessary strain on military and intelligence operations devoted to rooting out the enemy" and therefore encouraged the president to "drop the idea of trials altogether and simply continue to detain al-Qaeda members until the war is over." These differences meant that the role of the judicial system has fluctuated over the course of the global war on terror as presidential administrations unevenly have called on the courts to prosecute Guantánamo detainees, deny habeas petitions, and try terrorism-related cases facilitated by sting operations, confidential informants, and other aggressive policing tactics within the United States.

Under the Obama administration, Holder (2009) announced that he would "pursue prosecution in federal court of the five individuals accused of conspiring to commit the 9/11 attacks": Khalid Shaikh Mohammed, Walid Bin Attash, Ramzi bin al-Shibh, Ali Abdul Aziz Ali (also known as Ammar al-Baluchi), and Mustafa al-Hawsaw. Affirming that "many cases could be prosecuted in federal courts or military commissions," Holder reported that he reviewed each case to determine the best venue for prosecution. This decision aligned with a joint Department of Defense and Department of Justice (2009) protocol on the Determination of Guantánamo Cases Referred for Prosecution, which rebalanced the distribution of cases between military commissions and federal courts. The protocol explained, "There is a presumption that, where feasible, referred cases will be prosecuted in an Article III court, in keeping with the traditional principles of federal prosecution" (1).[35] Only when "compelling factors"—such as the nature and gravity of the conduct underlying the offenses and the manner in which the case was investigated and evidence gathered—make it "more appropriate to prosecute a case in a reformed military commission" could the government "prosecute there" (1).

Eighteen months after Holder's announcement, however, he was forced to turn the prosecution of the five defendants over to the Department of Defense after Congress passed the 2010 National Defense Authorization Act. In passing this yearly bill that funds the armed services, Congress inserted language that reduced the role of the federal courts in trying suspected terrorists by barring the Department of Defense from using its appropriated funds to release or transfer Guantánamo detainees into "the United States, its territories, or possessions." Preventing the transfer of Guantánamo detainees to the United States meant that these defendants could not be tried in federal court. Despite Congress's position, Holder (2011) stood by his original assessment, describing federal courts as "the best venue for these cases."

The congressional decision to ban Guantánamo transfers served as a response to President Obama's controversial plan to close the offshore prison and the perceived failure of the federal courts in securing terrorism convictions. Yoo (2010), for example, argued that the "near-total acquittal" of Ahmed Ghailani in 2010—who allegedly helped facilitate the 1998 U.S. embassy bombings in Kenya and Tanzania—"should, at a minimum, be the last grasp for President Obama's misguided effort to wage the war on terrorism in the courtroom." Although federal courts had tried other high-value defendants like Faisal Shahzad, *Ghailani* served as a test case to determine if defendants subjected to torture could be tried in federal courts. Greenberg (2016) reports that "the Ghailani case would give Holder's Department of Justice its first real opportunity to showcase its abilities to bring terrorists—even those being held at Guantánamo—to justice in accordance with the principles and guarantees of the Constitution" (193). Some worried that *Ghailani* would reinvigorate challenges to key global war on terror practices, such as torture, and questioned if federal courts were equipped to negotiate these thorny issues. Judge Lewis Kaplan, for example, ruled that Hussein Abebe could not testify against Ghailani because his name had been extracted through torture. Through this ruling, Judge Kaplan determined that evidence obtained through torture was inadmissible in federal court.

At the end of the trial, the jury found Ghailani not guilty on 284 of 285 counts, including 224 counts for those whose deaths were caused by the bombings. Ghailani's conviction on a single count—conspiring to destroy U.S. property and buildings—carried a sentence of life without parole. Despite this harsh sentence for a single conspiracy charge, Representative Peter King (R-N.Y.) described the verdict as a "tragic wake-up call to the Obama administration to immediately abandon its ill-advised plan to try Guantánamo terrorists" in federal court and, instead, "treat them as wartime enemies and try them in military commissions at Guantánamo" (qtd. in Savage 2010). Others, however, defended the use of federal courts to try Guantánamo detainees, citing Ghailani's guilty verdict and life sentence as evidence of success.

Four years after Ghailani's conviction, a New York City jury found Osama bin Laden's alleged advisor, Sulaiman Abu Ghaith, guilty of three terrorism-related charges and sentenced him to life in prison. For Holder, these convictions proved the federal courts could effectively try terrorism defendants (Weiser 2014; Horwitz 2014). For others, the potential acquittal or oversight of the use of torture in interrogations lurked behind each terrorism-related case tried in federal court.

Legal scholar Sara A. Solow (2011) reports, "Despite all of the attention that has been paid toward military commissions, the real adjudicative action vis-à-vis foreign terrorists since 9/11 has been Article III courts" (1491). By 2011, the domestic court system had resolved 431 of 578 cases associated with "a global jihadist ideology (i.e., al-Qaeda) or a local Islamist movement (i.e., Hamas)"; over 87 percent of these resolved cases resulted in a conviction—a rate that reflects all federal criminal cases (Center on Law and Security 2011, 7n1, 12). Given these statistics, legal scholar Christina Parajon Skinner (2013) argues that the "civilian system has, essentially, wholly replaced the military system in the government's preventative prosecution strategy" (328). If critics worried about how the use of punitive force, lingering constitutional issues, or evidentiary concerns would affect the outcomes of these trials, the federal courts demonstrated they could try terrorism-related cases in a way that arguably upheld constitutional obligations and barred evidence obtained through torture, without infringing on the courts' capacity to convict and harshly punish defendants. Still, the provisions added to the National Defense Authorization Act meant that Khalid Sheikh Mohammed and other Guantánamo detainees will be tried in long-delayed military commissions.

Despite the continued reliance on the federal courts to try terrorism defendants, presidential administrations have varied in how they have mobilized these legal forums in the global war on terror. In fact, the "strategy of prosecuting terrorism-related crimes has evolved in important ways over the course of the [first] decade" of the global war on terror (Greenberg 2011, 2). The Bush administration pursued a steady stream of indictments for low-level crimes, such as fraud and immigration violations. Under the Obama administration, the number of indictments both doubled and brought more serious charges, such as conspiracy to commit terrorism. In fact, "during the first two years of Barack Obama's presidency, the annual number of prosecutions for jihadist-related terrorism doubled" (2). Given this prosecutorial strategy, defendants convicted of such high-level offenses face prison terms 8.5 times longer than those charged with ordinary crimes like document fraud that were more commonly pursued under the Bush administration (Center on Law and Security 2011, 9). President Obama's aggressive use of the federal courts to try defendants marked a departure from President Bush's almost exclusive reliance on military commissions to prosecute Guantánamo detainees.[36]

To pursue this prosecutorial strategy, the federal government has relied on material support statutes originally passed in 1994 and then expanded under the 1996 Antiterrorism and Effective Death Penalty Act after the 1995 Oklahoma City bombing: Providing Material Support to Terrorists (18 U.S.C. § 2339A) and Providing Material Support to Designated Terrorist Organizations (18 U.S.C. § 2339B). Section 2339A prohibits the provision of "material support or resources" while "knowing or intending that they are used in preparation for, or in carrying out" specified terrorism-related crimes. Section 2339A also defines "material support or resources" as "any property, tangible or intangible, or service, including currency or monetary instruments or financial securities, financial services, lodging, training, expert advice or assistance, safehouses, false documentation or identification, communications equipment, facilities, weapons, lethal substances, explosives, personnel (1 or more individuals who may be or include oneself), transportation, except medicine or religious materials." As this legal definition illustrates, "material support" criminalizes a wide range of resources, such as providing English-language training to health care providers so they could read English medicine labels, or enhancing the legitimacy of a foreign terrorist organization through writings and other speech acts.[37] Section 2339A is marginally limited in its scope by narrowly criminalizing material support tied to an actual crime. Given this scope, Section 2339A does not require such material support to be given to a foreign terrorist organization to constitute a federal crime; such material support must merely support the furtherance of the specified crimes.

Unlike Section 2339A, Section 2239B makes it a federal offense to "knowingly provide[] material support or resources to a foreign terrorist organization, or attempt[] or conspire[] to do so." Later, Congress "amended § 2339B to make explicit that knowledge of a [foreign terrorist organization's] designation, not specific intent to further a group's illegal goals, [is] the proper legal standard for conviction under the statute" (Said 2015, 64). Furthermore, Section 2339B prohibits any form of support provided to a designated foreign terrorist organization, even if intended for peaceful or humanitarian purposes. In fact, the Supreme Court determined in *Holder v. Humanitarian Law Project* (2010) that efforts to train the Kurdish Workers' Party and the Liberation Tigers of Tamil Eelam on how to resolve conflicts peacefully constituted material support. This decision criminalizes advocacy groups and humanitarian aid workers seeking to promote peace by providing "service," "training," and "expert advice or assistance" to designated foreign terrorist organizations. Since it was enacted by Congress in 1996, Section 2339B has been "regarded as an attempt to close the loophole left open by previous terrorism-support statutes" to "combat the purportedly pressing problem of terrorist groups raising money for violence under the cover of charity" (Said 2015, 53).

Congressional revisions to this statute increased the maximum sentence from fifteen to twenty years for crimes committed after June 2015. Given Section 2339B's harsh penalties and broad targeting of individuals who conspire or attempt to provide material support to designated foreign terrorist organizations, the United States has used this statute more than any other in pursuing federal terrorism cases. The United

States continues to rely on material support statutes, which remain "the primary prosecutorial tool for federal terrorism prosecutions," with extra-territorial reach that can capture individuals acting entirely outside of the United States (Center on National Security 2017, 28).

Material support statutes and other laws facilitate the prosecution of terrorism defendants in federal court, rather than by military commission. Some legal scholars have argued that such prosecutions, and the resultant punishments, can deter, incapacitate, and/or rehabilitate suspected terrorists. Skinner (2013), for example, argues that "deterrence has a wartime role" and "was historically one of the principal reasons for punishing war criminals" (342). Although deterrence usually "has little relevance to combatants," the perceived "ideological fervor" driving the global war on terror makes deterrence a central tactic by "severing offenders' ideological ties to a larger terrorist network"; by disrupting these "ties of ideology and allegiance, the interest in perpetrating these crimes diminishes" (309). As authors of a government-wide strategy to deter terrorist networks, Matthew Kroenig and Barry Pavel (2012) similarly argue, "Deterrence holds great potential to help thwart future terrorist attacks," as "simple threats of imprisonment and death against these actors can deter terrorist activities" (22, 26). Law professor Samuel J. Rascoff (2014) further assesses that this deterrence strategy must be responsive to the differences in defendants as they assume a mix of roles such as financiers and foot soldiers for different groups employing different operational strategies toward different political ends. "Tailored deterrence" accounts for these variations while working to deny the benefits of terrorist attacks. Despite the growing popularity of this antiterrorism strategy, deterrence arguably "has been largely lost on lawyers, judges, and legal academics, resulting in significant gaps between the practice of national security in this arena and the legal architecture ostensibly designed to undergird and oversee it" (830). Notwithstanding the judicial focus on deterring terrorists, the scientific research on the relationship between terrorism prosecutions and deterrence is scant; more extreme measures such as extraordinary rendition, indefinite detention, and torture have not deterred armed political struggles.

Although often the subject of legal debate, the courts also consider rehabilitation as they try, prosecute, and sentence defendants in terrorism-related cases. Given the seemingly ideological character of terrorist violence, courts across the globe have sought to integrate "religious reeducation and psychological counseling" into the terms of incarceration (Porges 2010). Over time, these rehabilitative efforts have refocused on how to "modify a detainee's behavior, not change his religious beliefs," by offering a wider range of prison programs, such as art therapy, vocational training, and classes on Islamic culture and Sharia law (Porges 2010). To supplement these prison-based programs, some have sought to institutionalize the "aftercare" that formulate the conditions of supervised release, such as ongoing counseling and "consistent and sustained monitoring . . . to determine who the person keeps company with and who is his spiritual guide and mentor in the neighborhood mosque" (Wagner 2010). Ignoring the relationship between politics and violence, these rehabilitative approaches intend to correct the perceived psychological, cultural, and/or theological pathologies afflicting individual defendants. Judges even have sentenced nonviolent defendants to "deradicalization" programs, on the assumption that extremist ideologies drive the turn to violence. In this view, custodial and community rehabilitation programs can "deradicalize" individuals and thus "stem the tide of ideological extremism, the precursor of terrorism" (Gunaratna 2013, 2).

These rehabilitative efforts have not disrupted the punitive force of judges' sentencing decisions, evident in the long prison terms and supervised releases handed down to terrorism defendants, even in nonviolent cases. The Center on National Security (2017) reports that "the average ISIS sentence of 14.5 years more than triples the average federal sentence of 3.75 years" (1). These sentences often carry lengthy supervised releases that impose special conditions, such as monitoring their electronic devices, surrendering passports and other travel documents, and banning visits to "Sunni, Shiite, or extremist websites"[38] and association with "any individual with an affiliation to any organized crime groups."[39] These harsh sentences reinforce the popular belief that terrorism defendants pose an exceptional risk to public safety and national security and, as irredeemable subjects, deserve the longest prison terms allowable under the law.

The United States Sentencing Guidelines enable these punitive prison terms by recommending harsher sentences for individuals convicted of terrorism-related crimes through the application of the terrorism enhancement under § 3A1.4. The Guidelines account for both the seriousness of the offense and the offender's criminal history, which the courts use to calculate the appropriate sentences for defendants. To determine the seriousness of the offense, the Guidelines use a 43-point scale to classify different crimes, where more serious crimes merit a higher offense level. For example, trespassing crimes carry a base offense level of 4, whereas kidnapping crimes result in a base offense level of 32. The specific characteristics of a crime, such as a robbery, which has a base offense level of 20, can lead to a 5-level increase if the defendant brandished a firearm in the commission of the crime. The courts can further adjust the offense level by considering aggravating and mitigating factors. A defendant who minimally participated in the crime can receive a 4-point reduction in the offense level, whereas a defendant who obstructed justice can face a 2-point increase in the offense level. Under § 3A1.4, a felony offense "that involved, or was intended to promote, a federal crime of terrorism" automatically increases the offense level by 12 and provisions that if the resulting offense level is less than 32, the court should increase the offense level to 32. For example, if the offense level of a crime is 24, then the application of the terrorism enhancement increases the offense level to 36.[40]

To determine the offender's criminal history, the Guidelines assign each defendant one of six criminal history categories by accounting for the defendant's past misconduct. The Guidelines assign first-time offenders Criminal History Category I and repeat offenders Criminal History Category VI. A felony involving a federal crime of terrorism automatically increases a defendant's Criminal History Category to VI, the most extreme classification. The Guidelines' sentencing matrix calculates a defendant's Criminal History Category and offense level together, thereby recommending an appropriate sentence for each defendant. Although intended to impose mandatory sentences, the Supreme Court upheld judicial discretion, making the Guidelines advisory rather than mandatory.[41] Through these calculations, the terrorism enhancement empowers the courts to impose harsher sentences for individuals convicted of terrorism-related crimes while upholding judicial discretion, as judges can depart upward or downward from the recommended sentences.

If a court applies § 3A1.4, the Guidelines recommend a minimum sentence of 210 to 262 months, irrespective of the type of crime. One defense attorney explained:

If you get convicted for material support of terrorism—which can be speech based—you can go to a Career Criminal History of I where you have no prior criminal record to Career Criminal History VI which is the highest. You get 12 points added to your base level offense, which puts you up to 36—you're now at a minimum of thirty years to life, and even though the cap is twenty years, they can stack three, four, five different offenses to take a twenty-year cap and turn it into life or turn it into sixty years. (interview, March 2021)

For this lawyer, the terrorism enhancement created excessively long prison terms, especially for individuals whose nonviolent speech acts were criminalized as a form of material support to a designated foreign terrorist organization. Legal scholar Wadie E. Said (2015) similarly warns that under § 3A1.4, "the distinction between sentences for violent and nonviolent crimes narrows" and reinforces the idea that "terrorism is different and worthy of greater punishment" (123, 129). Judge Michael Davis, for example, sentenced Guled Omar to thirty-five years in prison after he discussed plans to travel to Syria with his high school friends to fight President Bashar al-Assad's brutal regime. Although Omar never left the United States, never wielded a weapon, and never engaged in an act of violence, Judge Davis described Omar as a "committed jihadist" who "may still believe in the extremist, violent, and deadly Jihadist ideology of ISIL and the Islamic State," ultimately deserving of a long prison term to incapacitate him.[42] Judge Davis's sentence corresponded to Omar's assessed Criminal History Category of VI and total offense level of 43. In the view of prosecutors, a long prison sentence would "incapacitate the defendant and protect the public" and "deter the continued threat that homegrown terrorists and those that support them pose to the United States and our allies" by "send[ing] a clear message to any would-be jihadists that such conduct is not tolerated by the U.S. government."[43]

Judge Davis's ruling reflects the judicial system's efforts to "incapacitate terrorists" through long prison terms. To do so, the courts not only prosecute suspected global war on terror fighters like John Walker Lindh but also use material support charges to facilitate preemptive prosecutions as in the case of Guled Omar. Prosecutors argued that Omar "was singularly committed to joining, fighting, and killing for ISIL," necessitating a sting operation to ensnare, arrest, and prosecute him before he engaged in any hostilities. In a policy brief, Erik Love (2012) writes that this strategy of preemptive prosecution "is based on the idea that preventing terrorism requires imprisoning certain suspects," like Omar, "due to their associations and/or beliefs" (6). *Omar* illustrates how synchronizing criminal law with global war on terror exigencies "can accelerate the point at which criminal liability attaches along a continuum that runs from an individual's mere inclination to act to the action itself" and premises such criminal liability "on association rather than on conduct as such" (Chesney 2009, 101). Preemptive prosecutions expand criminal liability to include radical beliefs, social networks, and speech acts marked as precursors to or indicative of terrorist activity. As an expression of carceral logics, the expansion of criminal liability abstracts political violence from its formative conditions and therefore individualizes armed resistance as the manifestation of an individual person's psychological, cultural, and/or theological pathologies. Locating the problem of political violence in such individual profiles severs politics from violence and justifies the criminal pursuit of individual actors, without attending to the material conditions, power relations, and governance regimes that give rise to armed resistance, as in Omar's desire to oust the Assad regime. As we will see throughout this book, prosecutors often have invoked political, cultural, and religious expressions to demonstrate a defendant's alleged predisposition to terrorism, even if they have yet to commit a criminal act of violence.

Because the government cannot charge individuals if they have not yet committed a crime, it uses two techniques to preemptively convict a terrorism suspect: first demonstrating that a suspect is associated with a group classified as a "foreign terrorist organization," then facilitating an elaborate sting operation "using aggressive informants to induce individuals to commit offenses they would never have committed without government prompting" (Norris and Grol-Prokopczyk 2018, 261). In this preemptive policing strategy, "instead of (or in addition to) focusing on previously ignored *offenses,* sting operations can target previously ignored *individuals,* potentially ensnaring harmless but impressionable defendants" (Norris and Grol-Prokopczyk 2018, 261). Many critics argue that these sting operations merely invent terrorists, a process akin to "ghost chasing" (Mueller and Stewart 2016, 2) or "creating bogeymen from buffoons" (Aaronson 2013, 233).

Preemptive prosecutions articulate with the anticipatory logics driving the Bush Doctrine. Integrating both criminological thinking and military strategy, this preemptive paradigm "shifts the temporal perspective to anticipate and forestall that which has not yet occurred and may never do so," a tactic that "takes precedence over responding to wrongs done" (Zedner 2007, 262). In this view, the "only option is to incapacitate terrorists *before* a plot has been initiated and *before* members of the public are harmed. Statutes that merely criminalize terrorist acts are inadequate because they target completed crimes" (Comerford 2005, 733). Using material support statutes, prosecutors can "criminalize *support* of the terrorist group" rather than simply target completed crimes. This preemptive strategy "allows prosecutors to act when an offender trains with, joins, and potentially lies in wait for instructions from, a foreign terrorist organization" (733). In this view, "maximizing early prosecutorial intervention" can enhance national security, albeit with some "civil liberty costs" (Chesney 2007, 427). Strengthening the role of federal courts as a counterterrorism tool, however, risks increasing the criminal-legal system's capacity to criminalize, punish, and incarcerate individuals who merely think about or express support for designated foreign terrorist organizations, as in the case of Omar (see also Dratel 2011).

Informed by "anticipatory reason" (Hong and Szpunar 2019), this approach to the global war on terror expands the role of the judicial system beyond trying Guantánamo detainees for war crimes; it specifically tasks the courts with preventing future terrorist attacks by preemptively prosecuting suspected terrorists for both completed crimes and inchoate activities. By mobilizing the judicial system in this way, material support statutes facilitate the punitive incapacitation of individuals convicted of terrorism-related crimes. The courts therefore prosecute a wide spectrum of terrorism defendants, including suspected global war on terror fighters like John Walker Lindh; individuals ensnared by elaborate sting operations whereby confidential informants encourage their targets to engage in fake terrorism plots concocted and financed by undercover law enforcement agents (Aaronson 2013); and individuals who provide material support or resources to terrorist organizations, such as Ashraf Al Safoo, who was convicted of conspiring to provide material support after allegedly using social media to "spread propaganda supporting violent jihad" at "the direction of and in coordination with ISIS" (U.S. Attorney's Office, Northern District of Illinois 2018). In this preemptive calculus, "security as a practice of government pivots not so much on a forbidding or enclosing of phenomena but on an embracing of the uncertain future by acting on the variations and circulations through a series of probabilistic interventions" (Goede 2012, xxii). In this way, federal courts facilitate the temporal shifts in anticipatory security practices that oscillate between punishing suspected armed insurgents who participated in hostilities and pursuing future terrorists who have not yet acted—but who, according to anticipatory logics, must be out there.

Specialized National Security Courts: An Alternative to the Current System?

Given the controversial use of military commissions to try detainees held at Guantánamo Bay and the denial of basic constitutional rights, "the criminal justice system represents the legitimate alternative to illegitimate exercises of presidential power" (Chesney 2009, 98). To maximize the credibility and authority of federal courts as the premiere venue for adjudicating terrorism-related cases, some legal scholars have called for reforming the current system. Robert Chesney (2009) argues that "the United States needs an optimally functional criminal justice apparatus for counterterrorism cases," necessitating reforms to strengthen the courts as a useful tool in the global war on terror (99). These reforms include expanding the legal prohibition against receiving military-style training from a designated foreign terrorist organization, further criminalizing attacks targeting civilians during armed conflicts, creating a graduated sentencing scale to more harshly punish defendants with the intent to harm compared to defendants who "act out of ignorance or foolishness," and calibrating the sentencing guidelines to increase the maximum sentence for providing material support to designated foreign terrorist organizations (100). Chesney's proposed reforms offer a pathway to optimize criminal prosecution as a counterterrorism tool by expanding inchoate criminal liability while imposing new procedural restrictions that enhance the criminal-legal system's legitimacy.

These calls for reform articulate with parallel demands to establish national security courts specially designed to try defendants for terrorism-related crimes. International law and national security expert Glenn Sulmasy (2009) argues that "the road to justice in the courtroom has been a strategic shortfall" in the global war on terror, thereby requiring a "hybrid model" that integrates the principles and practices of both military commissions and federal courts (1008). If designed for the unique needs of prosecuting global war on terror defendants, such a "hybrid court" can "strike the balance of military law, intelligence needs, human rights obligations, and the need for justice" (Sulmasy and Logman 2009, 302). In this view, nonstate actors like al-Qaeda fighters are "a mix of international criminal and traditional warrior," a hybrid status that requires the strategic "detention and adjudication of these individuals to be similarly tailored to the current circumstances by utilizing a court that neither embraces the law enforcement model or the law of war model, but rather a hybrid of these two prevailing paradigms" (Sulmasy and Logman 2009, 301).

Proposals for a hybrid court have recommended the use of appointed judges with expertise in the laws of armed conflict, as such training lends itself to both determining the legality of unique issues like the admissibility of evidence obtained through torture and balancing deference to individual rights with the protection of society. Furthermore, the Department of Justice National Security Division could assign qualified prosecutors and enlist active-duty Judge Advocate General (JAG) lawyers to serve as government-appointed defense attorneys. Last, these hybrid courts would rely on bench trials adjudicated by a panel of appointed judges, rather than jury trials given the impossibility of empaneling a jury of peers for alleged war criminals or international terrorists (Sulmasy and Logman 2009; Yoo 2006). These proposals for hybrid or specialized courts recommend a separate system to try, prosecute, and sentence defendants in global war on terror cases, particularly by integrating legal actors with expertise in national security and even military training. As Sulmasy (2009) contends, "justice" in the national security court is associated with punitive outcomes: convictions and long prison terms.

Such proposals for specialized courts seek to resolve the outstanding issues raised in adjudicating terrorism-related crimes in military commissions and federal courts. For example, terrorism-related cases tried in military commissions cannot guarantee "substantive due process, given the fact that defendants are accorded significantly fewer rights than those facing courts martial proceedings" (Setty 2010, 146). When tried in military commissions, defendants do not have a right to a speedy trial and the right to the exclusion of evidence obtained through unreasonable search and seizure. Furthermore, the Bush, Obama, and Trump administrations have detained defendants after their acquittal or after their completed sentences by alleging that such individuals continue to pose a national security threat.[44] These practices reflect the "structural inequities" that organize the military commission system and the executive authority to "pick and choose the venue in which it will try defendants," creating the "appearance and perception that the United States believes one system of justice is appropriate for its citizens and a lesser level of protection is, as a matter of policy, appropriate for noncitizens who are potentially dangerous" (Setty 2010, 147). In this view, such perceptions risk inspiring terrorists and providing a recruiting tool for their organizations while offering few pathways to ethically and effectively prosecute individuals charged with terrorism-related crimes. A specialized national security court staffed with military- or national security–trained legal actors provides a viable alternative to military commissions and federal courts.

The proposed solutions to these problems seek to reform the current criminal-legal system, often ignoring the "distorting effects" terrorism prosecutions have had on criminal law and procedure through exceptions to the conventional rules; reinforcing dominant understandings of terrorism that abstract political violence from its formative conditions; and expanding criminal liability to highly inchoate activities, radical beliefs, and associations (Said 2015, 4). One lawyer, for example, was disillusioned by efforts to reform the current criminal-legal system and to institute an alternative "parallel system that would be like drug rehabilitation or mental health where cases are diverted at the outset and people are allowed to heal and rehabilitate in the context of a non-punitive situation that's not controlled by law enforcement." Despite the initial promises of such an approach, this lawyer "lost a lot of confidence in separating out anything from law enforcement because of just the incredible jealousy that law enforcement has about anyone getting their hands on that piece of pie." Given the struggle over resources, this lawyer warned that law enforcement "will compromise. If there was some psychiatrist who was treating people as part of some diversion program and wanted to keep it confidential, the government would still monitor it, subpoena the records, wiretap the conversations, all sorts of things" (interview, October 2020). Given the exceptional status of suspected terrorists and the vast resources available to fight terrorism, this lawyer questioned the possibility of establishing alternatives to the current criminal-legal system (Kassem and Shamas 2017). Other legal actors have identified the need to consider "the level of suffering that the U.S. and the U.S.'s allies have caused around the world, particularly in Muslim communities around the world," and "understand about how many civilians have been killed because of U.S. foreign policy and you may not think of it as an equivalent and that you can say, with some moral authority, that the killing of civilians is somehow inhuman, you have to look at the context of [violence] that's not broadcast on CNN" (interview, November 2020). These legal actors recognized the role of the federal courts in the global war on terror, the messy interconnections between war-making enterprises and preemptive prosecutions, and the categorical differences between law-preserving violence enacted by "constituted power" and world-making violence instituted by "constituent power" (Benjamin 1978).

Such analyses understand the multiscalar power dynamics that organize the making of violence and its uneven criminalization. My focus here on the academic discourses, geographical imaginations, and social relations animating terrorism prosecutions can help enunciate a capacious political imaginary capable of assessing, challenging, and remaking the conditions of war, empire, and globalized punishment that shape people's everyday lives in violent yet banal ways. Such a political imaginary can inspire alternatives to the current adjudication of the global war on terror that do not merely reform military commissions, expand criminal liability, or establish specialized national security courts; rather, they work toward building a less violent and more liberatory world by addressing the root causes of political violence in a racialized world order defined by U.S. empire.

Offensive Lawfare: Rethinking How Law Animates Violence

Given the expanding, and increasingly anticipatory, role of the federal courts in the global war on terror, this book specifically explores the "central role" of judges in terrorism-related prosecutions (Brown 2012, 1). Presiding judges, after all, are tasked with admitting or excluding evidence, assessing the credibility and utility of proposed expert witnesses, ruling on motions, determining the applicability of the terrorism enhancement, considering plea bargains, and rendering sentences. In this way, judges play a powerful role in the adjudication of terrorism-related cases, which produce material outcomes for defendants and their families. By investigating the central role of judges, this book contributes to the emerging "granular examination" of terrorism prosecutions, especially because "the preponderance of attention to places such as Guantánamo, Abu Ghraib, and Bagram, and policies such as rendition, military commission trials, and indefinite detention overshadow the rights violations endemic to the federal system, with particularly severe impact over the past decade on Muslims facing terrorism-related charges" (Rovner and Theoharis 2012, 1337).

More pressingly, the focus on these offshore sites "has obscured the devolution of rights protection for people accused of terrorism-related charges here at home, the schisms of race and class that have long riven the criminal justice system and the disparate justice it produces, and the ways that the prison at Guantánamo Bay is not an aberration but part of a larger way of thinking about rights and security" (Rovner and Theoharis 2012, 1339). By placing the judicial system at the center of analysis, this book examines the distinct yet interconnected forms of globalized punishment that defend and expand U.S. empire, making plain the need to nourish an emergent anti-imperial abolitionist strategy that considers the relationship between war, empire, and prisons and that takes seriously political violence, even if we disagree with the politics animating that violence or the use lethal force. Such an approach would integrate an analysis of the "level of suffering that the U.S. and the U.S.'s allies have caused around the world" in its political strategy. Arresting cycles of targeted criminalization that define domestic policing practices in the context of imperial warfare requires ending military interventions, colonial occupations, and oppressive governance regimes that create the material conditions that armed militants challenge through their death dealing.

Contrary to such granular examinations, federal courts often "are held up as the 'anti-Guantánamo'—the converse of indefinite detentions, military commissions, and other second-class due process," without considering the gross injustices that occur in the judicial system in pursuit of global war on terror victories (Rovner and Theoharis 2012, 1413). Given the allure of deceptive "anti-Guantánamo" solutions that merely reinforce globalized punishment, understanding lawfare—and more specifically the role of the courts in the global war on terror—is critical to abolitionist organizing. As Maha Hilal (2021b) contends, abolishing Guantánamo includes both the closing of the physical prison and the dismantling of "the entire 'war on terror' paradigm," which "treats terrorism as an exceptional form of violence that necessitates extraordinary interventions" and positions Muslims as the universal enemy. Closing Guantánamo is intimately tied to the initiation of military interventions that necessitate offshore detention, the mobilization of the criminal-legal system as a global war on terror weapon, the creation of particular geopolitical conditions that give rise to political violence and the criminalization of this violence, and the invention of the concept of "terrorism" that reduces armed struggles to the expression of religious fanaticism or individual pathologies. In this context, the U.S. security state can continue to criminalize political violence responsive to despotic regimes and foreign interventions while authorizing unrestrained state violence waged in the name of self-defense through the law. Abolitionists therefore must attend to these interconnections by developing a more nuanced understanding of political violence and engaging in organizing efforts that intentionally connect struggles to end war, empire, and prisons in a "globalized order of racial violence" protected by and executed through the law (Li 2020, 26).

As a humble intervention, this book intends to initiate these conversations in the spirit of supporting a politics of solidarity in a way that is attentive to these interlocking "military-carceral modalities" and their brutal impacts on communities; this book reflects my own ongoing efforts to develop a more nuanced understanding of armed struggles and to think more strategically about undermining state violence. My court observations revealed how ready-made concepts like terrorism and jihadism structured always already racialized court discussions and judicial decision-making (Stoler 2016). These concepts, however, occlude rather than clarify our understandings of transnational armed struggles in a racialized and gendered world order defined by nation-states. These conceptual tools merely reinforce the perceived necessity of policing and security regimes in global governance, ultimately making abolitionist alternatives to the criminal prosecution of suspected terrorists nearly impossible. Studying the mobilization of these concepts in the courts allowed me to begin the process of rethinking terrorism, jihadism, and therefore abolitionism.

In the next chapter, I examine how certain understandings of geopolitical contexts, world affairs, and political violence have shaped the decision-making of judges and the legal strategies of federal prosecutors and defense attorneys. Lawyers strategically have asserted competing constellations of geographic knowledge that judges have drawn on to understand the factual evidence in terrorism-related cases and interpret defendants' actions. Judges' variance in their understandings of geopolitical struggles like the Syrian war have led to the uneven application of the terrorism enhancement and corresponding sentencing decisions. Because the geopolitical reasoning of judges has shaped judicial decision-making, the courts serve as critical sites of contestation where such geographical imaginations are debated, reinterpreted, and struggled over. By exploring the geopolitical logics that organize domestic court proceedings, I work to develop new ways of understanding political violence usually reduced to, and criminalized as, terrorism—a useful analytic that can inform anti-imperial abolitionist organizing.

2

DEFINING THE BAD GUYS
GEOPOLITICS, TERRORISTS, AND THE COURTS

IN 2019, *Washington Post* reporter Craig Whitlock released a cache of confidential documents related to the 2001 U.S.-led invasion of Afghanistan and subsequent twenty-year war. Comprising memos written by Defense Secretary Donald Rumsfeld and interviews with hundreds of U.S. political leaders, military strategists, and aid workers, the Afghanistan Papers revealed that high-level officials viewed the war as unwinnable and deceived the public by "distorting statistics" to "make it appear the United States was winning the war when that was not the case" (Whitlock 2019).[1] The Afghanistan Papers also showed that senior White House officials misunderstood the geopolitical contexts in which they operated, a confusion that fueled the government's conflicting military strategies and competing foreign policy priorities. For example, in a 2003 memo, Secretary Rumsfeld admitted, "I have no visibility into who the bad guys are in Afghanistan or Iraq."[2] Additional documents and interviews confirmed the uncertainty as to who, exactly, was the enemy of the United States: "Was al-Qaeda the enemy, or the Taliban? Was Pakistan a friend or an adversary? What about the Islamic State and the bewildering array of foreign jihadists, let alone the warlords on the CIA's payroll? According to the documents, the U.S. government never settled on an answer" (Whitlock 2019). Secretary Rumsfeld and others' equivocation reflected the rapidly shifting geopolitical contexts that have defined the global war on terror, such that the nation's enemies also have served as geostrategic allies.

Although popular analyses of the Afghanistan Papers have focused primarily on the war itself, the documents more broadly reflect the confused geopolitical imaginations that have shaped other facets of the global war on terror. This confusion spilled over to an often-overlooked participant in the government's prosecution of the global war on terror: domestic courts tasked with presiding over terrorism cases and sentencing people convicted of terrorism-related offenses. Indeed, judges presiding over these cases have taken dramatically different approaches based on divergences in their understandings of dynamic geopolitical contexts, such as the Syrian war.

At sentencing, some defense attorneys strategically responded to these divergences by introducing information to contextualize their defendants' actions, such as their experiences living under repressive regimes, the international community's support of "warlords on the CIA's payroll," and the rapidly shifting geostrategic alliances between rebel groups. Given the unique "genre" of terrorism-related cases, some defense attorneys offered judges a "primer" on the geopolitical contexts organizing their cases, such as the "ethnic cleansing" of Bosnian Muslims and Bosnian Croats that inspired thousands of mujahids to fight, in armed solidarity, in the Bosnian war (interview, October 2020).

Even as defense attorneys provided such contextualizing information to "better sell their client" at sentencing, they also believed that few judges "would be receptive to a downward departure given the *context*." Some even questioned whether the courts could understand the complexity of the geopolitical contexts of their cases, as in the case of the Syrian war, as most judges "*think* they get Syria," even when they "*don't have a clue* about Syria, about Assad, or about the Assad family." In this view, "there are arguments that can be raised that might spin off and discuss what's going on in Syria," but the complexity of the war and its "many different directions" could undermine their court strategy (interview, March 2021). Indeed, the courts have continued to "order higher and higher penalties out of a sense of revulsion at the existence of terrorism in the abstract," even as defense attorneys have "done a lot of explaining" to inform the courts of the "nuances" of each case—and, more specifically, the "underlying conflict to which [the defendant] is allegedly connected" (Said 2014, 528; interview, March 2021).

Defense attorneys also have sought to contextualize their cases for jurors, which "can work at trial," but "only if you have a way to get in evidence." This strategy was used in the first trial of the Arab American men known as the Holy Land Foundation Five who were charged with terrorism-related crimes after they established a Muslim charitable foundation. At trial, "the government stepped right into it" by opening the case "with the map of the Middle East." By introducing regional geopolitics, the government allowed the defense to go "full bore on it." In this case, "the conflict informed [the defense's] approach and informed their relationship with their clients" (interview, October 2020). In other words, telling their clients' story at trial required that defense attorneys understood the geopolitical contexts shaping their conduct and effectively communicated these material conditions to the jury. The Holy Land Foundation Five case demonstrates how defense attorneys have integrated contextualizing information to help judges and jurors understand defendants' actions and how such legal maneuvers can, but rarely do, succeed at trial.

From 1986 until 2001, the Holy Land Foundation sent aid to Palestinians throughout the Arab region and to war survivors in Bosnia, Chechnya, Kosovo, Turkey, and parts of eastern Africa. Commenting on the men's indictment, Attorney General John Ashcroft (2004) alleged that the Holy Land Foundation "was created for the purpose of providing financial and material support to Hamas," a "notorious terrorist organization that engages in violent attacks to intimidate and coerce the government of Israel and its civilian population." Although the zakat committees and individuals to which the Holy Land Foundation contributed were never designated as foreign terrorist organizations or listed as entities and individuals owned or controlled by Hamas, the government charged the men with providing material support to a designated foreign terrorist organization.

At trial, the defense used the jury selection process to "get rid of jurors" who "affiliated al-Qaeda with Hamas" by treating all Muslim institutions as a "monolithic thing" of "Muslim terrorist organizations" or viewed themselves as "potential victims" of a terrorist attack. Once the trial began, the defense team worked to ensure that empaneled jurors understood "that this wasn't a case about the United States, that it was *not* a threat to the United States, and that this was about Israel and Palestinians" (interview, October 2020). Having an "educated jury" with "a certain level of sophistication" in its analysis of Hamas and the Israeli occupation of Palestine led to a hung jury after the first trial. The defense viewed the mistrial as a significant victory because jurors "saw repeated pictures of burning busses, the result of suicide bombs," even though no defendant "was accused of burning a bus," and they "saw a videotape of demonstrators stomping on and burning an American flag," even though no defendant "was accused of stomping on and burning American flags" (Hollander 2013, 57). The defense's jury selection and trial strategy defused the impact of such inflammatory images, such that jurors "saw through all of it": the hearsay evidence, the prejudicial videos, the secret evidence, and the anonymous expert, all of which the defense viewed as unconstitutional (interview, October 2020; Hollander 2013, 56).[3]

On retrial, the jury found all five men guilty of terrorism-related crimes after the court permitted a lay witness from the Treasury Department's Office of Foreign Assets Control to testify that the defendants "should have known they could not give money to these zakat committees even though they weren't designated" as foreign terrorist organizations, allowed a former National Security staff member to testify that "Hamas violence threatens to increase the risks of another 9/11 style attack on the United States," authorized an informant's testimony alleging that "everyone in the West Bank knew Holy Land provided money to Hamas," and entered into evidence documents the Israel Defense Forces seized from the Palestinian authority purporting that the Ramallah Zakat Committee was a member of Hamas's fundraising network and that the foundation provided funds for it. While the U.S. Court of Appeals for the Fifth Circuit agreed with the defense that the district court erred in admitting this evidence, it also found that the evidence was "harmless because the testimony was cumulative to other testimony before the jury."[4] From the defense's view, "the law did not matter. The facts did not matter. What mattered was that these were Palestinian men providing charity and feeding Palestinian children and in the name of national security we simply could not let that happen" (Hollander 2013,

60). Another defense attorney explained how these cases represented a broader pivot in prosecutorial strategy as the government shifted from "targeting, going after, busting, and deporting leaders of movements that were involved in armed struggle that were foreign terrorist organizations or FTO individuals into a much more systemic attack on Palestinians or supporters of Palestinian liberation" (interview, March 2021). While defense attorneys could challenge the terrorism charges by contextualizing financial donations to Hamas, they could not contest the turn in prosecutorial strategy that led to the targeting of pro-Palestinian activists in the United States; the demonization of pro-Palestinian organizations; and the admittance of prejudicial, secretive, and unconstitutional evidence.

The diverging outcomes in these two trials communicated to criminal defense lawyers that "how the defense presented the case to the jury and also looked for jurors" were effective trial strategies. Yet defense lawyers also recognized that "there's very little that works" in defending terrorism prosecutions, especially as the courts continue to admit prejudicial evidence sometimes unconstitutionally discovered (interview, October 2020; see also Hollander 2013). Even though contextualizing terrorism cases "rarely worked" at trial, defense attorneys viewed it as one of the few "possibilities that exist for success"; they therefore became students of the geopolitical conditions relevant to their cases and then "tried to educate [other] lawyers on what resources are available and what has worked and what hasn't worked" so "they can then be more effective in representing their client" (interview, October 2020).

Although defense attorneys argued that extenuating circumstances, such as military intervention and occupation, justified a reduced sentence, the courts have continued to order harsher and harsher penalties for individuals charged with terrorism-related crimes. In fact, two of the Holy Land Foundation Five received sixty-five-year sentences, even though they never committed an act of violence and never donated to a zakat committee on a terrorist watchlist. Since the 2011 onset of the Syrian war, some judges similarly have affirmed popular portrayals of rebel groups in Syria as terrorist organizations engaged in heinous criminal enterprises and then sentenced defendants to long prison terms; this process reflects the general trend in terrorism sentencing jurisprudence whereby the courts "have in general displayed an unwillingness to carefully parse through the facts as they accept the government's characterization of a given defendant's threat level" and therefore "approve a sentencing scheme that authorizes the district court to drastically increase a sentence beyond what the jury's verdict authorizes on a judge's finding of a preponderance of the evidence" (Said 2014, 517).

These dynamics organized the 2016 sentencing of Adnan Farah, who discussed plans to travel to Syria with his friends to fight the Assad regime, given "the genocide that was happening over there."[5] Although Farah applied for and received an expedited passport, his family confiscated it. This family intervention effectively demobilized Farah: he never took any additional meaningful steps, such as purchasing airfare, to travel to Syria. During this time, however, Farah and his friends "talked and tweeted generally about the events in Syria as well as their desire to help victims of the civil war."[6] After a long sting operation, Farah and six of his friends were arrested and charged with conspiracy to provide material support to a designated foreign terrorist organization.

Farah later pleaded guilty and faced sentencing before Judge Michael Davis. In his sentencing memorandum, Judge Davis "categorically reject[ed]" Farah's claim that he "believed he would be providing humanitarian aid to the people of Syria." Judge Davis determined that "no reasonable person would believe that ISIL was an organization involved in charity, the protection of innocent Syrians, or the pursuit of fair government because no evidence was submitted to support such a contention."[7] In his ruling, Judge Davis dismissed the defense's efforts to contextualize Farah's actions in the ongoing Syrian war and the ensuing humanitarian crisis, observing that although Farah had no criminal history, the "undisputable facts demonstrate that a substantial sentence is necessary to reflect the seriousness of the crime, to promote respect for the law, protection of the public, and deterrence."[8] Having made this determination, Judge Davis sentenced Farah to ten years in prison and twenty years of supervised release.

In the case of Asher Khan, however, Judge Lynn Hughes rejected applying the Sentencing Guidelines, terrorism enhancement after Khan was convicted of crimes related to his attempt to travel to Syria to join ISIS's fight against the Assad regime. After his family concocted a story that his mother was in intensive care, Khan interrupted his journey to return home. He never set foot in Syria or engaged in any hostilities. In refusing to impose a harsher sentence, Judge Hughes pointedly asked, "So all of a sudden, the United States is policing people who want to hurt other governments?"[9] Judge Hughes reasoned that such policing could target other governments or even the United States, asking, "Is buying oil from an ISIS-controlled well, is that terrorism?" Throughout the sentencing hearing, Judge Hughes rejected conventional geopolitical scripts and convenient narratives that framed "talking about going and joining ISIS" to fight the Assad regime as a federal crime of terrorism.[10] In refusing to apply the terrorism enhancement, Judge Hughes sentenced Khan to eighteen months in prison and five years of supervised release, far short of the average sentence—32.2 years—for defendants who went to trial in cases related to ISIS (Center on National Security 2017, 8). Although rare, Judge Hughes's ruling illustrates that, while "it's very difficult for judges" to "distinguish between ISIS and Al-Nusra," some will "give a sentence that is significantly less than what the government asked for" if they could understand the geopolitical conflict from the perspective of the defendant and if they could move beyond the "monolithic concept of terrorism" (interview, October 2020).

As these cases illustrate, judges have varied in their interpretation of the Syrian war and associated efforts to fight the Assad regime. Such variances have led to the uneven application of the terrorism enhancement and differences in their sentencing decisions. As one defense attorney explained to me, "When you present your client's story . . . your ability to contextualize it in a way that broadens the scope beyond just a horrible criminal act or conspiracy . . . is very important." In this view, contextualizing cases is vital to judges understanding the "fundamental distinctions" between different types of violent actors, such as "a political insurgent and a terrorist"; "if you don't explain all of these issues, the judge sees one-size-fits-all and it's never going to be that" (interview, November 2020).

This legal approach recognizes that it can be "very difficult for judges" to distinguish different kinds of political groups, such as Ahrar al-Sham and al-Nusra, and different kinds of defendants, such as politically motivated actors and profit-seeking individuals. Given these difficulties, lawyers have tried to contextualize each case for the courts.

If successful, this strategy can destabilize the "monolithic concept of terrorism" and lead to sentencing decisions that account for the individual defendant's unique circumstances and actions (interview, November 2020).

Given these variances in sentencing terrorism defendants, scholarship on the adjudication of terrorism-related cases requires a deeper exploration of the courts to demystify the myth of uniform and unified judicial decision-making, even as security professionals assert coherent narratives celebrating terrorist convictions as global war on terror victories. In this chapter, I examine how the courts have differently interpreted prevailing (and dynamic) geopolitical contexts like the Syrian war, and how such diverging interpretations have shaped sentencing decisions, particularly given the uncertainty in defining the "bad guys" and given the ongoing military operations designed to achieve goals aligned with designated foreign terrorist organizations, such as fighting the Assad regime. Although scholars increasingly have examined how textbooks (Ide 2016; Christodoulou 2018; Loewen 1994), schools (Somoza-Rodríguez 2011; Conboye 2017; Nguyen 2014), and media (El-Ibiary 2011) have shaped and are shaped by dominant geopolitical imaginations, social scientists have yet to explore the courts as a key battleground in the global war on terror. In fact, the Obama administration framed the criminal-legal system as "a counterterrorism tool" by "incapacitating terrorists" through the "prosecution of hundreds of terrorism suspects" (Office of Public Affairs 2010). Through the prosecution of alleged terrorists, the "executive branch has enlisted the third branch—the judiciary—to pursue its war aims" (Skinner 2013, 309). Government officials have sought to mobilize the law as a weapon of war through the incapacitation of putative terrorists, the disruption of funding to alleged terrorist organizations, and the delegitimation of political violence waged by nonstate actors.

Despite the role of the judicial system in incapacitating terrorists and shaping multiscalar politics, critical approaches to "lawfare"—the use of law as a weapon of war—tend to focus on how the law mediates military campaigns in late modern war (Dunlap 2001, 5). Geographer Craig A. Jones (2016), for example, explains that the law "constantly intervenes in and gives shape to war" and "defines the contours of what shall count as legal and legitimate 'self-defense'" (222). These studies focus primarily on the weaponization of international law by insurgents and states alike to justify, legitimize, and conduct war, without paying particular attention to the role the courts play in demobilizing nonstate political actors, defining political conflicts, and adjudicating what constitutes lawful violence. This chapter therefore examines the courts as critical sites where certain understandings of geopolitical contexts, world affairs, and political violence inform the decision-making of judges, defense attorneys, and prosecutors and the extent to which these legal proceedings facilitate the global war on terror and its organizing logics.

Courts in the United States, however, are not simply containers that hold and act on particular constellations of geographic knowledge or advance the geopolitical interests of the security state. They also are important sites of contestation where such geopolitical imaginations are debated, reinterpreted, and struggled over by legal actors. Legal scholar George D. Brown (2012) describes how judges in terrorism-related trials are "captains of the ship" and play a "central role" in how courts function either as "centers of justice" or "a mere default forum in the 'war on terror'" (7). Recognizing that "legal spatializations are the result of the work of several agents and actors," this chapter explores the geopolitical reasoning of judges adjudicating terrorism cases and reflects on how dominant understandings of armed conflicts have informed terrorism sentencing jurisprudence (Jones 2016, 231). The judicial system is an important institution where such geopolitical knowledge takes shape and influences the decision-making of judges, jurors, prosecutors, defense attorneys, and defendants (Said 2015; Norris and Grol-Prokopczyk 2018, 2019; Ahmed 2017). Critically examining the courts and their corresponding geopolitical imaginations provides insight into how legal institutions participate in defining, and punishing, terrorist acts, and then mediate the global war on terror through these epistemic contestations. This analysis interrogates the ideological power of dominant geopolitical scripts, the judicial actions they authorize, and the ways these legal outcomes align with broader global war on terror exigencies.

Through this analysis, I argue that the judicial system relies on geopolitical frameworks that decontextualize and depoliticize armed struggles. These frameworks have helped facilitate the criminalization, demonization, and punishment of nonstate actors and expanded criminal liability to include radical beliefs, social networks, and speech acts,

in addition to political violence. Given the relationship between dominant constellations of geographic knowledge and carceral punishment,
imagining and creating abolitionist alternatives to terrorism prosecutions
first requires rethinking the complex geopolitical conditions in which
people live and retheorizing political violence. Understanding the weaponization of such geographic knowledge in and through the judicial
system can facilitate this reimagining.

Defeating Assad and Defining Lawful Violence: Adjudicating Geopolitical Conflicts

To stage these arguments, this chapter primarily draws on my observation of terrorism trials and my analysis of sentencing-related documents for dozens of terrorism-related cases in the United States. These
documents include sentencing transcripts and memoranda, motions for
downward departures, and related filings. My analysis of these court documents began as an exploration of the various facets of terrorism-related
cases, such as the length of prison terms and their variance by crime and
by association with specific designated foreign terrorist organizations,
the special conditions of supervised release for terrorist offenders, differences in terrorism sentencing occurring simultaneously with shifting geopolitical conflicts, and changes in the terrorism charges brought
against defendants. As I coded sentencing hearing transcripts, however,
I noticed a pattern in how judges discussed geopolitical conflicts, often
in fraught ways. I began refining my codes to account for the different
ways specific geopolitical imaginations showed up in these transcripts
and how they informed judges' understandings of the cases, crimes, and
defendants before them. Later, a defense lawyer explained that sentencing hearings are the primary venue to make arguments that contextualize
defendants' actions, making such proceedings central to understanding
how the courts act on certain interpretations of the geopolitical conditions organizing the cases before them (interview, November 2020).[11]

   In many instances, I recognized that judges struggled to understand specific geopolitical conflicts and, echoing the Afghanistan Papers,
sometimes expressed dismay at evaluating whom the United States considered to be an enemy at any given time. In addition, both prosecutors and defense attorneys presented materials that sought to inform the

courts about the geopolitical contexts central to their cases. As one lawyer explained to me, "I couldn't imagine getting a [terrorism] case . . . and not needing to master the origins, the evolution of a conflict, who's on what side, and who's *changed* sides . . . since it's all very fluid in the sense of, certain places, where people could be Taliban tomorrow and back in with the Afghan government the next day and Taliban the day after." Attorneys therefore used the courtroom to assert particular geopolitical knowledge to shape how judges and jurors interpreted the actions of the defendants before them. Without establishing an "appreciation for any of the nuances" in a case, judges typically "give some extraordinarily harsh sentences," so "understanding the conflict informs our approach" in court (interview, November 2020).

Given the importance of these geopolitical debates at sentencing, I examine the case of Aws al-Jayab, who traveled to Syria in 2013 and then joined Ansar al-Islam's fight against the Assad regime. After his arrest, al-Jayab pleaded guilty to one count of providing material support to a designated foreign terrorist organization and faced sentencing in front of Judge Sara Ellis. Given the role of the Syrian war in this case, the prosecution and defense alike used their sentencing memoranda to offer a more complete picture of the defendant and his actions. As we will see, these geopolitical framings assigned criminal liability to political violence funded, supported, and endorsed by the United States government and justified a carceral punishment. *Al-Jayab* therefore illustrates how such geopolitical knowledge can shape the outcomes in terrorism-related cases.

In its sentencing memorandum, the defense argued that al-Jayab's life history and experiences with war were central to understanding his decision to join Ansar al-Islam. The defense wrote that since al-Jayab's birth, "war, death, and destruction have shadowed him, leaving lasting physical and psychic scars." For the defense, "properly contextualizing those experiences requires considering the impact of multiple wars, international conflicts, humanitarian crises, the foreign policies of different nations, and the political motives that undergird this and every federal 'national security' prosecution."[12] For Judge Ellis to consider the nature and circumstances of the offense and the history and characteristics of the defendant when imposing her sentence,[13] she needed to locate that conduct in the "complex geopolitical and policy issues" in Syria.[14] Al-Jayab's biography and geopolitical context illustrated "why it is both dangerous and inaccurate to label this case as yet another example of 'violent jihad' in a way that disregards [the defendant's] unique personal history and motivations that led to the offense conduct."[15] The "one-size-fits-all" terrorism enhancement simply could not account for the circumstances surrounding al-Jayab's case. The defense therefore detailed how al-Jayab's childhood experiences with war, torture, and displacement informed his decision to fight in armed solidarity with Syrians challenging the Assad regime.

A Palestinian refugee, al-Jayab was born and raised in Iraq, where his childhood under President Saddam Hussein "involved seeking shelter from bombs, witnessing the death of friends and relatives, and being jailed and tortured."[16] In 1996, al-Jayab's mother died, leaving behind four-year-old al-Jayab and his newborn brother. Al-Jayab's father described his remarriage as "another page of despair" as his new wife subjected his sons to physical and emotional abuse.[17] In 2003, the United States invaded Iraq; al-Jayab "vividly remembers fleeing from rocket attacks; seeking shelter with others in crowded rooms as bombs rained down; seeing corpses in the street; and fearing death on a daily basis."[18] The "immediate aftermath of the forceful military removal of Saddam Hussein and his Ba'athist regime was the creation of a power vacuum that led to years of bloody sectarian violence that needlessly took numerous lives," ultimately creating consequences "worse than the invasion itself."[19] As Sunni Palestinian refugees, al-Jayab and his family were "targeted because of their minority status and religion by other groups, particularly Shia militia forces."[20] Between 2005 and 2007, fifteen members of al-Jayab's extended family were killed by Iraqi militia, along with thirty-six of his neighbors. Al-Jayab reported regularly seeing "dismembered limbs and corpses in the street" and witnessed his own cousin being "ripped apart" by an explosion.[21] In 2012, al-Jayab was kidnapped and tortured by Iraqi police for twenty-two days, on suspicion that he had participated in a car bombing four years earlier.[22]

After al-Jayab's release, he and his family fled to a Syrian refugee camp in early 2012, a time when "Assad and his forces unleashed a brutal campaign of violence against the civilian population that sought his ouster."[23] As in Iraq, al-Jayab "suffered a great personal loss when his cousin and best friend Mohammad Nasr Jayab was shot in the head and killed by a Syrian sniper on July 19, 2012."[24] Sociologist Yasser Munif (2020) reports that snipers "played a critical role in the Syrian conflict by initially preventing gatherings in public spaces, and later by terrorizing people living in areas controlled by insurgents" (73). It was during this time that al-Jayab came to identify with Syrian civilians oppressed by the Assad regime and "felt an affinity with their struggles and in many ways wanted to remain in Syria," especially because he had friends and family who "were united in the struggle against al-Assad."[25] Despite his desire to join this armed struggle, al-Jayab and his family immigrated to the United States as refugees.

Once in the United States, al-Jayab lived with different relatives and frequently moved. This "itinerant life" exacerbated his "sense of displacement."[26] To "alleviate the sense alienation and displacement" he experienced as a refugee, al-Jayab "continued to communicate with family members and friends in Iraq and Syria."[27] Their reports of Assad's atrocities fueled al-Jayab's desire to return to Syria; in the defense's perspective, "experiencing and surviving war as a civilian—and seeing many other innocent civilians be not so fortunate—instilled in [al-Jayab] a strong sense of opposition to injustice, as naïve as it may have been."[28] Although al-Jayab's "sympathy with groups aligned against Assad varied," his own opposition to the Assad regime "was constant, if for no other reason that he was a first-hand witness to its murdering of innocent civilians, including his own cousin."[29] Steeled by Assad's chemical weapon attack in August 2013, al-Jayab returned to Syria in November 2013.

As the defense wove the Syrian war into al-Jayab's biography, it described the dynamic alliances between different rebel groups fighting the Assad regime. Al-Jayab had returned to Syria during the 2013–14 era when "numerous rebel and opposition groups often worked cooperatively or at least shoulder-to-shoulder in their opposition to al-Assad and in defense of territory, cities, and civilian groups." In fact, "many of these groups were armed, supported, and funded by other countries, including the United States. The fluidity amongst most groups at the time spoke of a common objective: defeating al-Assad. This cooperation amongst groups often led to association with different groups," including those designated by the United States as foreign terrorist organizations.[30] Al-Jayab's defense team both asserted the importance of understanding the geopolitical contexts that shaped their client's actions and reframed rebel groups as legitimate actors struggling against an oppressive regime that used brutal violence, including chemical warfare, against its civilian population.

Although Syrians struggling for revolutionary change often viewed Islamic groups "as an extension of Assad's regime" (Munif 2020, 117), al-Jayab and others in the United States have tried to join ISIS, Jabhat al-Nusra, Ansar al-Islam, and Ahrar al-Sham to depose the brutal dictator. Yet the rise of such groups cannot be understood without considering "the disintegration of traditional frameworks of solidarity" and "the collapse of the nation-state's social and organizational frameworks (political parties, trade unions, and voluntary organizations) under the weight of Assadist tyranny" (al-Haj Saleh 2017, 187). In the wake of such disintegration, the proliferation and fragmentation of armed groups organized against the Assad regime defined the Syrian context. Given his own experiences under the Assad regime, al-Jayab felt compelled to join Ansar al-Sham, a member of the Islamic Front, and later "associated with Ansar al-Islam [a designated foreign terrorist organization] through Ansar al-Sham."[31]

Recognizing that the courts adjudicate what counts as legitimate violence, the defense rejected the realist assumption that the citizen-soldier who fights on behalf of the state holds a monopoly on legitimate violence. Like the United States, "rebel and opposition groups" fought to achieve specific geopolitical goals under the oppressive reign of a brutal dictator: capturing both territorial control and sovereign power. This analysis recast rebel groups as legitimate fighters rather than as terrorists because "many Western powers, including the United States, were covertly and overtly funding, arming, and training many rebel groups," whose fluid alliances and antagonisms regularly shifted.[32] Arguing that there were "often shifts in alliances between different groups and leadership structure within each group," the defense identified how U.S.-backed groups sometimes cooperated with designated foreign terrorist organizations, making associations and memberships less straightforward.[33]

Focused on these "complex geopolitical and policy issues," the defense concluded that "there is no evidence that points to Aws doing anything other than fighting in the Syrian War," which meant al-Jayab was "ultimately aligned against Assad's regime, aligning him with both Presidents Obama and Trump—the former who covertly support[ed] rebel forces fighting Assad and the latter who attack[ed] Assad directly."[34] Rather than dismiss these broader geopolitical contexts, the defense argued that al-Jayab's criminal offense "must be seen as a part of the Syrian War because, but for that conflict, Aws would have never left the United States."[35] Determining the criminality of al-Jayab's actions necessarily required the consideration of the geopolitical contexts and personal experiences that influenced his decision to travel to Syria. The defense therefore asked for a sentence "toward the low-end of the 57–71 month range."[36]

The prosecution challenged this framing of al-Jayab's actions at sentencing. For example, the prosecution argued that the defendant's claim that "he traveled to Syria to fight with his brothers against the brutal Syrian regime" obscured "the truth of the violent and dangerous nature of his conduct and should not be credited."[37] Al-Jayab "was a knowing and willing member of a designated foreign terrorist organization, intent on creating an Islamic State in the Syrian land and defeating the infidel, the United States."[38] To reinforce the conclusion that al-Jayab supported terrorist organizations, the prosecution described Ansar al-Islam and Jabhat al-Nusra as terrorist organizations engaged in "violent jihad" to acquire "Syrian land for the Islamic caliphate," while defining the Free Syrian Army as "an umbrella organization for various armed opposition groups fighting to depose the Syrian regime of Assad," with certain "elements of the [Free Syrian Army]" expressing support "for secular governance in Syria."[39] The prosecution concluded that "there is no doubt that the Syrian conflict is a complicated war with a range of parties engaged in violence. However, the complex contours of the Syrian conflict *are essentially irrelevant* to the defendant's conduct." Instead, the court needed to focus on the "defendant's own stated desires to join a foreign terrorist organization in order to engage in violent jihad," irrespective of the material conditions in which the defendant lived.[40] Such "jihadist" conduct merited a fifteen-year prison sentence.

After hearing these arguments, Judge Sara Ellis sentenced al-Jayab to five years in prison and twenty years of supervised release. Having dismissed al-Jayab's motion for combatant immunity before his plea deal, the court's interpretation of the Syrian war and the role of rebel groups was consequential in determining if al-Jayab was considered an illegitimate terrorist aligned with Ansar al-Islam or a legitimate citizen-soldier advancing the geopolitical interests of the United States. Indeed, Judge Ellis's five-year sentence suggests that the mitigating circumstances identified by the defense factored into her decision. Although Judge Ellis's sentencing opinion is not available to the public, her decision aligned with the defense's request of fifty-seven to seventy-one months, dramatically departing from the Sentencing Guidelines advisory range of thirty years to life imprisonment and from the prosecution's recommended fifteen-year sentence.

Al-Jayab illustrates how attorneys have competed over prevailing interpretations of the Syrian war by framing participation in the conflict as an exercise in terrorist violence, a humanitarian-motivated intervention, and/or a campaign to depose an authoritarian regime. Introducing mitigating circumstances at sentencing, such as a defendant's personal experiences with war and displacement and the geopolitical conditions shaping those experiences, can lead a judge to depart downward from the Sentencing Guidelines. Given the relevance of these contextualizing arguments in mitigating al-Jayab's sentence—which still exceeded the average time served for violent offenders in state prison (4.7 years)—the geopolitical reasoning of legal actors demands more attention by critical scholars (Kaeble 2018, 2).

Caliphate, State, or Nonstate?
The Making of the Unlawful Combatant

The *Al-Jayab* case provides insight into deeper debates about who counts as a legitimate actor, unlawful combatant, and terrorist in violent territorial struggles for administrative authority in a world order organized by states and statehood. In what is now commonly referred to as the Middle East, Anglo-French imperialism "divided the remnants of the Ottoman Empire into states with artificial borders," largely ignoring the "fragile ethnic, religious, and communal fabric characteristic of the region," of which "the current upheavals are a late outbreak of internal distress arising from that same historical injustice" (Valensi 2015, 59–60). Even the conceptual framework of the "Middle East" is a result of the chaotic and colonial imposition of borders on territory, regardless of people's own understandings of the land and their sovereign relationship to it. Furthermore, contemporary struggles over territorial governance have destabilized the state framework—a colonial imposition—particularly given the rise of both substate and suprastate formations that actively participate in the making of global, regional, and local politics. Political scientists, international law, and criminal-legal systems, however, continue to privilege the nation-state as the arbiter of world affairs and reinforce the state's exclusive right to the lawful use of violence. These privileges have facilitated the criminalization of nonstate actors like al-Jayab, even if doing so works counter to the state's own geopolitical pursuits and geostrategic alliances, including the "bewildering array of foreign jihadists" and "warlords" on "the CIA's payroll" (Whitlock 2019).

In the realist paradigm, nonstate actors like al-Jayab "make use of force that is not acceptable to the state in order to achieve their goals and thus challenge the state's monopoly over violence" (Valensi 2015, 62). This aligns with Max Weber's (1946) theorization that the modern state is "a human community that (successfully) claims the *monopoly of the legitimate use of physical force* within a given territory," meaning that "the right to use physical force is ascribed to other institutions or to individuals only to the extent to which the state permits it" (78). For Weber, the state holds the sole right to use violence, arbitrating who can enact violence and wielding such violence to assert, maintain, and legitimize its sovereign power and territorial control (2). State-centric laws of armed conflict have reaffirmed the state's monopoly on legitimate violence and reinforced a world order defined by sovereign states. Such processes criminalize nonstate actors and organizations that use violence to achieve specific geopolitical goals, such as seizing state power or capturing territorial control. In this framework, al-Jayab and the rebel group he joined must be understood as illegitimate political actors engaged in terrorism, regardless of their intentions to respond to the Assad regime's brutality and the ensuing humanitarian crisis. In a state-centric world order, the state is defined by its monopoly on legitimate force, rendering all other forms of violence illegitimate and unlawful.[41] Domestic courts reinforce the state's monopoly on violence by prosecuting individuals for their use of "acts dangerous to human life" to challenge state sovereignty and enact political change,[42] even as Additional Protocol I to the Geneva Conventions protects irregular guerrilla forces "fighting against colonial domination, alien occupation, or racist regimes."

Despite the rise of alternative paradigms within political science accounting for a wider range of actors and processes shaping the current world order, violent nonstate actors consistently have been framed as illegitimate, unlawful, and/or immoral as they disrupt the conventional dichotomy between the state and the nonstate under international law. For example, the United States designated ISIS as a foreign terrorist organization that, as a nonstate armed group, has engaged in unlawful warfare, even as the group evolved into a "state-like" entity—the Islamic State—in 2014. Although international law typically permits interstate wars as in the U.S.-led invasion of Iraq, the Islamic State's status as a "quasi state" or "proto-state" made it ineligible for participation in legal warfare (Brown 2018). At the time, the Islamic State was defined by the territorial control of western Iraq and northeastern Syria, the appointment of Abu Bakr al-Baghdadi as caliph, and the provision of social services—all defining features of a sovereign state. Despite the Islamic State's declaration of statehood, given its territorial control, political sovereignty, and government institutions that enforce laws and provide services (Mabon 2017), the international community largely denied the Islamic State's claim to statehood.[43] Under international law, the Islamic State cannot engage in lawful violence as a nonstate organization. As Christian Tomuschat (2015) writes, if the Islamic State constituted a state in the legal sense, "it would derive great advantages therefrom," including the right to invoke self-defense and thus the right to use armed force under Article 51 of the Charter of the United Nations (226). Given the state's monopoly on the legitimate use of physical force, denying the Islamic State status as a state under international law meant its military engagements could never constitute the legitimate and lawful use of force.

The Islamic State has challenged the realist assumption that the nation-state is the principal actor in international relations and world affairs. International law cannot account for emerging forms of governance that do not conform to a state-centric world order, even as conventional states "continue to invoke ad hoc supra-state justifications for armed intervention, such as the International Community, humanity, and civilization" (Li 2016, 372). Valensi (2015) argues that much like conventional state invocations, the Islamic concept of the *ummah* (community) is "fundamentally supra-national and supra-state," transcending the state by fostering transnational connections across geographic territories (71). Legal scholar Noah Novogrodsky (2018) similarly contends that the Islamic State challenges normative understandings of the world order given its territorial expansion, forcing the international community to "grapple with a non-State actor that controls land and lives and operates through select modalities" (59). Although these scholars demonstrate how the Islamic State disrupts realist understandings of the current world order, the international community continues to operate through a state-centric framework that delegitimizes and criminalizes nonstate actors and their use of violence in the pursuit of their political goals, even when aligned with and funded by the United States. The Department of Defense's *Law of War Manual* (2015), for example, asserts that "non-State armed groups lack *competent authority,*" and thus "there would not be a basis for non-State armed groups to claim the permissions that may be viewed as inherent in parts of the law of war" (81). By definition, nonstate actors cannot engage in legal or legitimate warfare, regardless of the geopolitical contexts in which they live, the funding they receive to support state-sanctioned military campaigns, or their conduct in armed conflicts.

Applying Western understandings of sovereignty and statehood to ISIS reaffirms the normative concept of the state as a fixed unit of sovereign space and a container of society, even though on-the-ground realities demonstrate how such understandings cannot account for territorial struggles, modes of governance, and forms of political life that defy sovereign borders. As political geographer John Agnew (1994) contends, "systems of rule or political organization need not be either territorial, where geographical boundaries define the scope of membership in a polity a priori . . . or fixed territorially," as "territoriality has been 'unbundled' by all kinds of formal agreements and informal practices, such as common markets, military alliances, monetary and trading regimes, etc." (54). Eschewing this "territorial trap," ISIS challenges these realist assumptions and thus the international community never affords it the right to violence, even when aligned with and working alongside the United States and its allies similarly engaged in violent armed conflicts.

Even as the Islamic State has challenged realist assumptions, social scientists continue to apply normative rubrics to evaluate rebel groups, their claims to statehood, and therefore their status as a sovereign entity.

Like Mabon's (2017) description of ISIS's political and social efforts as a state-building project, social scientist Timothy Clancy (2018) defines the Islamic State as an "emerging-state actor," arguing that the organization mobilizes local and global grievances to recruit fighters who use violence to "seize territory upon which it exercises sovereign control and begins openly governing," ultimately establishing legitimacy through the provision of social services (22). Some have defined ISIS as a "de facto state"—a "political authority functioning within a territory without international recognition"—that "uses jihadism as a survival strategy" (Özpek and Yağiş 2019, 23). Other scholars have argued that rebel groups responding to the Syrian war crisis enact a kind of "stateness" and gain legitimacy by providing bread and health care. These "state-like functions" or "state performances" position rebel groups as the political and administrative authority and legitimize their rule (Martínez and Eng 2018). These "deliberate actions," however fragile and fleeting, challenge the Assad regime's sovereignty, just as the Assad regime seeks to "eradicate rival performances" to maintain its statehood and global positioning (Martínez and Eng 2018, 247). Although some scholars demonstrate the "stateness" of ISIS, the organization never acquires a monopoly on violence, meaning it can only wage illegitimate and unlawful violence, regardless of the wider geopolitical contexts in which it operates. Using such realist rubrics also reinforces the current world order, even as the Islamic State has challenged "the nation-state as a normative governance unit" through their "post-national state ideology," their efforts to undo borders drawn by the Sykes-Picot Agreement, and their declaration of transnational political aspirations (Kaneva and Stanton 2020).

Despite these lively debates within political science and human geography, the international community—itself organized around a collection of nation-states—continues to define the concept of terrorism within a state-centric understanding of world politics in which states hold a monopoly on legitimate violence. Within this world order, the courts reinforce what constitutes illegitimate violence and unlawful actors through their adjudication of terrorism-related crimes. Yet the courts also function as contested sites where such geopolitical understandings are negotiated, reworked, and reproduced through the daily work of legal actors. The following section examines how the courts have interpreted the "stateness" and legitimacy of rebel groups, and how such interpretations bear on the courts' understanding and sentencing of the defendants before them. Although by no means an exhaustive analysis of every court case, this exploration illustrates trends in the competing geopolitical knowledges expressed in domestic courtrooms and their impact on judicial decision-making.

Detainee #001: The Global War on Terror's First Unlawful Combatant

The 2002 high-profile prosecution of John Walker Lindh illustrates how the courts can reinforce the realist dichotomy between lawful and unlawful combatants and, under the Third Geneva Convention, who is and is not eligible for immunity from prosecution. Before the September 11 attacks, nineteen-year-old Lindh traveled to Pakistan to attend a military training camp operated by Harakat ul-Mujahideen and, on completion in August 2001, expressed interest in fighting for the Taliban against the Northern Alliance in Afghanistan. Before deploying Lindh, Taliban officials required he undergo more extensive military training at the al Farooq training camp, "a facility associated with and funded by Osama bin Laden and al-Qaeda."[44] At the training camp, Lindh "voluntarily swore allegiance to Jihad."[45] After Lindh completed his training, a camp administrator asked if Lindh would take part in operations "against the United States, Israel, or Europe," but Lindh declined, stating he was interested in fighting only against the Northern Alliance.[46] Lindh was sent to Takhar in northeastern Afghanistan, where he joined Taliban forces before surrendering to the Northern Alliance in Kunduz two months later.

After his surrender, Lindh was transferred to Qala-i-Jangi, a prison that held hundreds of men deemed enemy combatants by the Northern Alliance. In prison, CIA agent Johnny "Mike" Spann and other intelligence officers interrogated Lindh and other captured soldiers. During this time, the detained men staged an uprising, attacking their captors and interrogators. The Northern Alliance used significant force to suppress the uprising, killing hundreds of prisoners. In the chaos, Spann was shot dead. Although he played no role in the uprising, Lindh suffered a gunshot wound to his thigh before hiding in the prison basement along with several other detainees. After the uprising, Lindh received medical care at Mazār-e Sharīf and then was transferred to Camp Rhino, a U.S. forward operating base in southern Afghanistan. National security scholar

Karen J. Greenberg (2016) reports that "Army photos from Rhino show Lindh naked, dirty, and duct-taped to a gurney, his eyes covered with a blindfold emblazoned with the word *shithead*"—with a bullet still lodged in his thigh (49). Lindh was then transferred to the navy ship, U.S.S. *Peleliu,* where he was denied legal counsel and brutalized by military interrogators before he signed a confession attesting to his membership to both the Taliban and al-Qaeda (50).

Upon return to the United States, Lindh was charged in federal court on ten criminal counts, including conspiracies to murder U.S. nationals and to provide material support to a designated foreign terrorist organization, even at a time when, as the Afghanistan Papers revealed, the United States could not discern "who the bad guys are in Afghanistan or Iraq." Lindh's lawyers filed a motion to suppress these coerced statements, but the night before the hearing, prosecutor David Kelly negotiated a plea agreement, meaning testimony about Lindh's treatment would not be entered into evidence. Although the plea agreement "did not please Donald Rumsfeld . . . no one, including Rumsfeld, wanted more details of Lindh's treatment at the hands of the military to come into public view, as they would have to at a suppression hearing" (Greenberg 2016, 51). Lindh's conviction proved the federal court system could manage criminal cases against terrorism defendants and therefore disrupt terrorist networks. This management included a plea deal to avoid going to trial, thereby ensuring that U.S. military conduct, such as torture, would remain outside of judicial review and public oversight.

Before signing his plea agreement, Lindh filed a series of motions to dismiss the indictment, mostly notably arguing that he was entitled to combatant immunity and therefore protected from prosecution. To evaluate a defendant's claim to combatant immunity, judges rely on the Geneva Convention (III) Relative to the Treatment of Prisoners of War, which outlines the four criteria an organization must meet for its members to qualify for combatant immunity status:

1. the organization must be commanded by a person responsible for his subordinates;
2. the organization's members must have a fixed distinctive emblem or uniform recognizable at a distance;
3. the organization's members must carry arms openly; and

4. the organization's members must conduct their operations in accordance with the laws and customs of war.[47]

Presiding over the case, Judge T. S. Ellis III dismissed the motion after concluding that the Taliban did not meet the Third Geneva Convention criteria for Lindh to qualify for combatant immunity status. In making this determination, Judge Ellis explained that although "Lindh and his cohorts carried arms openly in satisfaction of the third criteria for lawful combatant status," the Taliban "had no internal system of military command or discipline," "wore no uniforms or insignia and were effectively indistinguishable from the rest of the population," and "failed to observe the laws and customs of war."[48] Given these three violations, Judge Ellis determined that Lindh did not qualify for combatant immunity.

Reflecting on the case in a law journal, Judge Ellis (2013) explained that Lindh's status as a Taliban fighter "did not make him eligible for immunity from prosecution" for three reasons:

> (1) because the President had determined that Lindh was an un-lawful combatant and this determination, under well-settled law, was entitled to deference as a reasonable interpretation and application of the Geneva Convention; (2) because Lindh had not met his burden demonstrative that he was a lawful combatant given the criteria set forth in the Geneva Convention; and (3) because the Taliban/Al-Qaeda did not meet the Convention's criteria for determining entitlement to lawful combatant status. (1613–14)

In his sentencing memorandum, Judge Ellis further reasoned that "courts have long held that treaty interpretations made by the Executive Branch are entitled to some degree of deference," without conceding to "conclusive deference" which "amounts to judicial absentia."[49] Judge Ellis therefore assessed that the Taliban did not meet the criteria for determining entitlement to lawful combatant status, which aligned with the Bush administration's own declaration.

John Walker Lindh's July 2002 plea deal and Judge Ellis's October 2002 sentencing decision followed a January 2002 memorandum from White House counsel Alberto R. Gonzales to President Bush exploring the right to prisoner of war status in the global war on terror. In this memo, Gonzales (2002) advised the president that "the Department of Justice has issued a formal legal opinion concluding that the Geneva Convention III on the Treatment of Prisoners of War (GPW) does not apply to the conflict with al-Qaeda" (1). Popularly considered *hostes humani generis*—the enemy of humankind—al-Qaeda fighters do not qualify for protections under the Third Geneva Convention as members of a "stateless organization that *en masse* engaged in combat unlawfully in an international armed conflict without any legitimate or other authority" (Bialke 2004, 3). This means that international law "deems a transnational act of private warfare by al-Qaeda as *malum in se,* 'a wrong in itself'" (3). Stateless, al-Qaeda fighters can never claim lawful combatant status under international law and therefore do not qualify for prisoner of war protections guaranteed by the Third Geneva Convention. Under the Bush administration, such legal interpretations justified the indefinite detention of suspected al-Qaeda fighters at Guantánamo Bay.

Gonzales (2002) also reported that the "DOJ's opinion concludes that there are reasonable grounds for you to conclude that GPW does not apply with respect to the conflict with the Taliban" (1). Rather than focus on the criteria outlined in the Third Geneva Convention, Gonzales (2002) reported that these "reasonable grounds" included the "determination that Afghanistan was a failed state because the Taliban did not exercise full control over the territory and people, was not recognized by the international community, and was not capable of fulfilling its international obligations" (1). As a failed state, "the Taliban and its forces were, in fact, not a government, but a militant, terrorist-like group" (1). In this legal interpretation, the Taliban, much like al-Qaeda, "were armed militants," not "regular foreign armed forces," and therefore unentitled to prisoner of war protections under the Third Geneva Convention. Using his executive authority, President Bush "decided that GPW does not apply and, accordingly, that al-Qaeda and Taliban detainees are not prisoners of war under GPW" (1).

While "Taliban captives were at least *in theory* capable of qualifying for [prisoner of war] status," al-Qaeda captives "were not, even if they complied with the four criteria elements of the qualification equation" (Corn 2011, 263). Through these assessments, the executive branch categorically denied Taliban and al-Qaeda soldiers combatant immunity. Judge Ellis's determination aligned with these classifications.

While Gonzales detailed the military benefits of the unlawful combatant status in the midst of a "new kind of war," legal scholar Geoffrey Corn (2011) warned that the categorical denial of Taliban and al-Qaeda fighters "the legal status of prisoner of war and the accordant protections of the Third Geneva Convention" ultimately "deprives the individual of legal and moral equivalency with his privileged opponent: state actors" (253–54). Although the International Committee of the Red Cross proposed conferring prisoner of war status and the corresponding "elementary considerations of humanity" to "organized non-State armed groups" (Kellenberger 2008, 4), interpreting international humanitarian law in this way "would have deprived governments of the ability to hold [internal dissident forces] criminally accountable for their efforts to topple lawful government authority, because POW status would have prevented the state from prosecuting these dissident operatives for any offense for which its own forces could not be prosecuted, which would have included the harmful consequences of combatant conduct" (Corn 2011, 265). While some may laud efforts to confer humanity onto all kinds of armed soldiers, states "viewed the extension of POW status to nonstate actors as creating an unacceptable and ultimately unjustified intrusion upon their sovereignty" by limiting their "ability to punish individuals who act to harm the state" (Corn 2011, 265). The Third Geneva Convention risked infringing on the state's monopoly on the legitimate use of force to maintain its sovereign power and territorial control.[50]

For Corn (2011), "the determination to preserve the line between the authority to participate in armed conflict is almost certainly motivated by a desire to preserve the prerogative to sanction such unprivileged belligerents for participating in hostilities" such that "extending combatant immunity to non-state belligerents has and remains unthinkable" by state-sanctioned courts charged with making such determinations (255). Judge Ellis's ruling to dismiss based on combatant immunity by citing judicial deference and GPW criteria reinforces the legal line between lawful state soldiers and unlawful nonstate fighters. Such judicial decisions protect the sovereign interests of the state by protecting its monopoly on violence. In the years since Lindh's plea deal, other captured global war on terror fighters have asserted the defense of lawful combatant immunity. None, however, has been successful, as judges consistently have denied these claims by deferring to the executive branch for guidance on classifying nonstate fighters.

By exercising judicial deference to the Bush administration's classification of Taliban and al-Qaeda soldiers as unlawful combatants, the courts have functioned as "default forums" on the global war on terror. Although the executive branch's classification of (un)lawful combatants can be challenged in court and subjected to judicial review, the courts typically exercise judicial deference and therefore cosign the state's geopolitical maneuvering. By denying suspected fighters the protections afforded prisoners of war, the courts serve as important sites to interpret the legality and legitimacy of international conflicts and nonstate fighters.

"It Is No 'Crime' to Be a Soldier": The Doctrine of Combatant Immunity in Fluid Wars

Despite President Bush's determination that Taliban and al-Qaeda soldiers categorically constituted unlawful combatants, defendants facing criminal charges in domestic courts have since sought to assert their rights as lawful combatants and access combatant immunity. The judicial denial of lawful combatant status, and corresponding immunity from prosecution, continues to bear on terrorism-related court cases, particularly those related to the Syrian war. Although legal debates have focused primarily on the rights, treatment, and protection of global war on terror detainees under international humanitarian law, the principle of combatant immunity affects more than just the suspected soldiers indefinitely held (and tortured) at Guantánamo and tried in military commissions; it also shapes the legal defenses of returning fighters arrested, incarcerated, and prosecuted in the United States. Although judges have reasoned that "it is no 'crime' to be a soldier,"[51] Taliban, al-Qaeda, and other nonstate fighters do not qualify as lawful combatants and therefore face criminal charges for their participation in the global war on terror. At the same time, the Office of Legal Counsel determined that civilian employees like CIA agents who were ineligible for prisoner of war status but conducted drone strikes in foreign countries would be immune from prosecution, concluding that "lethal action carried out by a governmental official" could be considered "lawful" in "some circumstances" (Barron 2010, 12). As the judiciary has refused to confer legal protections guaranteed under international humanitarian law to nonstate soldiers while eliminating criminal liability for civilian employees using lethal force, defendants charged with terrorism-related crimes continue to submit the lawful combatant immunity affirmative defense at trial.

Although an unsuccessful legal strategy, motions claiming combatant immunity challenge the presumption that participation in transnational armed conflicts as a nonstate soldier constitutes a crime. For example, before Aws al-Jayab agreed to a plea bargain, he filed a motion to dismiss the indictment based on combatant immunity. In this motion, the defense described the complexities of the opposition to the Assad regime, reasoning that "the realities of the Syrian War are fundamentally important to the[] unique legal questions before the Court."[52] In this filing, the defense argued that al-Jayab was entitled to combatant immunity under common and international law, as "acts of legitimate opposition against [the] Assad regime and acts in defense of civilians cannot be considered murder abroad, and therefore those acts cannot serve as a basis for conspiracy or material support charges."[53] Citing common law, the defense first reasoned that President Obama "publicly called for military action and targeted strikes against Syria after Assad used chemical weapons" and extended combatant immunity to civilian personnel conducting drone strikes.[54] In other words, a government authority—the executive branch—gave the CIA, Islamic Front, and other rebel groups permission to engage in lethal action in Syria. In this context, the common-law variant of the public authority defense applied to al-Jayab and other nonstate soldiers who acted within the rules of warfare and in alignment with the geopolitical interests of the United States. The defense therefore argued:

> Unlike the executive determination of the Taliban's status, neither the Islamic Front nor Ansar al-Sham are designated foreign terrorist organizations; nor has there been any finding or declaration that those groups or Mr. Al-Jayab were unlawful combatants. Quite to the contrary, rather than declaring Syrian rebel opposition groups to be unlawful combatants, President Obama recognized them as legitimate representatives of the Syrian people in their fight against the Assad regime; secretly authorized the CIA to provide arms and training; and then, both in words and actions, supported those opposition groups.[55]

Given President Obama's alliance with the Islamic Front and other rebel groups, the defense concluded that "from a common law perspective, combatant immunity applies to legitimate acts of war during an armed conflict, and does not necessarily depend on the status of the individual actor or the nature of the conflict (i.e., as an international or non-international armed conflict)."[56] Under common law, al-Jayab's conduct did not constitute a crime.

The defense also argued that al-Jayab was entitled to combatant immunity under international law binding on federal courts, such as the Geneva Conventions. Citing academic scholarship on international law, the defense defined the Syrian war as an internal armed conflict that was "internationalized" by the U.S. military's intervention "in support of a nonstate actor against the state in which the conflict takes place." "Once internationalized, the conflict is subject to the standards applicable to international armed conflicts, including combatant immunity."[57] After arguing that the Syrian war met the type of armed conflict regulated by the Geneva Conventions, the defense asserted that members of the Islamic Front, like al-Jayab, "would be lawful combatants due to its organization structure, including military and political operations, and other distinguishing factors."[58] In this view, U.S. support for rebel groups was "evidence that it believed the belligerency against Assad was legitimate warfare and that fighters against Assad were entitled to combatant immunity for their legitimate acts of warfare against the regime."[59] The defense's motion provided additional legal analysis of the Syrian war and its many armed participants, ultimately asserting that as a member of a recognized force participating in an international armed conflict, al-Jayab was entitled to combatant immunity under common and international law.

Whereas the defense detailed the "unique and fluid" aspects of the Syrian war to substantiate its claim of combatant immunity,[60] the prosecution defined al-Jayab's conduct as a long-term plot to "return to Syria to fight on behalf of terrorist groups there" and described such military engagements as "violent jihad."[61] Through these arguments, the prosecution rejected al-Jayab's public authority defense, arguing that al-Jayab had not proven "he was engaged in otherwise-illegal conduct in Syria at the express direction of a U.S. government official."[62] Although the prosecution verified media reports documenting President Obama's financial, military, and strategic support of Syrian rebel groups, it argued that this defense "is tantamount to saying, 'President Obama told me to do it,'" and that the defendant failed "to show that a government official requested, directed, or authorized *the defendant* to engage in otherwise illegal activity."[63] Al-Jayab's public authority defense, however, rested on the fact that he "associated with an organized party that acted lawfully during a time of war" and that the Obama administration had announced that "similar groups were legitimate representatives of the Syrian people before Mr. Al-Jayab returned to Syria."[64]

Although the United States government supported, trained, and armed rebel groups opposing the Assad regime, it also designated some of these same rebel groups as foreign terrorist organizations (FTOs). Such reductive classifications often miss the fluid and shifting alliances between rebel groups. The prosecution's filing quoted messages al-Jayab sent explaining how he joined Ansar al-Sham; in this exchange, al-Jayab described Ansar al-Sham [not an FTO] as "the same as Ansar al-Islam [an FTO]. It is the one that leads the new Islamic Front [not an FTO] formed after merging with Jabhat al-Nusra [an FTO]."[65] The prosecution continued to cite al-Jayab's discussion of how "the Army of Islam [an FTO] and Ahrar al-Sham [not an FTO] and Al-Tawhid Brigade [not an FTO] became the al-Jabhah al-Islamiyyah [as-Suriyyah] [not an FTO] and Ansar al-Sham [not an FTO]. When they engage in battles [they are] led by Jabhat al-Nusra and Ansar al-Sham."[66] The prosecution even acknowledged that "as a result of these internal conflicts between terrorist organizations," al-Jayab "began to express his intention to return home."[67] Despite U.S. support for rebel groups and their shifting alliances, the prosecution ultimately described al-Jayab's participation in the Syrian war as "violent jihad"[68] fueled by his "jihadi ideals."[69]

To shape the court's understanding of these rebel groups, the prosecution differentiated the Islamic Front—defined as "an umbrella organization of Sunni Salafist groups fighting to depose the Syrian regime"—from the Free Syrian Army.[70] In doing so, the prosecution classified the Free Syrian Army as a legitimate "umbrella organization for various armed opposition groups fighting to depose the Syrian regime of Assad," which has "historically stated support for the secular governance in Syria," unlike the "violent jihad of Ansar al-Islam and Jabhat al-Nusra," which "hijack the struggles of the Syrian people for [their] own malign[ed] purposes."[71]

Given the collective use of violence, the prosecution differentiated the Islamic Front from the Free Syrian Army primarily by distinguishing their differing political aspirations: deposing Assad to "establish[] a global Islamic State" or unseating Assad to institute a "secular government."[72] The prosecution therefore distinguished lawful combatants from unlawful ones by specifically focusing on the political goals driving their violence rather than the criteria detailed by the Third Geneva Convention, which concentrate on the conduct of fighters, such as carrying their arms openly, wearing distinctive emblems, and abiding by the laws of war. By creating a clear legal line between mujahids and Free Syrian Army soldiers, the prosecution distilled the messy on-the-ground realities in Syria into a single conflict with three distinct sides: radical Islamists engaged in "violent jihad," the Free Syrian Army buttressed by the U.S. military, and the Assad regime. Depicting the Syrian war in this way belies the conflict's complexities, including Assad's strategic use of sectarianism and the proxy wars involving the United States, Russia, Saudi Arabia, and Iran (Hashemi 2016; Makdisi 2017; Munif 2020).

In addition to challenging al-Jayab's claim of an affirmative public authority defense, the prosecution argued that al-Jayab had "not met his burden to establish he is entitled to combatant immunity because he was fighting in a non-international armed conflict for militant groups that did not meet the prisoner of war criteria."[73] More specifically, the prosecution assessed that al-Jayab merely "speculate[d] that the U.S. government has supported and directed Syrian rebel groups fighting against the Assad government to such an extent that those groups have become State actors, thereby transforming the conflict into an international one," as the United States arguably "engaged only in non-international armed conflicts in Syria."[74] While the defense argued that U.S. military intervention "internationalized" the Syrian war, the prosecution maintained that the Obama administration "continued to characterize United States operations in Syria as against non-State actors (ISIS and al-Qaeda)."[75] Media reports, however, identified U.S. military strikes against "the two main players in Syrian war—President Bashar Assad's military and the Islamic State" (Myre 2017). Discerning if and when the Syrian war constituted an international armed conflict figured centrally in the legal calculus proffered by both the defense and prosecution. While defendants like al-Jayab understood and even criticized the shifting alliances between rebel groups and their conflicting geopolitical aspirations, the executive branch's uneven designation of foreign terrorist organizations at the same time as its financial, political, and operational support of these same rebel groups made it easier for the prosecution to define al-Jayab's conduct as "involving international terrorism."[76] Judge Ellis ultimately denied al-Jayab of combatant immunity, demonstrating the symbiotic yet fraught relationship between U.S. military operations globally and criminalizing practices domestically.

Nonstate actors like al-Jayab have sought to claim their right to combatant immunity by asserting particular interpretations of the geopolitical conflicts in which they fought, often demonstrating their alignment with the covert and overt military operations of the United States. In every terrorism-related case in which a defendant claimed combatant immunity, the courts have rejected these arguments, designating each defendant as an unlawful combatant and therefore unentitled to immunity from criminal prosecution.[77] Such denials reaffirm the state's monopoly on violence by categorically defining nonstate fighters as unlawful and illegitimate.

Organized around the assumption that the "complex contours of the Syrian conflict are essentially irrelevant" to the defendants' actions, these judicial determinations depoliticize political violence by abstracting armed resistance from its formative contexts, erasing the "very particular historical and political conditions that enable us to understand political violence" (Poynting and Whyte 2012b, 6). Such normative claims about the illegality of nonstate violence refuse to consider the radically different power relations and uneven distribution of precarity under which certain nonstate actors live as well as the geostrategic goals they pursue, including political claims to self-determination and alternative forms of governance (Butler 2004). For example, while "ISIS has a traceable past, a history and a political trajectory grounded in movements, organizations, governments, and political moments that form a long story in the Middle East" (Bennis 2015, 1), conventional imperial scripts reduce such armed struggles to a "clash of civilizations" (Huntington 1996) rooted in cultural conflicts stoked by "jihadi ideals." Historian Bernard Lewis (1990), for example, theorized the alleged "roots of Muslim rage," contending that there "is something in the religious culture of Islam," which can create "an explosive mixture of rage and hatred" in "moments of upheaval and disruption" and in turn "impel even the government of an ancient and civilized country" to "espouse kidnapping and assassination, and try to find, in the life of their Prophet, approval and indeed precedent for such actions" (59). This double movement—depoliticization and demonization—"is the means by which state and sub-state political violence can be represented as occupying entirely different moral universes. . . . The material connections between those forms of violence are thus merely expressed in the mode of 'terror' that both may or may not deploy, rather than being understood through the political struggles that sustain them" (Poynting and Whyte 2012b, 6). When the courts invoke, debate, and employ such imperial scripts, even in contested and contradictory ways, they reinforce how the courts "operate as an unjust social institution through their legitimation and use of police, jails, and prisons as well as through their own unique techniques of mass criminalization" (Clair and Woog 2022, 6).

Although the international community denied the Islamic State's claims to statehood, the political promise of the caliphate as an alternative governance regime inspired transnational fighters to join armed struggles across Syria and Iraq. Taking seriously the Islamic State's statecraft strategies and governance practices defies conventional imperial scripts that frame violent struggles for territorial control and sovereign power as an apolitical expression of theological, cultural, and/or psychological perversions, even if we disagree with the politics animating such violence. For example, drawing on interviews with returning Islamic State soldiers from Denmark, Jakob Sheikh (2016) reports that Abu Bakr al-Baghdadi's declaration of the caliphate in 2014 galvanized transnational soldiers, explaining, "While a battlefield primarily attracts fighters, a state also attracts immigrants, who want to settle down and build a future for themselves" (63). Interview participants defined the caliphate as a *dawla* (state or nation) and identified clear political aspirations "for state building" (63). One returning Islamic State fighter, for example, described how Syria was "more perfect" than Denmark because "the state is better at taking care of its citizens" (63). When asked, "Which state? The Islamic State?," the participant explained, "Yes. But I am not speaking about the group now. I am speaking about the state" (63). What this participant named is an explicit political struggle for statehood—including the development of economic, educational, and legal systems—in the racialized context of continued military incursions, colonial occupations, and authoritarian regimes. It was the *dawla*—and its political possibilities—that inspired participants to join the Islamic State. Given the "combination of direct and indirect violence that Syrians have experienced since 2011 [that] has led to catastrophic humanitarian conditions," the invocation of the *dawla* identifies a political project that cannot be depoliticized and demonized as an alleged "clash of civilizations" or shoehorned into a hegemonic world order defined by nation-states (Munif 2020, 28).

Determining the legality of such political violence often ignores the governing contexts and political aspirations organizing armed resistance, which then justifies how states respond to such acts. Defendants charged with terrorism-related crimes therefore worked to refute such reductive analyses in the courtroom by providing an understanding of the wider geopolitical conflicts in which they acted. Although most still receive harsh sentences, defendants have continued to assert these analyses to contextualize their actions for the record.

"You Can't Explain Syria to a Judge": Judicial Geopolitical Knowledge at Sentencing

Because terrorism defendants like al-Jayab were unentitled to immunity from criminal prosecution, their attorneys often integrated biographical information and geopolitical analysis into their legal arguments. Given the need to disrupt the conventional "monolithic concept of terrorism" circulating in public, political, and legal discourses (interview, October 2021), some defense attorneys challenged simplistic interpretations of the complex geopolitical contexts organizing armed conflicts and reductive caricatures of their clients as "jihadists" or "terrorists" (interview, March 2021). Even if defendants refused to renounce their political struggles, defense attorneys placed their actions "in the best context and the best light, especially when there's been no violence, there's been no injury, and there's been no real harm" (interview, March 2021).

Defense attorneys often viewed sentencing as the most effective venue to raise these arguments. In a case involving Liberation Tigers of Tamil Eelam (LTTE) fighters, "the judge would not let them use as a defense essentially the concept that they were in a civil war, and they were on the side of the oppressed rather than the oppressor," observing that "it's not relevant to the elements of the case." This meant that the defense "didn't really have an option with respect to trial," even though the judge was "a good judge for this kind of case: a guy with empathy, a guy with a lot of experience, someone who had been in a variety of different roles in his career so he could understand a lot of [the geopolitics]." Instead, the judge agreed that if they "plead guilty and get the leniency that comes with that," the defense could then "make all of our arguments that we would have made in this defense [if it went to trial], we make it into sentencing arguments." The defense therefore "spoke to a lot of experts" and "developed a forty-five page, very comprehensive history of the Tamil oppression by the Sinhalese in Sri Lanka." The defense viewed its sentencing memorandum as "compelling just on the facts alone" (interview, October 2020).

Furthermore, "by the time the case started, it was 2006; by the time the case goes to sentencing in 2010, LTTE's already been wiped by the Sri Lankan government." This meant that the defendants no longer posed a threat "since there's no outlet for any kind of violent opposition to the government anymore." Given the end of the Sri Lankan civil war in 2009, by the time the 2010 sentencing hearing convened, the courts "are really dealing with ordinary people doing something that every Jew in America wished [they] could have done in 1939 and now there's no more Nazi Germany so nobody really cares about it now." This strategy worked, as "the judge understood"; the harshest sentence the judge handed down was a one-year prison term for a single defendant, with "everybody else getting time served and released on their sentence date." The defense viewed these sentences as "an extraordinary result" that the government "didn't like" (interview, October 2020). Although "few judges" could understand the geopolitical complexities organizing contemporary armed conflicts and the shifting alliances between armed groups, having a "good judge for this kind of case" who could move beyond "that monolithic concept of terrorism" and "distinguish between ISIS, al-Nusra, and different groups, all of which are illegal, but at the same time, very different in some sense," can result in a more tailored sentence attuned to the specificities of the defendant and the geopolitical contexts in which they operated. In this legal strategy, defense attorneys recognized that a judge's geopolitical knowledge shaped their sentencing decisions.

Given the messy complexities that have defined the global war on terror, some defense attorneys described "trying to explain to a district court judge what *Syria* is about" as a "waste of time," even as they filed combatant immunity motions and submitted "lengthy memoranda" explaining mitigating circumstances at sentencing (interview, March 2021). In this view, even the most sophisticated political scientists have struggled to understand the Syrian war, making these legal actors hesitant to raise these issues with the court. For example, one attorney explained:

> I understand Syria is complex. What started out as a pure civil war ended up with ISIS tripping and going off craziness and it then spun off in so many different directions. There are [sentencing] guidelines adjustments for downward departures; there are arguments that come to the role [the defendant] played; there are arguments that can be raised that might spin off and discuss what's going on in Syria.

Rather than explore the messy geopolitical conditions in Syria, this attorney explained that "the sale you really have to make for a [sentencing] guidelines adjustment with the government or to work out a plea [deal], you've got to really sell your client to the government" (interview, March 2021). Others, however, saw value in trying to "explain all of these issues" at sentencing; otherwise, judges could adopt a "monolithic concept of terrorism" that failed to account for the different roles defendants played, the dire conditions in which they lived, and their political aspirations (interview, October 2020).

Just as defense attorneys mobilized different legal arguments to "sell" their client, judges brought with them varying levels of geopolitical knowledge and therefore differently interpreted "all of these issues." As we will see in the case against Bilal Abood, judges with a limited or competing understanding of an armed conflict sometimes could not "distinguish between a political insurgent and a terrorist" and therefore handed down harsher sentences. In fact, the lawyers I interviewed typically identified "the *only* judge" or "one of the only judges" they viewed as capable of understanding the complicated facts in terrorism-related cases. Acknowledging that "not all U.S. district court judges have the experience in the law of war, intelligence law, international law, human rights, etc.," some legal scholars have called for specialized national security courts to try terror suspects, with judges "selected for possessing specialized knowledge of the substantive law surrounding issues of terrorism and a high level of practical experience" (Sulmasy 2009, 1015). Although such specialized courts would introduce other issues by mixing law enforcement and war fighting, these suggestions illustrate the legal community's concern about judges' capacity to impartially hear terrorism cases.

Even judges with extensive background knowledge struggled to make sense of these complicated situations and the criminal liability attached to them, such that determining if someone engaged in terrorist conduct and then deciding the appropriate sentence for that conduct was a messy process. In this section, I examine Abood's case, as it illustrates how defendants used their sentencing hearings to contextualize their conduct and how judges sometimes struggled to make sense of this information extemporaneously. Informed by their own geopolitical knowledge and its application to the cases before them, judges imposed sentences that generally aligned with the recommendations of the prosecution and sidestepped the issues raised by the defense.

Unlike the findings in the *Al-Jayab* case, a federal court in Texas refused to determine if Abood qualified for combatant immunity after a five-day stint working alongside a cook for the Free Syrian Army. Instead, this case focused on Abood's truthfulness in interviews with FBI agents upon his return to the United States and his social media activity. In these interviews, Abood admitted to traveling to Syria for the purposes of fighting with the Free Syrian Army, which President Obama recognized as the "legitimate representative of Syrian people" (qtd. in Landler, Gordon, and Barnard 2012). Abood also denied pledging allegiance to ISIS. An FBI search of Abood's computers, however, showed that he "pledged an oath to Abu Bakr al-Baghdadi, the leader of ISIL" on Twitter, "view[ed] ISIS atrocities," and "use[d] his Twitter account to tweet and retweet information on al-Baghdadi."[78] The prosecution cited Abood's Twitter use to cast suspicion on his time with the Free Syrian Army, suggesting that his "activities and motivations" were terroristic.

Interpreting "the war between Sunni and Shia" as "everywhere, physically on the ground . . . and even on social media," Abood insisted that he had "no interest or support at all" for al-Baghdadi; he asserted that his tweets were merely meant to "piss the Shia off" because Shia Muslims used social media to "get the Sunnis mad."[79] Abood, who identifies as Sunni, argued that his tweets did not represent his political allegiance to ISIS but rather his desire to engage the Syrian war on social media by intensifying the antagonisms between Sunni and Shia Muslims. Rather than frame such antagonisms as archaic tribalism or anachronistic sectarianism, Munif (2020) reports that "Assad developed a tactical prowess in sectarian maneuvering that slowly made sectarian politics one of the pillars of the Syrian regime, and one of the strategies for political control" (21). This analysis illustrates how "the prism of sectarianism, rooted in an alleged enduring Sunni-Shi'a chasm, clouds rather than illuminates the complex realities of the region which have their roots in a series of developmental crises (both political and economic) that the region has been facing since independence" (Hashemi 2016, 74). Sectarian violence therefore cannot be reduced to "ancient sectarian hatreds"; it must be located in "the persistence of authoritarianism" and "the crisis of legitimacy facing ruling regimes that has followed as a consequence" (65). Authoritarian regimes like Assad's use the "political mobilization and manipulation of sectarian identities . . . as a key strategy for regime survival" (65). Viewed through this lens, the Assad regime intensified and instrumentalized sectarianism to maintain power, which Abood contributed to through his social media activity. Abood considered the fueling of such antagonisms as a tactic in "the war between Sunni and Shia."[80]

Even though Abood pleaded guilty to making a false statement to a federal agency, both the defense and prosecution disagreed at sentencing whether the terrorism enhancement applied. Despite Abood's having joined an internationally recognized military in a noncombatant role, the prosecution argued that the case "did involve international terrorism" because "we've got a man who went to Syria" and "people who pledge loyalty to these international terrorist groups or to their leaders, it's one in the same thing." In other words, "a pledge of loyalty to Abu Bakr al-Baghdadi is tantamount to a pledge of loyalty to ISIS."[81] In this framing, Abood's travel to Syria, in and of itself, constituted a federal crime of terrorism, even though he faced no charges for this travel, or even for his contributions to the Free Syrian Army.

In response to the prosecution's theory of the case, the defense described Abood as "for sure guilty of [being a] goofball, not a terrorist."[82]

Subscribing to the prosecution's position, Judge Kinkeade ultimately determined that the case "involved terrorism."[83] U.S. Attorney John Parker later celebrated Abood's four-year sentence as a global war on terror victory, explaining, "We remain more committed than ever to aggressively fighting all terrorism-acts in north Texas" (qtd. in Office of Public Affairs 2014). An FBI agent similarly stated, "It remains among the highest priorities of the FBI to identify individuals who seek to join the ranks of foreign fighters traveling in support of ISIL" (qtd. in Office of Public Affairs 2014). These conclusions positioned Abood's false statement as an act of terrorism, ultimately divorcing this act from the geopolitical conditions—the Syrian war—that informed Abood's social media activity and one-week enlistment in the Free Syrian Army.

During his sentencing hearing, Abood challenged these reductive conclusions by offering a more nuanced analysis of the Syrian war and the Free Syrian Army. For example, in discussing his five-day stint with a cook in the Free Syrian Army, Abood explained how quickly alliances and antagonisms shifted. From his perspective, the Free Syrian Army "start[ed] cooperating—because of the lack of ammunition, lack of money—they started cooperating with those extremist groups and fight[ing] alongside and cooperating."[84] Judge Kinkeade agreed with Abood's depiction of these dynamic contexts, responding, "It's almost hard to tell who the players are. . . . Who are the good guys, the bad guys. And now Russia is involved."[85] More to the point, Judge Kinkeade concluded that "it is a very complicated situation that our own government can't figure out. The world can't figure out . . . it's the dictator who's killing people. Everybody is killing people over there. They're all the bad guys. I mean, you know, I know at least at some point we wanted to try to help who were the supposed good guys over there. And, you know, it's—you know, it's kind of a difficult thing."[86] In fact, Judge Kinkeade observed that although President Obama failed to enforce his "red line" with Assad, "there was some movement among the CIA and other operatives . . . to try and find some friendly Mujahidin . . . to fight both against Assad and against ISIS. It's really before ISIS became kind of known."[87] Judge Kinkeade recognized Assad's atrocities and acknowledged that the United States relied on "friendly Mujahidin" to fight Assad's regime. Until 2017, the United States supported, funded, and weaponized forces affiliated with the Free Syrian Army, initially to fight the Assad regime and then later to neutralize the growing number of Islamist groups. Some U.S.-trained fighters eventually defected to more radical groups, compelling the Trump administration to shutter this CIA-led program (Balanche 2017; Walcott 2017). For Abood, the internet served as another battlefield to engage this multifaceted war by intensifying the sectarianism fueled by the Assad regime. To Abood, his tweets did not reflect his allegiance to ISIS but rather his desire to "piss the Shia off" and "make them mad"; in his perspective, this social media activity "has nothing to do" with the United States, "just between Sunnis and Shia[s]."[88]

Abood's discussion of his social media strategy reflected the Assad regime's propagation of a "sectarian narrative about Syrian society that it instrumentalized against various social and political groups" (Munif 2020, 56). Judge Kinkeade's comments, however, drew on more mainstream understandings of sectarianism. As historian Ussama Makdisi (2017) writes, "Sectarianism is often characterized as the violent and illiberal manifestation of competing, age-old antagonistic religious identities in the [Arab] region. This characterization is rooted in a static, one-dimensional understanding of identity, so that being Sunni and Shi'i, for example, are assumed to be constants etched into the fabric of the past" (2). In fact, "the evocation of the threat of 'sectarianism' is often analogous to the way the word 'terrorism' is used by modern states: not as an objective signifier of violence, but as an ideological signifier of a particular form of violence, invariably stripped of any meaningful content" (6). Although Syrian security forces certainly have produced and exploited sectarian logics, Judge Kinkeade's comments placed such struggles in opposition to U.S. democracy and modern development. For example, Judge Kinkeade described Syria as "the most dangerous country in the world" such that "it makes almost no sense that [Abood] wouldn't value freedom the way we value freedom."[89] Judge Kinkeade chastised Abood for his sectarianism, saying, "You value the fight between Shias and Sunnis more than you value freedom here in America. That's the strangest thing I've ever seen. I don't get it. I do not get that culturally."[90] Judge Kinkeade also questioned why anyone would return to "one of the worst places in the world," especially when "you get a chance to come and live in the United States."[91] In this exchange, Judge Kinkeade reinforced the "pious ethnocentrism of American exceptionalism" and reduced the Syrian war to an uncivilized cultural battle between religious sects, rendering participation in this battle an affront to "freedom," even as he recognized that some parts of the Free Syrian Army aligned themselves with ISIS as a military strategy rather than as a subscription to the rebel group's transnational aspirations (Loewen 1994, 128).

Judge Kinkeade also demonstrated a confused understanding of the Syrian war as he evaluated Abood's testimony. He asked questions such as, "ISIS is Shia, isn't it?" and asserted factual misstatements such as, "Kurds are Christian Muslims." He also depicted the entire region as a "hell hole," questioning why Abood would "go back to that hell hole of the Middle East. I know it's your home, but I don't care what anyone else says about it, it is the most dysfunctional place in the world."[92] Erasing the historical, political, and imperial contexts and evoking an Orientalist image of the region, Judge Kinkeade interpreted Abood's decision to join the Free Syrian Army as "awfully strange" and characterized a complex war as the expression of religious fanaticism and the rejection of Western values.[93] Judge Kinkeade's understanding of Syria, regional politics, and sectarianism necessarily shaped his interpretation of the factual evidence in the case and therefore informed his sentencing decision.

Given Judge Kinkeade's geopolitical analysis of the Syrian war, he concluded that Abood's tweets pledging allegiance to al-Baghdadi "involved terrorism." As he assessed whether the terrorism enhancement applied to the case, Judge Kinkeade expressed outrage over Abood's social media activity:

> It's what [Abood] said over the [social media]—which is certainly abominable what he said in tweets and that sort of thing and then lying about it. People can believe those sort of things and make those kind of [comments]. You just can't lie to FBI agents about that. And that's what—it offends me that [Abood] would pledge allegiance like that. It really does. And I don't mind saying that. But I think people can—as long as it's not violent, they can have those kinds of beliefs and can tell people that sort of thing. Now, he did lie about both where he went and where he was going, and he lied about whether he had tweeted that or not.[94]

Although Judge Kinkeade understood that Abood joined an internationally recognized and U.S.-backed military—the Free Syrian Army—

and engaged in First Amendment–protected speech acts, he also held Abood criminally liable for the false statements he made to FBI agents. In his plea, Abood admitted that he "did knowingly and willfully make and cause to be made materially false, fictitious, and fraudulent statements and misrepresentations in a manner within the jurisdiction of the Federal Bureau of Investigation which *involved international terrorism . . .* by falsely stating to federal law enforcement that he had never pledged allegiance to Abu Bakr al-Baghdadi, the leader of ISIL."[95] Although Abood contextualized his Twitter use in the Assad regime's intensification of "sectarian strife" for survival (Munif 2020, 56), the plea agreement reduced such speech acts to terrorism.

Using sectarianism as a framework to understand Abood's actions, Judge Kinkeade concluded that the case "involved terrorism" even as he conceded that "there's no evidence that [Abood] built any bombs, knows how to build any bombs."[96] While no evidence showed that Abood posed a viable threat to the United States, Judge Kinkeade sentenced Abood to a four-year prison term for his false statements to FBI agents, which he considered to "involve terrorism."

While defense attorneys explained that few judges could understand Syrian politics, they still sought to "contextualize" each case, such as explaining "what Syria is about" to the judge (interview, October 2020; interview, March 2021). In Abood's case, the defendant tried to "explain Syria" to Judge Kinkeade. Judge Kinkeade's comments suggest that he interpreted this contextualizing information through the concept of sectarianism, even concluding that Abood valued the fight between Shias and Sunnis more than he valued "freedom here in America."[97] Reducing the Syrian war to sectarian violence entrenched in ancient hatreds facilitated the court's interpretation of Abood's tweets as a pledge to ISIS, ultimately absolving the Assad regime's production and exploitation of sectarianism as a key strategy in its authoritarian rule. In Abood's case, Judge Kinkeade's geopolitical knowledge—tinged with anti-Arab and anti-Muslim "race thinking" that normalizes the repudiation of terrorism defendants irrespective of their actual conduct (Razack 2008)—shaped his ruling on the application of the terrorism enhancement. *Abood* demonstrates how dominant geopolitical scripts inform judicial decision-making, illustrative of what Gerard Toal (1996) refers to as geopower, or the "functioning of geographic knowledge not as an innocent body of knowledge and learning but as an ensemble of technologies of power concerned with the governmental production and management of territorial space" (7). Organized around the concept of sectarianism, this "geography of evil" is a "cartography designed to bring relief to 'us' while bringing 'them' *into* relief; at once a therapeutic and a vengeful gesture, its object was to reveal the face of the other *as* other" (Gregory 2004, 49). Although defendants have tried to disrupt these dominant geopolitical scripts at sentencing, many judges continue to interpret their conduct through familiar frames—sectarianism, terrorism, and jihadism—that sustain the global war on terror.

"A Worldview Equating Fundamentalist Islam with Terrorism": Grounds for Recusal?

Given the specialized expertise required to defend clients charged with terrorism-related crimes, attorneys have used their social networks to share knowledge and legal strategy. One defense attorney explained that terrorism cases often involved "very unusual aspects legally and factually," such as classified information obtained through Foreign Intelligence Surveillance Act (FISA) searches and surveillance. Defense attorneys therefore had developed a "really strong network of lawyers and experts and academics and other people to draw on for particular issues that arise," even if very few legal strategies worked in defending terrorism clients (interview, October 2020).

Given the central role of the judge in adjudicating terrorism-related cases, defense attorneys sometimes filed a motion asking the judge to recuse themselves, citing their political beliefs and economic interests that could interfere with their ability to administer impartial justice. Palestinian community leader Rasmea Odeh, for example, filed a motion arguing that U.S. District Court judge Paul Borman should recuse himself from her case. Charged with obtaining U.S. naturalization by fraud after she failed to disclose a conviction by an Israeli military court system—in which she was sexually assaulted and tortured by prison authorities to obtain a false confession related to bombings in Jerusalem by the Popular Front for the Liberation of Palestine—Odeh questioned Judge Borman's impartiality, given his "deep personal and active commitment to the support and Defense of Israel."[98] After initially denying the motion, Judge

Borman recused himself, citing his financial investments in SuperSol, the Jerusalem supermarket Odeh was accused of bombing in 1969. Defendants charged with terrorism-related crimes have sought relief by challenging the impartiality of judges.

Whereas Odeh questioned Judge Borman's impartiality at the beginning of her trial, Amina Farah Ali filed an appeal arguing that U.S. District Court judge Michael Davis's in-court statements reflected a bias that made a fair judgment impossible. In 2010, Ali was arrested in Rochester, Minnesota, after she raised money for al-Shabaab, a designated foreign terrorist organization. According to one lawyer, Ali had "lived in a refugee camp that was in Somalia. She came to the United States and unbeknownst to her, it was illegal to give food and clothing [to the camp]. She was putting [the food and clothing] together to send to Somalia when an FBI agent said, 'You can't do it.' Unfortunately, he never told her you can't raise money. She raised $35,000, which she then sent to the [refugee] camp, which was headed by al-Shabaab" (interview, March 2021). Ali and her friend Hawo Hassan collected and sent money and used clothing to Somali refugees living in camps run by al-Shabaab, after Ethiopia invaded and occupied Somalia at the request of Somalia's provisional Transitional Federal Government (TFG) to seize power from the Islamic Courts Union (ICU). The government viewed donations to Somali refugee camps as a federal crime of terrorism: providing material support to a designated foreign terrorist organization, namely al-Shabaab.

As legal scholar Nicole Stremlau (2018) explains, "The rise of al-Shabaab has been misunderstood and the history of the organization is often muddled with the global history of Islamic terrorism" (80). Al-Shabaab is better understood as the product of "local Somali politics," significantly defined by the colonial imposition of borders on east Africa, even as Somali communities "spread well into neighboring Ethiopia, Kenya, and Djibouti" (Stremlau 2018, 74). After the fall of Siad Barre's authoritarian regime in 1991, Somalia's formal government struggled to maintain territorial control and sovereign power beyond Mogadishu, which led to the formation of "a variety of entities or informal systems" that "attempted to provide security and governance" and conduct "statelike" governance through the delivery of social services like education, health care, and resource distribution (Stremlau 2018, 75). In 2000, "the courts first united to form what would be called the ICU" and eventually "evolved from a judicial system to a governing apparatus" that provided social services and enforced Sharia law (CISAC 2019). Led by "young, disciplined fighters recruited across clan lines—*al-Shabaab*," the Islamic Courts Union overtook Mogadishu and the warlords (Verhoeven 2009, 415). The ICU then expanded its authority across central Somalia and "gave immediate orders to remove all roadblocks, reopen schools, and confiscate all guns" (415).

The ICU's rule brought "very tangible benefits" to Somalis as "girls went back to school, transaction costs for business shrunk, entire neighborhoods were thoroughly cleaned, and Mogadishu's streets became safe again at night" (Verhoeven 2009, 415). Rooted in Sharia law and Islam, the ICU "became popular among communities in south Somalia, as citizens appreciated the security and peace it brought to the local, street level" (Stremlau 2018, 80). In the absence of the rule of law, the Islamic Courts Union "delivered the closest resemblance of institutionalized political authority within the collapsed state" (A. Ahmad 2009, 59) and operated as "one of the most ambitious and effective regional and credible state-like structures Somalia had seen since 1991" (Stremlau 2018, 78).

Threatened by the rise of the ICU, Ethiopian forces invaded Somalia at the invitation of Somalia's Transitional Federal Government, and ousted the ICU. While the ICU focused al-Shabaab's energies on the nationalist struggle and tempered its more global aspirations, the disintegration of the ICU transformed al-Shabaab into an independent organization that sought to expel Ethiopian forces, depose the TFG, and establish an Islamic emirate. After the Islamic Courts Union fled Somalia, al-Shabaab was "the only organization actively resisting the Ethiopians" and therefore attracted many young Somalis "who wished to defend their families and reclaim their country" (Wise 2008, 5). Al-Shabaab's militant efforts continued despite months of "bloody Ethiopian repression and irregular American missile strikes against 'high-value targets,'" once again destabilizing the region and triggering a humanitarian crisis. Although the United States designated al-Shabaab as a foreign terrorist organization, the everyday realities in Somalia reflected more complex circumstances defined by the 2006 Ethiopian invasion, which meant that Somalis varied in their understanding of al-Shabaab as the organization controlled access to refugee camps and humanitarian assistance. As in Palestine, designating groups that formally or informally control territory and resources as terrorist organizations renders the provision of any aid to those regions a "federal crime."[99]

As political scientist Rob Wise (2008) explains, the "Ethiopian occupation of Somalia, from December 2006 to January 2009, would fuel the development of al-Shabaab's ideology, recruitment, operational strategy, and partnerships, transforming the group from a small, relatively unimportant part of a more moderate Islamic movement into the most powerful and radical armed faction in the country" (4). Despite long-standing efforts to reduce al-Shabaab to a designated foreign terrorist organization, its political agenda must be understood in the context of the Ethiopian invasion, which "was directly responsible for the ideological transformation al-Shabaab underwent between the end of 2006 and the beginning of 2008" (Wise 2008, 4). Understanding Ali's urgent desire to send donations to Somalia, even if through the hands of al-Shabaab fighters, requires an analysis of the geopolitical contexts and material conditions in which Somalis lived, including the reliance on warlords and armed militias to provide security in the absence of an executive authority like the Islamic Courts Union.

At trial, the prosecution used wiretapped phone calls to show that Ali spoke with al-Shabaab members who shared their battle strategy and encouraged her to send money as early as 2007, before the United States designated al-Shabaab a foreign terrorist organization. For example, in one teleconference, al-Shabaab leader Mahad Karate made a financial appeal to his audience, saying, "The jihad that is currently underway is waged verbally; it is waged through physical means; it is waged financially. Today, what is needed from you is financial help. You are asked to financially sponsor the Muslim people, who are hungry, the orphans of the martyrs and the widows of the martyrs."[100] As Ali explained at her sentencing hearing, she never collected money for al-Shabaab, but she did use al-Shabaab as "the vehicle" to "get the money to the needy."[101] Ali's comments reflect how al-Shabaab controlled Somali territories and even access to humanitarian assistance. In fact, the World Food Programme eventually left Somalia in 2011, citing "international donor policies that prevented aid agencies from disbursing funds that might end up in the hands of al-Shabaab" and "al-Shabaab's decisions to ban most agencies working in areas it controlled" (Hammond 2014, 7). Despite the humanitarian crisis following the Ethiopian invasion, international aid agencies and diasporic families alike struggled to send resources to Somalia in legal ways, especially given al-Shabaab's territorial control, even if unrecognized by the international community. After twenty hours of deliberations, a jury found Ali guilty on one count of conspiring to provide material support to al-Shabaab and twelve counts of providing material support to al-Shabaab.

As in other cases, the defense and prosecution disagreed at sentencing whether the terrorism enhancement applied to the case. The defense argued that the terrorism enhancement should not apply to this case because "this is part of a civil war in civil conflict and that doesn't qualify as a federal crime of terrorism under the particular definition that's supplied for the purposes of the increase in the guidelines."[102] In this understanding of the 2006–9 Somali civil war, "there was no government, no recognized government of Somalia at the time, that the Transitional Federal Government was not a government, was not recognized by the United States."[103] Because a crime of terrorism involves the "violent acts or acts dangerous to human life" that appear to be intended to "intimidate or coerce a civilian population," "influence the policy of a government," or "affect the conduct of a government by mass destruction, assassination, or kidnapping," the defense argued that there was no recognized government to intimidate, coerce, or affect.[104] The prosecution, however, asserted that al-Shabaab "was bent on toppling the government, the Transitional Federal Government, by violence."[105] The prosecution cited a "ghoulish call"—one in which Ali described news of an attack on a TFG minister as "the best joy ever"—as evidence that Ali's offenses were calculated to influence or affect the TFG by intimidation or coercion.[106] While military strategists and U.S. citizens celebrated the assassination of Osama bin Laden and other high-level targets in the course of the global war on terror, the prosecution argued that this "joy" reflected the defendant's commitment to violent jihad—a war against infidels—even as Ali explained that she understood the term jihad to refer to "a method to use when you are trying to alleviate the sufferings of people who were either enslaved or mistreated or disrespected. Jihad is one method to use to remove that suffering."[107] Ali offered a more expansive understanding of jihad, which challenged the prosecution's claim that jihad primarily involves the use of death to punish "apostates," "infidels," and "traitors to Islam."[108]

Subscribing to dominant understandings of "jihad," Judge Davis concluded that the terrorism enhancement applied. In his view, Ali's "teleconferences in which she raised money to be sent to al-Shabaab were fully—were full of rhetoric extolling the virtues of violent jihad against infidels and apostates. Evidence at trial also demonstrated that the money raised by the defendant and others is al-Shabaab's lifeblood."[109] For Judge Davis, these facts "sufficiently support a finding that the crimes of conviction in this case were calculated to influence or affect the conduct of government by intimidation or coercion or to retaliate against government conduct."[110] Judge Davis sentenced Ali to 240 months in prison, followed by a lifetime of supervised release.

It was this very geopolitical reasoning, and its corresponding understanding of world affairs, that Ali and her friend Hassan challenged on appeal. Ali and Hassan argued that these judicial remarks "suggest a worldview equating fundamentalist Islam with terrorism, therefore deserving of punitive measures in order to preserve the illusionary concept of 'national security.'"[111] During jury selection, for example, Judge Davis asked prospective jurors whether "you or anyone that is close friends or relatives ever had any kind of experience with people from Somalia, the Horn of Africa, the Middle East, with Muslims, Persians, Iraqis, or Afghanistans" and whether anyone had "specialized knowledge or expertise in the issues of terrorism" or familiarity with "the Middle East, Iraq, Iran, Afghanistan, Egypt, Somalia, Kenya, Tunisia, Morocco, and Egypt."[112] Ali and Hassan alleged that such questions reflected Judge Davis's "group[ing] together" of Muslims as a monolith. Ali and Hassan also cited Judge Davis's questions at sentencing as further evidence of his partiality and bias—questions such as, "What does jihad mean to you?"; "Did you know about al-Shabaab describing itself as waging jihad against enemies of Islam?"; "Would you agree that al-Shabaab is an Islamist organization that follows a very conservative and strict interpretation of Islam?"; and "Are you telling me that you don't want to talk to me about that or you have no knowledge of [al-Shabaab's] strict beliefs?"[113] Last, Ali and Hassan referenced Judge Davis's comments in similar cases to illustrate how the court was predisposed to rule against them given his "worldview equating fundamentalist Islam with terrorism." For example, in another case, Judge Davis stated, "The community at large and the Somali community should know that the United States . . . has done an admirable job at investigating and prosecuting all the individuals that were involved in these terrorism activities."[114] These comments reflect the popular vocabularies used to describe Somali communities in Minnesota, including the "Islamic State of Minnesota," "Mogadishu, MN," and "a city gone mad" (participant observation, April 2017). This racial imaginary prefigures Somalis as terrorists. One Somali activist even referred to Judge Davis's comments in another series of cases and corresponding antiterrorism policies targeting Somali youth as "viable hate speech that's acceptable because we are Black and Muslim and poor and refugees" (participant observation, April 2017). Viewing Judge Davis's questions as an effort "to comprehend Ali's understanding of al-Shabaab's goals and actions" and his prior statements as "merely reflect[ing] the court's view of cases over which it presided," rather than "extreme favoritism or antagonism," the U.S. Court of Appeals for the Eighth Circuit denied Ali and Hassan's appeal.[115]

Hassan's lawyers also argued on appeal that "Somali history and the current political situation is a complex brew of colonialism, tribalism, and civil war that is not easily reduced to a succinct explanation."[116] Federal courts, however, have relied on blunt instruments like the terrorism enhancement and convenient geopolitical scripts offered by prosecutors to interpret the factual evidence in the case, make rulings, and hand down sentences, as illustrated in Judge Davis's comments in jury selection, at trial, and at sentencing. At sentencing, Judge Davis questioned Ali at length, asking if she "hated Ethiopians," if she would "guess that the Somali community supports al-Qaeda," and if she knew "that there was a Minneapolis young man that was a suicide bomber for al-Shabaab."[117] Evoking a sense of collective responsibility that holds all Muslims responsible for individual acts of political violence, Judge Davis's questions suggested Ali, and Somalis more generally, "hated Ethiopians" and "supported al-Qaeda," proof that Ali donated to al-Shabaab with the explicit intention to effect political change through the use of violence. Although the U.S. Court of Appeals for the Eighth Circuit determined that these judicial comments did not meet the legal threshold for personal bias or prejudice, they illustrate how "stereotypes about Muslims and fear of Islamic terrorism permeate the opinions of U.S. courts in many facets of the law" (Koprowski 2011, 200). For example, Judge Davis defined Somali armed resistance to the Ethiopian invasion as "jihad," rather than as a civil war with foreign intervention. As in the case of Ali, jihad has been called on to undertake certain conceptual work in the courts: defining the "bad guys," formulating a moral evaluation of the defendant's conduct, and assessing the applicability of the terrorism enhancement.

The epistemic power of the term jihad leaves us with few conceptual tools to understand the relationship between power, politics, and violence; it also empowers the courts to function as a "counterterrorism tool" and to "send a clear message to any would-be jihadists that such conduct is not tolerated by the U.S. government."[118] Such judicial opinions have given racism—understood as "a resource, an entitlement, almost a property right really, by which every white person is able to gain priority and preference over people who are not white"—the "law's imprimatur to that racial priority" (Bell 1991, 120). By creating and enforcing "hierarchies of personhood," U.S. law participates in the "ongoing cultivation of human waste" and the maintenance of legal fictions that normalize and codify racialized violence (Dayan 2011, 22). While judicial opinions certainly rely on anti-Muslim stereotypes and other racial biases (Chew and Kelley 2009; Sen 2015), such decision-making processes surface how the law creates gradations of personhood and therefore unevenly confers rights, protections, and humanity. This means that judges who reject imperial scripts still sentence defendants to significant prisons terms.

Defining the Bad Guys: Criminal Prosecution, Anti-Muslim Racism, and the Global War on Terror

Legal scholars have argued that judicial opinions organized by anti-Muslim racism may be "unavoidable" because judges "must function in a world of concrete answers" (Koprowski 2011, 184) and "produce definite outcomes—verdicts or judgments—within short time spans" (Good 2008, s57). Critical race theorists, however, have shown how the courts do not passively enact racialized decision-making processes as the law actively participates in the social construction of race and racial hierarchies, such that "the procedures and substance of American law, including

American antidiscrimination law, are structured to maintain white privilege" (Valdes, Culp, and Harris 2002, 1; cf. Good 2008; Koprowski
2011). Even as the United States has produced administrative briefs,
memos, and opinions making legal the torture, indefinite detention, and
targeted assassinations of Arabs and Muslims, it also has invoked the
law to categorically classify nonstate fighters, such as Taliban, al-Qaida,
ISIS, and al-Shabaab soldiers, as unlawful enemy combatants. Such legal
invocations establish a "minimal claim to legitimacy," which "works to
occlude the imperial vocation of law to exercise violence in order to
render the other's violence as lawless, uncivilized, and irrational" (Pugliese 2013, 6). The State Department, however, also insisted that "international obligations," such as the Geneva Conventions, applied to U.S.
citizens who, as "war volunteers," joined Ukrainian forces after Russia's
2022 invasion (Price 2022). Russian officials, however, described these
foreign fighters as "soldiers of fortune" not formally conscripted in the
Ukrainian military and therefore "not subject to the Geneva convention"
(qtd. in Kelly and Popeski 2022). While the State Department expected
that under international law "all those who have been captured on the
battlefield [will] be treated humanely and with respect and consistent
with laws of war," it denied these same prisoner of war rights to U.S.
Muslims who traveled to Syria to fight an authoritarian regime alongside U.S. soldiers (Price 2022). The differences in treatment illustrate
how race and racism have shaped the uneven interpretation and enforcement of international law.

In terrorism-related cases, the courts crystallize anti-Muslim referents by admitting cultural evidence about the motivations and aspirations of so-called transnational radical Muslim terrorists to clarify the
intent, effect, and cause of defendants' conduct. If military strategists
like Defense Secretary Donald Rumsfeld have struggled to discern "who
the bad guys are in Afghanistan or Iraq," judges, by design, also have difficulty in understanding the prevailing geopolitical contexts that inform
what defendants did, and why. With little direct knowledge of certain
armed conflicts and the "obliteration" of "local and concrete circumstances" (Said 1997, xxii), judges "end up relying on a mix of expert
opinion—as presented in court—and generalizations about foreign concepts" that often "employ negative views about Islam" (Koprowski 2011,
184). As Matthew Clair and Amanda Woog (2022) contend, judges play

a "central role" in "perpetuating and maintaining racial and economic hierarchies" such that "the courts—defined here as the assemblage of legal actors, practices, precedents, and incentives that make up the courtroom workgroup—are an essential component of the carceral state" (2). The criminal courts largely "function to both legitimate police while also funneling people into carceral spaces and other systems of control," which means that they cannot be recuperated through the establishment of a specialized national security court, the expansion of judicial discretion, or the introduction of geopolitical knowledge at trial or at sentencing (Clair and Woog 2022, 6). Because "the creation and articulation of laws function as a 'racial project'" (Schwabauer 2010, 659), the solution is not "better jurists" or stronger geopolitical literacies (Dayan 2011, xvi) but rather the dismantling of both the racial logics that animate the law and the criminal-legal system that sustains such racial formations.

Although the courts have played a central role in the execution of the global war on terror, anti-Muslim racism has organized the law since the creation of late eighteenth-century legislation regulating U.S. citizenship by naturalization and the forced arrivals of enslaved African Muslims. In other words, law "is central to the broader project of Islamophobia" such that Islamophobia "cannot be adequately theorized or explained without an account of the operations of the law" (Beydoun and Choudhury 2020, 7). It is to this legal history, and its contemporary hauntings in terrorism prosecutions, that I now turn.

3

THE RACIALIZATION OF LEGAL CATEGORIES
FROM THE CITIZEN TO THE TERRORIST

In 1790, Congress passed the Naturalization Act, which limited the right to citizenship by naturalization to "free white persons." Although clear in its racial restrictions, the Naturalization Act raised contentious legal debates about who qualified as a "free white person" under the law. The courts, for example, "ruled inconsistently on the whiteness of particular groups," with Arab immigrants unevenly classified as nonwhite in 1913 and 1914 court cases but white in similar 1909, 1910, and 1915 cases (Fitzgerald 2017, 139). These inconsistent rulings "demonstrate the unusually high level of judicial autonomy to define race in the U.S." (139). Shaped by judges' variable understandings of race, the courts contributed to the uneven racialization of immigrants and their access to citizenship during the Naturalization Era (1790–1952).

During this era, the courts sometimes granted naturalization to Arab Christians but not to Arab Muslims by categorically racializing Muslims as nonwhite. Christianity therefore functioned as a "prospective gateway toward citizenship for immigrants from the Arab World," as judges "who performed these religiously determined racial associations" sometimes "classified Christian immigrants from the Arab World as a racial group distinct from 'Arabs' solely on account of their Christianity" (Beydoun 2013, 33).[1] Understanding this racially restrictive legislation, Arab Christians "could—and did—invoke the fact of their Christianity to argue that they were white," which "sometimes secured citizenship for Christian petitioners, but did not always rebut the presumption that every immigrant from the Arab World was Muslim" (Beydoun 2013, 29). Such judicial opinions reflect how Islam came to be "viewed as irreconcilable with whiteness" (Beydoun 2015)—a legal history that "reveals that the current hostile climate for Muslims in the United States is part of a much larger story about establishing whiteness as a prerequisite to substantive citizenship and the conflation of Arab and Muslim identity in the law" (Ramahi 2020, 569).

Informed by eugenics research, judges sometimes referenced skin color and the one-drop rule as they assessed whether Arab petitioners qualified as "free white persons" under the law. Using these unstable referents, judicial opinions sometimes classified Arab petitioners as nonwhite and thus ineligible for citizenship. In 1913, Judge Smith denied Maronite Faras Shahid's application for citizenship after he immigrated from Zahlé in modern-day Lebanon, citing Shahid's failure to meet the racial prerequisites.[2] In his ruling, Judge Smith described Shahid as the color of a "walnut, or somewhat darker than is the usual mulatto of one-half mixed blood between the white and the negro races." Although Shahid invoked his Christianity to refute the assumption that he was Muslim, Judge Smith assessed that Shahid "writes his name in Arabic, cannot read or write English, and speaks and understands English very imperfectly" and "answers to the questions whether he is a polygamist or disbeliever in the affirmative." In this case, "Shahid's dark skin signaled to [Judge Smith] that he was either Muslim or the product of racial miscegenation with Muslims that diluted his Christianity and ultimately undermined his petition for American citizenship" (Beydoun 2018, 62). Despite this reasoning, Judge Smith also insisted that geography served as the deciding factor in this case because it was "impossible" to identify the "race or color of the modern inhabitant of Syria." Judge Smith further explained that the "geographical interpretation" of "free white persons" as "persons of European habitancy and descent" gave the naturalization statute "a construction that avoids the uncertainties of shades of color and invidious discriminations as to the race of individuals," a finding that made it unnecessary to examine Shahid's complexion "with a microscope" or "measure his skull or his limbs and features." For Judge Smith, "free white persons" meant "persons of European habitancy and descent," making "a modern Syrian of Asiatic birth and descent" ineligible for citizenship.[3] In denying Shahid's petition, Judge Smith concluded that the "applicant is not one the admission of whom to citizenship is likely to be for the benefit of the country."

Sociologist Ronald Fernandez (2008) writes that through this ruling, Judge Smith "enforced the notion that the United States was a white, Christian nation capable of excluding even Jesus Christ," even if the United States government could not, and still cannot, agree on "who, exactly, is a white person" (29). Judicial opinions affirmed the supremacy of "free white persons" under the law and reinforced the image of the Muslim and/or Arab immigrant as the inassimilable other. Judge Smith's ruling reflected common judicial decisions restricting Arab immigration and ensuing legal struggles to overturn these rulings.

A year later, Judge Smith again denied a Maronite Syrian-Lebanese immigrant naturalization.[4] In this 1914 case, George Dow filed a citizenship petition after immigrating to the United States from Batroun. Judge Smith denied Dow's petition, determining that "a Syrian of Asiatic birth is not a 'free white person' within the meaning of the naturalization statute." As in *Shahid,* Judge Smith used eugenics thinking to render his decision, describing Dow as "darker than the usual person of white European descent, and of that tinged or sallow appearance which usually accompanies persons of descent other than purely European." Judge Smith used skin color and the one-drop rule to determine Shahid's right to naturalization, despite also stating that "the right of the applicant is not determined by the question whether or not upon ocular inspection he may in the opinion of the judge be actually white in color." On appeal, Judge Smith again concluded that "Syrians are not white." On a second appeal, however, a new judge ruled that Syrians are "so closely related to their neighbors on the European side of the Mediterranean that they should be classed as white" and that "they must be held to fall within the term 'white persons' used in the statute." The judge therefore reversed the lower court's decision and granted Dow citizenship.

Five years earlier, Syrian immigrant Costa Najour successfully challenged a lower court's denial of his citizenship application on the grounds that he did not meet the requirements of the revised naturalization statute.[5] On appeal, Judge Newman granted Najour citizenship, writing in his decision, "I consider the Syrians as belonging to what we recognize, and what the world recognizes, as the white race." For Judge Newman, "fair or dark complexion should not be allowed to control [the decision]," making race, not skin color, the deciding factor in naturalization cases.

Informed by eugenics research, these judicial opinions reflect the dynamic racialization of Arab and Muslim immigrants at the beginning of the twentieth century. These early court battles secured a pathway to citizenship for some Arab immigrants through their uneven classification as members of the "white race" and their invocation of their Christianity. In the decades since, Arab American communities have fought to add a "Middle East/North Africa" racial category to the U.S. census, as such data shape the federal government's policies, funding priorities, and civil rights protections.

Despite the victories secured by Najour and Dow affirming that Arab Christians met the statutory definition of whiteness, these early judicial decisions also "positioned Islam as hostile to the United States and Muslims inassimilable with American society, an orientation that established a de facto bar against the naturalization of Muslim immigrants from the Arab World and elsewhere" (Beydoun 2013, 72). Because "Christianity was the lone portal toward whiteness and naturalization for Arab immigrants during the Naturalization Era," the early waves of immigrants from the Arab region primarily were Christian and "the judicial orientation toward Arab identity"—often conflated with Muslim identity—"created a burden for Christian petitioners, who were forced to prove in court that they were not Muslim" (Beydoun 2013, 72). The legal struggles that defined the Naturalization Era illustrate the tenuous racialization of Muslim immigrants, whom the courts often prefigured as nonwhite threats to U.S. society and security.

Engaged in active racialization processes, judges in these naturalization cases mobilized the organizing logics found in an earlier Supreme Court ruling in *Ross v. McIntyre* (1891), which assessed the applicability of U.S. law to sailors on U.S. ships in the territory of another country. In this case, Canadian sailor John Ross was arrested after committing murder while aboard a U.S. ship docked at a Japanese harbor; a U.S. consular court in Japan convicted Ross of murder and sentenced him to death. Although the U.S. president, Rutherford B. Hayes, commuted Ross's sentence, Ross sought a writ of habeas corpus, arguing that, having been born on Prince Edward Island, he was a British subject and

so the U.S. consular court had no jurisdiction over him. In its ruling, the Supreme Court stated that the authority of consular courts was
necessary to "discharge[] judicial and diplomatic functions," especially
as contact between Christians and Muslims intensified. In this view, the
alleged "rise of Islamism, and the spread of its followers over western
Asia and other countries bordering on the Mediterranean" made "the
exercise of this judicial authority" a "matter of great concern." According to the Supreme Court:

> The intense hostility of the people of Moslem faith to all other
> sects, and particularly to Christians, affected all their intercourse,
> and all proceedings had in their tribunals. Even the rules of evi-
> dence adopted by them placed those of different faith on unequal
> grounds in any controversy with them. For this cause, and by rea-
> son of the barbarous and cruel punishments inflicted in those coun-
> tries, and the frequent use of torture to enforce confession from
> parties accused, it was a matter of deep interest to Christian gov-
> ernments to withdraw the trial of their subjects, when charged
> with the commission of a public offense, from the arbitrary and
> despotic action of the local officials. Treaties conferring such juris-
> diction upon these consuls were essential to the peaceful residence
> of Christians within those countries, and the successful prosecu-
> tion of commerce with their people.[6]

In this judicial reasoning, Muslim governments unfairly tortured, punished, and incarcerated Christians, making Western consular courts necessary to guard against the "arbitrary and despotic action of local officials"
on Christians.

In addition to these jurisdictional concerns in the context of "the
rise of Islamism and the spread of its followers," the Supreme Court
ruled that Ross's enlistment as a sailor on a U.S. ship made him "an
American seaman, one of an American crew onboard of an American
vessel, and as such entitled to the protection and benefits of all the laws
passed by congress on behalf of American seamen, and subject to all
their obligations and liabilities."[7] Although the Supreme Court fore-
casted that "the occasion for consular tribunals in Japan may hereafter
be less than at present, as every year that country progresses in civilization, and in the assimilation of its system of judicial procedure to that of
Christian countries, as well as in the improvement of its penal statutes,"

it ultimately ruled that the U.S. consular court had jurisdiction over Ross and upheld his conviction.[8] In this ruling, the Supreme Court engaged, circulated, and reinforced the racist assumption that Muslims "resent the West" and "desire to reassert Muslim values and restore Muslim greatness," such that "Muslim rage" drives the "rising tide of rebellion against this Western paramountcy" (Lewis 1990, 47–49; Huntington 1996). As the United States waited for non-Western countries to "progress in civilization," it treated Islam as a threat to its Christian values and principles.

Through the *McIntyre* ruling and citizenship denials, the "judicial narrative that natives from the Arab World were antagonistic and inassimilable began to take shape" (Beydoun 2013, 47). More specifically, "U.S. courts not only institutionalized an image and understanding of Islam as an irreducibly foreign and inassimilable religion, but also one that was bent on threatening the Christian character of the United States," especially as judges "echoed the maligned view of Islam affirmed by the Supreme Court in *McIntyre*" (Beydoun 2013, 47). Although contemporary courts no longer deny Arab citizenship applications on the basis of race, they continue to treat Arabs and Muslims as national security threats. Wadie E. Said (2015) writes, "Since the early 1970s, the [U.S.] government has continually associated Arabs and Muslims with terrorism—a linkage that has produced heightened surveillance of those communities in the United States as well as restrictive immigration policies for nationals of certain Arab and Muslim countries" (13). Similarly refuting popular historicizations of anti-Muslim racism as a modern racial formation, sociologist Louise A. Cainkar (2009) argues that "the negative treatment of Arabs and Muslims in the United States after 9/11 was not caused by the 9/11 attacks themselves, but by preexisting social constructions that configured them as people who would readily conduct and approve of such attacks" (2). The figure of the Islamic terrorist therefore signals a colonial presence whereby "colonial counter-insurgency policies rest undiluted in current security measures" (Stoler 2016, 4). As colonial histories bear on the present, the September 11 attacks crystallized, rather than created, anti-Muslim racism and the specter of the Islamic terrorist, whose legacies stretch back to the early forced arrival of enslaved African Muslims, the Naturalization Era, and the anti-colonial struggles across the Middle East and North Africa (Alsultany

2008; Jamal 2008; Naber 2006; Alimahomed-Wilson 2019; Selod 2015; Hilal 2021a).

Terrorism experts draw on these racial legacies by reinforcing the image of the Islamic terrorist whose cultural and religious values threaten the United States and its democratic principles. Law professor Ileana Porras (1994) writes that "religious fanaticism serves the heuristic function of explaining terrorism" such that "ideas of terrorism and Islamic fundamentalism [have] come to be connected" (134). Sherene H. Razack (2008) similarly documents how "ideas about Muslim irrationality drawn from older Orientalist and colonial discourses now undergird an entire field of knowledge production known as terrorism studies," necessarily precluding any examination of the root causes of political violence and rendering ordinary criminal law insufficient to deal with such a menacing threat (47). By reducing political violence to the expression of cultural, psychological, and/or theological perversions afflicting individual actors, terrorism research erases the geopolitical contexts that incite armed resistance, such as the ethnic cleansing of Bosnian Muslims and the Ethiopian invasion of Somalia. Such material conditions motivate individuals to take up arms, donate money and used clothing to rebel groups, and express outrage on social media. Instead, dominant terrorism research makes Islam a convenient boogeyman, whereby religion, culture, and race function as proxies for risk and therefore aggravate already existing disparities in the criminal-legal system. Contested citizenship rulings during the Naturalization Era and controversial terrorism prosecutions after the September 11 attacks illustrate "the continuing presence of race in judicial sense-making and decision-making practices" as judges "order and classify defendants in implicitly or explicitly racial terms" (Oorschot 2020, 791–92). Anti-Muslim racism continues to structure court proceedings, especially as judges have drawn on racialized narratives, discourses, and frameworks to understand the terrorism cases before them (Crenshaw 1989; Breen 2018; Delgado and Stefancic 2012; Coates 2003).

Given the role of race in judicial sense-making practices, this chapter examines the racialized frameworks that legal actors have mobilized in court proceedings and that judges have reached for in their decision-making processes. As Colin Dayan (2011) writes, legal thought has "relied on a set of fictions that renders the meaning of persons shifting and tentative: whether in creating slaves as *persons in law* and criminals as *dead in law*, or in the perpetual re-creation of the rightless entity" (xii). Such fictions actively participate in "shaping the possibilities for how *differential futures* are distributed and who are, and will be, targeted as those to be exposed, both external and internal enemies in the making" (Stoler 2016, 13). Such an analysis takes seriously how race is "something evoked and produced *within* legal practices," not just "an outcome or product of legal forms or practices," as evidenced in the adjudication of naturalization cases (Oorschot 2020, 792). For example, in the sentencing hearing for Adnan Farah, who discussed plans to travel to Syria to join ISIS, Judge Davis worried that Farah would be "rejected" by his family because "he's been labeled a terrorist." Judge Davis reasoned that, if rejected, Farah would "fall back into religion because the religion says, 'See, you've been rejected, come back with us.'"[9] Assessing that Farah lacked a "safe harbor," Judge Davis explained that it would be "so easy to explode because either his family is going to reject him [for] what he's done, and if his family rejects him, then his only family is ISIL."[10] While Farah repudiated ISIS and admitted he "fell" for its propaganda, Judge Davis feared that Farah would "fall back into religion" and "explode" in the face of family alienation, which meant turning to ISIS. In other words, Judge Davis equated Farah's Muslim faith with ISIS.

In her study of how "judicial language and legal action perpetuate negative stereotypes about Muslims," Agatha Koprowski (2011) notes that "fears of Islamic terrorism permeate the opinions of U.S. courts in many facets of law," such as asylum hearings, where Muslims seeking relief encounter assumptions that "Islam is represented most accurately and most innately by the most repressive regimes," and terrorism prosecutions, where juries often "associate *all* Muslims who are indicted for crimes with radical Islamic terrorists" (200, 189–90). Rooted in the politics of empire, these racial logics draw on imperial scripts that historically have cast Arabs and Muslims as "monolithically barbaric and violent groups of misogynist men and abused women" and reflect "narratives informed by colonial Orientalism and more longstanding white European Christian animosity toward Islam" (Cainkar and Selod 2018, 167). This means that "to be a Muslim is to be a racial other in the U.S. racial formation in a religion–culture–race linkage, and as a part of an emergent global racial system" (Rana 2017, 261). Recognizing that "the racial category of Middle Eastern–, Arab-, or Muslim-looking people is imprecise, too fluid, and too wide a net" (Grewal 2014, 298), Cainkar and Selod (2018) argue that there "is no single racial naming of this made-up group of people, except that they are understood by the state and the public to be threats: terrorists and potential terrorists" (166). As in citizenship cases, judicial sense making in criminal court can establish, affirm, challenge, and/or revise dominant geopolitical scripts that racialize Muslims as the inassimilable and dangerous other, always already prefigured as the terrorist-monster—or, more sensationally, the jihadist (Puar and Rai 2002). This chapter therefore examines how different judicial understandings of terrorism and corresponding racial logics, and their articulation with broader social forces, have shaped legal outcomes.

"Influencing the Policy of a Government by Intimidation or Coercion": Defining Terrorism

As the Naturalization Era illustrates, racial domination requires the production and circulation of legal fictions to legitimize the dehumanizing functions of U.S. law, from their colonial inception to their contemporary expressions (Dayan 2011, xii). Far from aberrational or exceptional cases, terrorism trials confirm how the law "encapsulates, sustains, and invigorates" hierarchical statuses of personhood, evident in the lawful use of extraordinary rendition, indefinite detention, and torture. Judges presiding over terrorism-related cases have varied in their understandings of the conceptual frameworks organizing such legal fictions. For example, judges differently understood the concept of terrorism, which is simultaneously a legal category defined under the law, a political classification used to delegitimize nonstate violence, and a specter sensationalized in popular media. These judicial variances have shaped the uneven application of the terrorism enhancement, and subsequently the sentences defendants convicted of terrorism-related crimes receive. Despite the growing number of academic studies and court cases related to terrorism, the term remains a deeply unstable concept, with no academic, legal, or popular consensus on its definition. In the courtroom, "terrorism" was a term up for debate as attorneys offered competing understandings of the concept, which influenced how judges and jurors interpreted the actions of the defendants and generated uneven legal outcomes.

According to federal statute, terrorism refers to "violent acts or acts dangerous to human life that are in violation of the criminal laws of the United States or of any State, or that would be a criminal violation if committed within the jurisdiction of the United States or of any State."[11] Such activities also must "appear to be intended: to intimidate or coerce a civilian population; to influence the policy of a government by intimidation or coercion; or to affect the conduct of a government by mass destruction, assassination, or kidnapping." The federal statute distinguishes "international terrorism"—activities that "occur primarily outside of the territorial jurisdiction of the United States, or transcend national boundaries in terms of the means by which they are accomplished"—from "domestic terrorism"—activities that "occur primarily within the territorial jurisdiction of the United States."[12] The legal definition of terrorism under this statute understandably focuses narrowly on individual actors, their actions, and their intent, irrespective of the broader geopolitical contexts in which they operated or the political orientation informing their conduct.

The United States Sentencing Commission's *Guidelines Manual* advises judges to apply a "terrorism enhancement" if "the offense is a felony that involved, or was intended to promote, a federal crime of terrorism." Applying the terrorism enhancement results in a higher computation of the defendant's Criminal History Category (automatically assessed at Category VI) and elevates the defendant's Total Offense Level (automatically raised by 12), both of which increase the recommended sentencing range for each defendant. In other words, if the judge concludes that the defendant committed a federal crime of terrorism, the judge can apply the terrorism enhancement, which can drive a defendant's sentence upward. Judges, however, have varied in their interpretation and application of the terrorism enhancement, arguing, for example, that there are "degrees of terrorism," that this sentencing guideline amounts to "double-dipping" or doubly punishing a defendant for a single crime, and that the United States does not have the authority to determine who can, or cannot, pressure other governments through the use of violence.

In this section, I examine how judges have interpreted what constitutes terrorism, and how their variance has led to differential outcomes for the defendants before them. Although these courtroom deliberations raise important legal questions, such as the extent to which the prosecution must prove the requisite mens rea or intent to commit a terrorism-related crime, they also represent broader debates about defining and responding to terrorist acts in fraught geopolitical contexts, particularly when top military strategists have "no visibility into who the bad guys are." Given the complex relationship between geopolitics and the law, this geolegal terrain produces material effects by shaping judicial decision-making that can impact the length of prison terms for individuals convicted of terrorism-related crimes.

In many sentencing hearings, arguments related to the application of the terrorism enhancement functioned as explanatory moments where judges and attorneys asserted particular understandings of terrorism, inconsistently rejecting, accepting, and challenging conventional definitions and associated racial scripts within the context of the shifting global war on terror. The legal analysis staged by judges and attorneys alike often aligned with their commonsense understandings of terrorism and the courts' role in the global war on terror. Such reasoning therefore reflects struggles over legal definitions of terrorism as well as geopolitical and sociological interpretations of terrorist acts and the extent to which the courts can (or should) punish individuals for challenging state sovereignty through the use of violence.

"There Are Degrees of Terrorism": Legal Struggles over the Terrorism Enhancement

Emblematic of the legal contestations over what constitutes a terrorist offense, Judge Lynn Hughes refused to apply the terrorism enhancement in the case of Asher Khan, who tried to travel to Syria to join ISIS's fight against the Assad regime before his family tricked him into returning to Texas by alleging that his mother had been hospitalized. After he returned home, Khan allegedly helped a friend travel to Syria, where he later died fighting for ISIS. At sentencing, Judge Hughes explained that applying the terrorism enhancement doubly punishes conduct given the "ugly label" of terrorism; ignores the various "degrees of terrorism" requiring tailored, not uniform, sentences; and unnecessarily empowers the courts to "police[] people who want to hurt other governments."[13] Given these conclusions, Judge Hughes determined that he would "not enhance this crime, which is intrinsically terroristic by association to a bunch of other things that are listed in that statute."[14] Such judicial reasoning reveals the tensions between the legal recommendation to apply the terrorism enhancement if the offense "involved, or was intended to promote, a federal crime of terrorism"; the variable conduct proffered to involve a crime of terrorism; the positioning of the courts as a global war on terror weapon; and judicial discretion.

Throughout Khan's sentencing hearing, Judge Hughes rejected the enhancement's organizing logic that terrorism "is different from other crimes" and therefore deserving of "harsh sentences" (Brown 2014, 546). Judge Hughes objected to what he viewed as unduly "bumping" a defendant's sentence by applying the terrorism enhancement to criminal conduct already defined as terrorism: "It's the terrorism thing, the bump for terrorism but the charge itself is terrorism, so you can't . . . do that."[15] Using the example of an airplane hijacking to clarify his reasoning, Judge Hughes explained that "there is a specific statute that addresses hijacking. So, if it were whether it was motivated to prod a government or not, if you hijack an airliner, it should be addressed as the airline hijacking statute, you should be punished under that statute, not then call it terrorism."[16] The prosecution countered, arguing that if the hijacking were "for the purpose of coercing the state," then "you would get the [terrorism enhancement] bump."[17] Judge Hughes, however, observed, "It's the same—look, the whole idea of being a terrorist is you do something that we've called terrorism, and we keep calling— you know, the State of Texas calls a terroristic threat any hostile threat you make over the phone. And they're not all terrorists. Stupid, but not terrorists. So, I just think it's piling on, as reluctant as I am to use sports metaphors."[18] Here, Judge Hughes rejected the application of the terrorism enhancement on legal grounds (charging a defendant with a terrorism-related crime and then "piling on" by applying the enhancement) and on geopolitical grounds (contesting the government's definition of terrorism).

Despite Judge Hughes's discussion, the prosecution continued to advocate for the application of the terrorism enhancement, arguing that "this Court has the discretion to apply the enhancement when it thinks it's appropriate or to not apply it when it thinks it's not appropriate."[19] Judge Hughes responded, "I think the government might reluctantly concede that there are degrees of terrorism. . . . Somebody does—bombs a school, and another person bombs an armory. One of those strikes me as more reprehensible than the other."[20] More to the point, Judge Hughes observed that "there is more funding from Congress when you say 'terrorism,'" which made him reluctant to apply what he viewed as a political rather than legal label to the defendants before him.[21] For Judge Hughes, the terrorism enhancement and its blunt intensification of the recommended sentencing range could not adequately account for the differences in the acts that could be classified as terrorism or the implicit politics in labeling certain acts as terrorism. Other judges "half applied" the terrorism enhancement to resolve these tensions, such as agreeing to a downward departure by lowering a defendant's Criminal History Category from VI to I, thereby reducing the recommended sentencing range.[22]

Given Judge Hughes's reluctance to apply the terrorism enhancement, the prosecution argued that Khan undertook additional terrorism-related actions, such as sharing a speech delivered by ISIS leader Abu Bakr al-Baghdadi on social media. Judge Hughes, however, explained, "I'm sorry. You're talking about sharing press releases and speeches. That cannot be terrorism. . . . You can't pile on everything that happens after he made a really awful choice . . . and say it adds to it. No."[23] Later, the prosecution asserted that ISIS "gets its fighters" through online propaganda that radicalizes and recruits young people, thereby framing Khan's use of Facebook, WhatsApp, and other encrypted technologies as contributing to the rebel group's violence. Judge Hughes, however, objected to this interpretation of Khan's online activities, reasoning:

> Everybody in this room uses cell phones and everything else. They read books. . . . There are murders and crimes in this country that are provoked by religious beliefs of all kinds, and they are provoked by anger, and romance. They are provoked by all kinds of things. That doesn't make people who sit around and talk about their grievances with people either conspirators or recruiters for anybody. . . . They are acting like everybody else in the United States.[24]

Despite Judge Hughes's consistent reasoning, the prosecution argued that Khan's noncriminal behaviors, such as using encrypted applications like WhatsApp, supported his broader conspiracy to provide material support to ISIS. When pressed by Judge Hughes, the prosecution suggested that despite the legality of these activities in themselves, they served as "indicia of where [Khan's] mind was."[25] In doing so, the prosecution asserted that acts that would not be illegal on their own nevertheless had the interpretive power to assist the court in understanding the specific intent—and ultimately the terroristic character—of Khan's actions.

Throughout the sentencing hearing, Judge Hughes refused to define owning an ISIS flag, consulting with a travel agent, and using encrypted messaging apps as "indicia" of terroristic intentions. When the prosecution insisted that "buying items from ISIS" constituted "material support to ISIS from a financial standpoint," Judge Hughes interrupted to say, "Wait a minute. I buy stuff from all kinds of stores where I don't know who owns them, don't care who owns them, and I certainly don't support what I know to be the politics of many vendors. I want the stuff."[26] This exchange illustrates how the courts serve as sites where legal actors debate what constitutes the legal definition of terrorism and demonstrates the requisite mens rea.

Although Judge Hughes rebuffed this part of the prosecution's strategy at sentencing, his other comments aligned with the criminal complaint that alleged that Khan "conspired to provide himself and his friend . . . as fighters for a designated foreign terrorist organization, namely the Islamic State in the Levant (ISIL)."[27] Directly addressing the defendant, Judge Hughes said:

> Mr. Khan, what you were proposing to do was go over and help a really awful group of people. And no matter how nobly you construed getting rid of Assad would have been, if you have to behead civilians to get Assad, aren't you worse than Assad or equal to him? . . . Terrorism *in the more historic sense, not necessarily a legalistic sense,* has done awful things to the United States and abroad. . . . I don't think we need to lock you up for 15 years, and I have been pleased with your progress while you have been under my care.[28]

On the basis of the unsubstantiated conclusion that fighting alongside ISIS to depose Assad required "beheading civilians," Judge Hughes assessed that such conduct would render Khan "worse than" or "equal to" Assad. Yet Judge Hughes also rejected the broader tendency to impose harsh sentences for crimes that met the legal definition of terrorism through the application of the terrorism enhancement. Judge Hughes ultimately sentenced Khan to eighteen months in prison, followed by five years of supervised release.

Because Judge Hughes refused to apply the terrorism enhancement, the government appealed Khan's sentence. In its ruling, the U.S. Court of Appeals for the Fifth Circuit noted that Judge Hughes came to three conclusions that informed his sentencing decision: that applying the enhancement would constitute "double dipping," that there are "degrees of terrorism" such that some crimes do not satisfy the enhancement's requirements, and that the enhancement does not pertain to conduct intended to influence a foreign government. The Fifth Circuit concluded that in relying on these "three rationales," the district court "did not make factual findings as to whether Khan's conduct would have otherwise satisfied § 3A1.4's requirements."[29] According to the Fifth Circuit, supporting ISIS "is some evidence that Khan's conduct was calculated to influence or affect the conduct of the United States because ISIS's terrorist acts are intended to intimidate or coerce the United States."[30] The Fifth Circuit therefore ruled that the district court "committed procedural error in concluding, as a matter of law, that the terrorism enhancement does not apply and therefore failing to determine whether, as a factual matter, the enhancement applies."[31] The Fifth Circuit remanded the case back for resentencing.

Despite the Fifth Circuit's ruling, Judge Hughes resentenced Khan by imposing the same term: eighteen months in prison and five years of supervised release. In his ruling, Judge Hughes applied the terrorism enhancement while citing reasons to depart downward from the recommended sentencing guidelines, such as Khan's lack of criminal history, his academic studies, and his contributions to a Department of Homeland Security–sponsored antiterrorism training. In handing down this sentence, Judge Hughes explained, "The Constitution must work through reason not through anger or power. Our justice [system] serves the narrowest of goals, it does not serve revenge" (qtd. in Banks 2019).

The government appealed the sentence again, with the Fifth Circuit finding that Judge Hughes erred when he "characterized and discounted

Khan's conduct effectively so as to contradict the facts Khan admitted in his plea agreement," including that "Khan had facilitated and fully supported the purposes and atrocities of ISIS." Citing how Judge Hughes "downplayed" the nature of what Khan "intended to accomplish," the Fifth Circuit again remanded the case for resentencing. In doing so, the Fifth Circuit invoked its "extraordinary" power to reassign the case to a different judge, finding that the district court's sentence was "substantively unreasonable," that the "sentencing judge seems immovable from his views of the sentence he imposed," and that the judge "displayed bias against the government and its lawyers."[32] In December 2021, Judge Charles Eskridge sentenced Khan to 144 months in federal prison, followed by sixty months of supervised release.

Despite the circuit court's rulings, Judge Hughes followed similar reasoning in his 2018 sentencing of Iraqi refugee Omar Al Hardan, who was charged with and convicted of attempting to provide material support to a foreign terrorist organization after he expressed support for political rivals Al-Nusra Front and ISIS, sought to travel to Syria to fight on behalf of ISIS, and participated in an hour-long tactical weapons training with an AK-47 alongside a confidential human source. As in *Khan,* Judge Hughes observed, "Saying stupid, insane, even violent things on Facebook, or other social media, cannot be a crime or we'd have to fill half the country with prisons. It seems to be standard operating procedure. . . . You're free to own in America an ISIS flag. . . . And you can watch videos of how to make atomic bombs, as well as improvised [explosive] devices. That's all well and good."[33] Judge Hughes also explained to Al Hardan, "The games you and your father played with blowing up toy airplanes and yelling Allahu Akbar, I'm not going to punish you for that."[34] Although Judge Hughes concluded that none of these activities constituted a crime, he also observed that they served as "an indication of what [Al Hardan was] thinking about, and none of it was new, none of it was impulsive."[35] Judge Hughes refrained from punishing Al Hardan for these acts while also interpreting these behaviors as evidence of the defendant's radical ideology and thus terroristic intent. This meant that while Judge Hughes refused to apply the terrorism enhancement, he still sentenced Al Hardan to sixteen years in prison and a lifetime of supervised release, "on the narrow grounds of planning, training, and attempting to get a travel document you weren't entitled to."[36] Judge Hughes described his decision as "a cold, rational, and fully informed analysis," despite the charged "emotional and political context."[37] Judicial refusals to apply the terrorism enhancement do not insulate defendants from long prison terms, as evidenced in Al Hardan's sixteen-year sentence.

Judge Hughes's variable rulings in *Khan* and *Al Hardan* show that judges can contradict their own conclusions in similar terrorism-related cases, particularly as legal actors strategically assert specific understandings of terrorism and terrorist groups at sentencing. As Judge Hughes's rulings indicate, the courts serve as sites of epistemic struggle, such that the frameworks judges use to determine if a defendant's conduct "involved a federal crime of terrorism" shape legal outcomes. Such epistemic struggles therefore have material consequences for defendants in terrorism-related cases, evident in Judge Eskridge's decision to sentence Khan to 144 months in prison—126 months more than Judge Hughes's overturned sentence.

Appellate Review: Shaping Terrorism Sentencing Jurisprudence

As in the appellate decision in *Khan,* the U.S. Court of Appeals for the Fourth Circuit directed District Court judge Claude Hilton to conduct a "fresh analysis" as to whether the terrorism enhancement applied in the case against Ali Asad Chandia, a third-grade teacher convicted of providing material support to Lashkar-e-Taiba (LET). The criminal complaint alleged that Chandia worked as a driver for LET officer Mohammed Khan in Virginia and helped ship $50,000 worth of paintball pellets to Pakistan. Recognizing that an offense must meet two elements to constitute a federal crime of terrorism—the commission of one of a list of specified felonies and the specific intent "to influence or affect the conduct of government by intimidation or coercion, or to retaliate against government conduct"—the Fourth Circuit ruled that the district court "appeared to assume (erroneously) that the enhancement automatically applies to a material support conviction" and remanded the case back to the district court for resentencing. Unlike terrorism cases involving "violent terroristic acts," the Fourth Circuit observed that helping ship paintball pellets to Pakistan "cannot, standing alone, support application of the terrorism enhancement," without a factual finding on the intent element. Furthermore, if the district court found that Chandia had the requisite intent, it "should identify the evidence in the record that supports its determination." In other words, the district court could apply the terrorism enhancement only if a preponderance of evidence established the requisite intent to affect or retaliate against the conduct of the government. The Fourth Circuit therefore concluded that without a factual finding on intent, Judge Hilton erred in applying the terrorism enhancement and sentencing Chandia to fifteen years in prison.

On remand, Judge Hilton again applied the terrorism enhancement and resentenced Chandia to fifteen years in prison, which Chandia appealed a second time. On appeal, the Fourth Circuit ruled that the district court had failed to resolve the factual disputes relevant to the application of the terrorism enhancement, evident in Chandia's objection to the presentence investigation report describing LET as an organization whose "primary" focus was "conducting violent jihad against the Government of India."[38] Because Chandia "contended that LET is a popular organization in Pakistan that operates schools and hospitals and provides vocational training," the district court needed to resolve the dispute about "which of LET's purposes Chandia intended to serve by providing material support."[39] Chandia's intent was "relevant to the terrorism issue" such that the district court needed to "resolve this factual dispute and explain whether the resolution leaves motives attributable to Chandia under the terrorism enhancement." The Fourth Circuit remanded the case for resentencing.

For a third time, Judge Hilton applied the terrorism enhancement and resentenced Chandia to fifteen years in prison, after establishing factual findings showing Chandia knew that LET was an organization engaged in acts of terrorism. On the third appeal, the Fourth Circuit upheld Judge Hilton's sentence and ruled that the district court did not commit significant procedural errors and its conclusions were not the result of clear error. Through an "in-depth examination of the adequacy of the record" by the district court to support its application of the terrorism enhancement in *Chandia,* the Fourth Circuit "vacated [the first two] sentences based on the district court's unsupported application of the enhancement, but permitted its imposition on remand" after the court found the necessary intent (Brown 2014, 544). Even though the appellate court reversed Judge Hilton's *Chandia* ruling twice, it ultimately upheld the court's application of the terrorism enhancement and fifteen-year sentence.

Although some legal scholars have cited *Chandia* to show that appellate courts do not "reflexively affirm the application of the terrorism enhancement" by district courts (Wassenberg 2017, 93), others have explored the "sharp tensions that have emerged between trial and appellate courts in the application of the enhancement" such that appellate courts "express the need to control [sentencing] discretion and to advance the policies embodied in the enhancement" in terrorism-related cases (Brown 2014, 522). In fact, a 2012 review of all thirty-eight terrorism cases with reported decisions available online found that "in approximately thirty-one instances, the application of the enhancement was affirmed on appeal"; in two additional cases, the appellate courts overturned the district court's ruling that the terrorism enhancement did not apply (Said 2014, 503).[40] Only two of the thirty-eight reported decisions governing the applicability of the enhancement resulted in the appellate courts "upholding a district court's refusal to apply it" (504). Moreover, the appellate courts reversed the lower courts' application of the terrorism enhancement in only three instances, two of which were *Chandia* and the other *United States v. Parr*,[41] in which the appellate court remanded the case to the district court to reconsider whether the facts determined that the offense "promoted"—rather than "involved"—a federal crime of terrorism and therefore supported the application of the enhancement (Said 2014, 504). Last, in cases where district courts substantially departed downward from the enhancement-based sentencing guidelines, appellate courts have reversed (Floyd 2021). The courts continue to apply the terrorism enhancement, rulings that appellate review almost always uphold and rarely reverse.

Given these trends in district court sentencing and appellate review evident in *Khan,* legal critics warn that the terrorism enhancement "serves as a kind of statutory basis to embolden courts of appeals to overturn a sentence as too lenient"; in doing so, appellate courts endorse the "expressive exercise" of "condemning terrorists qua terrorists as being worthy of the most serious sentences allowed by law" and "demonstrating their participation in the project of protecting national security" (Said 2014, 481). Because appellate courts typically "cite no evidence or studies to justify sentencing enhancements," they create the impression that a court review "may overturn a sentence in a terrorism case simply because it disagrees with the district court" and that judges "rely on their own views of what they imagine to be, regardless of whether those views jibe with current reality or, at the very least, the particular circumstances of the individual being sentenced" (481). Terrorism sentencing jurisprudence reveals that "there is a fair segment of appellate judges who believe that terrorism is different, maybe even exceptional," thereby justifying "a departure from the normal standards" (525). Through these decisions, appellate review largely has affirmed the role of the courts as a global war on terror weapon.

Although appellate courts "appear to tilt in favor of the enhancement and the approach it embodies" (Brown 2014, 540), district courts remain split over when the enhancement applies. Variances in judicial understandings of terrorism largely account for this split, as some courts broadly have applied the terrorism enhancement "by reasoning that terrorists are distinct from other criminals and refractive to rehabilitation," while other courts have refused to apply the enhancement or justified a downward departure "based on a defendant's unique history, the nature of the offense, and the potential for rehabilitation" (Floyd 2021, 144–45). Legal scholar George D. Brown (2014) explains that the "central, and unresolved, question for trial judges at the sentencing phase of a terrorism trial is whether to focus on the special approach [to terrorism offenses], which the enhancement represents, or whether to treat the defendant like any other defendant" (540). While judicial variances reflect the deeply embodied nature of the criminal-legal system and the discrepancies in popular, political, and legal understandings of terrorism, conviction rates confirm the centrality of the courts in the global war on terror. In fact, out of 570 terrorism cases, 455 defendants have been convicted and only seventeen acquitted, dismissed, or exonerated (Center on National Security 2022). Even with variances in judicial decision-making and appellate review, the courts typically have treated terrorism offenses as exceptional crimes requiring a departure from the normative standards of sentencing jurisprudence, most evident in the application of the terrorism enhancement.

Proving Intent: The Invention of the "Wider Global Salafi Jihad Movement"

Given the Fourth Circuit's finding in *Chandia* that the district court needed to identify evidence relating to the specific intent element to substantiate its application of the terrorism enhancement, prosecutors successfully have argued that a defendant's perceived political ideologies or religious beliefs can serve as a reliable proxy for intent. For example, Adham Amin Hassoun was charged with attempting to provide material support to designated foreign terrorist organizations after he sent financial donations to, among others, Bosnian and Chechen Muslims subjected to the genocidal violence inflicted by Bosnian Serbs and Russians. The prosecution argued that "the jury essentially adopted allegations of [Hassoun and his coconspirators'] belief in the 'politico-religious' framework for violent jihad," meaning "the defendants could only have done what the jury convicted of them of doing, with proper intent, if they subscribed to the Salafist philosophy or theology," the "politico-religious" engine driving "violent jihad."[42] By framing Hassoun's financial donations as a kind of economic jihad, the prosecution described Hassoun as a participant in "a covert American support cell that funded, recruited for, and supplied various mujahidin groups overseas with the intent to prepare for acts of murder, kidnapping, and maiming," ultimately advancing the "wider global Salafi jihad movement" in Afghanistan, Algeria, Bosnia, Chechnya, Egypt, Lebanon, Somalia, Tajikistan, and Tunisia.[43] In this view, adherence to an alleged "global Salafist movement" reflected an intent to support "violent jihad" and "displac[e] un-Islamic governments with Sharia."[44]

In objecting to the application of the terrorism enhancement, Hassoun first contested the prosecution's premise that his financial donations contributed to an allegedly unified global Salafist movement engaged in "violent jihad" to establish "Islamic governments." To do so, Hassoun challenged the prosecution's "sweeping over-generalization, based upon an exaggerated, distorted, and one-sided, biased view of the Islamic religion."[45] Hassoun explained how the United States, "together with Muslim countries, poured millions of dollars into the training and arming of the Arab mujahedeen who fought in the jihad against the Soviet Union."[46] The deeply localized struggle in Afghanistan could not be categorically denounced as a criminal expression of "global Salafi-jihad" simply because pious transnational fighters participated in the U.S.-backed anti-Soviet resistance; this imprecise category collapsed different armed groups and denied the different political dimensions organizing each armed struggle. For Hassoun, participation in or support of a specific armed conflict could not imply allegiance to all other political conflicts claiming the label of jihad. Hassoun therefore challenged the reductive analysis that his alleged subscription to "Salafist philosophy" offered a way to interpret his charitable contributions as funding the "global Salafist movement" that murders, kidnaps, and maims to achieve its "politico-religious" agenda, rather than as financial support for survivors of anti-Muslim aggression.

Disputing the presupposition that he was "under the influence of al-Qaeda," Hassoun also argued that the prosecution never proved that the monetary checks he wrote "were ever transmitted to any location overseas for the purpose of 'establishing Islamic states' or for the purpose of 'intimidating [or] coercing' governments through 'violent jihad'— or through any means."[47] Hassoun explained that when he "sent or discussed sending money or other items to particular places, atrocities were being committed against Muslims in those places and/or relief operations were underway to aid Muslim victims and refugees in those places. A desire to aid Muslims who are under attack [and] respond by 'opposing' their attackers is *not* equivalent, legally or factually, to having a purpose of 'intimidating [or] coercing' governments nor is it equivalent to 'violent jihad.'"[48] As one witness testified, Hassoun "told us that Jihad is to protect innocent people, either by going and help or give money or give, collect food, clothes, or just praying for the people. . . . He always said to pray for them, give clothes, whatever they need."[49] Through these arguments, Hassoun rejected the premise that he was driven by "Salafist philosophy or theology" to commit "violent jihad," arguing that his efforts sought to alleviate the suffering of Muslims under siege. As the prosecution worked to frame Hassoun's donations as fueling "Bosnian jihad," the defense sought to dispel the myth of Hassoun's murderous desires and underscore the humanitarian crisis wrought by genocidal warfare.

Hassoun further challenged the application of the terrorism enhancement by illustrating how the prosecution had failed to establish the "motivational element" required under the Sentencing Guidelines.[50] More specifically, Hassoun argued that "the government cannot carry its burden of proving by *clear and convincing evidence* that his *motivation* in committing any 'offense' of which he was convicted was 'to influence or affect the conduct of a government by *intimidation or coercion,* or to *retaliate* against government conduct."[51] In this view, a "desire to aid

Muslims by 'opposing' their attackers is, at most, a desire to help Muslims *defend themselves*—and that is not the same as the very specific motivation required by the 'terrorism' enhancement."[52] Although the prosecution used Hassoun's alleged adherence to "Salafist philosophy" as evidence of his intent, the defense argued that no factual findings demonstrated his intent to intimidate, coerce, or retaliate against a government.

Having heard these arguments, Judge Marcia Cooke determined that Hassoun had acted in response to "the plight of Muslims throughout the world," given his own firsthand knowledge of "what happened to a country when internal politics turned violent" (qtd. in Hogle and Leinonen 2019). She also found that Hassoun did not pose a threat to the United States and that his activities involved "no violent acts, had no identifiable victims, and were never directed against the United States or Americans" (qtd. in Hogle and Leinonen 2019). Despite these findings, Judge Cooke applied the terrorism enhancement and sentenced Hassoun to 188 months in prison and twenty years of supervised release.

As *Hassoun* illustrates, material support charges have been "used aggressively by the U.S. government—often improperly—to criminalize First Amendment protected speech and other non-violent acts the government deems connected to terrorism" (Hogle and Leinonen 2019). In this view, Hassoun was charged with and convicted of crimes "related to his support for Muslims suffering and defending themselves in military conflicts abroad in the 1990s" (Hogle and Leinonen 2019). Questioning the application of the terrorist label to Hassoun and his coconspirators, legal scholar Wadie E. Said (2015) provocatively asks, "Is support for the besieged Bosnian Muslims in the face of Serb ethnic cleansing the same as support for al-Qaeda? Does solidarity with Chechen rebel groups—even their violent activities—indicate approval of the 9/11 attacks?" (110). The blunt analysis offered by the prosecution and adopted by the court in *Hassoun* "effectively criminalized the transmission of aid by religious Muslims wishing to alleviate the plight of their religious brethren suffering under objectively dire conditions of violent oppression, even when the groups receiving the aid have not been designated as terrorists" (110). When confronted with racialized frames through which to interpret geopolitical struggles, the courts have treated innocuous behaviors, such as donating humanitarian aid to Muslim relief organizations—or, in the case of coconspirator Kifyah Jayyousi, sending satellite telephones to Chechnya—as terrorism, without needing to provide affirmative evidence of such a finding. Furthermore, such legal proceedings conflate Bosnian Muslims, Chechen rebels, and al-Qaeda operatives, reductively defining all as terrorist groups through the invocation of the specious specter of a "wider global Salafist movement." Amassing terrorism cases into this "collective basket" ignores the "wide gradation of criminal [and noncriminal] behavior within the category of material support," obscures the concrete conditions that incite humanitarian and political solidarity with besieged populations, and erases the distinctions between armed groups and their sometimes competing geopolitical goals (Baltes et al. 2016, 355–56).

On appeal, the government defended the judge's finding that the "record demonstrates that [Hassoun and his codefendants'] support activities were intended to displace 'infidel' governments that opposed radical Islamist goals" and that they conspired to "advance violent jihad, including supporting and participating in armed confrontations in specific locations outside of the United States, and committing acts of murder, kidnapping, and maiming for the purpose of opposing existing governments."[53] Although Hassoun and his coconspirators did not commit acts of violence, the U.S. Court of Appeals for the Eleventh Circuit agreed that these monetary donations supported "Islamist jihad organizations" in Afghanistan, Chechnya, Kosovo, and Somalia, with the intent to "displace" and "oppose" their respective governments. By framing Hassoun's charitable contributions as financial support for "Islamist jihad organizations," the government effectively marked Hassoun as a terrorist. In doing so, the government denied the suffering of Muslims inflicted by state-sanctioned warfare, framed the provision of humanitarian aid to alleviate such suffering as economic jihad, and criminalized nonviolent humanitarian and political solidarity with rebel groups using violence to end ethnic cleansing. The court inferred Hassoun's intent based on the flawed understanding that al-Qaeda and its so-called Salafist ideology had infiltrated and radicalized Muslim communities in the United States, even if this meant concluding that Hassoun supported disparate designated foreign terrorist organizations that crossed borders, continents, languages, cultures, and geopolitical aspirations.

Even after completing his prison term, the terrorist label continued to haunt Hassoun. Immediately after Hassoun's release in 2017, the

Trump administration detained him, citing an immigration statute. After eighteen months of administrative detention, President Trump then classified Hassoun as a national security threat who could be subjected to incarceration without charge or trial, as authorized by Section 412 of the USA PATRIOT Act, which requires the mandatory detention of suspected terrorists (Hogle and Leinonen 2019). Labeled a terrorist, Hassoun was indefinitely detained despite the federal court's earlier determination that Hassoun did not pose a threat to national security. In 2020, Judge Elizabeth Wolford ordered Hassoun's release, discrediting the prosecution's evidence alleging that Hassoun posed a national security threat.[54] The federal government then initiated Hassoun's deportation. However, as a Palestinian born in Lebanon, Hassoun was stateless. Rwanda later granted Hassoun asylum on humanitarian grounds.

Hassoun's case illustrates how terrorism is a "sticky" sign that acquires meaning through repetition: "if a word is used in a certain way, again and again, then that 'use' *becomes* intrinsic; it becomes a form of signing" (Ahmed 2004, 91). Through such repetition, the word "terrorism" and its association with Islam elicits derision and disgust that "sticks" to Muslim bodies. The stickiness of such signs "depends upon an economy of recognition in which some bodies more than others will be identified as terrorist bodies, regardless of whether they have any official links with terrorist organizations" (Ahmed 2004, 98). In this way, the stickiness of a term like terrorism is "an effect of the histories of contact between bodies, objects, and signs" such that the marking of an individual as a terrorist cannot be considered to be an objective determination but an identificatory process shaped by past histories of contact that "have already impressed upon the surface of the object," as in early twenty-first-century naturalization rulings (Ahmed 2004, 90). Edward Said (1997) similarly explains that "what one reads and sees in media about Islam represents the aggression as coming from Islam because that is what 'Islam' is"—an epistemic process that obliterates "local and concrete circumstances" and instead shows "what Muslims and Arabs by their very flawed nature *are*" (xxii). Partially mediated through the legal system, this epistemic process erases the material conditions in which people live and maps fear and terror onto Muslim bodies such that Muslims are made knowable as always already potential national security threats.

This reductive conflation criminalizes Muslims and Arabs as incipient terrorists, ignores the "gradations" of terrorism-related cases, and obscures the variable geopolitical contexts in which people act (Baltes et al. 2016). Given this epistemic terrain, legal actors must actively work to humanize their clients and contextualize their cases in ways intelligible to judges and jurors. For example, Javed Iqbal faced a sixty-nine-month prison term after selling "different bundles of [TV] channels for people in the United States," television packages that included programming from the Lebanese Broadcasting Corporation (interview, November 2020). As a salesman, Iqbal bundled the most popular channels to increase subscriptions, including adult entertainment, Christian broadcasting, and Al-Manar, colloquially known as "Hezbollah television." One terrorism lawyer explained that like many salespeople, Iqbal was motivated to sell popular subscriptions to increase his revenue: "There was no political element to his [sales]. But they charged him with material support to Hezbollah because he's promoting this propaganda" (interview, November 2020). The court agreed to a shorter prison term "because of [Iqbal's] lack of political ideology," meaning "the terrorism enhancement wouldn't apply because there was no terrorism motive. It was all for profit. So they acknowledged that. And he did much better at sentencing than the average guy would be because of that and so that's one where understanding the context of the *lack* of any ideology was important" (interview, November 2020). Iqbal's sixty-nine-month sentence reflects how contextualizing a defendant's actions can shape the court's understanding of the case by destabilizing the "monolithic concept of terrorism" and therefore result in a relatively lighter punishment; still, Iqbal's sale of television subscriptions resulted in his arrest, conviction, and incarceration.

Despite these legal strategies, the "monolithic concept of terrorism" oftentimes prevailed in court. One judge required Muslim defendants convicted of terrorism-related crimes to identify themselves as terrorists, asking in several sentencing hearings: "Sir, are you a terrorist or not?"; "You agree that you were a terrorist?"; and "Would you look upon yourself as a terrorist?" Forced to show their acceptance of responsibility and remorse, defendants typically responded by affirmatively stating, "I am a terrorist, Your Honor." This judge used his judicial authority to mark defendants as terrorists. Through domestic court proceedings infused with uneven power relations, the terrorist label sticks to Muslim defendants, sometimes generating associative vocabularies, such as defining ISIS as "pure evil," "inherently evil," "forces of evil," and "vile." In these instances, any perceived support of ISIS constituted a commitment to murderous criminal violence, irrespective of the broader humanitarian crises in which violent and nonviolent support was given. In this context, the court functions as both a site of repetition and a place where such acquired value takes on meaning, thereby informing how judges and jurors interpret the terrorism defendants before them.

The courts, however, are not overdetermined by hegemonic understandings of terrorism or dominant racial formations that work in and through the law. Judge Hughes, for example, refused to accept that ISIS uniquely sought to establish a "worldwide caliphate," observing that "so do a lot of non-ISIS people."[55] In other cases, legal actors debated the usage of the term terrorism, recognizing that "the word terrorist is used to label the enemy" and that "terrorist" has "no standard definition" (Sutton 2007; see also *United States v. Asher Khan, Rumsfeld v. Jose Padilla*, and *United States v. Muhamed Mubayyid*). Domestic courts therefore have served as complex sites of contestation where legal actors debate the meaning of terrorism and the frameworks to interpret the actions of the defendants before them. As more than mere containers of dominant geopolitical imaginations or counterterrorism tools, the courts are rife with contradiction and contestation, and therefore ripe with political possibility.

As these cases demonstrate, the courts have functioned as key sites of struggle over the definition, usage, and application of terms like "violent jihad" and "global Salafist movement." Although the courts often have relied on a "monolithic concept of terrorism," expert discourses related to terrorism have never stabilized and remain variously infused with moral, political, and legal evaluations that can be activated strategically in the courtroom. Terrorism scholars admit that terrorism has "no precise or widely accepted definition and it is often used pejoratively" such that its usage "seems to depend on point of view—it is what the 'bad guys' do" (Jenkins 1974, 135–36). In *Hassoun*, for example, legal actors mobilized jihad as a conceptual frame to define various violent and nonviolent activities as participation in or promotion of "extreme violence," with the "ultimate goal of creating Islamic governments under

Sharia in present and former Muslim lands."[56] Although concepts like jihad have provided the courts with organizing guides to interpret the criminality of defendants' activities and intentions, such concepts are always already embedded in relations of force that require further inquiry. As Foucault (1972) argues, "We must question those ready-made syntheses, those groupings that we normally accept before any examination, those links whose validity is recognized from the outset" (22). Political concepts, after all, are designed to "distribute power" and "assess the value of humankinds" (Stoler 2016, 120, 117).

Anthropologist Ann Laura Stoler (2016) entreats scholars to challenge such ready-made syntheses through "concept-work," which attends to "the relations of force in which concepts are embedded, the fictions of their 'stability' that entail violences of their own," and considers "what concepts implicitly and often quietly *foreclose,* as well as what they encourage and condone" (17–19). Applying "concept-work" to terrorism prosecutions means interrogating the conceptual work that jihad and other such terms are called on to undertake in the courts and, in the process, recognizing how imperial formations "prodigiously produce specialized lexicons of legal, social, and political terms, concepts, and enduring vocabularies that both innocuously and tenaciously cling to people, places, and things" (20). Such concepts, and "the processes of occlusion they afford and the misrecognitions to which they give rise," make defendants legible in strategic ways while obscuring the historical, geographical, and political dimensions to their actions—or, in other instances, the specious charges applied to them (19). Although legal actors can throw such ready-made narratives into question or register the dubious categories used to classify defendants, concepts like terrorism and jihadism continue to cue epistemic processes that effectively criminalize Muslim, Arab, and other defendants of color, irrespective of their actual conduct or the material contexts in which they acted.

On How to "Look Like a Jihadi": Conceptual Habits in the Courtroom

The successful prosecution of terrorism defendants typically has relied on government expert witnesses whose testimony reifies monolithic, and often racialized, understandings of jihad. In *Hassoun,* for example, prosecutors called on terrorologist Rohan Gunaratna to testify as an expert witness on al-Qaeda's "principal aim" to "create Sharia based on Islamic states"; on the use of "jihad" to refer to the "fight to create Islamic states wherever Muslims lived"; and on the role of "migrant communities" in "Australia, Europe, and North America" in providing "money to conflict zones."[57] Defendants also have called on terrorologists whose expert testimony could refute the reductive definitions offered by prosecutors and contextualize armed resistance. Such testimony, however, often recited the same monolithic understandings of political violence used against defendants. In *United States v. Amer Alhaggagi,* prominent terrorologist Marc Sageman testified on behalf of the defendant, arguing that Alhaggagi "doesn't look like a jihadi and he doesn't behave like a jihadi."[58] Sageman suggested, "You can look like a jihadi: you have short pants because you have to have your pants above your ankles. A lot of people wear shalwar kameez, which are the Pakistani look. Some people have one of those rolled-up hats, which the Tajiks use. It's called pakul—P-A-K-U-L—hat."[59] To prove Alhaggagi was not a jihadist, Sageman argued that the defendant did not "look like a jihadi," a maneuver that reaffirmed the concept of both a jihadist—a radicalized Muslim extremist—and a "jihadist look," with observable and identifiable markers. While jihad "can of course mean many things" (Li 2020, 23), its activation by terrorologists in the courts has reinforced mainstream understandings of jihadists, making it difficult for judges and jurors to "dislodge" what they imagine to already know about the defendants before them (Stoler 2016, 8).

Informed by this expert testimony, legal actors often subscribed to conventional definitions of jihad, which shaped their interpretation of the cases before them. In *United States v. Mohammed Hamzah Khan,* Judge John Tharp Jr. concluded, "To want to join the Caliphate is to want to join jihad, which is war," with the intention to "exterminate anyone who disagrees with their religious dogma."[60] In *Al-Jayab,* the prosecution argued, "Jihad is defined in the Merriam-Webster dictionary as a holy war waged on behalf of Islam as religious duty."[61] In *Hassoun,* the prosecution used the term jihad to refer to ideologically motivated violence driven by "global Salafi-jihadist views," including "blood-thirsty activities" like "assassination, hostage takings, suicide bombings, and beheadings to achieve their goals of political and religious change."[62]

Framed by these sensationalized understandings of jihad, vocabularies like "jihadi ideals" have entered court documents as indicators of the defendant's political, moral, and ethical character, such as a "loathing of the United States."[63] Attorneys therefore have offered competing understandings of jihad to interpret the criminality and, often, morality, of defendants, their actions, and their intentions. Although the concept of jihad appears to clarify the intent driving, and criminal liability attached to, certain acts, as an empty signifier, it does little to explain "the wide range of very different kinds of political conflict" waged under the banner of jihad or the variable conduct alleged to constitute jihad, such as sending financial donations to refugee camps (Li 2020, 24).

In the case against Sami Osmakac, the concept of jihad featured prominently in court proceedings as the prosecution used the term to demonstrate the defendant's criminal intent. Following an elaborate sting operation, the FBI arrested Osmakac after he allegedly purchased weapons from an undercover agent and planned to attack crowded locations in Florida. At trial, the defense argued that Osmakac was entrapped by the FBI and that his psychiatric disabilities made him vulnerable to manipulation: "[Osmakac] has a severe mental disease and he has this low intelligence and the FBI . . . took advantage of him. They overwhelmed him. . . . He had no chance. Even someone probably that knew what they were doing would have very little chance in that kind of situation where they're sandwiched between both sides with the FBI on both sides pushing on him, controlling him."[64] The prosecution, however, argued that the evidence conclusively demonstrated Osmakac's "overwhelming intent to conduct this terroristic attack that he planned in Tampa, Florida," after first failing to travel to Afghanistan to "join violent jihad."[65] This case pivoted on whether the FBI created or uncovered a jihadist.

To support its contention that Osmakac sought to "join violent jihad," the prosecution called terrorologist Evan Kohlmann to testify as an expert witness who could "explain to the Court and to the jury the definition of terms and phrases" used throughout the investigation, including mujahidin and jihad.[66] In the prosecution's perspective, such expert testimony would inform the jury about these terms so they could understand the factual evidence in the case and therefore be better prepared to evaluate Osmakac's criminal liability. In its closing statement, the prosecution assessed that Kohlmann's testimony demonstrated Osmakac's "overwhelming viewpoint to commit jihad, to commit martyrdom."[67] Kohlmann's expert testimony contributed to the prosecution's successful conviction of Osmakac.

As a self-identified "expert on the vocabulary of a radical extremist," Kohlmann first defined the terms Osmakac used and their connections to "contemporary violent extremists."[68] For example, Kohlmann explained that while the "traditional definition of hijrah refers to making a religious journey," in the "context in a particular sect of Muslims, Salafis," the term "has taken on the meaning of also journeying abroad to participate in Islamic society, including participating in fighting on a frontline for Islamic causes."[69] Referring to a government exhibit, Kohlmann concluded that Osmakac's use of the phrase "big hijrah" signified "the journey to the afterlife, the journey to paradise . . . making the big journey."[70] On cross-examination, however, Kohlmann admitted that in another conversation, Osmakac used the word "hijrah" to refer to "moving to an Islamic country" and "get[ting] a wife and some other things like that."[71] Although Kohlmann described hijrah as "an essential term within the context of Islam," he also asserted hijrah is "a term used in similar but not the same context by contemporary violent extremists" such that Osmakac's mention of "big hijrah" indicated his desire to be "martyred" for an "Islamic cause" (161). Kohlmann's testimony aligns with other terrorologists who contend that the Islamic State has "manipulated" the concept of hijrah to "attract Muslims from countries [the Islamic State] perceives as *Dar al-Harb* [house of war or lands hostile to Islam] (but mainly the West) to the Islamic State," migrations that allegedly pose "security problems" (Uberman and Shay 2016, 18–19). By defining Osmakac's use of hijrah in this way, Kohlmann imbued the defendant's statements and actions with meaning: they reflected a commitment to "tying radical ideas to violence."[72] In other words, Osmakac's vocabularies could be used to determine if he "fit the profile of a 'homegrown' terrorist network" or "fit the characteristics associated with the profile of a contemporary violent extremist."[73]

Derived from the Arabic root *ha/ja/ra*, "to leave," *hijrah* "is classified into two types: *hijrah makaniyah* (moving from one place to another) and *hijrah ma'nawiyah* (changing yourself better to get closer to Allah and to get pleasure from Allah)" (Muna 2002, 92). Referring to Prophet Muhammed's migration from Mecca to Medina in 622 CE, hijrah signifies "a carefully planned migration which marks not only a break in history—the beginning of the Islamic era—but also, for Muhammed and the Muslims, a new way of life," with the travelers who accompanied Prophet Muhammed called the Muhajirun (the migrants) and those in Medina who became Muslims called Ansar (the helpers) (Nawwab 2021). Although terrorologists have fixated on how rebel groups have used social media to attract young Muslims to undertake hijrah, this approach misses the many other ways Muslim millennials have engaged hijrah activities online, as with Indonesian celebrities using hijrah to denote "the change or movement into a better version of oneself" and documenting the "hijrah movement" with viral hashtags like #hijrah (Noormega 2019; Muna 2002). Despite these more robust understandings of hijrah and the different ways Muslim millennials have engaged the concept, Kohlmann's testimony primarily distinguished how "most Muslims" used certain words from how "radical extremists" adopted the maligned "alternate meanings" of these terms. In doing so, Kohlmann suggested Osmakac's invocation of hijrah could only reflect a commitment to violence. Kohlmann's testimony affirmed a commonsense understanding of the idioms and tropes conventionally cast as "Islamic," without assessing how their users deployed such concepts and without "attending to the patterns of historical movement that bring people together such that categories like ansar [and hijrah] could emerge as something they all regarded as compelling" (Li 2020, 32). Decontextualized, these terms provide little insight into the phenomenon they are called on to explain while occluding the histories, practices, and politics underpinning the conduct on trial.

In addition to his discussion of hijrah, Kohlmann also explained in his expert report that the contemporary invocation of jihad almost always reflected a "hardline sectarian religious perspective" indicative of "homegrown terrorism."[74] In this view, Osmakac's use of terms like jihad and hijrah reflected his adoption of a "radical sectarian ideology" that "has put him at odds with other members of his own local community," an alleged causal factor of terrorist violence.[75] By treating the use of jihad, hijrah, and other Islamic concepts as an indicator of future terrorist activity, Kohlmann's research erroneously infused these terms with predictive value, emptied them of their theological and political contents, and abstracted them from the material contexts in which speakers employed them, including an elaborate sting operation designed to ensnare a target in a concocted terrorist plot.

As "primary definers," terrorologists "establish the initial definition or *primary interpretation* of the topic in question" and then "*set the limit* for all subsequent discussion by framing what the problem is. This initial framework then provides the criteria by which all subsequent contributions are labelled as 'relevant' to the debate or 'irrelevant'" (Hall et al. 1978, 59). In *Osmakac,* this meant that expert testimony narrowed how the court came to understand the defendant's actions and intentions through a lens of "homegrown terrorism," even as a mental health expert testified that Osmakac had "delusions of martyrdom" and diagnosed him with "depressive disorder, depression, psychotic disorder, [posttraumatic stress disorder], the schizophrenia disorder, depression, isolation, suicidal, homicidal ideation, paranoia, auditory and visual hallucinations."[76] As the prosecution alleged, Osmakac maintained a "consistent viewpoint" that "there's a division between people who believe in Islam, as he does, and everyone else"; given this viewpoint, Osmakac believed "the only thing to be done is to commit violent jihad until the world agrees with his viewpoint."[77] In this reading of Osmakac's worldview, jihad meant "the next world war."[78] Rather than view Osmakac's actions as the result of an FBI sting operation that exploited his radical belief system and psychiatric disabilities, the court viewed his conduct as intending to promote a federal crime of terrorism, applied the terrorism enhancement, and sentenced him to forty years in prison.

Despite the prevalence of this primary definition of jihad in legal proceedings, the term, "most often and sensationally glossed as Islamic 'holy war,'" can refer to different meritorious efforts, "from a spiritual struggle for self-improvement to armed confrontation" (Li 2020, 23). Yet academic scholars and media pundits have both misapplied the term jihad to a wide range of nonviolent activities to criminalize Muslims and essentialized the concept by reducing it to violence waged by religious fanatics and occluding the conditions that incite armed resistance. Such an approach elides the various ways jihad is understood and mobilized as a political concept, such as Lebanese women who engage in "gender jihad" by undertaking the political project of establishing gender equity (Deeb 2006; Huq 2009). Religion professor Bruce Lawrence (1998) frames jihad as invested in seeking justice, arguing that "jihad has come to mean the advocacy of social justice in a widening circle that also includes economic participation and prosperity for Muslims in the modern context, not just for Muslims alone" (159). Given these multifaceted ways differently situated actors have theorized and employed the concept of jihad, Hamdar (2009) concludes that "jihad in Islam comes in many forms, but its association with holy war is an interpretation that many Muslims and non-Muslims alike make in error" (89). Although these analyses destabilize essentialist understandings of jihad, we still have few tools available to us to "make sense of the acts of sacrifice that do occasionally take place in the name of Islam between people who seem to lack any other tie of commonality or interest" (Li 2020, 25). In terrorism prosecutions, the courts reflected this epistemic terrain as they actively engaged in debates to understand defendants marked as jihadists. Despite these lively debates, the "monolithic concept of terrorism" typically organized court proceedings and sentencing decisions, evidenced in the prosecution, conviction, and sentencing of Osmakac and Hassoun.

Even as terrorologists have offered expert testimony reducing Islamic concepts and Arabic vocabularies to indicators of terrorist activity, the courts have offered alternative explanatory frameworks to understand the factual evidence before them. In some cases, judges made their struggles to understand jihad and its relationship to the defendant's actions visible in court proceedings. Judge Janet C. Hall expressed concerns with popular interpretations of jihad in the sentencing hearing of Babar Ahmad, who was convicted of conspiring to provide material support to foreign terrorist organizations after publishing two articles on his website that encouraged readers to send money to the Taliban in February and November 2001—the first publication before the September 11 attacks staged by al-Qaeda, and the second after the United States believed the Taliban agreed to harbor Osama bin Laden in Afghanistan. Refusing to conflate jihad with terrorism, Judge Hall observed:

> So, there has been the use in this case of the phrase "violent jihad"
> and the use of the word "terrorism" and the use of the word

"Jihad." In my view, the Jihad does not equal terrorism. All terrorists appear, over the last 20 years, to carry out acts under a banner of Jihad. They claim that. In my view, they misappropriate that phrase. And indeed, their use of the word "Jihad" is a perversion of what Islam teaches. . . . My understanding is that the concept of Jihad in Islam is struggle, and it's both an internal and a defensive struggle, but it's never what happened on 9/11.[79]

Given this understanding of jihad, Judge Hall refused to classify Ahmad as a terrorist and determined that the defendant was never "interested in what is commonly known as terrorism."[80] Even in her refusal, however, Judge Hall's reasoning articulated with popular "culture talk" that reifies the "good Muslim/bad Muslim" trope, whereby some Muslims correctly interpret and invoke (nonviolent) jihad while others use the term to justify their maligned interests (Mamdani 2004, 18). Manzoor-Khan (2022) explains that under these racial logics, "Even those who say terrorism is only the problem of a minority of Muslims, concede that it *is* a Muslim problem" (21). In the absence of other conceptual tools, the mere refusal to equate jihad with "what happened on 9/11" does not necessarily offer alternative analyses, such as how jihad is used to organize political violence in pursuit of different geopolitical goals responsive to specific material conditions, such as imperial warfare and colonial occupation—including the September 11 attacks.

Despite these conceptual limitations, Judge Hall also refused to reduce political violence to terrorism by recognizing how many took up arms "under the banner of Jihad" to resist military interventions and other colonial incursions that produced racialized violence, dispossession, and displacement. At sentencing, Judge Hall considered the geopolitical contexts in which Ahmad operated, particularly in the wake of the Bosnian war and the Chechen wars that brought "many Muslims from the United Kingdom" to "central Europe, Bosnia, Chechnya, and Afghanistan at various times in the '80s and '90s and into 2000."[81] It was through this geopolitical analysis of armed transnational solidarity that Judge Hall came to describe Ahmad's 1997–2002 publications as

relating to the struggle in Bosnia by Muslims against the Serbs and their efforts to ethnically cleanse Bosnia of Muslims. . . . And then later, in Chechnya . . . the two-step attack by Russians on Chechens and the response by Chechens supported by foreign Mujahi-din . . . to fight back or to drive out Russians from Chechnya. And then lastly, of course, it eventually turns to Afghanistan where the Taliban, of course, if we go back with our history, was initially fighting the Russians with support by the United States. That eventually evolved into an internal struggle between the Taliban and the Northern Alliance as to who would be in control of which parts of the country, then finally evolved into a dispute with the United States and the Taliban, in particular surrounding the fact that the Taliban allowed Osama bin Laden to return to Afghanistan and, in effect, protected him, allowing him to continue his operations and to develop and grow al-Qaida.[82]

Rather than reduce Ahmad's publications to terrorist propaganda, Judge Hall observed how Muslims mobilized transnationally to respond to anti-Muslim violence waged by state actors across the globe, from Bosnia to Chechnya to Afghanistan, often in ways that aligned with the geostrategic interests of the United States. In fact, Judge Hall affirmed that "the Chechens were not terrorists at the time they were trying to expel the Russians, which is the time that Mr. Ahmad was doing what he was doing on the web with respect to Chechnya."[83] Given this understanding of jihad, Judge Hall refused to classify Ahmad as a terrorist and determined that the defendant was never "interested in what is commonly known as terrorism."[84]

Like some of her peers, Judge Hall used her understanding of jihad and the contexts in which violence circulates to reason that there are degrees of terrorism; in her legal estimation, not everyone "guilty of a material support count is in that category of terrorists" that recidivate.[85] Affirming that "there must be distinctions between and among people who do acts that make them guilty of material support," Judge Hall considered the nature of the offense rather than the terrorism label affixed to it.[86] One terrorism lawyer even described Judge Hall as

one of the few judges, maybe the *only* judge I can remember, who understood the fundamental distinctions in this particular group of defendants. She was able to distinguish between a political insurgent and a terrorist, between someone who targets civilians and someone who is involved in a military oppositional endeavor. And so she was able to understand [Ahmad's] motivations. . . .

She understood. And she essentially gave [Ahmad] a sentence of maybe—he did about another six months, and he was back in England. (interview, November 2020)

By contextualizing Ahmad's actions within his longer life history in Bosnia and the geopolitical conflicts he survived, the defense destabilized the monolithic concept of terrorism, such that the judge could understand "why you've done what you've done" (interview, November 2020). Ahmad's sentence, however, still amounted to 150 months—a significant prison term for two online publications produced in rapidly shifting geopolitical contexts defined by anti-Muslim aggression.[87]

As some judges recognized that "all terrorists wave the banner of Jihad, but not all Jihad is terrorism," their courts became important sites of struggle over understanding, interpreting, and responding to concepts like jihad.[88] In the absence of alternative frameworks to understand political violence and transnational mobilizations, "the fears and distortions swirling around the meaning of jihad" have continued to justify the harsh punishment of defendants, as evidenced in Ahmad's 150-month sentence for two online publications soliciting support for Chechen rebels and Taliban fighters (Euben 2002, 5). As political scientist Roxanne L. Euben (2002) explains, the "familiarity, even preoccupation, with the phenomenon of jihad would seem to provide a unique opportunity to take up the challenge to consider seriously the implications of death for politics"; this opportunity, however, "goes almost entirely unnoticed" given the West's abstraction of the term from "the ethico-political contexts through which it is defined and made to signify a more general irruption of the irrational, archaic, and pathological" (6). Judge Hall, for example, reasoned that terrorists "have acted out against this country" by "twisting and warping the Koran," that "Islam was hijacked by Osama bin Laden" who mobilized "false doctrinal support for jihad," and that Ahmad "wrongly supported the Taliban . . . at a time when he knew the Taliban was protecting Osama bin Laden and al-Qaeda."[89] By relying on hegemonic explanatory models circulated by expert witnesses, the courts can reject reductive understandings of jihad without dislodging Orientalist mystifications that depict jihad as "a by-product of and an atavistic reaction against modernity" that requires a carceral response (7).

Using the Courts to Incapacitate Jihadists: Prosecuting Youth as Terrorists in Minneapolis

As legal actors have debated terms like jihad and hijrah, judges also have varied in their understanding of the role of their courts in the context of the global war on terror. Some judges have identified how the courts can, and should, demobilize and incapacitate fomenting "jihadist cells" before the commission of an act of violence. In fact, throughout the global war on terror, the executive branch consistently has relied on the judiciary "to pursue its war aims," particularly through terrorism prosecutions (Skinner 2013, 309). The judiciary's extensive role in the global war on terror, the expansion of criminal liability "to the earliest point now countenanced under American law," and the racialized understandings of Islamic concepts and Arabic vocabularies have accelerated pre-emptive prosecutions that criminalize inchoate activities, religious beliefs, and social networks to "ferret out terrorism in Muslim communities" (Sherman 2009, 1486; Aaronson 2013, 16).

The confluence of these relations of force has made the racialized strategy of preemptive prosecutions central to the global war on terror, evident in the cases of nine Somali youth brought by federal prosecutors after an elaborate sting operation in Minneapolis: Zacharia Abdurahman, Hamza Ahmed, Abdirahman Daud, Adnan Farah, Mohmed Farah, Hanad Musse, Guled Omar, Abdirizak Warsame, and Abdullahi Yusuf. With the help of the young men's friend, Abdirahman Bashir, who worked as a paid undercover informant, federal authorities listened to hours of conversation between the young men. During this time, the young men watched ISIS propaganda videos, discussed plans to travel to Syria to fight the Assad regime, and tried to purchase fake passports from an undercover FBI agent.

Although the young men differed in their commitment to travel to Syria—with some making active plans to leave the United States and others simply engaging in bravado-laden discussions with their peers, often at the provocation of Bashir—they all faced terrorism-related charges for their actions. Twenty-two-year-old Guled Omar expressed equivocation with the group's plans to join ISIS in Syria but later declined to cooperate with law enforcement and refused to plead guilty. Omar therefore faced several terrorism-related charges, including conspiracy to commit murder abroad. After his jury conviction, Omar was sentenced to a thirty-five-year prison term, followed by a lifetime of supervised release. Despite his lengthy sentence, Omar never stepped foot in Syria, never wielded a weapon, and never committed an act of violence.

At Mohamed Farah's sentencing hearing, Judge Michael Davis reinforced the dominant narrative that the young men posed an imminent terrorist threat. Judge Davis concluded that "it's clear . . . there is a jihadist cell in this community" and that "we have to incapacitate this cell."[90] Having testified on behalf of the government, United States Attorney Andrew Luger affirmed this observation, explaining in a press release that the defendants "wanted to fight for a brutal terrorist organization, kill innocent people, and destroy their own families in the process" (Office of Public Affairs 2016). In this view, the conviction of all nine boys "should serve as a wake-up call that it will take the entire community to stop terror recruiting in Minnesota" (Office of Public Affairs 2016). Through these highly publicized cases, Judge Davis concluded that a "jihadist cell" had infiltrated Somali communities in Minnesota and posed an active threat to national security, necessitating the mobilization of the criminal-legal system to incapacitate "committed jihadists." In this way, Judge Davis's courtroom served as a key counterterrorism tool to protect the United States from the threat of terrorism.

Pejoratively referred to as the "ISIS trials," these cases demonstrate how the criminal-legal system has advanced the global war on terror and reaffirmed the state's monopoly on violence. The cases also illustrate how particular constellations of geopolitical knowledge and racial logics coalesce in domestic courtrooms, ultimately shaping the adjudication of terrorism-related crimes and facilitating the global war on terror. Legal actors used the "ISIS trials" as an explanatory moment demonstrative of the imminent terrorist threat lurking in Minnesotan communities and necessitating a strong punitive response from the criminal-legal system. Rather than focus on the aggregate outcomes of terrorism-related cases, the next section examines how issues of national security and normative assumptions about jihad influenced these outcomes, which were determined by an individual judge who acted on legal, sociological, and geopolitical interpretations of the defendants and crimes before him.

A "Spiritual Struggle": Wannabe Terrorists, Jihadists, or Emerging Political Actors?

The high-profile cases in Minneapolis featured critical debates about how the court should understand the defendants: as "jihadists," as youth "deeply troubled by the brutal war in Syria" and "motivated by their desire to fight the Assad regime," or as "wanna-be terrorists" merely expressing "teen braggadocio" and largely incapable of enacting their plans to join ISIS.[91] In a joint evidentiary hearing, Judge Davis explained that through the pretrial probation office, the court hired the director of the German Institute on Radicalization and De-radicalization Studies, Daniel Koehler, to evaluate the defendants, train probation officers in assessing terrorism defendants, and provide additional information to facilitate the sentencing of the defendants.[92] Although the government called expert witnesses to testify in *Hassoun* and *Osmakac,* it was Judge Davis who sought the expertise of a terrorologist to inform his sentencing decisions. As in other terrorism-related cases, expert knowledge on terrorism defined these legal proceedings.

As a part of his paid work, Koehler provided the court with an evaluation of each defendant and his prospects for rehabilitation. At Judge Davis's request, Koehler also testified at the joint evidentiary hearing about concepts like radicalization, jihad, and Salafism. Judge Davis asked Koehler to explain "the basic elements of Salafi and Jihadi ideology."[93] As in other terrorism-related cases, terms like jihad—and, later, hijrah, Tawhid, caliphate, and ummah—offered a conceptual lens to assess defendants, their alleged degree of terrorist radicalization, and therefore their prospects for rehabilitation.

As we will see, Koehler's testimony aligns with terrorism taxonomies invented and popularized by Western academics who have mobilized the Salafi-jihadi label as a typological category. This label classifies alleged Salafi adherents as an embodied manifestation of menacing Islam and therefore validates efforts to obliterate this perceived enemy of the state. This paradigm equates Salafism, a conservative theological movement within Sunni Islam, with a political ideology that drives violence. Yet as Li (2020) notes, "Salafism lacks any inherent political content: Salafis have all sorts of different relationships with the state and—like the general populations to which they belong—exhibit no demonstrable proclivity toward violence as a single group. And even when Salafis are engaged in violence, they do so as part of a wide variety of political projects" (105–6). Mobilizing the reductive conclusion that not all Muslims are terrorists—but that some, especially Salafis, are—reinforces the notion of the radical Muslim terrorist (Islam 2021). As a constant referent, Salafism does the conceptual work to mark certain Muslims as terrorist threats without necessarily castigating all Muslims. The interchangeability of "Salafi groups" and "jihadi groups," evidenced in Judge Davis's question, collapses the terms and treats them as synonymous: religious fanatics engaged in illegitimate warfare.

Through this racialized lens, subscription to Salafism could serve as evidence of a defendant's propensity for violence. Koehler explained that he categorized defendants as at a "low stage of risk and radicalization" if they "[did] not think or act or talk in a way that would suggest [they are] still very much convinced of these certain ideological aspects that we talked about that are part of Salafi/Jihadi ideology."[94] In other words, Koehler used adherence to "Salafi/Jihadi ideology" as a defining metric in his risk assessments, even though social scientists routinely have disproven the organizing assumption that radical beliefs facilitate the turn to violence (Sharma and Nijjar 2018; Walker 2021; Kundnani 2012; Patel 2011).

Using prepared PowerPoint slides to supplement his testimony, Koehler divided Salafis into four distinct groups: "purists" who are both "completely apolitical and nonviolent," "political missionaries" who preach against any form of violence, "political missionary groups" that support the use of violence in limited situations, and finally "Jihadi groups" that "perform[] the individual jihad."[95] Although Koehler sought to dissolve the notion of a monolithic Salafi ideology, his testimony reinforced the concept of jihadi Salafism or Salafi jihadism, which still assumes "the culprit is Salafism" (Li 2020, 106). Furthermore, this classification of Salafis—purists, political missionaries, and jihadists—"renders politics and violence as mutually exclusive, which is to say it treats state violence as normal while conflating all forms of nonstate violence as deviant" (Li 2020, 230n4). In other words, nuancing the typological category of Salafi-jihadism does little to dislodge the organizing assumption that Salafism drives violence or disrupts the continued cleaving of politics from violence.

Koehler also described how "Salafi/Jihadis" have engaged in a "spiritual struggle or internal struggle between the Shias and the Sunnis."[96] To understand this spiritual struggle, Koehler explained that "Jihadi groups" believe that "performing the individual jihad . . . the military version of jihad is an individual duty. From group to group, it's even seen as the most important element of your Muslim identity so you cannot be a true Muslim without performing jihad," which means "to fight the forces of evil, to fight the forces of infidel, and to spread the realm of Islam across the world which is the core idea behind Jihadi groups."[97] In this view, "the basic ideology behind every single Jihadi group which, is first of all, the problem that the true Islam is under global attack by the force of evil and infidel, Israel, the U.S., Europe, Russia, China, other countries that do not follow the true path of Allah."[98] Furthermore, jihadi groups uniformly agree that the "only solution to that global struggle against Islam which is the individual duty of violent militant Jihad to fight back and conquer these territories that are thought of lying in the house of war or house of unbelief or disbelief."[99] Koehler concluded that "all Jihadi groups share the future vision: the goal to re-erect, recreate the caliphate as the home state for all true Muslims. It is not unlike . . . the state of Israel for the Jewish people."[100] In this view, "jihadi groups" have used violence to gain territorial control and sovereign power outside of the current world order. Koehler, however, described such violence as a response to religious commandment, ultimately ignoring the formative conditions that inform the variable political aspirations of such groups and erasing the radically different political aspirations of al-Shabaab, al-Qaeda, ISIS, and other armed militias.

Assuming a unified and unifying jihadist ideology, Koehler argued that all jihadi groups believe that

> to revive the true Muslim community and the ummah—give them back their statehood that they have been granted by Allah and that they deserve—they have to govern over other people, over other religions and ethnicities; they have to, in their minds, spread the interpretation of Muslim by force and conquer other territories and, of course, defeat other blasphemous religions and interpretations of Islam or other religions as such.[101]

By affirming that all jihadi groups subscribe to this viewpoint, Koehler imbued the jihadist label given to the defendants with interpretive power: the defendants' actions sought to "revive the true Muslim community . . . by force." As an explanatory framework, this understanding of jihadi groups provided insight into the intentions of the defendants—a useful tool to determine their risk profiles.

To reinforce popular understandings of jihadi groups, Koehler described geopolitical struggles across the Arab world as an expression of sectarianism. Koehler argued that as a Shia Muslim, Syrian president Bashar al-Assad "has been known to oppress, violently suppress, Sunni groups within the Syrian population for decades because his father did that," even committing "mass atrocities" and using "chemical weapons against the civil population."[102] Koehler also reported that "after the U.S.-led coalition brought down the Saddam Hussein regime, the power again shifted back to the Shia which are a minority that took over rule in Iraq and also started to suppress and sideline Sunni, Sunni groups in Iraq."[103] Koehler described armed conflicts to gain or maintain territorial control and sovereign power as an "internal spiritual struggle between the Shias and Sunnis"— devoid of any serious political orientation.[104]

Koehler's court-requested testimony is critical because although it defined the Syrian war as a response to an oppressive Assad regime and recognized a broader strategy to capture territorial control and sovereign power in ways that challenged current borders, it also reduced these conflicts to a "spiritual struggle," with little consideration of how the Assad regime used sectarianism to maintain its administrative authority or how the U.S.-led invasion of Iraq created the conditions for, and then institutionalized, sectarian factions. As political scientist Nader Hashemi (2016) explains, in Arab republics, the "driver of politics is not a defense of theological doctrine or loyalty to the collective interests of a religious sect. The core allegiance for ruling elites is to their political thrones and their various clients, whether Sunni or Shi'a, who can help sustain their power" (74). Given the colonial imposition of borders after the fall of the Ottoman Empire, ruling elites have engaged in sectarianization—"the deliberate manipulation of religious identities"—in pursuit of this political power (74). Rather than take seriously the political strategies of authoritarian regimes in the wake of colonial rule, including sectarianization, Koehler reduced jihadists to religious fanatics engaged in a spiritual struggle between Shias and Sunnis. By reducing political violence to religious perversions and abstracting it from the material conditions in which people act, Koehler treated violence and politics as separate rather than co-constitutive spheres. Koehler therefore dismissed the clear geopolitical grievances, goals, and aspirations of rebel groups even though they often were aligned with and supportive of the geostrategic agenda of the United States as well as equally vested in gaining territorial control and sovereign power through the use of lethal force.

According to Koehler, "jihadists" fight "the forces of evil" as a spiritual duty "given to [them] by Allah."[105] Marking individual actors as jihadists driven by religious commandment "delegitimizes the political actions of those stuck with the label" and "denies any political dimension to their use of violence—and, paradoxically, only serves to reconfirm that this violence is political, even as it takes moralistic forms (as 'evil') or technocratic ones ('extremism')" (Li 2020, 25). In this way, "terrorism is a label of definition, a means of excluding those so branded from human standing. . . . Once so defined, those affected may become international lepers" such that their "objectives, ideology, and historical reason for being will be dismissed out of hand" (Perdue 1989, 4). Koehler's blunt analysis, even while seeking to nuance the court's understanding of Salafism, reduced deep political conflicts—intensified through the strategic use of sectarianization by authoritarian regimes—to the perverse theology of its armed participants and therefore occluded the broader geopolitical contexts and geostrategic priorities organizing the use of lethal force. While we may disagree with the politics animating violence or the use of lethal force, this conceptual framework justifies deploying military-carceral modalities to confine and kill suspected nonstate soldiers and their supporters, without attending to the root causes of armed resistance, such as despotic regimes and colonial incursions.

Consonant with Koehler's testimony, the prosecution acknowledged that the term jihad "is fraught with the possibility of misunderstanding," all while strategically using it to refer to "acts of violence against non-Muslims, a category that includes many people who are Muslim, but are considered by ISIL to be either insufficiently zealous (most Sunnis), or else to hold beliefs that ISIL does not recognize as Muslim at all (the Shi'a)."[106] Rather than engage the geopolitical contexts, conditions, and aspirations under which rebel groups have operated, the prosecution framed the defendants' actions as expressions of violent Salafi jihadism, even though the defendants had never traveled to Syria, joined a rebel group, or committed an act of violence. They merely discussed, in politically charged conversations, their outrage over the Syrian war, their reactions to the continued siege on Muslims, and their responsibility to act. Referring to the defendants as jihadists, however, encouraged the court to evaluate the young men's nonviolent conduct as contributing to illegal and illegitimate violence aimed at establishing a global caliphate.

As a reductive explanatory framework, Salafi-jihadism allowed the prosecution to define the defendants' actions as a "long-term conspiracy that contained within it three distinct efforts by the conspirators to reach Syria," through which the young men sought to contribute to "the murderous practices of ISIL and the terrorist organization's global aspirations."[107] By vacating the political, economic, and humanitarian contexts that informed the young men's drive to depose Assad and protect Muslims under attack, the prosecution described the young men's unsuccessful efforts to travel to Syria as "extremely violent and dangerous behavior," particularly given ISIS's "extraordinary violence, not to say sadism."[108]

The prosecution also used Salafi-jihadism to define every aspect of the young men's actions as nefarious, if not criminal. For example, the young men used an encrypted text messaging application, Kik, to communicate privately. Mohmed Farah explained that he began using Kik to communicate with "friends, people from school," without the intention to "hide" their discussions. Once the young men "learned what [Kik] was and how it could be used," they "started using it to communicate with our friends overseas," outside the purview of any government surveillance. Although it is understandable that communities under surveillance, including Muslim youth and political dissidents, turn to encrypted applications to protect their communications, in the context of the global war on terror, the courts have interpreted these actions as a part of a grander scheme of logistical subterfuge to evade law enforcement until they mobilize their terrorist plans.[109] By interpreting the young men's desire to depose Assad and alleviate the suffering of Muslims as driven by Salafi/jihadi ideology, the court scrutinized every aspect of their behavior in relation to the perceived conspiracy to engage in "extraordinary violence."

Given this theory of the case, the defense offered an alternative framework to understand the Syrian war, the role of rebel groups, and the young men's desires to depose Assad. Mohamed Farah's defense attorney argued that his client "believed he was pursuing just causes, such as the protection of innocent Syrians being attacked by a ruthless dictator."[110] Guled Omar's defense attorney similarly asserted that the defendants did not seek to "influence the conduct of the governments of Syria or Iraq"; instead, "the Defendants' principal motivations, viewed most favorably to the Government, were to join a religious struggle against an Islamic sect or, more generously, to safeguard and protect Sunni Muslims in the Middle East."[111] The defense attorneys argued that their clients tried to travel to Syria to "safeguard and protect" Muslims subjected to Assad's atrocities rather than to engage in terrorism or Salafi jihadism. The prosecution, however, challenged this framing, describing these humanitarian statements as "just more lies from the defendant."[112] Here, the prosecution and the defense competed to assert a particular geopolitical understanding of the Syrian war, and consequently a specific interpretation of the defendants' actions and intentions.

In Mohamed Farah's sentencing hearing, Judge Davis generally adopted the prosecution's position, ultimately concluding that "there was a terrorist cell in Minneapolis of more than nine people that were dedicated to the Jihadi ideology of ISIL or the Islamic State, that the— you and your co-conspirators tried to fake it until you could make it."[113] Judge Davis also addressed Somali Minnesotans from the bench, observing that "this community has to understand there's a Jihadist cell in this community. Its tentacles spread out. Young people went to Syria and died. . . . There's no denying there's a Jihadist cell. You might want to publicize that these are just young kids that are misguided, but the Court is thankful that there was a trial so all the evidence could come out. It is on the record. There's no denying it."[114] Judge Davis concluded that the "young kids" were driven by the "Jihadi ideology of ISIL," a determination that refused to take seriously the humanitarian suffering inflicted by the Assad regime, the use of lethal force by state militaries to depose the authoritarian ruler, the rapidly shifting alliances between rebel groups, and the role of the FBI's undercover informant, Bashir, in the sting operation. Interpreting failed attempts to travel to Syria as a terroristic, not political or humanitarian, effort driven by Salafi/jihadi ideology, Judge Davis sentenced Mohamed Farah to thirty years in prison, followed by a lifetime of supervised release.

The way Judge Davis approached these cases illustrates how competing geopolitical scripts inform how the courts interpret defendants' (nonviolent) actions and thus shape sentencing decisions. Although defense attorneys offered a nuanced understanding of why pious young men might seek to depose Assad, Judge Davis ultimately interpreted their plans as expressions of "the Jihadi ideology of ISIL" defined by "sadism" and "murderous violence." Reflecting on the cases, Judge Davis provocatively observed, "This was a terrorist cell. Everyone's danced around it. Let's talk about what happened here. We had a number of individuals, between 9 and 20, that were involved in a Jihadist ideology."[115] Although none of the nine young men traveled to Syria, took up arms, or committed an act of violence, each received a long prison term, even as the U.S. military continued to fund and support covert and overt operations to depose Assad through alliances with a "bewildering array of foreign jihadists" and "warlords" (Whitlock 2019). The young men's long prison terms, however, do little to disrupt the historical, social, and geopolitical contexts in which violence circulates, from military interventions to colonial occupations to despotic regimes.

"Why Didn't You Go Join al-Shabaab?": Geopolitical Incoherence and the Courts

Despite Judge Davis's emphatic statements and subsequent sentencing of the young men, court transcripts also reveal a more confused and often chaotic understanding of the geopolitical contexts surrounding these "ISIS trials." In Zacharia Abdurahman's sentencing hearing, Judge Davis questioned why Abdurahman tried to join ISIS, rather than al-Shabaab, ultimately assuming that every designated foreign terrorist organization operated under the same jihadi ideology and therefore worked toward the same murderous ends. Dismissing the differing political orientations of these rebel groups and the variable material conditions in which they operated, Judge Davis reduced the Syrian war and Somali civil war to the "slaughter of human beings, all in the name of a religion, a Jihadi religion."[116] Rather than use the differences between and within al-Shabaab and ISIS as evidence that rebel forces respond to different political conditions and work toward disparate geopolitical goals irreducible to a unifying jihadi ideology, Judge Davis merely viewed al-Shabaab and ISIS as interchangeable: Abdurahman could fight for either simply by mobilizing the same ideological framework.[117]

Given this understanding of armed militias, Judge Davis questioned Abdurahman's failed allegiance to his "parents' homeland" and cast suspicion on his motivations for traveling to Syria. Despite the ongoing U.S.-led military operations aimed at ousting Assad and the shifts in al-Shabaab's political aspirations and military tactics, Judge Davis interpreted Abdurahman's actions as mere expressions of jihadi ideology rather than the active pursuit of a geopolitical agenda aligned with the geostrategic interests of the United States. Abdurahman therefore struggled to respond to the judge's fraught understandings of the Syrian context and the young men's desire to depose Assad, as the following exchange illustrates.

> JUDGE DAVIS: I have some intelligence, so let's talk about these dots. You say you were concerned about Syria, but your parents fled Somalia, right?
>
> ABDURAHMAN: Yes, Your Honor.
>
> JUDGE DAVIS: And there's been a Civil War going on in Somalia since, what, 1992 and before, right?
>
> ABDURAHMAN: Yes, Your Honor.
>
> JUDGE DAVIS: That's your parents' homeland, right?
>
> ABDURAHMAN: Yes, Your Honor.
>
> JUDGE DAVIS: There are suicide bombers killing other Somalis in Somalia, right?
>
> ABDURAHMAN: Yes, Your Honor.
>
> JUDGE DAVIS: And we've had a group of Somali Americans right from this community go over and try and join al-Shabaab. Did you know that?
>
> ABDURAHMAN: Yes, Your Honor. Yes, I do.
>
> JUDGE DAVIS: Why didn't you go join al-Shabaab?
>
> ABDURAHMAN: Your Honor, I did not relate to them. There's— there was no way I would go out and seek al-Shabaab videos out.
>
> JUDGE DAVIS: Why not?
>
> ABDURAHMAN: Because I did not believe at that time for what they stood for.

JUDGE DAVIS: And what did you think they stood for?

ABDURAHMAN: I believed that they were not doing a legitimate struggle. It had—it had—it was just Somalis versus Somalis. It was—they was just doing something that was—that was—that was just out of touch. It did not make no sense to me.

JUDGE DAVIS: Well, let's back up here. Al-Shabaab pledged allegiance to al-Qaeda? Is that right? Do you know that?

ABDURAHMAN: Yes. Yes, sir.

JUDGE DAVIS: And you know that al-Shabaab believes in strict interpretation of Sharia law?

ABDURAHMAN: Yes, Your Honor.

JUDGE DAVIS: And you know that ISIL or Islamic State believes in strict conservative interpretation of Sharia law, right?

ABDURAHMAN: Yes, Your Honor.

JUDGE DAVIS: So, what's the difference?

ABDURAHMAN: Your Honor, the best way I could explain it is that the reach that ISIL had al-Shabaab did not have. The influence that they had, the propaganda they had, none of that was attractive to somebody like me.[118]

In this exchange, Abdurahman diligently worked to refute the judge's narrow interpretation of his actions and the geopolitical contexts that informed these actions. Despite earlier efforts to explain his desire to respond to the "atrocities" committed against Sunnis in Syria and his understanding of ISIS's "execution videos or videos of battle warfare" as "a retribution to what the regime and what these people are doing," Abdurahman reluctantly conceded that ISIS propaganda ultimately influenced his actions.

Through this questioning, Judge Davis sought to fit Abdurrahman's actions into frames of analysis already available to him, namely that the current world order privileges the (arguably secular) citizen-soldier and discourages fighting in "other people's wars" (Li 2020, 4). Because al-Shabaab seemingly subscribed to the same jihadi ideology as ISIS, Judge Davis questioned why Abdurahman discussed joining ISIS in Syria rather than committing to fight in Somalia, given his filial ties to the land. Judge Davis's inquiry reflects a kind of methodological nationalism that makes it impossible to understand individuals like Abdurahman who participate, or seek to participate, in transnational armed struggles, even as U.S. soldiers regularly contribute to military campaigns across borders, languages, and political ideologies, and as the international community recognized European "war volunteers"—who traveled to Ukraine to militarily contest Russia's 2022 invasion—as lawful foreign fighters (Li 2020; Horton, Nakhlawi, and Mekhennet 2022). In fact, Abdurahman never evoked the underlying assumption in Judge Davis's evaluation—that he sought to establish an Islamic state with strict adherence to Sharia law—and instead asserted a desire to protect fellow Muslims from Assad's murderous drive. Such analyses, however, proved unintelligible to Judge Davis, who reached for readily available narratives to interpret and evaluate Abdurahman's actions, his morality, and ultimately his criminality. Prevailing geopolitical imaginations therefore have undertaken important conceptual work by narrowing the ways the courts understand, interpret, and respond to the actions of the defendants before them. Even when defendants like Abdurahman cited the protection of Muslims as a motivating factor in their efforts to join the Syrian war, the courts often have reduced these political goals to the fanatical expression of a unifying and unified jihadi ideology and a corresponding desire to establish a "worldwide caliphate," making al-Shabaab and ISIS interchangeable groups.

During his sentencing hearing, Abdurahman negotiated the court's reduction of regional geopolitics to expressions of religious fanaticism, which meant that his responses to Judge Davis needed to conform to dominant understandings of jihadi ideology and ignore the broader political struggles that have shaped the Syrian war. Emblematic of how "primary definers" set the terms of the debate, Abdurahman needed to organize his defense around the "definitions of the powerful," meaning the expertise circulated by terrorologists, like Koehler, imbued with epistemic authority by the courts (Hall et al. 1978, 57). Even when aligned with the United States' own geopolitical goals and consonant with its military operations, the concept of engaging in an armed conflict outside of the model of the citizen-soldier was unintelligible to the court and thus an ineffective explanatory defense. In this view, al-Shabaab, al-Qaeda, and ISIS pursued the same goals, used the same tactics, and engaged the same political ideology; Abdurahman's analysis needed to fit this interpretive frame to effectively argue his case.

Judge Davis continued to reach for dominant geopolitical frameworks that reduced extrastate political violence to an irrational sectarian conflict mired in religious fanaticism, ignoring the deeper historical struggles for state power and territorial control. When Judge Davis sought to understand how, in his estimation, Abdurahman came to "hate" Shia Muslims "so much that [he] could kill them and not think of them as being human just because they were Shias," Abdurahman worked to place the Syrian war in a broader geopolitical context:

> Your Honor, when I—when I started—when this whole conspiracy started, I seen Shias mass killing Sunnis and carrying sectarian flags. This was no ordinary war. This was a war of creed. This was a war, to me, at that time, belief and unbelief, a war between pure and evil. I looked at Syria, it's mostly a Sunni country with a Shia dictator. Most of the casualties and people dying were Sunni. Most of the refugees fleeing that country were Sunni. I looked at Iraq, it was the same thing.

When Judge Davis interjected to say, "Well, I think some people would disagree that Assad is Shia," Abdurahman further explained:

> Me, personally, I knew that I believed that Assad was a Shia because he belonged to a minority sect in Syria and who had mercenaries hired from different Shia countries, like Lebanon, Iran, and this was all evident. Now, I cannot justify the reasons why, why I believe that their killing was lawful . . . but everybody in the world knows that the situation in Syria is very grave and that people are dying.[119]

Rather than engage Abdurahman's discussion of the Syrian war, its transcendence of conventional borders, or the Assad regime's strategic use of sectarianization to maintain power, Judge Davis returned to his earlier interpretation that both al-Shabaab and ISIS shared the same jihadist ideology—and by inference the same political goals—when he observed, "People are dying in—have been dying in Somalia." Satisfied with his understanding of the broader geopolitical context and the defendant's behavior within it, Judge Davis then pointedly asked Abdurahman, "You agree that you were a terrorist?" By collapsing al-Shabaab and ISIS into a single frame of analysis and erasing the Assad regime's brutality, Judge Davis's geopolitical reasoning reinforced the state's monopoly on violence, reaffirmed that radical beliefs like jihadist ideology facilitated the turn to violence, and rearticulated the specter of a globally threatening militant Islam.

Conclusion: Waging Offensive Lawfare and Misunderstanding Political Violence

The harsh sentencing of the Minneapolis boys illustrates how the activation of particular constellations of geographic knowledge have material consequences for defendants and their families, especially when judges view their courtrooms as key sites to "incapacitate terrorists." Judge Davis's adjudication of the "ISIS trials" aligns with some legal scholars and military strategists who view the courts as a counterterrorism tool critical to winning the global war on terror. For example, legal scholar Mary B. McCord (2017) argues that "prosecution in an Article III federal court is not just an option to [take custody of an enemy combatant], it has been the most successful long-term option since 9/11." Colonel Mark W. Holzer (2012) similarly advocates for the use of offensive lawfare in the global war on terror, including legal efforts "to deny enemy forces sanctuary, to blunt their abuse of courts, and to use both foreign and domestic courts to better support our national security strategy." For Holzer, the courts serve as an important "battlespace" of "21st century warfare," particularly by targeting communities viewed as representative of the nation's foreign enemies. Rather than rely solely on military tribunals to detain "enemy combatants," military strategists and legal experts have advocated for the use of criminal sentencing in federal courts to serve "conflict-related aims" (Skinner 2013, 311).

Within and through domestic courts, concepts like jihad are "made meaningful in distinctively legal ways" to advance the global war on terror (Delaney 2015, 98). Such concept-work articulates with broader processes of anti-Muslim racism, which "involve, among other things, the depoliticization of Muslim opposition to empire, a culturalist naturalizing of conflict between 'Islam' and the 'West,' and a dehumanizing legitimization of violence against Muslims, producing a vast death toll in Afghanistan, Iraq, Pakistan, Palestine, Somalia, Yemen, and elsewhere" (Kundnani 2017, 35). As a "lay ideology" that furnishes a "common sense" explanatory framework that displaces "political antagonisms onto the plane of culture" (Kundnani 2016, 1), Islamophobia "pervades legal institutions and enactments" (Beydoun and Choudhury 2020, 7). For example, in sentencing Guled Omar on terrorism-related charges, including conspiracy to commit murder abroad, Judge Davis adopted the prosecution's position that although Omar never developed an actual plot to commit murder and never traveled to Syria, talk of "joining a violent organization like ISIL inherently involved a willingness and intent to commit murder on ISIL's behalf."[120] Such an observation emptied Omar's conversations of their political content, obscured the material conditions that incited armed resistance in Syria, and blamed religious beliefs for expressions of transnational solidarity with besieged Muslims and for outrage over ongoing military interventions, colonial incursions, and despotic regimes.

For Judge Davis, Omar "believed in and may still believe in the extremist, violent, and deadly Jihadist ideology of ISIL and the Islamic State, period"—a status that justified a thirty-five-year prison term. This determination aligned with prosecutors who provocatively concluded that "the defendant has blood on his hands, Your Honor. He's got blood on his hands from people he's helped get overseas who are dead."[121] Even though Omar never traveled to Syria and only discussed, with equivocation, a desire to fight Assad's brutal regime, Judge Davis determined that Omar's conversations demonstrated an intent to take human life. As this example illustrates, judges can come to inscribe Muslim defendants as terrorists in and through legal proceedings, an epistemic process with material effects: stigmatization, alienation, and incarceration. Denied combatant immunity, Omar is serving a lengthy prison term, forever marked as a terrorist with a "willingness and intent to commit murder."

In sensationalist news stories, local media captured the anguish of Omar's heartbroken mother, Fadumo Hussein, in the aftermath of her son's sentencing. She painfully explained, "I don't know who to talk to in my community. I don't know where to take my family anymore. I am asking for help from my people, no matter what" (qtd. in McEnroe 2015). These epistemic struggles are more than a legal exercise; they directly shape the lives of defendants and their families, who must grieve the loss of their loved ones to long prison terms and manage the stigma and alienation that terrorism convictions produce.

Judge Davis's characterization of Omar's murderous intentions tracks with legal trends that punish different acts similarly, often in conflict with other legal conclusions that there are degrees of terrorism. In *United States v. Tarik Shah* (2007), for example, the defendant was charged with and convicted of terrorism-related crimes for seeking, unsuccessfully, to provide medical services to al-Qaeda, after a sting operation. In *United States v. Mohamed Warsame* (2009), the prosecution charged the defendant with providing material to support to a designated foreign terrorist organization after offering English-language lessons at an al-Qaeda clinic in Afghanistan so that nurses could read English medicine labels.[122] Judge John R. Tunheim observed that these English-language lessons had "direct application to an FTO's terrorist activities, as it would likely speed the healing and eventual return of militants to al-Qaeda training camps." Although the court found "nothing that adequately demonstrates that Warsame was part of a specific plot against the United States, and very little that suggests he was especially useful to al-Qaeda," the defendant still faced a ninety-two-month prison term—a downward departure from the recommended 180-month punishment under the Sentencing Guidelines. Through sentencing decisions that criminalize and harshly punish even the provision of humanitarian aid and medical services, the courts "act as partners with the executive [branch] in advancing the global war on terror" (Skinner 2013, 365).

Despite these legal trends, judges have discretionary power to depart downward in sentencing a defendant, particularly if the Criminal History Category overrepresents the seriousness of their criminal history or likelihood of recidivism. Such discretion has created uneven sentencing outcomes for defendants convicted of terrorism-related crimes, although most still face long prison terms even when judges grant downward departures. In *United States v. Yassin Aref,* Judge Thomas McAvoy opted to depart downward at sentencing. Convicted of terrorism-related charges related to his brokering of a loan between an FBI informant and struggling pizza shop owner Mohammed Hossain, Aref was sentenced to a fifteen-year prison term, the statutory maximum for § 18 U.S.C. 2339B offenses at the time—significantly less than the recommended sentencing range of 292 to 365 months, even though judges have the power to impose the statutory maximum for each count and order the sentences to run consecutively rather than concurrently to reach the recommended Guidelines range.[123] Judge McAvoy reasoned that the application of the terrorism enhancement would result in a Criminal History Category of VI, which "does substantially overrepresent the seriousness of the defendant's criminal history." Judge McAvoy further explained that

Aref "has no prior criminal history and received zero total criminal history points." Furthermore, "credible and reliable evidence indicates that Mr. Aref came to this country with his family, with a limited understanding of the English language, and provided for his family, until his arrest, through lawful employment in various capacities."[124] The *Aref* case illustrates how judicial discretion can, but usually does not, disrupt standard sentencing decisions as even downward departures result in long prison terms. In addition, cases like *Aref* "are the exception to the rule," as few cases result in a downward departure from the Sentencing Guidelines (Ahmed 2017, 1532n50).

Although judges can use their discretion to sentence defendants more leniently, appellate courts often overturn these decisions using language from *Meskini* (2003) that "even terrorists with no prior criminal behavior are unique among criminals in the likelihood of recidivism, the difficulty of rehabilitation, and the need for incapacitation," thus necessitating long prison terms. Despite this legal conclusion, both social science research and the experiences of defendants who completed their prison terms demonstrate that terrorist recidivism "is not a thing" (interview, November 2020). As a blunt instrument, this legal approach treats all terrorism defendants as posing the same national security threat, regardless of their individual conduct. Defense attorneys therefore have worked to disrupt this "monolithic concept of terrorism."

In a limited number of cases, however, judges refused to adopt dominant narratives about terrorism and rejected the impetus to mobilize their courts as default forums in the global war on terror. In the case against Asher Khan, Judge Hughes resisted applying the terrorism enhancement and sentenced the defendant to just eighteen months in prison and five years of supervised release. After the appellate court decided that Judge Hughes "committed a procedural error in concluding, as a matter of law, that the terrorism enhancement does not apply" and remanded the case, Judge Hughes resentenced Khan to an eighteen-month prison term. Such judicial decisions, however, remain an exception, as the "average ISIS sentence of 14.5 years more than triples the average federal sentence of 3.75 years," and the average sentence of those who go to trial (32.2 years) exceeds the average for those who pleaded guilty (11.2 years) in ISIS-related cases (Center on National Security 2017, 1, 4). Khan, after all, faced resentencing in front of a new judge after the appellate court ruled, on a second appeal, that Judge Hughes's sentence was "procedurally and substantively unreasonable"; Khan is now serving a twelve-year prison term.

As these cases demonstrate, judges have varied in their understandings of geopolitical struggles like the Syrian war, the relevance of these formative conditions in making sense of defendants' actions, and the conceptual frameworks organizing legal proceedings. Despite the state's desire to engage in offensive lawfare through the courts, how judges understand broader geopolitical contexts like the Syrian war have shaped their application of the terrorism enhancement, their ruling on combatant immunity motions, their conception of defendants' capacity for rehabilitation, and their sentencing decisions. The courts therefore remain contested sites where particular understandings of geopolitical contexts, world affairs, and armed struggles take shape and affect the decision-making of judges, prosecutors, and defense attorneys, even as they continue to incapacitate alleged terrorists, disrupt perceived terrorist financing, and create symbolic victories in the global war on terror. Although security professionals have sought to mobilize the domestic court system to "degrade Islamic extremist capabilities and activities," the variable outcomes of these cases demonstrate that the courts remain a contested space rather than a monolithic state institution with homogenous decision-making processes (Holzer 2012). Far from a blunt counterterrorism tool, the courts are sites of epistemic, legal, and geopolitical contestation.

This epistemic terrain has led to the uneven application of the terrorism enhancement and therefore variable sentencing decisions. Because judicial geopolitical reasoning shapes legal outcomes, defense attorneys and prosecutors alike have used the legal tools available to them to assert competing constellations of geographic knowledge that can inform how judges interpret the cases before them, such as infusing Islamic concepts and Arabic vocabularies like jihad, hijrah, and Salafism with predictive meaning. In this way, legal arguments often articulate with imperial ideologies through which "cultural or religious differences become sufficient explanation for exclusion, and, with the fetishization of marginality, a surrogate for politics" (Kundnani 2016, 6). The courts therefore serve as critical sites of contestation where such geopolitical imaginations are debated, reinterpreted, and struggled over.

Evident in Judge Davis's description of Guled Omar as a "hardcore al-Shabaab extremist," the invocation of racialized concepts like Salafi-jihadism and the reduction of political violence to individual pathologies illustrate the continuing presence of anti-Muslim racism in judicial sense-making and decision-making practices. Yet in her consideration of the Serbian siege on Bosnian Muslims, Judge Hall demonstrated that prevailing racial and geopolitical logics are not overdetermining in judicial opinions, as judges can reach for alternative conceptual frameworks to understand the factual evidence in the cases before them. By locating Babar Ahmad's online publications in the context of the Bosnian war, Judge Hall viewed incarceration as an insufficient response to terrorism crimes enacted in the face of ethnic cleansing while still imposing a 150-month sentence. Juxtaposing Judge Davis's and Judge Hall's reasoning demonstrates that how we understand political violence necessarily shapes what we view as appropriate responses to that violence. Such judicial sense making therefore illustrates the need to develop a more capacious abolitionist imaginary that reckons with the figure of the terrorist; takes seriously the relationship between power, politics, and violence; integrates an analysis of war and empire; and challenges essentializing narratives reducing armed struggles to cultural, theological, and/or psychological perversions putatively inherent in Islamic faith and Arab culture. A critical understanding of the relationship between power, politics, and violence clarifies how the courts, and the broader criminal-legal system, cannot attend to the underlying relations of force, material conditions, and geopolitical contexts that incite armed resistance; they also cannot undo the structural racism organizing the law and its enforcement. Considering the experiences of Guled Omar, Babar Ahmad, and al-Qaeda fighters, the figure of the terrorist reaffirms the urgent necessity to dismantle prevailing military-carceral modalities and integrate an anti-imperialist analysis into abolitionist struggles by attending to the root causes of political violence.

As carceral states, empires have long used the courts to police the boundaries of racial belonging, expand colonial enterprises, and reinforce sovereign power, as in court rulings during the Naturalization Era. As a colonial project, the global war on terror similarly uses the criminal-legal system to reorganize Afghanistan and Iraq according to U.S. interests and to create new spaces primed for capitalist expansion. As one node in a broader carceral archipelago, domestic courtrooms can reinforce, challenge, and/or undermine these imperial aims by circulating dominant geopolitical narratives and their implicit racial logics that legitimize the global war on terror and its abusive systems, whether at Guantánamo Bay, Fallujah, or Minneapolis.

Despite popular struggles challenging anti-Muslim racism and its cascading effects—such as the indefinite detention and torture of Guantánamo detainees, the use of elaborate sting operations to ensnare otherwise law-abiding Muslims in criminal enterprises, and the criminalization of nonstate armed militants challenging repressive regimes in a world order defined by U.S. empire—the courts have relied on expert knowledge to understand the complicated facts and evidence raised in terrorism-related cases. As Koehler's testimony illustrates, the reliance on terrorism experts occludes other ways of knowing, understanding, and responding to political violence. Abolition therefore requires the elimination of the racial logics, imperial scripts, and primary definers that inform the production of hierarchies of personhood through the law. The next chapter therefore explores how expert knowledge has reinforced anti-Muslim tropes that narrow rather than expand how judges understand armed struggles, exemplifying the urgent need for new conceptual frameworks to make sense of political violence and imagine anti-imperial abolitionist futures for armed militants and their supporters.

4

TERROROLOGISTS
EPISTEMIC INJUSTICE IN TERRORISM PROSECUTIONS

IN CRIMINAL PROSECUTIONS, attorneys can call on expert witnesses to explain, contextualize, and analyze complicated facts and evidence for judges and jurors. Judges determine the admissibility of such testimony by evaluating the scientific rigor of the proposed expert witness's research using certain standards and rules of evidence. The *Daubert* test, for example, assesses whether the expert's testimony will be based on "scientifically valid reasoning" and will be properly applied to the facts at issue. As gatekeepers, judges decide which expert witnesses are qualified to testify and narrow the scope of their testimony. Since many terrorism cases have involved complicated facts, the courts have relied on terrorism scholars to help judges and jurors make sense of the evidence before them, such as the nature, structure, and methods of terrorist organizations.

Although the *Daubert* test provides a concrete method to evaluate potential expert witnesses, legal scholars argue that "in the terrorism prosecution, the government's expert can enjoy an informational advantage that the defense is hard pressed to challenge," even when terrorism scholars lack academic credentials, methodological training, and language fluency (Said 2015, 96). For example, in a 2014 *Daubert* hearing to evaluate the admissibility of proposed expert witnesses, Judge Mary Scriven queried the credentials of terrorologist Evan Kohlmann. Kohlmann's expertise focuses on the development of a list of characteristics that make up the terrorist profile, such as subscribing to al-Qaeda in the Arabian

Peninsula's *Inspire* magazine. According to Kohlmann, if a person exhibits more than one of these characteristics, then it is likely that the person is a "violent extremist" or "homegrown terrorist." In evaluating Kohlmann's credentials, Judge Scriven observed, "It's been determined by at least one Court that your work is not control tested or peer reviewed in the technical *Daubert* sense."[1] Indeed, Judge Scriven concluded that Kohlmann's research on the "factors or characteristics of a so-called homegrown terrorist," such as consuming terrorist propaganda, "are nothing other than the products of Mr. Kohlmann's analysis, personal analysis."[2] Judge Scriven further noted that "there's no scientific analysis associated with this, no peer review that's ever tested this evaluative notion that all of these factors as a confluence of factors establishes proof or even indicates homegrown terrorism exists in an individual."[3] Using the *Daubert* test to inform her evaluation, Judge Scriven questioned the methodological rigor of Kohlmann's research.

Despite Judge Scriven's hesitations, the prosecution argued that the court could not understand the testimony of undercover FBI agents about the defendant's adherence to the "countersurveillance" instructions outlined in *Inspire,* such as using different cell phones to evade law enforcement, without "someone like Mr. Kohlmann testify[ing] that these are things that are specifically preached to individuals who adhere to Islamic radicalism."[4] Despite her misgivings about Kohlmann's credentials, Judge Scriven determined that such countersurveillance met one of Kohlmann's factors indicating a homegrown terrorist. Although Judge Scriven observed that this factor "doesn't really exist in any other world other than Mr. Kohlmann's world," she determined that, as to "the ultimate factual issues and how they tie back to the literature, I think he's perfectly competent to testify."[5] Even though much of Kohlmann's research failed to engage "any scientific analysis" and did not meet the basic *Daubert* standard of peer review, Judge Scriven permitted Kohlmann to testify. Such a determination aligned with prosecutors who viewed the inclusion of this expert testimony as a necessary step to help the court understand the evidence before it.

Across the United States, judges have relied on self-identified terrorism experts like Kohlmann to inform their decision-making. In doing so, judges have conferred epistemic authority onto such experts as they produce and share knowledge about terrorism in court proceedings.

Terrorism experts therefore have served as key actors in the adjudication of terrorism-related cases by offering the frameworks through which judges and jurors come to understand the cases before them.

Despite this judicial trend, social scientists have questioned the credentials of terrorism experts, the validity of their research, and their allegiances to powerful institutions, including police, military, and intelligence agencies. In fact, one defense attorney reported that in addition to Kohlmann, "there's a couple of other guys who are cultivated within the law enforcement community to be experts because they can't get a real academic to be as strident and monochromal as [Kohlmann]" (interview, November 2020). In this view, the law enforcement community "cultivates" or "grows" its own experts because other academics refuse to testify in such a narrow and scientifically specious way (Yang 2010). To better understand how terrorologists have shaped the adjudication of terrorism-related cases and the epistemic issues such practices raise, this chapter investigates the emergence of terrorism studies, the influence of the government on its development, and the use of terrorism expertise in the courtroom. The courts legitimize, circulate, and consume "orthodox terrorism expertise" as they make sense of the factual evidence in terrorism-related cases (Miller and Mills 2009). Because orthodox approaches to the study of terrorism abstract political violence from its formative conditions, the use of such expertise narrows how terrorism is made knowable in domestic courtrooms and strategically shapes how judges and jurors understand defendants (Reid 1997; Burnett and Whyte 2005; Stampnitzky 2011; Miller and Mills 2009). Drawing from "technocratic assessments that are of use to powerful state and corporate agents," such expert testimony offers a coherent grand narrative to secure convictions and normalize harsh sentencing (Burnett and Whyte 2005, 13).

By endorsing these experts as the authority on terrorism, the courts commit a distinctly epistemic type of injustice by denying defendants their credibility and capacity as knowers of their own lives and the political contexts in which they operate. Uncorroborated by terrorism experts, defendants' interpretations of their actions and experiences have been dismissed as "a series of lies," as immaterial to court proceedings, or as beyond the comprehension of the court.[6] This chapter examines how such forms of epistemic injustice have shaped the adjudication of terrorism-related cases and limited how the general public has come to understand these alleged crimes.

Terrorism Studies: Establishing a New Field of Expertise

In her groundbreaking study on the "invention of terrorism and the rise of the terrorism expert," sociologist Lisa Stampnitzky (2013) documents how the massacre at the 1972 Munich Olympics facilitated the establishment of terrorism as a new object of study (21). During the Olympics, eight members of the Palestinian political organization Black September kidnapped Israeli athletes and demanded the release of 236 political prisoners held in Israel and West Germany. An ensuing rescue effort led to the killing of all eleven hostages and eight Black September members. Hundreds of journalists contributed to the first televised crisis broadcast globally; media reports described Palestinian political violence as an act of terrorism. After the televised events at Munich, "terrorism began to take shape as a problem in the public sphere and as an object of expert knowledge" (Stampnitzky 2013, 23). Although hostage taking and airline hijackings occurred throughout the 1950s and 1960s, the Munich Olympics ushered in a new problem to be studied, understood, and addressed: terrorism.

During the 1970s, the concept of terrorism took shape through the work of an increasing number of self-styled experts who conducted research studies, offered media commentary, provided court testimony, and consulted on the development of antiterrorism strategies in the United States. Although terrorism is a deeply contested and unstable concept, it has become the dominant framework for understanding and responding to purportedly illegitimate political violence waged by nonstate actors since the 1970s. In this way, terrorism emerged as a phenomenon that could be made knowable and thus managed.

To support the emergent field of terrorism studies in the United States after the Munich Olympics, the federal government provided substantial funding for scholars conducting terrorism-related research. It also contracted think tanks to carry out specific research projects and helped disseminate key findings through new industry- and academic-oriented conferences and journals. For example, in 1972, the government contracted the Rand Corporation to conduct policy-oriented research on international terrorism, which led to the development of a controversial terrorism database and establishment of empirical evidence to "justify the increased use of force, rather than negotiations, to end hostage episodes" (Reid 1997, 103).

Rand is a nonprofit organization with origins in the U.S. Army Air Forces, federal funding earmarked for terrorism-related studies, and administrators like Defense Secretary Donald Rumsfeld with professional ties to the military and political elite. Given these origins, Rand's terrorism-related research has "developed within institutions (such as the police, the security services, private corporations, and so on) which are neither neutral or impartial on the question of how political violence is defined or framed" (Miller and Mills 2009, 422). Rand's terrorism database, for example, "explicitly excludes acts of state terror committed by any government against its own citizens, and acts of violence occurring in war or war-like situations" while also including "non-violent activities and protests against state violence" (Burnett and Whyte 2005, 10). Rand's database plays a critical role in defining what acts constitute terrorism, ultimately protecting the state's monopoly on legitimate violence. As Rand's contracted work illustrates, federal funding and political priorities shaped the initial development of the field of terrorism studies by narrowing the types of research questions selected, the methodologies employed, and the definitions of terrorism mobilized to fit the hegemonic imperatives of policy makers and governing institutions.

After the September 11 attacks, the federal government again "tried to stimulate research through a dramatic rise in funding of terrorism research," which led to a "rush of newcomers into the field," most of whom still lacked training in the scientific method (Sageman 2014b, 566). Similar to the previous era, federal funding for terrorism research typically "reflected policy makers' narrow concerns, based on lay assumptions and understandings of the 9/11 terrorists" (566). The injection of federal funds into the field incentivized scholars to develop research studies according to the agendas of grant-awarding bodies and to "uncritically adopt the perspectives and values of policymakers" (Jackson, Gunning, and Smyth 2007, 14). In addition to this federal funding, "hardline supporters of Israel's quest to extend its reach into Palestinian territories" have further "subsidized" and "bankrolled" this federally funded "Islamophobia industry," as "the threat of Islam and Muslims creates an atmosphere of less resistance for their policies against Palestinians" (Lean 2012, 11). Although a "critical turn to the normative discipline of terrorism has mushroomed since the events of 9/11, dominant knowledge production of terrorism research remains founded, to a large extent, on positivist problem-solving theory which renders 'terrorism experts' being too closely linked to, or employed by, government organizations that reinforce (positivist) orthodox terrorism conceptualizations" (Al-Kassimi 2019, 2). These analyses highlight the troubling relationship between imperial exigencies and knowledge production processes; in the context of U.S. empire, power and politics have shaped how self-styled experts have made terrorism knowable.

Social scientists argue that the relationship between terrorism studies and the federal government has politicized this line of research, transforming the pursuit of new knowledge into an exercise in justifying, legitimizing, and advancing state interests. As neither "a purely political or a purely analytical concept," expert discourse on terrorism "exists in an interstitial space between the realms of politics and science," particularly given the field's "origins as an adjunct to the developing counterterrorism apparatus of the state" (Stampnitzky 2011, 7). Furthermore, the adoption of a "problem-solving" approach to the study of terrorism "implies that its referent object is state-centric" and therefore "takes security to mean the security of the state, rather than that of the individual" (Al-Kassimi 2019, 4). The federal funding and prioritization of terrorism research have shaped the development of the field by encouraging untrained enthusiasts to undertake research studies primarily focused on nonstate actors who commit acts of violence against Western societies and to limit the types of data and methodologies used to understand political violence (Reid 1997; Miller and Mills 2009).

In addition to the influence of these institutional arrangements on terrorism-related research, the field often functions as a closed network or "invisible college" of "interconnected public terror experts whose views are strikingly similar and whose activities are linked to state and corporate priorities" (Miller and Mills 2009, 425). Terrorologists themselves have referred to this "core group at the center of the emerging terrorism studies world" as the "terrorism mafia," although such members constitute only a small percentage of the overall field (Stampnitzky 2013, 42). This core of terrorism scholars is "intimately connected—

institutionally, financially, politically, and ideologically—with a state hegemonic project," which "has serious implications for the integrity and independence of research on terrorism" (Jackson, Gunning, and Smyth 2007, 8). Li (2015) similarly contends that "the field's intimate relationship with the national security state has left it without the autonomy needed to develop into a serious intellectual project" (15).

The consumers of such terrorism research consist primarily of the public and the state, rather than the scientific community that tests, verifies, and challenges knowledge production processes. Given the state's commitment to counterterrorism operations, it has served as both the "primary *sponsor* of knowledge-production" as well as the "primary *consumer* of research" (Stampnitzky 2011, 7). This means that new findings within terrorism studies "are not debated in the academy in a collegial way, but on television and the Internet as arguments to advance political agendas" such that "the voice of true scholars is drowned in this hysterical cacophony of political true believers" (Sageman 2014b, 566). Given the field's character as an invisible college and its ties to the political elite, terrorism studies operates at the nexus of converging interests, including the military, the media, and state institutions like the criminal-legal system and intelligence agencies.

Despite the primacy of these terrorism researchers in the policy arena and in domestic courtrooms, social scientists have identified serious methodological limitations in this scholarship, noting how many academic publications are "written by people who have never met a terrorist, or have never actually spent significant time on the ground in the areas most affected by conflict" (O'Leary and Silke 2007, 393). Andrew Silke (2004) reports, "Due to reasons of personal safety, political sensitivity, and perceived methodological difficulty, researchers have largely shied away from action and actor-based research, largely leaving those topics to a handful of individuals who encounter the terrorists as part of their professional work and for whom research is both a peripheral and generally sporadic activity (for example, prison psychiatrists)" (9). Rather than interview or collaborate with individuals labeled as terrorists, researchers primarily use secondary sources, which inevitably results in "a very lopsided literature which says surprisingly little on some very important aspects of the subject" (9). Given their lack of language training, inexperience in non-Western contexts, and limited access to the very actors they study, many terrorologists rely on English-language websites and press releases as their main sources of data (Li 2020, 34). Such methodological practices do not meet the academic standards for rigorous research and fail to center the voices of those involved in the very phenomenon researchers seek to understand. In the process, terrorism scholars often impose Western academic interpretations of political violence with a "morally condemnatory tone" while ignoring the historical, social, and geopolitical contexts in which such actions emerge (Jackson, Gunning, and Smyth 2007, 5).

Even when researchers conduct interviews with those allegedly involved in terrorism, their focus often narrows to individual pathologies, such as the "psychological factors that drive individual motivation, action, and decisional processes" (Horgan 2003, 31). This approach continues to abstract political violence from its formative conditions. In conducting these qualitative research studies, terrorism scholars have described how "disturbingly 'normal' most terrorists seem when one actually sits down and talks to them," after expecting to meet "wild-eyed fanatics or crazed killers" rather than "highly articulate and extremely thoughtful individuals" (Hoffman 1998, 7). Prominent terrorologist John Horgan (2003), for example, warns that it "can be more disturbing" to encounter a "terrorist" who is "no different in appearance and public behaviors than if an overly 'fanatical' person were sitting across from the interviewer" (47). In these cases, terrorism experts reveal their normative assumptions about the psychological, cultural, and theological pathologies implicit in their research, such that they are "struck" by the rationality, intelligence, and behavior of their "terrorist" interviewees (Hoffman 1998, 7). Such findings make terrorism seem even more frightening and unpredictable: Terrorists cannot be detected from the general public if they appear to be "normal" citizens instead of "wild-eyed fanatics." Unfortunately, terrorism scholars rarely engage in reflexive practices that critically examine how power relations shape the research encounter and the production of new knowledge.

Although many mainstream experts theorize terrorism as a "social and political process," they still study "terrorism and terrorists from criminological and psychological perspectives" by examining the motivations, pathologies, and actions of individual actors (Horgan 2003, 30–31). This approach typically denies the political dimensions of violence by treating the terrorist as the unit of analysis, thereby forgoing more complex analyses of the racialized world order defined by sovereign states and its articulation with the production of nonstate violence. Scholars, however, would never reduce U.S. soldiers who enlisted after the September 11 attacks to pathological fanatics duped by government propaganda. Such military mobilizations would be placed in the broader geopolitical context, such as the September 11 attacks. Terrorism studies often denies terrorists their status as political actors by reducing them to "wild-eyed fanatics or crazed killers."

Despite these methodological and conceptual limitations, the field has grown rapidly, as evidenced by the increasing number of research studies, conferences, academic journals, and think tanks on terrorism over the last fifty years. Even with this growth, scholars have yet to agree on a universal definition of terrorism, an elusive problem that has left the "focus of the field . . . scattered and fragmented" (Silke 2004, 4). Terrorism scholars today admit that their field remains woefully stagnant, undertheorized, and overly reliant on flawed methodologies and data sets (Sageman 2014b; Kundnani 2014; Stampnitzky 2011). Although scholars indict different sources for this incoherence, the field remains chaotic and largely dominated by self-styled experts who "are not versed in the scientific method, and often pursue a political agenda" (Sageman 2014b, 566). Terrorism studies has yet to cohere as a field of study organized around a central and stable concept of terrorism, and with institutional credentialing practices that regulate who counts as an expert.[7]

Terrorologists, however, have managed to establish, legitimize, and circulate a "homogenized grand narrative of terrorism (the 'new terrorism' thesis)" (Burnett and Whyte 2005, 2). To do so, a "small but highly influential group of experts" developed the new terrorism thesis, which the courts, media, and counterterrorism strategists have used to make sense of political violence (2). In the process, terrorologists have established new academic journals and mediated what constitutes rigorous research. For example, former Rand administrator Bruce Hoffman serves as editor in chief of *Studies in Conflict and Terrorism,* a prestigious academic journal established by another Rand administrator, George Tanham. Through the production of peer-reviewed academic articles, these journals validate, legitimize, and circulate the "new terrorism" thesis. Despite the field's incoherence, a small group of tightly networked, federally funded, and heavily publicized researchers dominate the public face of terrorism studies, ultimately serving as producers and arbiters of legitimate knowledge in the public arena. Even if terrorism scholars disagree on the very definition of terrorism, these anointed experts dictate how the U.S. public and powerful institutions like the criminal-legal system come to understand and respond to the problem of terrorism.

Through expert testimony, the theories supported by the government and advanced by elite researchers enter domestic courtrooms, informing how judges and jurors interpret the actions, beliefs, and behaviors of individuals charged with terrorism-related crimes. This expert testimony smooths over the field's incoherence, contradictions, and debates by presenting a single, unified understanding of terrorism as an irrational, unscrupulous, and incorrigible campaign of lethal violence waged by fanatics seeking to install a new world order according to their religious dogmatism. Terrorologists therefore have shaped how the courts understand and adjudicate terrorism-related crimes.

The New Terrorism Thesis:
Coherence in an Incoherent Field

In the 1990s, historian Walter Laqueur (1996, 1999) began developing a new framework for understanding "postmodern terrorism" or "new terrorism." Documenting the "changing face of terrorism," Laqueur (2006) identified a "new breed of terrorism" distinct from previous forms of terrorism enacted by "social revolutionaries driven to desperate actions by intolerable conditions, oppression, and tyranny" (48). Rather than pursue "clearly defined political demands," new terrorists intend to destroy society and eliminate entire communities (Laqueur 1999, 81). Laqueur distinguished "traditional terrorism" and its inherent political aims, such as "gaining independence, getting rid of foreigners, or establishing a new social order," from new terrorism's purported intent to "liquidate all satanic forces, which may include the majority of mankind, as a precondition for the growth of another, better, and in any case different breed of human life" (81). Given these murderous desires, "in its maddest, most extreme form, [new terrorism] may aim at the destruction of all life on earth, as the ultimate punishment for mankind's crimes" (81).

Laqueur concluded that a "pathological complexion" defined new terrorism and predicted that "political and ideological motivations in the traditional sense, however far-fetched, will recede" as "fanaticism" intensifies (226). In this view, new terrorists abandon the political pursuits of traditional terrorists and embrace indiscriminate violence to institute a new world order informed by their cultural, psychological, and theological pathologies. Despite disagreements within the field of terrorism studies, prominent terrorologists have established a coherent grand narrative through the new terrorism thesis, stabilizing popular understandings of and state responses to nonstate actors and organizations using violence to achieve specific political goals.

In this orthodox framework, new terrorism is defined by key features distinct from previous armed struggles, including: the perceived access to weapons of mass destruction trafficked through the "nuclear black market"; the seemingly indiscriminate and apocalyptic use of violence increasingly targeting civilian populations; and the erosion of the highly hierarchical organizational structures of terrorist groups (Laqueur 1999, 71). This thesis proposes that the indiscriminate, incorrigible, and intractable characteristics of new terrorism make it more difficult to contest and eliminate, ultimately authorizing more aggressive and more lethal counterterrorism operations to thwart this new threat.

Through the production of the new terrorism thesis and related theoretical frameworks, "the concept of terrorism became inherently associated with a moral judgment about the acts that we place in the category: terrorism *is* unacceptable violence" (Stampnitzky 2013, 8). President George W. Bush (2001a, 2001c) popularized this moral interpretation of terrorism by repeatedly referring to terrorists as "evildoers" driven by "evil plans." In a speech to the nation in the aftermath of the September 11 attacks, President Bush argued that these "evil people" have "no justification for their actions. There's no religious justification, there's no political justification. The only motivation is evil." The threat posed by such evil justified the use of "every means of diplomacy, every tool of intelligence, every instrument of law enforcement, every financial influence, and every necessary weapon of war—to the destruction and to the defeat of global terror network" (Bush 2001a). Osama bin Laden, however, reasoned that the men that God helped [commit the September 11 attacks] did not intend to kill babies; they intended to destroy the strongest military power in the world, to attack the Pentagon that houses more than sixty-four thousand employees, a military center that houses the strength and the military intelligence. The [Twin] Towers [were] an economic power and not a children's school or a residence. The general consensus is that those that were there were men that supported the biggest economic power in the world. They have to review their books. We treat others like they treat us. If they kill our women and our innocent people, we will kill their women and their innocent people. (qtd. in Alouni 2005, 200)

Bin Laden argued that the September 11 attacks targeted key sites of U.S. military and economic power as well as the electorate responsible for backing political leaders who authorize anti-Muslim aggression. Meanwhile, President Bush (2001c) celebrated a brutal military campaign in Afghanistan that would "make it more difficult for the terror network to train new recruits and coordinate their plans." In this framework, "when it is made knowable, the new terrorism—the mode and scale of attack, its indiscriminate targets and, crucially, its incorrigibility—constitutes a potential threat against which a proportionate response is justified" (Burnett and Whyte 2005, 6). As the new terrorism thesis popularized among policy makers and the public, it legitimized the use of "every necessary weapon of war" to ward off the threats posed by such immoral and undeterrable evildoers.

The apocalyptic possibility of weapons of mass destruction featured prominently in emerging terrorism research during the 1990s. During this time, "the terrorism research world seemed transfixed with the threat of terrorists using weapons of mass destruction," an agenda incentivized by an uptick in government funding for related research (Silke 2004, 24). Laqueur (1999) emphatically warned that "no matter how small the numbers of fanatics become, the dawning era in which weapons of mass destruction will be widely accessible could make them more dangerous than a much larger number of terrorists using the traditional tools of their trade" (155). The perceived threat of weapons of mass destruction have preoccupied military strategists, policy makers, and academics over the last thirty years, even though the United States

remains the only state actor that has waged nuclear warfare—twice—
and used other brutal weapons, such as Agent Orange, in its military
campaigns. This research primed the United States for President Bush's
(2003) false accusations that Iraq possessed "weapons of mass murder,"
which his administration used to justify its 2003 invasion to depose
Saddam Hussein and "disarm Iraq."

Terrorologists argue that the growing role of religious fundamentalism in armed conflicts has driven the turn to indiscriminate lethal
violence by new terrorists (Hoffman 1998). Although the use of weapons of mass destruction conflicted with the principles of old terrorism,
contemporary terrorist groups "may be ready to accept any degree of
destruction, even of itself, as justifiable," primarily because their "hate
and fanaticism are in some cases so deeply ingrained that they are willing to use any weapon, however barbaric" (Laqueur 1999, 81). In this
framework, the confluence of new terrorists' access to weapons of mass
destruction and religious fundamentalism made the prospect of "indiscriminate mass murder" imminently possible (81). Facilitated by anti-
Muslim tropes, the moral evaluation built into the concept of terrorism
facilitates these understandings of the seemingly inevitable and depraved
use of weapons of mass destruction by terrorists.

Terrorologists also contend that the hierarchical structure of terrorist organizations slowly devolved into highly decentralized groups
of transnational actors loosely bound by a common ideological imperative. In this view, "traditional militants were linked in tight, central-
ized, structured conspiracies," whereas new terrorists activated "diffuse
and decentralized networks" (Crenshaw 2000, 411). Defined by a "network of networks," al-Qaeda mobilizes a "global network of operational
cells, preparative cells, support cells, and affiliated groups" to "sustain its
global terror campaign on a number of fronts simultaneously" (Wilkinson 2007, 30). For terrorologists, this decentralized model is more dangerous because it is more difficult to manage and control than traditional
networks. This conceptualization of terrorism has legitimized an aggressive, military-driven approach mixed with a preventative mindset to
"find informants with inside information about terrorist plots so as to
stop any attacks coming to fruition" (Said 2015, 34). The United States
thus has focused on pursuing potential terrorists and terror cells domestically while waging war globally.

Drawing from this homogenized grand narrative of terrorism, prominent terrorologist Paul Wilkinson (2007) defined al-Qaeda as the "archetype of the new terrorism," given its "absolutist and grandiose ideology," "record of mass murder of civilians" fueled by a "high propensity" for "nuclear terrorist weaponry," and commitment to "recasting the entire international system" (29–30). Terrorologists therefore have made "new terrorists" knowable as more lethal and less discriminating violent actors with greater access to weapons of mass destruction. The explanatory power of this conceptualization of terrorism renders those marked as terrorists as illegitimate, barbaric, and immoral nonstate actors willing to inflict massive death and destruction to achieve their fanatical goals. In this way, "the language of terrorism and defeating 'the Muslim terrorist' has enabled Western states to hide and depoliticize histories of racial violence and contexts of imperialist profit-making which nonstate actors' attacks often respond to" (Manzoor-Khan 2022, 39). Through the recitation of this "monolithic concept of terrorism," the courts have played a central role in neutralizing and incapacitating terrorists, particularly "homegrown" or "lone wolf" actors, who threaten the current world order (interview, November 2020; see also Brown 2014).

For some terrorologists, the moral evaluation that organizes the new terrorism thesis strategically can delegitimize and discredit violent political actors, particularly by applying the terrorist label to individuals. Military historian Caleb Carr (2007) describes terrorism as "among mankind's most outrageously unacceptable belligerent practices, which include piracy, slavery, and genocide" and depends on a "cyclical pattern of atrocity, accusation, rationalization, recrimination, and revenge that has allowed the practice to remain alive" (48). Given this type of "outrageously unacceptable" violence, Carr contends that the terrorism label must do the conceptual and political work of delegitimizing such "belligerent" activity. Marking an individual actor as a terrorist effectively denies the political dimensions of their use of violence. This means that discrediting political violence is part of the aim of applying the terrorist label, a tactic often mobilized in the courts to delegitimize defendants, criminalize their actions, and justify harsh punishments.

The criminal-legal system has affirmed this framing of terrorism by empowering the courts to sentence individuals convicted of terrorism-related crimes to longer prison terms, a practice reflective of the seemingly exceptional, illegitimate, and grotesque nature of terrorist violence. In 1994, Congress asked the U.S. Sentencing Commission to amend its sentencing guidelines manual, which advises the courts on how to enhance the penalties in cases involving a federal crime of terrorism.[8] The manual now recommends that the courts make a victim-related adjustment to sentencing decisions for terrorism-related crimes, which tracks with the legal finding that "an act of terrorism represents a particularly grave threat because of the dangerousness of the crime and the difficulty of deterring and rehabilitating the criminal."[9] This means that "terrorists and their supporters should be incapacitated for a longer period of time."[10] The manual, and legal interpretations of it, adopts an orthodox approach to terrorism and terrorists: incorrigible, unscrupulous, and irredeemable.

Despite the field's incoherence, the new terrorism thesis has made terrorism knowable, with defining features such as the organizational structure of terrorist groups, the use of indiscriminate violence, the easy access to weapons of mass destruction, and the enduring commitment to religious fundamentalism. The new terrorism thesis strategically has shaped how the U.S. public, policy makers, and military planners understand terrorist threats and the possibilities for thwarting these threats. By offering a conceptual framework for understanding terrorist violence as "global, indiscriminate, and incorrigible," terrorologists have created a rationale for a new counterterrorism approach, including the "rapid expansion of antiterror policing resources and new policing powers, and their use against Muslims, asylum seekers, and protestors" (Burnett and Whyte 2005, 6). Sociologist James Petras (2006) provocatively argues that in advancing the new terrorism thesis, terrorologists may be "far from the killing fields," but "their spirit will be there, on the front lines and in the torture chambers, guiding the hands that place the hoods over the unredeemable nihilists, Muslims, Marxists, or national patriots" (158). Through his analysis of hundreds of publications by self-styled experts on terrorism and terrorists, Petras (2004) further contends that "the dehumanization process is central to the whole terrorist–political–academic enterprise for the purpose is to present 'the terrorist' with no redeeming features, with no 'place' in the world, no 'time' to exist; in other words, worthy of physical extermination." Critical scholars like Petras indict terrorologists as key operatives in the global war on terror as they provide the frameworks that justify military aggression, indefinite detention, preemptive prosecutions, torture, and blanket surveillance in the name of national security. The epistemic influence of terrorologists also has infiltrated domestic courts, where such experts have informed how judges and jurors understand the terrorism-related cases before them.

Terrorism Expertise and the Courts: Determining and Conferring Epistemic Authority

Legal scholar Wadie E. Said (2015) reports, "In prosecutions with complicated facts, the use of an expert witness allows a party to explain and contextualize its arguments, because an expert may provide an opinion and analysis of the evidence, something a lay witness may not do" (96). In terrorism-related cases, terrorologists like Rohan Gunaratna, Rita Katz, Daniel Koehler, Evan Kohlmann, Matthew Levitt, and Marc Sageman have been called on to provide judges and jurors with contextual information about terrorism and terrorist organizations. Expert testimony can inform how the courts interpret defendants' actions, behaviors, and ideologies.

Given the complexity of terrorism-related cases, the courts often conferred epistemic authority onto terrorologists, but without interrogating their testimony. For example, in the *Daubert* hearing I mentioned at this chapter's outset, Judge Scriven determined that Kohlmann's expert testimony could "assist the jury in understanding certain terms they may be unfamiliar with in the context of this case, including *Kuffar, Jihad, Takfiri, [Hijrah]*."[11] During the court's evaluation of the admissibility of this expert testimony, Kohlmann explained that "Salafi-Jihadis and Takfiris is basically almost the same thing. Sorry, Takfiris is T-A-K-F-I-R-I-S." Rather than evaluate the veracity of such an assertation, the judge readily accepted the expert's testimony on Takfiris, admitting, "I can't even say it."[12] Given the judicial deference to such expert witnesses on the intricate and often complex details of political violence—typically contested, rather than settled, knowledge—the courts have admitted such testimony "without any real scrutiny" (Goodman 2010a, 670). Although social scientists and legal scholars have documented how these experts contribute to and profit from the "cottage industry" of terrorism studies (Stampnitzky 2013; Li 2020; German 2013; Patel 2011; Kundnani 2014; Said 2015; Goodman 2010a), self-styled terrorologists maintained epistemic authority in the courtroom. When judges and jurors cannot even pronounce the names of groups or concepts under discussion, they can concede interpretive authority to terrorism experts—a deference that narrows the possible analyses offered and understood in court.

Despite such judicial deference, scholars have questioned the expert status of terrorologists. Unlike other academic disciplines, "no licensing body exists to certify 'proper' expertise, and there is no agreement among terrorism experts about what constitutes useful knowledge" (Stampnitzky 2013, 12–13). In fact, "there are few barriers to entry," which means that "a high proportion of those writing on the topic have no significant background in the topic" such that even "experts themselves have complained that the field is filled with 'self-proclaimed experts'" (Stampnitzky 2011, 6). Furthermore, terrorologists who subscribe to the dominant state narrative about terrorism—that the United States is at war with irrational, evil, and incorrigible fanatics opposed to Western values—have enjoyed more media attention and have featured more prominently in terrorism-related court cases, even when less frequently cited than other scholars with more credentials, training, and publications (Burnett and Whyte 2005; Stampnitzky 2013; Miller and Mills 2009). In fact, a defense attorney reported that at one terrorism trial, "there was a guy who was a government expert who acknowledged, 'Yes, there are wars of liberation and then there's terrorism.' And those guys have never been used again! Because they give too much ground, and they give ground because it's true" (interview, November 2020). Prosecutors expect terrorologists "not to give ground," even though "real experts, real academics with integrity" provide a more nuanced understanding of political violence (interview, November 2020). Unfortunately, research shows that experts whose "ideological lineage, academic approach, connections, and practice is firmly within the military-industrial-academic complex" dominate the field (Miller and Mills 2009, 423).

Given the current state of the field, the hierarchical status of terrorism experts is not always determined by the rigor or sophistication of their research but rather by the extent to which they subscribe to and confirm the state's global war on terror agenda. These epistemic allegiances transform prominent terrorologists into "technicians" of the global war on terror, rather than merely scholars of political violence (Burnett and Whyte 2005, 13). Some terrorism scholars even refrain from contributing to court proceedings, viewing the study of terrorism as incompatible with the demands of an expert witness testifying on "objective and factually correct" evidence (Crace 2008). Despite these concerns about the integrity of terrorism research, self-styled experts continue to influence national security policies, military operations, and court proceedings, particularly when their research aligns with the geopolitical goals of the state.

The Daubert Standard and Terrorologists: Determining the Admissibility of Expert Testimony

Given the controversial role of expert witnesses in the adjudication of terrorism-related cases, several legal scholars have contested the admissibility of terrorologists, and defendants have sought to preclude such testimony from trial by citing federal standards used to determine the reliability and relevance of evidence. For example, the Federal Rules of Evidence outline the standards that inform how the courts rule on the admissibility of expert testimony. Federal Rule of Evidence 702 specifically provisions that a witness may testify as an expert only if the following hold:

1. the expert's scientific, technical, or other specialized knowledge will help the trier of fact to understand the evidence or to determine a fact in issue;
2. the testimony is based on sufficient facts or data;
3. the testimony is the product of reliable principles and methods; and
4. the expert has reliably applied the principles and methods to the facts of the case.

In *Daubert v. Merrell Dow Pharmaceuticals, Inc.,* the Supreme Court clarified the admissibility of expert testimony under Rule 702, instructing presiding judges to conduct an assessment that considers the qualifications of the proposed expert, the reliability of the methodologies employed, and the fit or connection between the scientific research and the factual issues in the case. More specifically, the *Daubert* factors used to determine the scientific validity of expert testimony include "whether the theory or technique in question can be (and has been) tested, whether it has been subjected to peer review and publication, its known or potential error rate and the existence and maintenance of standards controlling its operation, and whether it has attracted widespread acceptance within a relevant scientific community."[13] In reviewing this case, Justice Blackmun emphasized the importance of evaluating scientists' methodologies, arguing, "It is *how* conclusions are reached, not *what* the conclusions are, that make them 'good science.'"[14] Under *Daubert,* the courts must conduct a multifaceted analysis to determine the admissibility of expert testimony; scientific knowledge is admissible if it is derived from sound scientific methodology. This means that judges serve as gatekeepers by preventing the jury from hearing unreliable scientific research—a difficult role to fulfill, particularly when judges struggle to understand the subject matter, such as Takfiris, under consideration.

Focused on evaluating the hard sciences, the Federal Rules of Evidence and the *Daubert* standard do not provide clear guidance on the evaluation of social science research presented by experts such as anthropologists, sociologists, historians, and political scientists. Evidence professor Maxine D. Goodman (2010b) contends that "the *Daubert* test is arguably and predictably ill-suited for testing theories that arise from a non-scientific methodology," such as a historian whose methodology "does not involve testing a hypothesis and then replicating the test to check the hypothesis" (838). This means that the courts cannot "differentiate between the purveyor of junk history from the reliable historian" (838). Law professor Edward Imwinkelried (1994) similarly argues that the courts "have failed to develop their own objective reliability standards for propositions of nonscientific expert evidence," relying more narrowly on the expert's qualifications, reputation, and helpfulness to the trier of fact (2281). Rather than evaluate the reliability and validity of the methods used by social scientists, the courts sometimes scrutinize the witness's credentials as a proxy for their research expertise. In fact, "certain federal courts disregard the reliability requirement altogether (and focus almost exclusively on qualifications)," particularly in reviewing social science research (Goodman 2010a, 642). In terrorism-related cases, the courts have admitted expert witnesses without evaluating the rigor and efficacy of their social science methodologies, even as terrorologists themselves admit that their field relies on "poor research methods" (Silke 2004, 12; Sageman 2014b; Li 2020; Kundnani 2014; Said 2015; Horgan 2003).

In the absence of a rigorous review of an expert's scientific methodology in terrorism-related cases, the courts have assessed the expert's credentials, qualifications, and peer-reviewed publications as well as the relevant scientific community's acceptance of this research. These assessments, however, fail to consider the unique characteristics of the scientific community of terrorism scholars, which operates as an "invisible college" of like-minded scientists and a highly controlled "in-group" influenced by federal funding and geopolitical priorities (Miller and Mills 2009, 425). Terrorism studies thus functions as a "strange field" as it "fails to fulfill the expectations" of what constitutes a scientific field through the development of academic departments and professional organizations that "establish control over the definition of their particular problem and the production and certification of legitimate experts" (Stampnitzky 2011, 6). In fact, there is "little regulation of who may become an expert, and the key audience for terrorism expertise is not an ideal-typical scientific community, but rather the public and the state" (Stampnitzky 2011, 6–7). *Living with Terrorism* author Richard Clutterbuck even admits, "My becoming a so-called expert on terrorism simply evolved from the fact that I spent a lot of time talking about it" (qtd. in Kahn 1978, 55). Under *Daubert,* the courts must consider a witness's scientific qualifications, which is difficult to assess given the field's lack of credentialing practices and subsequent rise of self-appointed experts conducting nonscientific research studies using secondary sources such as English-language websites.

The nature of the field also complicates the *Daubert* standard that a witness's scientific research must be peer reviewed because those who conduct peer reviews and control academic publications are also self-styled terrorism experts who use similar methodological approaches. As a closed network, terrorism studies often publishes research that has not been tested and verified by the broader academic community. These conditions make it difficult for the courts to effectively evaluate the admissibility of terrorologists under *Daubert,* especially when the courts limit their assessments to the credentials, qualifications, and publications of proposed experts. In doing so, the courts ignore the extensive reports systematically disproving terrorism research (Sageman 2014b; Said 2015; Li 2011, 2020; Patel 2011; Monaghan 2014; Nguyen 2019; Kundnani 2014; Kumar 2012). Legal scholars warn that "a review of expert testimony in terrorism prosecutions reveal several troubling trends in how the government and courts evaluate an individual's expertise and scope of testimony," often qualifying expert witnesses with university credentials but without linguistic training or cultural experience in their fields of study (Said 2015, 96).

Other critics have expressed concerns about the relationship between terrorism experts and the federal government, particularly given the field's deep relationship with police, military, and intelligence agencies. For example, defense attorney William Swor cautions that terrorism experts "all work for the government or they work for government-funded agencies or government-contracted projects," so "when the government calls them, they are a ready source of government-approved information" (qtd. in Bartosiewicz 2008). "Unabashedly ideological," these self-styled experts "furnish law-enforcement agencies, the media, and the public with their insights on Muslim extremism, and they have emerged to significantly affect the way the 'war on terror' is framed, investigated, and prosecuted" (qtd. in Bartosiewicz 2008). Such research "cannot be regarded as objective scholarship in a traditional sense," particularly when funded by federal agencies like the Department of Homeland Security and the National Institute of Justice (Burnett and Whyte 2005, 13). For example, terrorologist Marc Sageman (2014a) has criticized Evan Kohlmann, the government's most high-profile and most frequent expert witness. Sageman (2014a) describes Kohlmann's research and testimony as "so biased, one-sided, and contextually inaccurate that they do not provide a fair and balanced context for the specific evidence to be presented at a hearing." A defense attorney similarly explained:

> Kohlmann is full of shit. If he got paid a million dollars, he'd put a headband on and sing kumbaya, OK? *He worked for the CIA!* All right? So the Evan Kohlmanns that think they're the best and the brightest and the prettiest among us—this whole development of experts, of high-paid expert witnesses who will over the years make *millions of dollars*—became the voice of the government. They knew what the government wanted; they gave them that. (interview, March 2021)

In this view, terrorism experts like Kohlmann conduct research that aligns with the needs of the U.S. security state.

Other legal scholars have questioned Kohlmann's credentials. One defense attorney described Kohlmann as "some guy from [Georgetown], who has never been overseas, who spells Hamas 'hummus' and doesn't see the difference, and who testified, as he admitted, about the wrong terrorism case [in *United States v. Yassin Aref*] as an expert witness" (interview, March 2021). Wadie E. Said (2015) explains that "courts have qualified [Kohlmann] as an expert witness in over two dozen prosecutions in the United States," despite Kohlmann's not knowing Arabic, not having military or intelligence experience, and "tracking al-Qaeda and ideologically related groups, mostly on the Internet," without identifying a methodology for verifying the "open source intelligence" he gathers (96–97). Although the courts have not applied strict scrutiny to Kohlmann's expertise and testimony, he "has achieved celebrity status as a specialist in tracking terrorists," so "the courts routinely admit Kohlmann to testify on the background, origins, and structure of terrorist organizations, despite forceful defense objections concerning the reliability of Kohlmann's methodology" (Goodman 2010a, 656). Notwithstanding these critical appraisals by his colleagues that question the rigor of his research, Kohlmann continues to provide expert testimony in terrorism-related court cases.

Although scholars have examined the legal issues such witnesses raise, like the *Daubert* standard used to determine the admissibility of expert testimony, the reliance on experts like Kohlmann often denies defendants and their attorneys who represent them their status as legitimate and credible knowers of the social worlds they inhabit, their political aspirations, and their driving motivations. In other words, by calling on expert witnesses who have studied, but not experienced, the political, social, and cultural contexts in which defendants have operated, the courts defer epistemic authority to third-party outsiders rather than those intimately involved in the political struggles criminalized and prosecuted by the state. This epistemic injustice is compounded by the lack of collaborative or participatory research with, rather than on, alleged terrorists, such that their perspectives, experiences, and knowledges are never solicited or made central to the study of political violence and armed struggles. Although some seek to professionalize, or standardize, terrorism studies to fit the vetting, credentialing, and disciplining traditions used to legitimize academic fields, the current state of terrorism expertise raises important epistemic questions about who has the authority to explain terrorism and whose knowledge informs national security operations.

Given this context, the courts play a critical role in adjudicating what constitutes legitimate scientific knowledge related to terrorism by conferring epistemic authority on certain self-styled terrorologists and by conceding their interpretations of political violence to the frameworks advanced by these expert witnesses. Court proceedings therefore participate in epistemic struggles to endorse and legitimize certain academic approaches to the study of terrorism. Once admitted, these expert witnesses play an instrumental role in shaping how judges and jurors understand the cases before them, often granting experts more epistemic authority than defendants. As one defense attorney explained to me,

> Kohlmann, his generation of experts, tell jurors what jurors have heard on TV. And have heard in the paper. And have read about. And heard from their neighbors. So they work it. They milk it. They manipulate it. They flex it. If the government opened up a terrorism case and said, "The Brooklyn Bridge doesn't exist. It's a gamma ray shield," and the government got an expert witness who said, "It's a gamma ray shield," the jury would buy it! It's a gamma ray shield. (interview, March 2021)

Expert witnesses testifying on behalf of the prosecution often repeat racialized narratives circulating in popular media that jurors draw on to make sense of the cases before them. In other words, expert witnesses confirm what jurors already believe about terrorism and terrorists, making this testimony seem both credible and useful, without any extra scrutiny needed.

Given the role of expert witnesses in terrorism-related cases, defendants strategically have challenged the inclusion of terrorologists using the limited legal tools available to them, such as *Daubert* motions and cross-examination. Unfortunately, the expert status of terrorologists often supersedes these legal challenges, such that commonsense understandings of terrorism and terrorists circulate with epistemic authority in the courtroom.

*Motions to Preclude: Contesting the Expertise of
Terrorologists in the Courtroom*

In 2003, the U.S. government charged Uzair Paracha with providing material support to al-Qaeda. Prosecutors anchored their case against Paracha in his business relationships with Majid Khan and Ammar al-Baluchi, two alleged al-Qaeda members.[15] After graduating from a Pakistani business college in 2002, Paracha moved to New York, where he advertised his father's luxury apartments in Pakistan to Pakistani Americans. Before leaving for the United States, Paracha met with al-Baluchi, who sought to invest in a Karachi apartment complex planned by Paracha's father.[16] Referred to as "al-Qaeda's Moneyman," al-Baluchi was arrested in 2003 for allegedly facilitating the wire transfers that financed the September 11 hijackers (Shannon 2003). During this time, a family friend also introduced Paracha to Khan, who wanted help obtaining immigration paperwork to enter the United States. Shortly after this meeting, Khan was arrested on charges related to his alleged work with Khalid Sheikh Mohammed, often referred to as the mastermind of the September 11 attacks. Given these associations, United States Attorney Michael Garcia concluded that "Paracha attempted to help an al-Qaeda operative enter the United States to carry out terrorist attacks within our borders," a plan facilitated by al-Baluchi's financial support for the assistance Paracha promised Khan (qtd. in Department of Justice 2006).

Before Paracha's trial began, the defense read into the record stipulated testimony by both Khan and al-Baluchi that was based on unclassified summaries of their statements given while in custody at Guantánamo Bay, as provided by the government. The parties stipulated that Khan and al-Baluchi would have testified that they never informed Paracha of their involvement with al-Qaeda and that Paracha was unaware of their operational plans. Al-Baluchi, for example, stated that Paracha was "totally unwitting of al-Baluchi's al-Qaeda affiliation, or of al-Baluchi's intention to use [Paracha's father] for the broader operational plan involving Majid Khan."[17] Al-Baluchi's testimony also confirmed that "Uzair Paracha knows nothing about operations" and that "neither al-Baluchi nor Majid Khan indicated to Uzair Paracha at any time that they were *mujahidin* or al-Qaeda."[18] Because both Khan and al-Baluchi were detained at Guantánamo Bay, these summary statements replaced their in-court testimony. As in other cases, the inclusion of summary statements provided by the government, rather than witness testimony, prevented the defense from raising questions about the treatment of witnesses detained in offshore prisons or the veracity of the summaries.

Confronted with clear evidence that Paracha did not contribute to al-Qaeda's operational plans, the prosecution used Evan Kohlmann's expert testimony to implicate Paracha. Kohlmann reported that al-Qaeda operated through an "amorphous" structure that, outside of Osama bin Laden's inner circle, consisted of independent cells with specialized roles for different individuals holding "very limited information" about the organization as a whole.[19] In this view, Khan and al-Baluchi would, by design, not know about Paracha's involvement in al-Qaeda. Although Khan and al-Baluchi denied collaborating with Paracha on any of their operational plans, the prosecution used Kohlmann's testimony to conclude that Paracha's contributions simply were unknown to his coconspirators. Even though the prosecution could not demonstrate Paracha's role in al-Qaeda or in an active terrorist plot, Kohlmann's testimony suggested that a lack of evidence did not indicate innocence; it merely reflected al-Qaeda's insular cell structure.

Kohlmann's testimony influenced how the jurors and judge interpreted Paracha's actions and subsequent guilt. Judge Sidney Stein reasoned that, given Kohlmann's testimony, "it was entirely consistent with Paracha's guilt . . . for other low-level operatives like Khan and al-Baluchi to remain in the dark as to the extent of the defendant's knowledge."[20] Furthermore, the prosecution argued at trial that the question as to whether Paracha knowingly aided al-Qaeda was "the heart of this case" and the "one thing that is seriously at issue." Judge Stein's decision to allow Kohlmann to testify on the background, origins, and structure of al-Qaeda shaped how he and the jurors came to understand the facts of the case. Paracha's conviction demonstrates how jurors granted Kohlmann epistemic authority, using his understanding of al-Qaeda's organizational structure to verify Paracha's status as an al-Qaeda operative. Uncorroborated by other evidence, such as bank records that could confirm al-Qaeda paid Paracha to help Khan enter the United States, Kohlmann's testimony outweighed the testimony of al-Baluchi, Khan, and Paracha, all of whom insisted that Paracha was not an al-Qaeda member and had not contributed to any of its operations.

Before the jury trial, Paracha had challenged the admissibility of this expert testimony by contesting the reliability of Kohlmann's methodology, which included the use of hearsay evidence obtained through the collection and analysis of secondary sources like websites. In a *Daubert* hearing, both parties debated the relevance, reliability, and role of the expert witness. The defense noted that there was no legal standard to evaluate the methodologies of social scientists, pointedly asking: "What makes a witness an expert in terrorism? The amount of times they appear on the TV show? What they studied in college? Who they interviewed in a mosque in connection with a graduate program? How many times they stay on the Internet? That qualifies a person as an expert?"[21] In this view, these activities "would not qualify a person as an expert in any fields because the Court would have no independent way . . . of determining the ultimate reliability, the gatekeeping reliability, of what the witness is being offered."[22] The defense challenged Kohlmann's admissibility by questioning both the expert's credentials and the court's capacity to evaluate his research. Judge Stein responded to these arguments by saying, "I agree with you that to a certain extent I am limited in testing the reliability."[23]

Given the defense's arguments, Judge Stein commented, "I'm not quite sure why the government seems to be relying so heavily on this expert when you have so many admissions from the defendant that presumably will come in as admissions when you put the law enforcement people who took the admissions on the stand."[24] The prosecution, however, worried that the defense would "attack the credibility of the agents who are going to testify about the confession and the statement made by Mr. Paracha," which would include an admission that "Uzair Paracha said, 'Yes, I knew Majid Khan and al-Baluchi were al-Qaeda.'"[25] The prosecution argued that if the defense "intend[s] to attack the agents' credibility as to what Uzair Paracha said and what he knew, [then] it goes to show that—or we should be permitted to prove that in fact Ammar al-Baluchi and Majid Khan did participate in attacks against the United States," necessitating the inclusion of Kohlmann.[26] Because Paracha alleged that he made false confessions to FBI agents under duress, the prosecution needed to introduce additional evidence that could tie Paracha to al-Qaeda through expert testimony. In similar cases in which a defendant denied membership to a foreign terrorist organization, "expert testimony was needed to show the affiliation," the planned strategy of the prosecution.[27]

The defense warned that the inclusion of such expert testimony could create "hierarchical testimony." With such testimony, "the danger is that the jury will put more onus or more weight on the expert testimony's—expert witness's testimony," at the expense of the testimony from lay witnesses like Khan and al-Baluchi.[28] This exchange reveals how credibility and expert status are inextricable, such that jurors often grant experts epistemic authority often denied to other kinds of witnesses like Khan and al-Baluchi, whose credibility is circumscribed by their nonexpert and "terrorist" statuses.

In a written opinion, Judge Stein observed that "an essential element of the government's burden of proof on all counts of the indictment is Paracha's knowledge of Khan and al-Baluchi's association with al-Qaeda and his knowledge that his actions would or could support the al-Qaeda organization and not simply its individual members."[29] Given this burden of proof, "testimony tending to undermine the government's assertion that Paracha knew or had reason to believe that his alleged coconspirators were al-Qaeda associates is vital to Paracha's defense," such as the "unclassified summary of statements" where "al-Baluchi has stated that neither Paracha nor his father had knowledge of al-Baluchi's affiliation with al-Qaeda or al-Baluchi's intent to use [Paracha's father] for a larger operation involving Majid Khan."[30] Majid Khan also "denied that Uzair Paracha was motivated to help Khan out [of] a desire to help al-Qaeda" and even "believed that Paracha was disinterested in extremism."[31] Citing national security concerns related to bringing Khan and al-Baluchi into the courtroom, Judge Stein reasoned that "the unclassified summaries of Khan and al-Baluchi constitute an adequate substitution for their live testimony."[32]

Although Judge Stein entered these statements into the record, he rejected the defense's proposal that the court instruct the jury that Khan and al-Baluchi "are providing assistance to the U.S. government and that the government has found the witness credible" because the court does not know if the witnesses "are in fact providing assistance to the government rather than misleading it" and that jurors must determine witness credibility.[33] At trial, the court informed jurors that Khan and al-Baluchi provided written statements while in custody and were questioned "on multiple occasions" about "their relationship with the defendant."[34] The court also reported to the jury that the witnesses "are segregated from each other and are not able to coordinate their statements" and "have had no contact with the defendant since his arrest."[35] These jury instructions ultimately concluded, "It is your decision, after reviewing all of the evidence, whether to accept the testimony of these two witnesses just as it is with other witnesses and to give that testimony whatever weight you find it deserves."[36] While the court sought to reaffirm the jury's role in determining the credibility of each witness through these instructions, incarcerated witnesses who cannot testify in court because of national security concerns carry an epistemic charge that can deflate their credibility.

To manage the possibility of prejudice at trial, Judge Stein also instructed the prosecution to "ask jurors to use their good judgement, common sense, and life experiences in judging the credibility of the witnesses' statements just as they would with any other witness."[37] Yet Khan and al-Baluchi are not just "any other witness." Although Khan was released in 2023, al-Baluchi continues to be held at the Guantánamo Bay detention camp, which confines prisoners that Defense Secretary Donald Rumsfeld publicly referred to as "the worst of the worst" (qtd. in Stein 2011).

Legal scholars have shown how certain referents shape a witness's credibility. Bennett L. Gershman (2005) documents how "a jury's evaluation of a witness's credibility may be distorted by the jury's subjective assessment of the witness's background, narrative, language, and demeanor" (328). Writing on a terrorism jury trial, Laura K. Donohue (2007) warns that "jurors may be biased against defendants sharing an ethnic or religious background of those engaged in violence"—a bias that could "influence their ability to evaluate evidence, the way in which juror deliberations unfold, and the verdict" (1324). "Even unconsciously," Donohue further cautions, jurors "may want to return a decision consistent with community sentiment—a community potentially angry and scared and mourning the loss of their own" and "may be afraid of being the future target of attack, making them less likely to entertain doubt as to the guilt of the accused" (1324). In examining the so-called Detroit sleeper cell terrorist prosecution that convicted five individuals of allegedly plotting an attack on Disneyland, Gershman

(2005) found that "extrinsic sources of jury error including suppressed evidence, dishonest and unreliable testimony, partisan experts, coaching, obstructed cross-examination, and inflammatory arguments" can "impair a jury's decision," no matter how "fair-minded and competent" (4). In fact, a federal judge later vacated two of the convictions, citing prosecutorial misconduct.

In addition to these referents that can undermine a witness's credibility, Federal Rule of Evidence 609 allows both parties to use a witness's criminal history to "attack a witness's character for truthfulness by evidence of a criminal conviction," particularly if such felonies involved "some element of deceit, untruthfulness, or falsification bearing on the witness' credibility."[38] This means that a witness's criminal history can undermine their credibility. Legal scholar James McMahon (1986) warns that the use of prior conviction evidence "has the potential to create several problems, particularly unfair prejudice" and "detract from a jury's dispassionate consideration of the evidence" (1066, 1067).

If a witness can be impeached through prior convictions, through a critical examination of their demeanor, or through assumptions about their accent or background, then a witness's status as a Muslim terrorist incarcerated in a Guantánamo Bay detention facility also can affect the credibility jurors afford such a witness. Lay witnesses in Paracha's case lived at the intersections of these discrediting statuses, creating an epistemic charge that denied them of their trustworthiness, believability, and reliability in the courtroom. Representative of the "hierarchical testimony" the defense forewarned, Kohlmann's explanation of al-Qaeda's insular organization structure outweighed Khan and al-Baluchi's declarative statements denying Paracha's affiliation with and contributions to al-Qaeda.

Limiting such extrinsic factors is critical to returning a fair and accurate jury verdict. The government enjoys the distinct advantage of using state-sponsored expert witnesses, whom jurors often view as having "an aura of special reliability and trustworthiness."[39] An expert's credentials, ability to testify persuasively, and conclusions that "invariably interlock with other evidence in the case" can "reinforce the jury's confidence in the expert's opinion," even when the expert offers "ludicrous" analyses based on "almost laughable" opinions (Gershman 2005, 327). A witness's expert status can confer epistemic authority without jurors rigorously evaluating the testimony's reliability and its relevance to the case at hand. Such a risk is "particularly great when . . . a prevailing social climate of prejudice and hostility toward one party may predispose lay juries to accept purportedly scientific claims that confirm prevailing hostile views."[40]

Given the epistemically and emotionally charged nature of terrorism cases, the court's gatekeeping functions—determining who may or may not testify as an expert—play an important role in securing just and accurate verdicts. In *United States v. Abu Hamza al-Masri* (2014), Judge Katherine Forrest observed that "testimony regarding terrorist attacks by al-Qaeda and bin Laden is no doubt prejudicial and inflammatory to some degree," but she still allowed an expert witness to discuss al-Qaeda. In *United States v. Abu-Jihaad* (2008), Judge Mark Kravitz found that "conversations referring to support of *jihad* were no more inflammatory than the charges in the indictment," suggesting that terrorism-related charges themselves—of which the defendant is innocent until proven guilty—are inflammatory. Despite such "prejudicial and inflammatory" testimony, judges continue to confer epistemic authority onto terrorologists by admitting them as expert witnesses without rigorously assessing the reliability and validity of their research. At the same time, terrorism defendants and terrorist witnesses struggle to prove their credibility to the courts, especially if they offer different interpretations of the factual evidence at hand, as in the summary statements—not court testimony— by Khan and al-Baluchi confirming that Paracha was not an al-Qaeda operative. Journalist John Crace (2008) reports that, given their intellectual commitment to providing expert testimony that is "governed by the principle of professional, scientific neutrality," many scholars refuse to appear in terrorism trials "precisely because they feel their subject does not lend itself to such high levels of impartial scrutiny." Although some scholars view their terrorism research as incompatible with the demands of an expert witness, some eagerly participate in court proceedings, which can introduce extrinsic sources of jury error.

In the *Paracha* case, Judge Stein admitted Kohlmann as an expert witness, although the court limited this testimony to the "origins and structure of al-Qaeda, its leaders, and its use of cells and individuals to provide logistical support."[41] In qualifying Kohlmann as an expert, Judge Stein affirmed the rigor and reliability of Kohlmann's methodology, explaining it consisted of "gathering multiple sources of information, including original and secondary sources, cross-checking and juxtaposing new information against existing information, and evaluating new information to determine whether his conclusions remain consonant with the most reliable sources."[42] Judge Stein also noted that Kohlmann's methodology "is similar to that employed by his peers in his field," concluding, "Although Kohlmann's methodology is not readily subject to testing and permits of no ready calculation of a concrete error rate, it is more reliable than a simple cherry-picking of information from websites and other sources."[43] Judge Stein, however, did not indicate that he conducted a systematic analysis of Kohlmann's methodology, as he merely acknowledged that "Kohlmann's methodology, as he describes it, is similar to that employed by experts that have been permitted to testify in other federal courts involving terrorist organizations."[44] Judge Stein compared Kohlmann's methods to other terrorism scholars as one metric to evaluate Kohlmann's research. Prior court decisions to admit Kohlmann confirmed Judge Stein's confidence in Kohlmann's expertise.

Judge Stein further reasoned that Kohlmann's "opinions and conclusions are subjected to various forms of peer review and that the opinion he proposes to offer here regarding al-Qaeda's origins, leaders, and certain tradecraft are generally accepted within the relevant community."[45] Rather than conduct a rigorous analysis of Kohlmann's research methodology, Judge Stein used Kohlmann's scientific community and peer-reviewed publications as a proxy, even after the University of Pennsylvania declined to publish Kohlmann's book, *Al-Qaida's Jihad in Europe: The Afghan–Bosnian Network,* after receiving a scathing peer review by Sageman. In fact, CIA case officer Philip Giraldi (2011) reports, "Within the intelligence community and the Pentagon, Kohlmann, like many of his expert colleagues, is widely considered a phony who has somehow ingratiated himself with those who want an affable young media resource who will say just the right things when it comes to terrorism, keeping the public suitably alarmed while exuding a facile expertise." Despite Judge Stein's conclusion, many in Kohlmann's own scientific community do not accept his research methodology or his findings. Furthermore, scholars warn that "even where articles are peer-reviewed, the peers reviewing may lack the expertise," especially because "few terrorism experts are really qualified to authoritatively comment on the internal structures of different terrorist groups across different contexts" (Ranstorp 2009, 15). Kohlmann even misrepresented the status of his book at trial, stating it had been published by Oxford University Press, "a university publisher, which means it is an academic book."[46] *Al-Qaida's Jihad in Europe,* however, was published by Berg, an imprint of Oxford International Publishers, which has no relationship with Oxford University and is not an academic press. Despite outstanding concerns about the relevant scientific community's ability to vet and peer review Kohlmann's research, Judge Stein concluded that such evidence was admissible.

In 2018, Judge Stein granted Paracha a new trial in light of new evidence, including Khalid Sheikh Mohammed's admission that he played a central role in al-Qaeda and that Khan and al-Baluchi were uninvolved in the organization's operations. According to Judge Stein, "The newly discovered evidence contains statements by all three men professing that, contrary to the factual assumptions upon which this trial proceeded, Khan and al-Baluchi are themselves not members of al-Qaeda," a finding that would enable Paracha "to argue on retrial not only that he never *knowingly* aided the terrorist group, but that he never aided al-Qaeda *at all.*"[47] The government declined to reprosecute Paracha, who returned to Pakistan with his conviction vacated.

Even with this vacated sentence, the courts continue to admit Kohlmann as an expert witness. Legal scholars therefore have unrelented in challenging the government's reliance on "a self-made al-Qaeda expert" as one of its key witnesses, arguing that such testimony "undermines severely the credibility of the proceedings and makes mockery of the principle of scientific expertise" (Ranstorp 2009, 28). In *Paracha,* Kohlmann's testimony deftly assisted the prosecution in arguing that the insular structure of al-Qaeda meant that Khan, al-Baluchi, and Paracha could be coconspirators without knowing about each other's involvement in the organization. Kohlmann thus was central to securing Paracha's conviction, despite the continued legal and scientific challenges to the reliability and rigor of his research.

Although scholars have assessed the limitations of the *Daubert* factors in terrorism-related cases (Said 2015, 2012; Aaronson 2013; Li 2020; Goodman 2010a, 2010b), these analyses miss how courts commit a distinctly epistemic type of injustice by simultaneously denying defendants their credibility as knowers of their own lives and deferring interpretive authority to self-made expert witnesses who have little contact with the violent political actors at the center of their research. Judge Stein, for example, explained that the "prosecution was able to sap the probative force of . . . the exculpatory testimony" of Khan, al-Baluchi, and Paracha "by reference to the testimony of its expert witness, Evan Kohlmann, on the insular 'cell' structure of al-Qaeda."[48] Imbued with epistemic authority in the courtroom, Kohlmann's expert testimony outweighed the combined lay testimony of Khan, al-Baluchi, and Paracha, all of whom carried with them the epistemic stigma of the terrorist label.

Writing on different forms of epistemic injustice, philosopher Miranda Fricker (2007) describes such denials as "testimonial injustice," where "prejudicial dysfunction in testimonial practice" can result in an expert witness receiving more credibility (credibility excess) and a defendant receiving less credibility (credibility deficit) (17).[49] Power relations can affect "how much credibility a hearer affords a speaker" such that "prejudice will tend surreptitiously to inflate or deflate" a person's epistemic credibility (Fricker 2007, 17). Charles Mills (2015) argues that in the context of racial domination, epistemic injustice participates in the reproduction of "a general skepticism about nonwhite cognition and an exclusion from accepted discourse of nonwhite categories and frameworks of analysis," which denies people of color "credibility" and rejects "the alternative viewpoints that could be developed from taking their perspective seriously" (222). Writing on colonial epistemologies, Ann Laura Stoler (2009) similarly explains how "hierarchies of credibility" establish "scales of trust that measure what forms of witness, words, and deeds, [can] be taken as reliably relevant," while recognizing that such hierarchies "are sometimes inverted" (23). As recipients of court testimony, judges and jurors interpret the credibility of witnesses, often granting experts more authority than defendants even when the experts lack experiential and empirical evidence to support their claims. This delegitimizing function of the terrorist label, and its articulation with prevailing racial formations, carries with it an epistemic charge that affects the credibility of a terrorism defendant or a lay witness charged with or convicted of terrorism-related crimes. Meanwhile, judges and jurors often grant terrorism scholars credibility excess, which shapes how they come to understand and ultimately determine the guilt of individuals charged with terrorism-related crimes.

Granting Kohlmann epistemic authority through his designation as an expert witness in *Paracha* provided the justification to admit Kohlmann in future cases, despite Paracha's vacated conviction. In fact, courts across the country have cited Judge Stein's ruling to admit Kohlmann as an expert witness. In *United States v. Oussama Abdullah Kassir* (2009), Judge John Keenan referenced the *Paracha* case, concluding that "Kohlmann's expertise and reliability have not diminished, and the standard under Rule 702 and *Daubert* remains the same. Therefore, his testimony on the origins, history, structure, and leadership and various operational methods of al-Qaeda and other terrorist groups is sufficiently reliable."[50] In *United States v. Sulaiman Abu Ghayth* (2014), Judge Lewis Kaplan also affirmed Judge Stein's findings and determined that Kohlmann "is qualified under Rule 702" and "has been qualified in twenty-five federal criminal trials."[51] As these cases demonstrate, once a court has admitted a terrorologist as an expert, that expert "will be qualified as such" in future cases, "to the point where defendants have given up trying to challenge his suitability as an expert" (Said 2015, 98).

Evan Kohlmann is not the only controversial terrorologist the courts have relied on to interpret factual evidence for judges and jurors. Other terrorism scholars like William Braniff, Rohan Gunaratna, and Matthew Levitt have testified on the government's behalf, where they also have faced similar critical appraisals as Kohlmann. In the trial of Noor Salman—charged with aiding and abetting her husband, Omar Mateen, in his 2016 Pulse nightclub shooting—defense attorneys sought to limit or preclude the expert testimony of William Braniff. In its *Daubert* motion, the defense argued that "the Government has not established that Mr. Braniff's methodology or experience is reliable as applied to his particular opinions in this case" and that "the Government has not explained in its expert disclosure how Mr. Braniff's experience led to the conclusions he reached, why his experience was a sufficient basis for these opinions, or how he applied his experience to reach his conclusions."[52] In this motion, the defense questioned Braniff's credentials, noting that the prosecution had not established his authority as an expert with a record of sound empirical evidence related to the case. Citing

Federal Rules of Evidence 401, 402, 403, and 701, the defense also opposed Braniff's testimony related to terrorist organizations, contending it was not relevant to Salman's alleged criminal actions and would be more prejudicial than probative.

In response, the prosecution argued that Braniff used the same methodologies as other experts in the field that "[have] been accepted by other courts when qualifying terrorist experts," including

> online research specifically studying websites operated by terrorist organizations and their followers; visiting jihadist chatrooms; reviewing lectures and books by known jihadist leaders; analyzing publications and periodicals published by terrorist organizations; consulting with other experts in the field, as well as with law enforcement officials; and cross checking information from primary and secondary sources for accuracy and authenticity.[53]

According to this record, Braniff has never conducted firsthand research, like interviewing ISIS fighters. Terrorologists themselves have identified serious concerns with the field's "almost total reliance on secondary and tertiary source material to inform theoretical development" (Horgan 2003, 30). Similarly, in an amicus brief, terrorism scholars and evidence experts argued that the Supreme Court's "intervention is needed to provide guidance to the lower courts in assessing expert reliability in the unique context of terrorism cases, where firsthand evidence is often lacking."[54] Given his lack of firsthand evidence, Braniff has relied on secondary sources such as websites, chat rooms, and periodicals. In response, the prosecution argued that other courts had qualified Braniff as an expert because they had verified his expertise.

Because the terrorologists who gain prominence in the field of terrorism studies and domestic courtrooms typically subscribe to orthodox approaches to the study of terrorism, their inclusion in the adjudication of terrorism-related crimes necessarily narrows how judges and jurors come to understand the cases before them. The prevailing frameworks terrorologists advance in the courts often correspond to dominant images in popular media that define terrorists as fanatical evildoers, ultimately abstracting political violence from its formative conditions and reinforcing racist tropes that reproduce a commonsense understanding of terrorism (Gramsci 1971). Rooted in "racial hierarchies and racialized transnational (dis)locations" that organize U.S. society, popular culture articulates with knowledge production processes and national security operations to naturalize "brown as deviance," a category "harnessed and extended to any behaviors, places, spaces, and performances that challenge the hegemonic Whiteness of U.S. neo-nationalism" (Silva 2016, 29). This means that judges and jurors can reach for dominant frameworks to interpret the actions and intentions of defendants rather than relying on nonexpert witness testimony that can offer alternative interpretations, as in the case of Uzair Paracha. Given the importance of terrorologists in securing guilty verdicts, prosecutors diligently worked to defend the status of their expert witnesses and to challenge any legal contestations seeking to limit their role in court proceedings.

"Dueling Experts": Epistemic Struggles to Limit the Role of Terrorologists

Although defendants have challenged the expert status of terrorologists, prosecutors also have filed *Daubert* motions contesting the admissibility of expert testimony. In *United States v. Mohamed Osman Mohamud*, for example, Judge Garr King weighed competing objections, explaining, "The defense objects to government witness Evan Kohlmann. The government objects to defense witnesses Dr. Marc Sageman, Dr. Fathali Moghaddam, and Dr. Elizabeth Cauffman."[55] Judge King admitted all four as expert witnesses, concluding that they each could "provide insight into the terrorism community that would assist the jury."[56] In his determination, Judge King recognized the methodological limitations of both Kohlmann and Sageman: Kohlmann's "latest publications have not been in peer-reviewed journals," with "no known error rate and no formal control group" for such research. Sageman's research also lacks "documentation for his analysis."[57] In fact, Judge King observed that "terrorism does not lend itself to strict scientific study that the court would expect in the testing of a new medication," but "the issues raised by counsel on either side" did not "discredit the experts' methodologies to the point the court should exclude their testimony."[58] Judge King, however, barred these expert witnesses from testifying "on the ultimate label they would affix to [the] defendant," such as terrorist or violent extremist, because these labels "are code words for predisposition."[59]

The courts have sought to manage competing testimony by terrorologists, particularly as Sageman and Kohlmann's professional relationship deteriorated, making the conceptual ruptures in the field of terrorism studies more visible. To do so, the courts have admitted both witnesses as "dueling experts" who offer competing understandings of the factual evidence of each case.[60] For example, in *United States v. Ibrahim Harun Hausa* (2017), the defense moved to admit Sageman as an expert who could offer an informed opinion on Kohlmann's credentials.[61] The prosecution, however, argued that such testimony "would usurp the jury's role in assessing witness credibility" and "run afoul of Rule 403 of the Federal Rules of Evidence by [sowing] confusion in the courtroom."[62] The prosecution also explained that "the credibility and reliability of witness testimony is a question of fact to be determined by the jury, not another expert witness"; the "proper tool" for challenging an expert witness's testimony is cross-examination, not another witness.[63] If the court admitted Sageman to testify "as to the credibility and qualifications" of Kohlmann, it would "simply open the door for a third or fourth expert such as Bruce Hoffman to be called by the government to criticize Sageman."[64] Attorneys have proposed the admission of dueling experts and used cross-examination to offer competing testimony that jurors would consider in their deliberations. One defense attorney reported that such aggressive cross-examination using the expert's own scholarship against him "is effective" (interview, October 2020). Another defense attorney, however, argued that such "pissing matches" distracted the jury from the actual facts of the case and placed too much emphasis on the concept of terrorism (interview, March 2021). Still, he often sought to aggressively cross-examine expert witnesses like Kohlmann and to introduce his own experts. Such legal maneuvers demonstrate the field's chaotic incoherence and deep divisions between trained academics and self-styled experts.

The proposition of including such dueling experts, however, assumes that terrorologists are best suited to provide credible and reliable testimony. Rather than destabilize the concept of the terrorism expert, the proffered use of Sageman to challenge Kohlmann's credibility (and then Hoffman to challenge Sageman's) reaffirms the prevailing notion that terrorism is an object of study that can be made knowable.

In this approach, the courts determine who counts as the "real" or most credible terrorologist rather than questioning the relevance, reliability, and utility of terrorism scholarship more broadly. The field of terrorism studies itself is rife with conflict, given its lack of credentialing and gatekeeping functions that define most academic disciplines. Ranstorp (2009) argues that the field of terrorism studies even "suffers from the very absence that drives academic knowledge forward—against-the-grain theories and rigorous intellectual debates and critiques among scholars" (15). The contest over expert witnesses in domestic courtrooms reflects the broader debates about what constitutes expertise in the field of terrorism studies: "the field of terrorism studies has been characterized by weak and permeable boundaries, a population of 'experts' whose backgrounds and sources of legitimation are highly heterogenous, and a lack of agreement not just over how expertise should be evaluated but even over how to define the central topic of their concern" (Stampnitzky 2013, 46). Given this current state of the field, "as long as terrorism experts within academia do not have the power to regulate who is treated as an expert in the broader world, and as long as experts on terrorism are still 'disciplined' by the taboo on 'understanding' terrorism, they will have difficulty bringing rational explanation to bear on how Americans think about the problem" (Stampnitzky 2013, 200). Although the contestations over the study of terrorism have appeared in court documents— even documenting Sageman's changing relationship with Kohlmann, which went from meeting for "drinks and discussion" to "attack[ing] Kohlmann so vehemently"—they typically rehearse familiar arguments: individual experts do not have the credentials, training, and sophisticated methodologies to conduct rigorous and reliable research useful to judges and jurors.[65] Academic critics also challenge terrorologists using similar arguments, noting that sought-after expert witnesses do not know Arabic or other relevant languages, rely on internet sources, spew "junk science," and were "grown hydroponically in the basement of the Bush Justice Department" (Yang 2010).

In these cases, the standard trial strategy of filing a *Daubert* motion to contest an individual expert often reinforces terrorism studies as a legitimate field of study that can offer judges and jurors ways to understand and interpret the factual evidence before them. Because trial attorneys must challenge a proposed terrorism expert, their contestations typically do not question the utility, rigor, and reliability of terrorism studies as an entire field. Instead, attorneys question an individual terrorologist's credentials, training, methodology, and publication record, leaving unchallenged the unregulated field of terrorism studies. Defense attorneys have sought to admit a dueling expert to contest expert testimony, even though all these experts come from the same field of study and employ similar research methods. Furthermore, terrorologists themselves have defined their field as a "failure," particularly given the "lack of credentialing qualifications and a consequent plethora of 'self-appointed experts,' critiques of insufficient research methodology, assessments of a lack of intellectual progress, and the inability of experts to establish a unified, stable definition of the concept of 'terrorism'" (Stampnitzky 2011, 9). Terrorologists also admit that "the search for an adequate definition of terrorism is still on," meaning that such scholars do not even agree on what they are studying, let alone if it can be rigorously understood and made relevant to court proceedings (Schmid and Jongman 1988, xxi). Although different parties may question the credibility of an individual terrorologist in court, such contestations never challenge the status of terrorism research. The courts understandably do not question the concept of terrorism expertise; they merely debate whose terrorism expertise counts as legitimate knowledge.

On rare occasions, legal challenges have questioned the role of terrorologists in court proceedings, including identifying other individuals capable of explaining and contextualizing a party's arguments. In *United States v. Abu Hamza al-Masri* (2014), the defense sought to "limit the testimony of proposed prosecution expert Evan Kohlmann," citing the unreliable sources Kohlmann used to formulate his opinion on the Islamic Army of Aden-Abyan (IAA), a Yemeni-based al-Qaeda affiliate. In 2014, Abu Hamza al-Masri faced eleven criminal charges for providing material support to terrorist organizations, including aiding the IAA in a plot to abduct Western tourists. In 1998, al-Masri allegedly sent six IAA operatives to Yemen for training, who subsequently were intercepted and arrested on December 23. Three days later, using a satellite phone provided by al-Masri, IAA leader Zein al-Abidine Almihdhar allegedly worked with al-Masri to devise a plot to kidnap Western hostages and then demand the release of the six operatives, including al-Masri's stepson. British intelligence officials reported that during the

December 28 kidnapping, al-Masri and Almihdhar continued to talk by satellite phone, although some evidence presented to the court demonstrated al-Masri's "affirmative efforts to assist the U.K. with its anti-terrorism and law-enforcement activities."[66] Given the complicated facts of the case, the prosecution argued that Kohlmann could help the jury understand the history, structure, and leadership of al-Qaeda. Judge Katherine Forrest concurred, reasoning that the defendant "is charged with providing support to terrorists and a terrorist organization, al-Qaeda. Testimony regarding the structure and leadership of that organization is probative and helpful in determining whether [the] defendant in fact supported the organization."[67] For Judge Forrest, Kohlmann's testimony could help the jury understand the facts of the case.

Al-Masri's defense team contested the admissibility of Kohlmann's expert testimony, specifically challenging the terrorologist's reliance on the 1999 testimony of Yemeni detainee Abu al-Hasan al-Midhar to formulate his opinion on the IAA. Citing a State Department report, the defense documented how Yemeni authorities regularly tortured detainees through beatings, electric shock, and exposure to extreme temperatures. In this view, such torture was designed to elicit confessions, even though "the link between coerced statements and unreliability generally is undeniable."[68] The defense concluded that "Mr. Kohlmann's opinion on the Islamic Army of Aden-Abyan is unreliable because his key source—Mr. Abu al-Hasan—was likely subjected to physical and/or psychological abuse, including torture."[69] Yet the defense also disputed the need for *any* terrorism expert, not just Kohlmann's credibility. The defense specifically argued that "the jury will not need Mr. Kohlmann to provide information about the kidnapping in Yemen because the government is calling two fact witnesses—hostages from the incident—that will testify first-hand to those facts."[70] Unlike other cases, this legal challenge was also an epistemic contestation that directly questioned the role of expert witnesses in helping the jury understand events experienced by other people. This legal challenge, however, was unsuccessful, as Judge Forrest concluded that Kohlmann's testimony "would be no more disturbing than the crimes charged and not be unduly prejudicial" and its relevance "would outweigh any prejudice."[71]

Ultimately, the legal challenges raised by defendants rarely resulted in the exclusion of terrorologists from testifying against them. Sometimes judges limited the scope of such testimony, as in the *Paracha* case, but such limitations did not offset the impact of terrorism scholars on how the courts understood the factual evidence before them and often helped secure guilty convictions. For example, between 2004 and 2008, Kohlmann took the stand in seven cases, all of which ended in guilty verdicts (Bartosiewicz 2008). Because the courts conferred expert status onto terrorologists, jurors typically granted them epistemic authority by interpreting them as more credible and more impartial than lay witnesses, as evidenced in the *Paracha* case. One defense lawyer even reported that Evan Kohlmann "is fawned over" by judges and jurors alike (interview, November 2020). In terrorism-related cases, the courts commit a distinctly epistemic type of injustice by treating defendants and other terrorist witnesses as less credible, less reliable, and less trustworthy than experts. The legal challenges available to defendants cannot disrupt such epistemic injustice.

Challenging the Concept of Terrorism: A Role for the Courts?

As we have seen, domestic courts have legitimized, circulated, and consumed orthodox approaches to the study of terrorism by admitting terrorologists as expert witnesses. In this capacity, terrorologists have offered specific interpretive frameworks, such as the new terrorism thesis, that judges and jurors can use to make sense of the cases before them. Because terrorologists also "are ubiquitous in mainstream media coverage on political violence," expert testimony circulated in domestic courts often corresponds to the dominant terrorism discourses that fill popular news outlets (Miller and Mills 2009, 414). Rather than introduce new ways of conceptualizing terrorism, expert witnesses have reiterated commonsense understandings of political violence, which can resonate with how jurors already conceive of terrorism: as an irrational and incorrigible act of violence committed by Muslim fanatics. Such resonance can, by proxy, confirm the credibility and veracity of each expert.

The prominence of the new terrorism thesis in courtrooms and news outlets has forced attorneys to contend with these dominant interpretive frameworks, which circumscribe how defendants and their actions can be made knowable to judges and jurors. In the *Paracha* case, expert witness Evan Kohlmann drew on the new terrorism thesis to describe al-Qaeda's purported organizational hierarchy and operational methods so that the prosecution could establish Paracha's involvement in a terrorist plot. The *Paracha* case illustrates how flimsy, yet successful, this conceptual approach is in securing a guilty verdict in terrorism-related cases; it also demonstrates how difficult it is to challenge the tenets of the new terrorism thesis, which can recast the ordinary activities of Muslims, such as engaging in a business partnership, as criminal efforts to provide material support to a designated foreign terrorist organization.

Although legal challenges have contested the inclusion of such terrorologists, these contestations are limited to the legal tools available to defense attorneys, such as *Daubert* motions. Unfortunately, these legal motions do not provide the courts with the tools to challenge the keystone of these cases: the concept of terrorism. Defense attorneys have sought to counter, limit, or reframe the centrality of orthodox views on terrorism by challenging the credibility of terrorologists, introducing their own expert witnesses, and placing political violence within its formative conditions, such as U.S. empire. Given the limited legal tools available to defense attorneys, these strategies represent an epistemic struggle to make terrorism knowable in new ways. By arbitrating who can testify and on what, judges have played a critical gatekeeping role in determining which interpretive frameworks can enter the courtroom and thus how terrorism can be understood. Terrorologists, however, maintain narrative authority in the courtroom, which means these challenges often fail to disrupt the epistemic injustices that define terrorism trials.

Prosecuting Muhamed Mubayyid: The Epistemic Charge of Terrorism in Ordinary Criminal Cases

In 2008, Muhamed Mubayyid was convicted of engaging in a scheme to conceal material facts from the United States, conspiring to defraud the United States, making a false statement on a tax return, and obstructing and impeding the Internal Revenue Service (IRS). The crux of the case rested on IRS Form 1023, an application for tax exemption under 501(c)(3) of the Internal Revenue Code, which grants tax exemptions to charitable foundations. The prosecution charged Mubayyid and his alleged coconspirators, Emadeddin Muntasser and Samir Al-Monla, after

Muntasser failed to report on Form 1023 that their charitable foundation, Care International, produced and circulated publications as a part
of its fundraising activities, including its newsletter, *Al-Hussam,* which
allegedly promoted "pro-jihadi viewpoints."[72] The prosecution further
charged that Mubayyid and his coconspirators misled the IRS when
Muntasser reported on Form 1023 that Care was not "the outgrowth
of (or successor to) another organization," particularly given Care's perceived origins in the Al-Kifah Refugee Center. Last, the prosecution
argued that the yearly filing of Form 990, in which Mubayyid failed
to inform the IRS of "any activity not previously reported," amounted
to the concealment of material facts in violation of a federal statute
because Mubayyid did not submit the *Al-Hussam* newsletters or report
Care's noncharitable activities "involving the solicitation and expendi-
ture of funds to support and promote jihad and mujahidin."[73] The prosecution argued that the *Al-Hussam* newsletters and Care's origins would
have "had a natural tendency to influence or be capable of influencing
the IRS in making *its* determination of whether Care International qualified for tax-exempt status," making the alleged concealments a crime.[74]
This technical tax case rested on how the defendants reported their noncharitable activities and described their organization's history on official
IRS forms.

Even though these charges did not include any terrorism-related
crimes, the prosecution pursued Mubayyid's conviction on the belief that
he and his coconspirators used Care to funnel money to "Muslim holy
warriors ('mujahidin') engaged in violent, religiously-based military conflict overseas ('jihad')."[75] The prosecution alleged that Care was an "outgrowth" of the Al-Kifah Refugee Center, an alleged "outpost" of Maktab
al-Khidamat that Sheikh Abdullah Azzam and Osama bin Laden established to "support jihad in Afghanistan and around the world" (Levitt
2008). Mubayyid and his coconspirators allegedly employed "economic
jihad" by raising money to support "radical Islamist groups" through Care
(Levitt 2008). The failure to report Care's purported origins in the Al-
Kifah Refugee Center, its promotion of "pro-jihadi viewpoints," and its
publication of the *Al-Hussam* newsletter constituted criminal activities.

Reflecting on the case, the government's expert witness, Matthew Levitt (2008), concluded that although the government charged
Mubayyid with "ordinary criminal activities" related to Care's tax forms,

this legal strategy "should not cloud the fact this was a terrorism case at heart." Presiding Judge Dennis Saylor, however, observed:

> The role of this court, at least in this context, is necessarily narrow. It is not to help—or, for that matter, to hinder—American foreign policy. It is not to help or hinder American law enforcement priorities. It is not to make broad "statements," "send messages," or bestow symbolic "victories" or "defeats." Instead, the role of the court is to make a relatively narrow and focused inquiry: whether the evidence presented at trial, taken in light most favorable to the government, is sufficient to support a conviction as to each defendant as to each count. And it is to examine that evidence with a cold eye, not with inflamed passion—and without regard to any greater cause that this case may be deemed to represent, no matter how worthy that cause may be.[76]

Although prosecutors have pursued terrorism-related cases by charging individuals with "ordinary criminal activities," Judge Saylor cautioned that the role of the trial court was not to advance the global war on terror through these strategic prosecutions; instead, it narrowly tries criminal cases with a "cold eye" disentangled from U.S. foreign policy pursuits. Despite Judge Saylor's comments, terrorism, along with its pulsating anti-Muslim overtures, infused Mubayyid's trial, revealing how orthodox approaches to terrorism are reinforced, circulated, and called on to do conceptual work even in "ordinary criminal cases" through the use of expert witnesses who define concepts like terrorism, jihad, and mujahidin for the courts.

With Judge Saylor "working very hard to keep references of terrorism out of the case," the prosecution mobilized concepts like mujahidin to frame Mubayyid's actions as a kind of economic jihad rather than as charitable or noncharitable activities.[77] These terms maintain the same moral evaluation as the concept of terrorism, noted in how jihad has been sensationalized in popular U.S. media as Islamic holy war despite its actually signifying a range of struggles, from internal spiritual efforts aimed at self-reformation to armed anticolonial conflicts. In the United States, the term jihad has collapsed different political projects into a single frame of reference, such as "fighting against non-Muslims in situations of occupation or civil war," "revolting against Muslim rulers," and waging war against the United States "in an attempt to force a military withdrawal from Muslim-majority countries and end its support for repressive regimes" (Li 2020, 23). Li (2020) argues that the U.S.-led global war on terror "has conflated all of these phenomena wholesale under the rubric of a single overarching threat, reserving special concern for those who have crossed borders as part of their armed commitments" (23). In the *Mubayyid* case, the prosecution drew on this dominant conceptual framework by defining jihad as a "violent, religiously-based military conflict overseas" waged by "foreign fighters."[78] Mobilizing the term jihad requires little analysis that engages the broader contexts in which such armed conflict might unfold, such as the brutal anti-Muslim military campaigns in Afghanistan, Bosnia, and Chechnya, or the various political projects taken up under the banner of jihad.

In the courts, terms like jihad and mujahidin are open for debate, although they often reinforce rather than challenge familiar frames of analysis that mark defendants as illegitimate and violent nonstate actors. Indicative of these debates and the conceptual work these terms are called to undertake, Judge Saylor noted that "the indictment defines 'jihad' to mean 'violent, religiously-based military conflict overseas,'" whereas the defendants "dispute this definition, contending that 'jihad' in fact means 'utmost effort' or 'struggle' and refers to the obligation of all Muslims to promote and defend Islam."[79] Even from the initial indictment, the *Mubayyid* case rested heavily on how the judge and jurors understood jihad and mujahidin and their relation to Care's activities, despite its being a technical tax case. Given the perceived relevance of jihad and mujahidin to this case, Judge Saylor permitted terrorologist Evan Kohlmann to testify as an expert witness, despite defense counsel's concerns that "if he testifies, the specter of terrorism will be cast over this entire case in a way that is completely unfair."[80]

Disputing Orthodoxy: Legal Challenges to Terrorism Expertise

In response to the prosecution's trial strategy, Mubayyid's defense team sought to exclude terrorologists from testifying, contending that such expertise was not relevant to a technical tax case. In a motion to preclude Evan Kohlmann and Matthew Levitt from testifying, the defense argued, "This is a tax case. . . . This is not a terrorism case. There is no charge that Care was a terrorist organization. . . . There is no charge that the money collected by Care was spent on anything other than the stated purposes of providing humanitarian relief to people in dire need and publishing and distributing books and newsletters protected by the First Amendment."[81] As a technical tax case, the defense further reasoned that while the jury "may well benefit from the assistance of experts in tax law" and "experts who can describe for them the conditions in Afghanistan, Pakistan, Bosnia, and Kosovo in the period following the Soviet withdrawal which created the humanitarian crisis Care was founded to address," the jury "most definitely does not need" the "testimony of experts in terrorism committed by individuals and organizations nowhere mentioned in the indictment, engaged in crimes not charged in the indictment, in parts of the world and by organizations that the defendant had absolutely nothing to do with."[82] The defense concluded that through expert testimony, "the prosecution wants to tell the story of the battle in Bosnia, leaving out the suffering to which Care addressed its efforts, and inviting the jury to convict Care for crimes it has not been charged with committing. That is wrong."[83] Asserting that the introduction of terrorism experts into a tax case "is plainly irrelevant and prejudicial," the defense noted that "we have . . . found *not a single tax case in which terrorism experts have been permitted to testify.*"[84] Citing the fitness prong of *Daubert,* the defense argued that expert testimony by terrorologists was not relevant to the factual evidence at hand and that Levitt and Kohlmann both lacked expertise in the issues related to the case.

Finding terrorism expertise irrelevant to questions of tax law, the defense also questioned the expert reports furnished by Levitt and Kohlmann. For example, although Levitt argued in his expert report that "CARE International (CARE) is an outgrowth of the Al-Kifah Refugee Center, a part of the Maktab al-Khidamat (MAK) support network founded by Osama bin Laden and Abdullah Azzam," the defense noted that "whether Care is an 'outgrowth' of the Al-Kifah Refugee Center is a question of tax law unrelated to Dr. Levitt's knowledge of Middle Eastern terrorism" and that "there is absolutely no indication that Dr. Levitt has done any research independent of this case on the relationship between Care International and Al-Kifah."[85] Because Form 1023 asked if Care was "an outgrowth of (or successor to)" another organization, the defense argued that the legality of Care's response was a matter of tax law, a topic unbefitting a terrorologist's expertise. In fact, IRS tax exemption specialist Gerald Sack testified that Care's *Al-Hussam* newsletters would have prompted the IRS to "go into development mode"—that is, it would seek additional information from the applicant—but not trigger an immediate denial.[86]

The defense also disputed expert reports that offered ahistorical and apolitical renderings of humanitarian crises in Afghanistan, Bosnia, and Chechnya—political conflicts that Levitt and Kohlmann used to demonstrate the role of charitable organizations in economic jihad. The defense noted that Kohlmann's expert report "totally distorts the history of the wars in these countries," such as the humanitarian crisis wrought by the genocidal killing of Bosnian Muslims during the Bosnian war.[87] The defense further charged that Kohlmann "does not lay out the historical context. He does not lay out the humanitarian disaster. He talks only about extremist groups, and he also warned us of his account with wildly—with wild speculation, and it was quite clear from his testimony about how he does research on his vast internet site."[88] In sum, the defense viewed Kohlmann's expert report as "replete with summarization, speculation, infelicitous adjectives, notorious, violent, illicit through. He speculates. Everything he says about Al-Hussam is either speculation or repetition."[89]

Although the defense challenged Kohlmann's expertise, its concerns lay squarely with orthodox approaches to terrorism that abstract political violence from its formative conditions, such as brutal military campaigns against Muslims, ongoing humanitarian crises, and military conflicts supported by the United States. In addition, the defense viewed Kohlmann's expertise on foreign mujahids as irrelevant to the tax questions defining the case, especially because the prosecution failed to present evidence connecting Care to the "atrocities and battles in Bosnia (as well as in Libya, Chechnya, Algeria, and Egypt)."[90] In court proceedings, the defense worked to challenge Kohlmann's orthodoxy, including his ahistorical analyses; Kohlmann's expert status, however, insulated him from these direct challenges.

Reframing Charitable Giving as Economic Jihad: Terrorologists in Ordinary Criminal Cases

Although Judge Saylor sought to limit specific references to terrorism, the concept showed up in other ways, particularly through expert testimony on economic jihad, mujahidin, and terrorist financing. Despite the prosecution's failure to present any evidence proving Care funded foreign mujahids, the role of Muslim charitable organizations in "terrorist fundraising" featured prominently in expert testimony. In this way, terrorologists were instrumental in reframing this "technical tax case" as a "terrorism case at heart."

In his sweeping expert report, Matthew Levitt examined charities purportedly used as "front organizations" for "terrorists," concluding that Care is a "textbook example" of a charity offering a "veil of legitimacy for terrorist fundraising" and "grassroots support for the terrorist groups in the region."[91] Levitt then described other so-called terrorist organizations that allegedly engaged in economic jihad, again determining that Care is "a prime example of how mujahidin, terrorist groups, and their supporters use charity as a cover to provide a veneer of legitimacy to otherwise illicit activities."[92] In this way, the prosecution positioned Levitt as "the primary financing person, the person who is talking about how the mujahidin were financed."[93] In doing so, the prosecution made economic jihad—defined as terrorist financing—central to the case, even though it charged the defendant with tax law violations. In fact, the prosecution never charged Care with "terrorist fundraising" or with operating as a "front organization" for financing terrorist plots. Levitt's report and testimony, however, suggested that Care solicited and expended funds to support foreign mujahids.

Evan Kohlmann's expert testimony similarly established uncorroborated links between "ostensible charitable organizations" like Care and the funding of foreign mujahids. At trial, the prosecution specifically asked Kohlmann to provide an overview of conflicts in Afghanistan, Bosnia, and Chechnya; detail how "the mujahidin, the foreign fighters" contributed to these conflicts; and explain the role of the "ostensible charitable organizations" in providing "support for these different mujahidin organizations."[94] Through his testimony, Kohlmann presented Care as yet another Muslim charitable organization that "provided financing for fighters involved in the conflict," reinforcing the centrality of economic jihad in this technical tax case.[95] The racial logics organizing the criminal-legal system make such unsubstantiated conclusions possible, and legally effectual, by tethering Islam to violence and by defining terrorism as a Muslim phenomenon (Volpp 2002; Beydoun and Choudhury 2020; Razack 2008).

In addition to detailing the alleged role of Muslim charitable organizations in funding armed resistance, Kohlmann discredited foreign mujahids who arguably fought under religious, rather than nationalist, doctrine. In his description of the Bosnian war, for example, Kohlmann explained, "Initially, starting off, there were no Bosnian mujahidin," as "the main body of Bosnian Muslim fighters were fighting under the Army of Bosnia-Herzegovina, which was a nationalist force."[96] However, "starting in the summer of 1992, as the foreign mujahidin began arriving in Bosnia, they decided that they would need to form an official organization for themselves, which they called Kataeb al-Mujahidin, the Mujahidin Brigade."[97] The constitution of this battalion "formalize[d] the reception of foreign fighters arriving from places such as Afghanistan" and "encourage[d] the recruitment of Bosnian Muslims, who had previously been very nationalist, to convince them to adopt a new religious perspective, a new political perspective, and to join the mujahidin fighting in the field," in pursuit of capturing and defending "territory that they considered genuinely part of the Bosnian Muslim state."[98] Here, Kohlmann distinguished legitimate Bosnian Muslims fighting under a nationalist force from illegitimate transnational fighters (foreign mujahids)—even as both types of forces responded to the "ethnic cleansing" of Bosnian Muslims, and even as the broader Yugoslav wars (1991–95) saw "the participation of foreign fighters on all sides" and atrocities committed by soldiers of all stripes (Arielli 2012, 1). By discrediting Muslim transnational fighters responding to dire humanitarian crises and genocidal campaigns, Kohlmann foreclosed alternative ways of understanding political violence, such as exploring how the invocation of global Islamic solidarity works to "enact an alternative to the interventions of the 'International Community'" by negotiating the "interstitial spaces of the international legal order of sovereign states" (Li 2016, 372–73). Instead, terrorologists like Kohlmann deny the political dimensions to violence and criminalize armed resistance, irrespective of the material conditions in which violence circulates. Applied to the *Mubayyid* case, Kohlmann's testimony discredited all efforts to finance, promote, and support foreign mujahids by charitable organizations, even though the prosecution never charged Care with providing material support to a designated foreign terrorist organization.

Rather than challenge Kohlmann's depiction of foreign mujahids as illegitimate nonstate actors driven by religious doctrine, the defense used its cross-examination of Kohlmann to affirm the humanitarian crises that organizations like Care sought to mitigate through their charitable and noncharitable activities. The defense asked Kohlmann if he was aware that "Serbs slaughtered Bosnian Muslims" in what "the State Department has referred to . . . as one of the worst single reported incidents of genocidal mass murder—mass killing of members of an ethnic or religious group in Europe since 1945?"[99] Kohlmann confirmed that in the 1990s, "there were refugee crises involving Muslims" in Afghanistan, Bosnia, and Chechnya. Despite Kohlmann's tepid response, the defense detailed the pressing humanitarian crises that generated immense human suffering, which organizations of all stripes sought to mitigate. The defense argued that "the evidence of a Muslim genocide and the enormous suffering brought about by Serbian and Croatian forces is directly relevant to this case . . . because it is the jury's job . . . to determine whether Care was engaged in the mission described in its founding documents submitted to the IRS."[100] Such evidence could "make plain that there was more than one explanation for how foreign funds could be spent in Bosnia and why they would be sent there."[101] Rather than dispute Kohlmann's analysis of foreign mujahids, Mubayyid's defense team highlighted the dire conditions that motivated charitable organizations to contribute to "humanitarian relief" efforts.[102]

In addition to this legal strategy, the defense sought to admit an expert witness who could testify about U.S. support for foreign mujahids, particularly in Afghanistan. Leaving the prosecution's framing of foreign mujahids as illegitimate nonstate actors unchallenged, the defense argued that Care's actions aligned with the U.S. government, making it material to the case at hand. For example, the IRS employee who reviewed Care's tax exemption forms stated that "if the application had indicated that the fundraising requested specific money for the support of mujahidin," then he would have "made the determination not to grant Care exempt status," a conclusion "based on the United States public policy aspect."[103] The defense therefore asked in a pretrial motion, "How can [U.S.] public policy be irrelevant if, according to the government, it would have been the basis for the denial of tax-exempt status?"[104] At trial, the defense argued that "if the court is going to allow testimony that the mujahidin were financed by Muslims in other countries . . . then we have to be allowed to bring out they were funded by the United States. In fact, Mr. Kohlmann will agree that they were vigorously and enthusiastically supported by the United States."[105] If demonstrating that Care's charitable and noncharitable giving aligned with U.S. public policy, such that these activities would not bear on the IRS's decision, the court should permit testimony on the "United States public policy aspect."

The prosecution contested evidence related to "the United States government's political policies" and references to its "defense and intelligence service activities abroad."[106] The prosecution argued that such evidence "is not probative of any issue in this case going to an element of an offense or to be a legal defense."[107] More specifically, the prosecution explained that "*the alliance of the defendants' activities with U.S. foreign policy* does not mean the failure to disclose those activities could not be material to the IRS" and that "the jury will be improperly influenced by the suggestion that if the U.S. government supported the goals of the mujahidin, then the Defendants' failure to disclose their relationship to the mujahidin is meaningless."[108] Despite entering substantial evidence about foreign mujahids, the prosecution sought to narrow the defense's testimony to the mere tax questions at hand. The prosecution actively centered economic jihad, mujahidin, and martyrs throughout this case while also seeking to limit how terrorism could be made knowable in the courtroom.

To restrict court testimony in this way, the prosecution contradicted itself, arguing that "this case does not present a political question, nor should the defense be permitted to invite speculation as to whether the IRS' decision-making would have been mooted because of official foreign policy decisions by the Office of the President and other departments."[109] In fact, the prosecution proffered that "the point of this prosecution is that the defendants concealed from the government crucial information which could have affected the IRS determination of Care's tax exemption status," meaning "the defendants' geopolitical views are not on trial as being seditious or antithetical to American foreign policy; rather it is the fact that they failed to disclose their activities, origins, and purposes, which could have influenced the government's granting and maintenance of Care International's 501(c)(3) tax-exempt status."[110] The prosecution also moved to exclude evidence of Care's charitable activities, asserting that "nowhere in the indictment does the government allege that Care did not engage in charitable activities," meaning that "the evidence that Care purportedly solicited money for widows and orphans in addition to the mujahidin is simply irrelevant."[111] The "presentation of hundreds of pages of documents, almost entirely based on only one of Care's activities, orphan sponsorship, would unnecessarily stray the focus of the inquiry from the charges in question and would only serve to confuse or mislead the jury," particularly because "the only issues [alleged in the indictment] is whether Care engaged in other noncharitable activities that the defendants decided to conceal from the government."[112] The double standard here is evident. Kohlmann could testify that foreign mujahids contributed to transnational conflicts around the globe with the support of Muslim charitable organizations that provided "financing for fighters involved in the conflict" and "vocal support advocacy on behalf of these groups, suggesting that their causes were just and were right."[113] Yet the defense could not locate such fighting within a broader geopolitical context defined by the United States' own support of mujahids.

The prosecution's desire to make jihad a central feature of this case while limiting how jihad could be made knowable to jurors demonstrates the epistemic struggle to assert particular understandings of jihad, mujahidin, and terrorist financing, which ultimately informs how jurors determine the criminality of the defendant and his actions. Terrorologists like Kohlmann and Levitt therefore play a critical role in asserting the interpretive frameworks to understand a case's factual evidence such that an ordinary criminal case transforms into a "terrorism case at heart." Although Judge Saylor sought to restrict references to terrorism at trial, the prosecution found other ways to introduce such evidence, particularly through expert testimony invoking jihad and mujahidin as organizing conceptual frameworks.

In response to these arguments, Judge Saylor observed, "I think to be completely fair and somewhat deferential to the defense, I'm going to permit testimony, limited testimony that the United States provided military aid to mujahidin, provided that the timeframe is made clear and that there was publicity, in the 1980s at least, concerning the mujahidin as freedom fighters in the United States if the witness is aware of it."[114] Judge Saylor allowed this testimony because he recognized how the concept of mujahidin and its moral standing shifted in the United

States, explaining that "if you asked the average well-informed American in 1981 who were the mujahidin, they would say freedom fighters. And we boycotted the Moscow Olympics in 1980 in their support. And if you ask the average American in 2003 who the mujahidin are, they would say they are terrorists."[115] At trial, Kohlmann verified that the United States provided "billions of dollars to Afghan fighters" through both "humanitarian relief" and "weapons shipments."[116] Minutes later, however, Kohlmann reaffirmed that "charitable organizations . . . provided financing involved in conflict . . . [and] provided means by which recruits from other countries . . . could reach these various zones."[117] Through his testimony, Kohlmann demonized foreign fighters as unlawful enemy combatants driven by religious commandment, without questioning the ideological motivations that brought U.S. soldiers to fight in Afghanistan. Kohlmann's portrayal of mujahids reflects how "participating in armed forms of solidarity without the permission of any nation-state—fighting in 'other people's wars'—is treated as suspect in a world order that favors the model of the citizen-soldier as the paradigm for legitimate violence" (Li 2020, 4). Despite Kohlmann's testimony, Judge Saylor clarified that "there's no evidence that Care provided military equipment or fighters in these areas."[118]

Because the prosecution also charged Care with failing to report its organizational origins on its IRS forms, it also called on Kohlmann to establish Care's lineage, particularly its roots in Maktab al-Kihdamat (Office of Human Services) founded by the so-called father of global jihad, Abdullah Azzam. To begin, Kohlmann described how "mujahidin organizations" recruited foreign fighters, noting that Azzam is "largely credited with having brought many of the foreign fighters that eventually joined the mujahidin, or fought alongside the mujahidin, to Afghanistan. He was—his major focus was on the concept of jihad, or holy struggle, and he encouraged many young men from around the world that it was their duty to go fight in Afghanistan against enemies of the Afghan people of Islam and to join that battle."[119] This testimony distorted how Azzam "operated according to a logic of solidarity, maintaining a resolutely localized sense of authority in the Afghan jihad—a struggle that sought control of a state *within* the international legal order and openly aligned with members of that order, not least the United States" (Li 2020, 85). Kohlmann also reported that to support these recruitment efforts, Azzam established Maktab al-Khidamat, and that "in North America, Maktab al-Khidamat was known as the Al-Kifah Refugee Center."[120] In this view, Azzam established Maktab al-Khidamat to recruit and finance foreign mujahids; Maktab al-Khidamat then opened a North American branch, the Al-Kifah Refugee Center, which would later become Care. Kohlmann's testimony supported the prosecution's charge that Care was an "outgrowth" of the Al-Kifah Refugee Center—a status Care was legally obliged to report to the IRS.

For the prosecution, this evidence "bears on the principal concern of the IRS. If you're engaged in noncharitable activity, that goes—that is critical in court to the Form 1023 application form as well as to the successor outgrowth."[121] In other words, Care's relationship to the Al-Kifah Refugee Center may have affected the IRS's review of its Form 1023 application. Kohlmann's testimony was crucial in establishing the purported lineage of Maktab al-Khidamat, the Al-Kifah Refugee Center, and Care and their alleged commitment to supporting mujahids through charitable and noncharitable activities.

After listening to this testimony, Judge Saylor explained that "it is, at least, unclear enough in my mind as to whether there is evidence that Al-Kifah was actually supporting fighters as opposed to engaged in the same activities as Care, as to which there is certainly evidence."[122] In this view, the prosecution's evidence did not support its charge that Al-Kifah funded mujahids engaged in armed conflict in Afghanistan. In fact, Judge Saylor's written instructions to the jury before deliberations reiterated, "There is no evidence . . . that Care or the defendants provided or financed weapons, armaments, or lethal aid to any party, and you may not speculate or conjecture as to the possible existence of such evidence."[123] The jury, however, found Mubayyid guilty on all counts.

Levitt (2008) celebrated the conviction, concluding, "Like other radical organizations, Care took advantage of the otherwise laudable Islamic tradition of charity and good works not only to teach its particular version of Islam but also to actively support terrorist operations." In fact, Levitt argued that the courts could effectively incapacitate "terrorists," noting that the "ultimate effect of the tax law conviction was to expose and hold accountable a fundraising network that raised significant amounts of money for al-Qaeda and its affiliated groups." In this way, "sometimes the best strategy for a terrorism prosecution is to focus on the underlying and mundane criminal activity." Levitt's celebration clearly demonstrates how the government has used this pretextual prosecution strategy to "neutralize terrorists" and therefore execute its global war on terror (Kris 2011, 58). This legal approach expands criminal liability by targeting mundane activities, such as charitable giving recast as economic jihad; relying on anti-Muslim tropes to secure convictions; and advancing a "corpus of immigration law and law enforcement policy that by design or effect applies almost exclusively to Arabs, Muslims, and South Asians" (Ahmad 2004, 1262).

Despite Levitt's victory lap, the defense sought an acquittal, specifically contesting the prosecution's inclusion of "graphic, inflammatory, repeated, cumulative evidence referring to blood-curdling activities."[124] For the defense, the use of such evidence in a "technical tax case" was more prejudicial than probative.[125] In this view, if the government could prove "that any of the money went to the fighters, the mujahidin, or for the cause of jihad," then "we wouldn't be here right now. They would've charged material support. They couldn't. They didn't."[126] Unfortunately, the inclusion of Care's connections to "blood-curdling activities" transformed an ordinary criminal case into a terrorism trial. Although Judge Saylor overturned the conspiracy to defraud the United States charge related to the perceived hiding of Care's "pro-jihadi activities," the U.S. Court of Appeals for the First Circuit reversed this decision, reinstating the jury's verdict.

Echoing Levitt's expert testimony, many political leaders and law enforcement agents celebrated the guilty verdicts as critical victories in the global war on terror, demonstrating how a technical tax case can serve as a referendum on extremist causes, even absent credible evidence. Assistant Attorney General for National Security Kenneth Wainstein celebrated the convictions of Mubayyid and his coconspirators, describing the guilty verdicts as "a milestone in our efforts against those who conceal their support for extremist causes behind the veil of humanitarianism," like the defendants who "used an allegedly charitable organization as a front for the collection of donations that they used to support violent jihadists" (qtd. in Department of Justice 2008). As the government continues to broaden what constitutes the provision of "material support" to designated foreign terrorist organizations, such as medical services[127] and English-language lessons,[128] it also transforms the prosecution of "ordinary criminal cases" into terrorism trials.

Given the epistemic authority of terrorologists in the courtroom and the limited legal tools available to challenge such authority, Mubayyid's defense team strategically contested the credibility of proposed expert witnesses, the relevance of these witnesses, and their analyses. These contestations reveal how the courts authorize, circulate, and legitimize orthodox approaches to terrorism, necessarily narrowing how judges and jurors come to understand the concept and its application to defendants. In other words, prosecutors strategically invoke orthodox approaches to the study of terrorism to constrict the conceptual frameworks judges and jurors reach for to make sense of the cases before them. Defense attorneys must respond to and challenge such orthodoxy, which limits the epistemic maneuvers they might undertake in the courtroom to reinterpret and reframe their clients' actions. In *Mubayyid,* prosecutors used expert witnesses like Matthew Levitt to assert a conceptual framework—economic jihad—that jurors could use to interpret Care's activities and the defendant's actions, even in the absence of corroborating evidence.

Conclusion: Epistemic Injustice and Terrorism Prosecutions

As these terrorism-related cases demonstrate, domestic courts legitimize, circulate, and mobilize orthodox terrorism expertise by admitting terrorologists who rehearse dominant interpretive frameworks judges and jurors can use to understand the cases before them. Although the field of terrorism studies remains hotly contested and deeply incoherent, self-styled terrorologists like Evan Kohlmann have shaped the adjudication of terrorism-related cases by making terrorism knowable in specific ways. In their testimony, terrorologists often have abstracted political violence from its formative conditions and offered ahistorical renderings that tether Islam to violence. Even though terrorologists maintain controversial ties to powerful institutions such as the military, deploy questionable research methods, and self-determine their expert status, the courts often have viewed terrorism scholars as more knowledgeable, reliable, and credible than lay witnesses or the defendants themselves.

Terrorologists continue to play a powerful role in domestic courtrooms despite the contested status of terrorism studies within academia. Even when judges limit references to terrorism, the courts function as a key site in the global war on terror through "the strategic utility of charging terrorists and their supporters for ordinary criminal activities that the government can easily prosecute" (Levitt 2008). Unfortunately, the specter of terrorism infects these cases with enormous prejudice, making it impossible to evaluate evidence without using orthodox approaches to terrorism, and their articulation with familiar anti-Muslim narratives circulating in popular media, as a way to interpret defendants' actions.

Cases like *Paracha* demonstrate how defendants, as subjugated knowers, often are denied epistemic authority to narrate their lives, to locate their experiences in the prevailing geopolitical contexts they negotiate daily, and to provide alternative interpretations of the events that led to their arrests. Instead, court-endorsed experts like Kohlmann have been called on to do this epistemic and conceptual work, advancing the reductive yet effective new terrorism thesis which provides judges and jurors with the interpretive tools to make sense of the evidence before them. In *Paracha,* alleged al-Qaeda operatives Majid Khan and Ammar al-Baluchi vehemently denied collaborating with defendant Uzair Paracha to plan and execute a terrorist plot. Despite their corroborating testimony, Kohlmann's description of terrorist organizations allowed the prosecutors to suggest that al-Qaeda's insular cell structure made it possible for one operative to be unaware of another. The prosecution thus relied on a terrorologist to prove that a lack of evidence merely reflected the defining features of terrorist organizations, such as their diffuse and decentralized structure, rather than Paracha's innocence. Kohlmann and his colleague Matthew Levitt functioned similarly in the *Mubayyid* tax case by making mujahidin and economic jihad central features of this tax case, despite the judge's own jury instructions reiterating that no evidence demonstrated that Care provided financial aid to foreign mujahids. The *Paracha* and *Mubayyid* cases illustrate how domestic courts commit a distinctly epistemic type of injustice by denying defendants their credibility and capacity as knowers of their own lives, particularly as they negotiate the stigma the terrorism label induces, and by conferring epistemic authority onto terrorologists.

Given that the defendants' status as Muslim men of color marked them as potential terrorists, we must remember that "differential positionings in terms of power, social location, and cognitive expectation shape perception" such that the courts view defendants charged with terrorism-related crimes as less credible than terrorologists (May 2014, 95). These power asymmetries confer epistemic authority onto terrorologists, typically at the expense of defendants, and confirm dominant narratives about incipient Muslim terrorists, who must be incapacitated through their arrest, conviction, and incarceration and through the attaching of criminal liability onto a long continuum of behaviors like radical beliefs, financial transactions, and personal associations. Feminist scholar Vivian M. May (2014) reminds us that "it is essential to account for how knowledge derived from and crafted in marginalized locations entails a double struggle: the struggle to articulate what cannot necessarily be told in conventional terms, and the struggle to be heard without being (mis)translated into normative logics that occlude the meanings at hand" (99). Such struggles reveal the "material and epistemological asymmetries of power" that emerge in domestic courts trying terrorism-related cases (99). In these cases, defendants and their attorneys must negotiate this uneven epistemic terrain, particularly when terrorologists place their narratives within normative logics that define terrorism as unscrupulous, incorrigible, and irredeemable acts of violence committed by evildoers, without reference to the prevailing historical, geopolitical, economic, and social contexts to understand such violence.

Unfortunately, defendants rarely have destabilized dominant understandings of terrorism or effectively countered expert testimony. In the *Mubayyid* case, for example, Levitt centered economic jihad in his testimony, arguing that many Muslim charities operated as front organizations to fund foreign mujahids, irrespective of the brutal anti-Muslim campaigns in Afghanistan, Bosnia, and Chechnya or of the actual activities of Care, which never included funneling money to the front lines. The inclusion of terrorologists in court proceedings thus intensifies, rather than transforms, such epistemic asymmetries, such as "disparities in cognitive authority, imbalances in historical memory, and inequities of rhetorical space" (May 2014, 97). Yet in the absence of other ways of knowing terrorism, judges and jurors will continue to reach for and use dominant anti-Muslim frameworks, such as the new terrorism thesis, to understand the cases before them. Terrorologists therefore play an instrumental role in securing convictions, even in ordinary criminal cases like *Mubayyid,* by confirming hegemonic understandings of terrorism and by providing the interpretive lenses through which prosecutors can demonstrate a link between defendants and terrorist plots.

Legal deliberations and judgments have reinforced and legitimized orthodox approaches to the study of terrorism—epistemic processes that have limited how defendants can contest the charges against them. The shadow of terrorism looms even in ordinary criminal cases, shaping how defendants can challenge these charges, how their actions can be made knowable to the jurors, and who holds epistemic authority to interpret the factual evidence in each case. Legal challenges, such as motions to preclude expert witnesses, typically contest individual terrorologists and generally cannot disrupt popular conceptions of terrorism, which correspond to expert testimony. In fact, in mock terrorism trials, researchers found that jurors considered the prosecution's expert witnesses to be "presenting 'the facts' in an impartial way" while dismissing the defense's expert witnesses as "unbalanced" (Battye and Rossner 2017, 212). The jurors therefore demonstrated "a high value accorded to expert knowledge and the light such knowledge could potentially shed on other evidence" (Battye and Rossner 2017, 210). Although the strategic cross-examination of terrorologists can introduce other ways of understanding terrorism and reveal an expert's analytical shortcomings, doing so rarely returns a not-guilty jury verdict. Cross-examination, after all, typically does not disturb the expert status of terrorologists or reaffirm the credibility of defendants and other lay witnesses. In bench trials and sentencing hearings, judges too rely on dominant understandings of terrorism, as defense attorneys report the futility of trying to explain contextualizing information, such as the geopolitical context of the Syrian war, to judges (interview, March 2021).

In considering such forms of "testimonial injustice," Fricker (2007) explains that "when it comes to the verdict, the jurors go along with the automatic distrust delivered by the prejudices that structure their perception of that speaker," such as individuals marked as terrorists, while also conferring epistemic authority onto expert witnesses (25). Although Fricker further argues that "the primary characterization of testimonial injustice . . . remains such that it is a matter of credibility deficit and not credibility excess," terrorism trials rest on an epistemic double movement: simultaneously denying defendants and lay witnesses their status as credible knowers, *and* affirming the expert status and thus knowledge of terrorologists (21). Such testimonial injustice persists, even as social scientists have "adopted a skeptical view of the dominant discourse and modes of study of those deemed 'terrorists'" and "challenged commonly held understandings about the nature and causes of terrorism" (Jackson, Smyth, and Gunning 2009, 1). With limited legal tools available to them, defendants can do little to challenge the epistemic authority of terrorologists, to offer alternative interpretations of the factual evidence before the court, and to prove their innocence.

Given the centrality of terrorism prosecutions in the global war on terror, terrorologists will continue to shape domestic court proceedings. In this legal context, reaching for justice means more than challenging terrorologists; it requires radically altering the epistemic terrain such that defendants can be heard as credible and reliable narrators of their own lives and that terrorism can be knowable in new ways. Legal scholars have argued for reimagining jury selection processes in terrorism-related cases, or even suspending jury trials altogether (Donohue 2007). Unlike ordinary criminal cases "where jurors have no stake in the outcome," terrorism trials "position the jurors as potential victims," which can impinge on a jury's ability to render a fair and accurate verdict (Tait and Goodman-Delahunty 2017, 274). One defense attorney even reported difficulty in securing a jury "where each juror's view of this is not shaped by their personal experience on 9/11," and, in "cases where there's this aura of terrorism," requested that judges ask potential jurors questions such as, "Do you know someone in the fire department? Do you have relatives in the police department?" In his view, if a juror's sibling "is a firefighter and on the job on 9/11, she's going to come to this case with a set of biases" (interview, November 2020). These legal challenges, however, cannot address the epistemic charge of terrorism trials that allow, for example, the recasting of a technical tax case as a major global war on terror victory by arresting alleged circuits of economic jihad.

Currently, the dominant racialized frameworks that the courts mobilize to understand terrorism or jihad secure convictions, even of individuals like Uzair Paracha with no proven links to al-Qaeda. The *Mubayyid* case demonstrates how prosecutors also use these frameworks to criminalize the provision of humanitarian aid by Muslim organizations responding to humanitarian crises, military incursions, and genocidal violence. Kohlmann's testimony made foreign mujahids knowable through a pathologizing lens, thus anchoring their participation in jihad in their presumed perversions of religious doctrine; this approach erases how foreign mujahids have articulated a substantive critique of Western aggression and the international community's failure to respond to violent political crises around the globe while developing a political vision for an alternative world order that acknowledges and defends their interests. In this sense, "contemporary transnational jihads need to be understood as taking place *in a world of sovereigns:* these invocations of jihad may draw on the rich and diverse textual traditions of Islam, but they do so under the structural conditions of a world order based on sovereign nation-states" (Li 2016, 375). Dominant terrorism discourses, however, make it impossible to conceptualize "roving participants in transnational jihad" as more than "the enemy of mankind" who "stand opposed not just to 'the West' but to multiculturalism, to tolerance, to the very idea of common humanity itself" (Li 2020, 3). Without alternative frameworks circulating in academic literature, popular media, and dominant discourses, the courts will continue to legitimize and mobilize orthodox terrorism expertise while also committing multilayered forms of epistemic injustice that deny defendants and defense witnesses their credibility. Such normative understandings of political violence and armed resistance limit the legal strategies available to defendants like Paracha and Mubayyid, making it imperative to integrate alternative frameworks into social movement work, popular discourse, and media reports.

Given the influential role of orthodox terrorism expertise in court proceedings, social scientists and abolitionists alike must center other conceptual tools useful in understanding and responding to political violence in ways that do not pathologize individual actors, rely on the criminal-legal system, justify war, and absolve the structurally powerful in creating the conditions that incite armed resistance. Such concept-work can challenge the state's invocation of terrorism, which by design facilitates the criminalization, prosecution, and incarceration of Muslim communities in the name of national security. For example, Suhaiymah Manzoor-Khan (2022) explains that the September 11 attacks must be understood not as an expression of Islamic fanaticism but rather as part of a "political pattern of violent responses to U.S. foreign policy" and a "manifestation of a type of political violence used by many nonstate groups against imperialist powers throughout the twentieth century" (28). However, with few conceptual tools to help us understand political violence, terrorologists will continue to provide the interpretive frames that justify the continued use of policing and security regimes and impute individual actors without addressing the root causes of armed resistance, including U.S. foreign policy and imperialist interventions. This absolution empowers, and is empowered by, the criminal-legal system's relentless pursuit of individual actors, without ever reckoning with the politics animating violence, as well as the continued reliance on orthodox approaches to the study of terrorism that occlude the role of power and politics in the making of armed resistance.

To nourish a political strategy that attends to the coherence of globalized punishment, war, and empire evident in terrorism prosecutions, abolitionists must engage scholars like Manzoor-Khan to develop and deploy alternative frames of analyses that offer us new ways of thinking about political violence outside of state-sponsored concepts like terrorism. Locating armed struggles and preemptive policing in their historical and geopolitical contexts shows us the limits of criminal prosecution and its use as a weapon of war. The punishment of individual actors—whether participants actively engaged in armed struggles, equivocally committed supporters, criminalized political dissidents or Muslim charities, or youth ensnared in sting operations—does little to undermine the material conditions that give rise to political violence. If we are serious about ending global violence and building a safer world, "we must reject this notion of security altogether and end the Islamophobic War on Terror" (Manzoor-Khan 2022, 40). Creating a less violent world requires attending to the root causes of armed resistance and nurturing alternative forms of governance, self-determination, and care that do not capitulate to state interests or expand police power.

In the absence of alternative conceptual tools, the state's theories will continue to dominate domestic courtrooms and newsrooms, the public's political imaginary, and national security policies and practices. Radicalization is one such state theory that continues to organize popular, political, and professional understandings of nonstate actors who use violence to effect political change. Radicalization theories intensify the contributions of orthodox terrorism studies by further reducing political violence to the expression of individual pathologies. In this view, political violence is a choice freely made by individual actors, irrespective of the brutal conditions under which some live. It is to these radicalization theories and their influence on terrorism trials to which I now turn.

5

PROSECUTING LONE WOLVES
THE LEGAL LIFE OF
RADICALIZATION THEORIES

IN 2016, Minnesota District Court judge Michael Davis presided over a sentencing hearing for the six young men who pleaded guilty to terrorism-related crimes after they discussed travel plans to join ISIS's fight against the Assad regime.[1] Before the hearing, Judge Davis ordered each defendant to submit to a risk assessment that would be conducted by a radicalization expert, Daniel Koehler. To inform his sentencing decisions, Judge Davis asked the expert examiner to produce a written report that would describe the "specific driving factors of radicalization for [each] individual defendant," offer insight into the "prognosis of possible chances of success for intervention and de-radicalization process," and outline recommendations for a "disengagement and de-radicalization program tailored to the individual defendant's circumstances and underlying radicalization factors."[2] In these related cases, the judge turned to a court-appointed terrorism expert to evaluate each defendant's degree of radicalization, his prospects for rehabilitation, and his future dangerousness.

Using the expert's risk assessments as a guide, Judge Davis ordered a tailored sentence for each defendant. For example, Judge Davis determined that Abdullahi Yusuf "displayed a medium to low risk of future offending and a comparatively advanced stage of disengagement," justifying a minimal sentence of time served (one year, eight months, and twenty-two days).[3] In the case of Adnan Farah, however, Judge Davis concluded that the defendant "has a medium to high risk of future offending and a comparatively advanced stage of radicalization," necessitating a ten-year prison term.[4] Informed by the expert's reports, Judge Davis determined that the defendants posed different risks and therefore required different prison terms, even though they had been convicted as coconspirators in the same criminal enterprise.

Across his sentencing memoranda, Judge Davis offered contradictory comments on the relationship between prisons and the terrorist radicalization process—inconsistencies that partially depended on the defendant's cooperation with law enforcement and the judge's use of the expert reports to justify these sentencing variations. In Adnan Farah's case, Judge Davis reasoned that, given both "the risks of re-radicalization for defendants convicted of terrorism offenses, and the fact that no program exists, either within or outside of the federal prison system, that meets the standard of a qualified disengagement and re-radicalization program," Koehler's "medium to high" risk assessment did not "support a more substantial variance from the applicable guideline range."[5] In this view, the public safety risks posed by individuals charged with terrorism-related crimes required harsher prison sentences, especially if evaluated to display a "comparatively advanced stage of radicalization." Without a deradicalization program to deter Farah from the perceived pathway to terrorism, the court needed to incarcerate Farah to protect the public. However, after helping law enforcement mount a case against his friends, Abdirizak Warsame faced only an eighteen-month prison term, even after allegedly being elected emir of the group and being classified by Koehler as "high risk."[6] Citing Koehler's report, Judge Davis determined that "a lengthy period of remaining untreated in prison *increases* the risk of further radicalization" and "obviously, increased radicalization, in this case due to lack of treatment, is anathema to 'public safety.'"[7] In this view, prison served as an incubator of terrorist radicalization, making a long prison term potentially dangerous. As the *Yusuf, Warsame,* and *Farah* cases illustrate, judges have used the concept of radicalization to evaluate the threat a defendant poses, assess their capacity for rehabilitation, and inform their sentencing decisions.

Given the currency of state-sponsored radicalization theories, scholars have explored how the concept of radicalization has shaped preemptive policing practices, reinvigorated interest in sting operations, and justified emerging antiterrorism initiatives (Shafi and Qureshi 2020; Kundnani 2012; Sharma and Nijjar 2018; Szpunar 2017; Patel 2011; Walker 2021; Sadequee 2018). Little attention, however, has been cast on the legal life of radicalization theories, such as their influence on sentencing decisions and their role in nullifying the entrapment defense—where defendants argue that they committed a crime only because of coercion by a government official—by establishing the defendant's predisposition to terrorism (Szpunar 2017). Because this legal defense must show the defendant lacked a predisposition to engage in criminal conduct, radicalization research offers a conceptual tool to connect innocuous behaviors, such as religious worship, international travel, and political protest, to a predisposition to terrorist violence. Drawing on older colonial narratives that have racialized Muslims as "inferior to whites, potentially violent and threatening, and therefore deserving of policies that target them as a distinct group of people and criminalize them without out evidence of criminal activity," radicalization research has reinforced the role of the criminal-legal system in mobilizing, reproducing, and remaking the racial formations that animate U.S. empire, including anti-Muslim racism (Jamal 2008, 116; see also Volpp 2002; Naber 2006; Selod 2018; Alimahomed-Wilson 2019). As Arun Kundnani (2016) writes, Islamophobia functions as a "lay ideology" of empire that "offers an everyday 'common sense' explanatory framework for making sense of mediated crisis events (such as terrorist attacks) in ways that disavow those events' political meanings (rooted in empire, racism, and resistance) and instead explain them as products of a reified 'Muslimness'" (1). To advance this ideological work, the study of radicalization offers one "set of fictions" on which colonial regimes depend to sustain technologies of domination and propel state-sanctioned degradations in and through the courts (Dayan 2011, xvi).

To examine the legal life of radicalization theories, this chapter explores how this concept has further justified the use of terrorism stings to inoculate individual actors, neutralized the legal defenses that can challenge charges stemming from such stings, and therefore nullified the oversight of these preemptive policing operations. Without a judicial check on terrorism stings, police officers can continue targeting financially, psychologically, and/or socially vulnerable individuals. As investigative journalist Trevor Aaronson (2013) reports, the individuals ensnared in FBI terrorism stings almost always involve a police informant "who came up with the idea and provided the necessary means and opportunity for the terrorist plot," meaning that while the police may "have captured a few terrorists since 9/11," they have "manufactured many more" (17). Even FBI agents have referred to this "expensive, exhausting, bewildering, chaotic, and paranoia-inducing process" as "ghost-chasing" (Mueller and Stewart 2016, 2).

Although social scientists repeatedly have demonstrated the racial impetus driving these theories and their methodological limitations, legal actors have called on the concept of radicalization to offer judges and jurors a racialized framework to make sense of and respond to the cases before them. In this way, radicalization research has contributed to and articulated with a "legal history of dispossession" that deprives people of personhood and renders them "dead in law" (Dayan 2005, 46; see also Cacho 2012). As Dayan (2005) explains, the "terms of the law and their rationalization of custody and control not only devise a philosophy of personhood"; in "creating the legal subject, [they] also summon forms of punishment that are activated when people of a certain 'nature'—those labeled as unfit, subhuman, barbaric, or in numerous prison officials', as well as Donald Rumsfeld's, phrasing, 'the worst of the worst'—are to be restrained in their liberty, deprived of rights, and ultimately, undone as persons" (46). Posed as an objective science that allegedly taxonomizes, psychologizes, and analyzes the terrorist threat, radicalization research reinforces the racialized role of the courts in the global war on terror and shapes case-level decisions by making defendants legible as "the worst of the worst" and therefore "dead in law." Through an examination of radicalization research and its mobilization in the courts as technologies of anti-Muslim racism, this sociological analysis of the law challenges the "penology of racial innocence" that obscures "the many ways racial power operates in and through the ever-expanding criminal justice system" (Murakawa and Beckett 2010, 698). Excavating the legal life of radicalization research illustrates the relationship between the law and racial power, including the inherent contradictions in and contestations over the courts and their role in the global war on terror.

Theorizing Radicalization: Homegrown Terrorism, Anti-Muslim Racism, and Preemptive Policing

In the years after the September 11 attacks, police strategists argued that "while the threat from overseas remains," terrorist plots "conceptualized and planned by 'unremarkable' local residents/citizens" posed a new threat to the United States (Silber and Bhatt 2007, 5). This threat demanded new conceptual tools that could inform the development of new policing practices. Supported by federal funding, law enforcement agencies and academic scholars began mapping the perceived process by which an "unremarkable" person transforms into a violent terrorist and designing new policing models to interrupt this process. Taking the individual actor as their unit of analysis, radicalization researchers established an expansive, albeit controversial, subfield within terrorism studies (Gartenstein-Ross and Grossman 2009; Borum 2011; McCauley and Moskalenko 2017, Horgan 2008).

The earliest studies on terrorist radicalization investigated the relationship between radical ideas, individual psychology, and violent acts. The ever-elusive search for a terrorist profile, however, has ignored the historical, geopolitical, and social contexts that give rise to armed resistance, including the state's own contribution to "the conditions in which terrorist action by non-state actors occurs" (Jackson, Gunning, and Smyth 2007, 7). For example, in developing his formative "new terrorism" thesis, historian Walter Laqueur (1999) wondered if "certain individuals have a predisposition toward engaging in terrorist operations" (38). Later, Laqueur (2004) suggested that a "cultural-psychological predisposition" could explain why "out of 100 militants believing with equal intensity in the justice of their cause, only a very few will actually engage in terrorist actions." By focusing on the perceived cultural or psychological pathologies of individual actors, this approach engages what Robert Cox (1981) describes as problem-solving theory, which "takes the world as it finds it, with the prevailing social and power relationships into which they are organized, as the given framework for action" and then strives to "make these relationships and institutions work smoothly by dealing with particular sources of trouble," such as nonstate actors who threaten state security (128–29). The problem-solving approach to the study of terrorism fixates on understanding state security problems to then solve those problems, but without "questioning the extent to which the status quo—the hierarchies and operation of power and the inequalities and injustices thus generated—is implicated in the 'problem' of terrorism and other forms of subaltern violence" (Jackson, Gunning, and Smyth 2007, 9). Applied to the problem of "homegrown terrorists," this approach pivots on the perceived psychological, theological, and/or cultural perversions of individual actors, ultimately bypassing a study of the politics that animates the use of violence and the broader power relations, geopolitical contexts, and material conditions that give rise to armed resistance.

Over the next decade, law enforcement agencies and academic scholars theorized possible predispositions to terrorist violence (Wiktorowicz 2005; Moghaddam 2005; Horgan 2008; Gartenstein-Ross and Grossman 2009), with continued "tendencies towards acontextuality and ahistoricism" (Jackson, Gunning, and Smyth 2007, 24). In doing so, radicalization researchers have overlooked scholars who have explored the relationship between power, politics, and piety in the making of violence through theorizations of anticolonial violence (Abraham 2014) and counterforce (Kawash 1999), which consider how "militant minorities" have deployed the use of force as a form of political action (Hyams 1975, 175; see also Asad 2007; Munif 2020; Fanon 1963; Benjamin 1978; Jackson 2019). Instead, prominent radicalization research typically mapped the cultural, psychological, and/or theological conditions that facilitated the turn to violence, thereby pathologizing individual actors as "irredeemably wicked and cruel" (Hyams 1975, 11).

In 2006, the FBI published one of the earliest "working models" of the radicalization process (2). The FBI developed this model on the premise that "homegrown Islamic extremists are a growing threat, and are identified as legal U.S. persons whose primary social influence has been the cultural values and beliefs of the United States, who also have the intent to provide support for or directly commit a terrorist attack inside the United States" (3). Specifically focused on Muslims, the report identifies a four-stage "radicalization cycle" defined by a changing relationship with Islam: preradicalization, identification, indoctrination, and action (3). The preradicalization stage begins with Muslim converts and Muslim "faith re-interpreters" who, through "introspection and evaluation," come to "follow a more extremist form of Islam" (5). Next, an individual enters the identification stage, "where an individual identifies with a particular extremist cause and accepts a radicalized ideology that justifies, condones, encourages, or supports violence or other criminal activity against the U.S. government, its citizens, its allies, or those whose opinions are contrary to [their] own extremist agenda" without ever engaging in violence (7). Although individuals at this stage may begin moving toward violence, others may simply "solidify" their "extremist identity" (7). Once "a convert has accepted the radical ideology," they may progress to the indoctrination stage, where their participation in group activity can convince them that "further action is required to support the cause" (8). In the final stage, individuals engage in "terrorist activities in support of the cause," which can include violent or nonviolent actions like providing financial assistance aimed at "inflicting damage to the enemy" (8). In the FBI's radicalization model, terrorism is an apolitical expression of an "extremist form of Islam," as radical religious beliefs drive the turn to violence.

To apply this model to local policing efforts, the FBI (2006) also developed a "preliminary list of indicators" to "identify an individual going through the radicalization process," such as "wearing traditional Muslim attire," "growing facial hair," "frequent attendance at a mosque or a prayer group," "travel to a Muslim country," and "increased activity in a pro-Muslim social group or political cause" (10). Police officers could use these indicators in their daily patrols to surveil the "nodes and venues where radicalization can occur," including "mosques, prisons, universities, and places of employment," and then identify individuals in the process of terrorist radicalization (3). Given its explicit targeting of Islam, the FBI's theorization of the radicalization process crystallizes around anti-Muslim referents.

In 2007, the New York City Police Department (NYPD) also published an influential report, *Radicalization in the West: The Homegrown Threat*, written by Mitchell D. Silber and Arvin Bhatt. This report similarly theorized the radicalization process to inform the daily work of beat police. Like the FBI, the NYPD outlined a four-stage radicalization process defined by a changing relationship with Salafi Islam: preradicalization, self-identification, indoctrination, and jihadization. The NYPD argued that each stage of the process had a "distinct set of indicators and signatures," such as "wearing traditional Islamic clothing," "growing a beard," and "giving up cigarettes, drinking, gambling, and urban hip-hop gangster clothes" (Silber and Bhatt 2007, 31). In this view, the "remarkable consistency in the behaviors and trajectory" of the radicalization process offered a "tool for predictability" such that police officers could use these signs of terrorist radicalization to identify potential threats on their beats (7). The NYPD specifically targeted perceived "radicalization incubators," including "mosques, cafes, cab driver hangouts, flophouses, prisons, student associations, non-governmental organizations, hookah (water pipe) bars, butcher shops, and bookstores," transforming these Muslim, Arab, and South Asian community spaces into critical sites of surveillance (22). The spatial shift inherent in this analysis—from the battlespaces of Afghanistan and Iraq to community spaces within the United States—has intensified domestic responses to the perceived terrorist threat, particularly through the use of predictive policing, sting operations, and preemptive prosecutions that disproportionately have targeted Arabs and Muslims.

Even terrorologist Marc Sageman (2008)—a vocal critic of radicalization research in court proceedings—explored the "centrality of the radicalization process in the formation of a global Islamist terrorist" by focusing on "how people in groups influence each other to become terrorists" (11, 13). Through his study of "leaderless jihad," Sageman developed his "bunch of guys" thesis, arguing that "the global Islamist terrorist social movement forms through the spontaneous self-organization of informal 'bunches of guys,' trusted friends, from the bottom up" (69). Although Sageman disproved many myths, like the "commonly held belief that terrorists are simply psychopaths or sociopaths," he also concluded that joining a "global Islamist social movement" generally emerges from "friendship and kinship" rooted in "Salafi ideology" (63, 66). By focusing on social networks and religious beliefs, this analysis dismissed the broader geopolitical, economic, and social conditions that have incited political violence as social bonds supersede "any ideological commitment" (70).

Presuming that radical ideas drive violence, Sageman's "bunch of guys" thesis has shaped local law enforcement strategies by tracking Muslim social networks, eliminating anti-Muslim discrimination that can cause terrorist messaging to resonate with Muslims, modifying social welfare policy "to provide Muslims options other than joining terrorism out of boredom and idleness," and enlisting Muslims in domestic anti-terrorism initiatives as the "fight against terrorism is a community affair" (Sageman 2008, 163–66). Sageman's analysis demonstrates that how we understand terrorism necessarily shapes what we view as effective methods to thwart such threats. Largely funded by the state, radicalization research encourages us to consider terrorism as the product of individual pathologies accelerated through social networks, not governance regimes, and therefore fosters support for the predictive policing and expansive surveillance of Muslim communities in the name of national security. Informed by radicalization theories, law enforcement agencies argued that these new policing models could catch incipient terrorists before they commit an act of violence, ultimately enhancing national security.

These initial reports led to an explosion of publications on the concept of "domestic radicalization and recruitment to jihadist terrorism" and facilitated changes in how law enforcement agencies responded to the perceived threat of homegrown terrorism (Jenkins 2010, 9). Rather than "identify and apprehend a perpetrator *after* a crime has been committed," the United States sought to establish "a more preventative approach—intervention *before* an attack occurs" (9, 10). To do so, police officers and confidential informants have patrolled local neighborhoods and infiltrated intimate sites like gyms, schools, and mosques to identify individuals perceived to be vulnerable to or in the process of terrorist radicalization. Monitoring these sites of everyday life through a lens of radicalization has further stigmatized Muslim communities and criminalized otherwise innocuous behaviors, such as attending school-sponsored camping or white-water rafting trips (Silber and Bhatt 2007, 46), participating in "pro-Muslim" social groups like Muslim Student Associations (FBI 2006, 10), and expressing hopelessness or experiencing economic stressors (National Counterterrorism Center 2014, 19–20). Furthermore, security professionals have treated radical beliefs as "a proxy—or at least a necessary precursor—for terrorism," even though "most people who hold radical ideas do not engage in terrorism, and many terrorists—even those who lay claim to a 'cause'—are not deeply ideological and may not radicalize in the traditional sense" (Borum 2011, 8). By anchoring the radicalization process in a changing relationship with Islam and identifying Muslim spaces as terrorist incubators, these reports have "mimicked long-standing Orientalist constructions of Muslims as inherently fanatical and prone to violence" and justified an ever-expanding security agenda targeting Muslims (Monaghan 2014, 498). These radicalization models have shaped popular and professional understandings of the "homegrown threat" and informed the daily work of police officers, who continue to patrol popular Muslim spaces to identify potential threats before a crime is committed.

The challenge to "identify, preempt, and thus prevent homegrown terrorist attacks given the non-criminal element of its indicators" has led to the creative development of interventions in the "pre-criminal space" by intensifying the relationship between law enforcement agencies and community members (Silber and Bhatt 2007, 87). The spatio-temporal concept of the precriminal space denotes the period before an individual engages in criminal activity and therefore represents an opportunity to deter the individual through interventions conducted by community members and social service providers. By redefining non-criminal behaviors as precriminal, the social construction of the precriminal space has facilitated the targeting of Muslim communities, as certain noncriminal behaviors exhibited by Muslims are identified, reported, and treated as precursors to criminal violence.

In popular antiterrorism models, precrime policing depends on community participation and even views family and friends as "more likely than the authorities to know when someone is turning dangerously radical and heading toward self-destruction," necessitating positive police–community relationships to facilitate information-sharing for the "successful containment of domestic jihadist terrorism" (Jenkins 2010, ix). For example, the Illinois Criminal Justice Information Authority (2016) created a training program to "educate a broad cross-section of communities on how to off-ramp individuals who exhibit warning signs of radicalization to violence as well as those who exhibit behaviors signifying they may be in the early stages of planning an act of ideologically inspired targeted violence" (2). To intervene in the precriminal space, these antiterrorism models have relied on "third-party policing," which refers to "police efforts to persuade or coerce nonoffending persons to take actions which are outside the scope of their routine activities, which are designed to indirectly minimize disorder caused by other persons or to reduce the possibility that crime may occur" (Buerger and Mazerolle

1998, 301). Although community members "do not technically qualify as the police," they are imbued with "a kind of regulatory power bound up with the threat of coercion, in other words, a form of police power" (Bell 2015, 20). Posed as a liberal alternative to conventional antiterrorism methods like sting operations, participatory approaches to countering homegrown terrorism have legitimized and expanded policing institutions that historically have targeted communities of color. More perniciously, these antiterrorism models specifically have called on Muslims to surveil, monitor, and report their own community members on the "presumption that Islam is inherently violent, alien, and inassimilable" and on the "belief that expressions of Muslim identity are correlative with a propensity for violence and terrorism" (Beydoun and Choudhury 2020, 7). While law enforcement agencies have promoted these preventative programs as an alternative to criminal investigations and preemptive prosecutions, Muslim communities have shown how intervening in the precriminal space has expanded police powers, infringed on their civil rights and civil liberties, and cast suspicion on innocuous behaviors (Alimahomed-Wilson 2019; Shafi and Qureshi 2020).

The rapid expansion of these participatory antiterrorism efforts reflected a broader change in global war on terror strategy under the Bush administration. As one National Security Council staffer reported, during the "2005–6 era," security professionals recognized that "you can't just confront terror on the battlefield. . . . If you really want people to stop blowing themselves up, we need to prevent them from finding these ideologies appealing. Try to reduce the pool of recruits. Transform someone's worldview. Address underlying conditions. Try to prevent them from engaging in violence" (participant observation, May 2017). A former Defense Department employee similarly argued that the United States could not simply "kill or capture" its way to victory; the "durable" terrorist threat necessitated a complex mixture of kinetic and non-kinetic tactics to "prevent the regenerating capacity" of insurgent networks by persuading civilians to denounce political violence and neutralizing known threats (participant observation, May 2017). As U.S. soldiers began engaging in counterinsurgency operations to "win the hearts and minds" of Iraqis, the federal government initiated new domestic initiatives in collaboration with Muslim leaders to fight the perceived threat of homegrown terrorism within the United States.

Applied to the domestic context, security professionals viewed the provision of social services, like religious education and mental health care, and the mobilization of community policing models as effective strategies to disrupt the radicalization process and prevent the "regenerating capacity" of terrorist organizations. According to this national security approach, service providers like teachers and mental health professionals play a vital role in preventing homegrown terrorism by identifying, reporting, and working with individuals vulnerable to or in the process of terrorist radicalization. For example, Minneapolis Public Schools announced plans to hire "experienced youth workers" to monitor school cafeterias and other nonclassroom spaces where they could "spot identity issues and disaffection" believed to be the "root causes of radicalization" among Somali youth (Kiernat 2015). In Maryland, school staff reported Arab students experiencing "homesickness," "acculturation related stress," "feelings of alienation," and "economic stressors," on the presumption that these psychological states "suggest they *may be* at risk of violent extremism" (World Organization for Resource Development and Education 2014, 4). As these examples illustrate, the concept of radicalization has justified a widening array of antiterrorism tools to combat the homegrown threat, often working from the premise that Muslims are more prone, or predisposed, to terrorism (Nguyen 2019; Alimahomed-Wilson 2019; Beydoun and Choudhury 2020; Walker 2021).

Informed by radicalization research, these antiterrorism tools treat everyday behaviors, experiences, and feelings like "disaffection" and "economic stressors" as early warning signs of terrorist radicalization. Sociologist Sabrina Alimahomed-Wilson (2019) explains that under the radicalization paradigm, "normal behavior becomes suspicious when practiced by Arabs and Muslims in the United States, which would otherwise be acceptable, mundane, and unremarkable if practiced by white Christians, thus constituting a form of 'racialized state surveillance'" (873). As both a product and driver of anti-Muslim racism, radicalization research has infused the everyday behaviors of Muslims with predictive meaning; in this paradigm, both community members and police officers can identify who is vulnerable to terrorist radicalization simply by observing Muslim spaces and peoples.

Rejecting Radicalization Research: Limitations, Inconsistencies, and Incompatibility

Early radicalization research developed terrorist typologies by identifying the trajectories and characteristics common among violent political actors. With a specific focus on belief systems like Salafism, these early models portrayed radicalization as a predictable process with telltale signs indicating who is likely to become a terrorist. Law enforcement agents could learn these warning signs and use them in their daily patrols to identify potential threats. Radicalization research therefore directly influenced local policing practices, particularly by treating the everyday behaviors of Muslims as suspicious activity.

In this way, radicalization research has drawn on and sustained a global racial system that prefigures the Muslim as a security threat and reinvigorates the moral panics that justify global, regional, and domestic policies and practices to control, contain, and enclose Muslims (Rana 2011, 51; see also Naber 2006; Bail 2015; Salaita 2006; Qureshi 2017; Shafi and Qureshi 2020; Bunglawala 2017). This racial project naturalizes the subjugation of Muslims and organizes the law, ultimately marking Muslims "as outside political community" because "they are assumed to carry *within* them the possibility of threat to the nation" (Razack 2008, 19). Further institutionalizing anti-Muslim racism, state security policies and practices informed by radicalization research "cannot be abstracted outside of the political context in which they emerged: the War on Terror directed against 'radical Islam' and/or 'extremist' Muslims" (Shafi and Qureshi 2020, 16).

As radicalization theories began dominating the national security arena and intensifying anti-Muslim policing, social scientists and legal scholars challenged the assumptions, methodologies, and analyses organizing this research (Alimahomed-Wilson 2019; Kundnani 2014; Huq 2007; Nasir 2019; Walker 2021). For example, media studies professor Deepa Kumar (2012) incisively concluded, "One does not need a PhD in sociology or psychology to see that this is an inherently racist behavioral model fraught with double standards" (156). Legal scholar Faiza Patel (2011) similarly reported that although "the NYPD and FBI have put forward radicalization theories that are congruent with efforts to penetrate American Muslim communities," these theories "are unduly reductionist and are contrary to research conducted by governments, social scientists, and psychologists" (5). Reflecting on the state of radicalization research in court testimony, terrorologist Marc Sageman (2015) admitted that "attempts to discern a terrorist 'profile' or to model terrorist behavior have failed to yield lasting insights." In reviewing these assessments, the Brennan Center for Justice (2019) concluded that radicalization research has been "discredited by decades of scholarly research."

Through these critiques, scholars have identified serious flaws in radicalization research, such as the field's deep ties to the military, its problem-solving drive to "explain the 'terrorist other' from within a state-centric paradigm," its methodological limitations, and its abstraction of political violence from its formative conditions (Gunning 2007, 371). As Burnett and Whyte (2005) argue, "It is more important now than ever before for academics interested in combating the roots of terrorism . . . to challenge the embedded knowledge that draws upon the imprimatur of the academy in order to provide the bankrupt intellectual leadership for this violent and socially corrosive war on terror" (15). Taking seriously this charge, this section examines the methodological limitations of radicalization research and the ways that the concept of radicalization misunderstands political violence, both of which bear on how the courts interpret terrorism-related cases.

Junk Science: The Methodological Limitations of Radicalization Studies

To develop its radicalization model, the NYPD analyzed five terrorist plots to detect the "point where we believe the potential terrorist or group of terrorists begin and progress through a process of radicalization" and to identify the behaviors that signal progression in this process (Silber and Bhatt 2007, 5). To do so, the NYPD "dispatched detectives and analysts to meet with law enforcement, intelligence officials, and academics at each of these [five] locations" (15). Although this fieldwork did not engage the individuals charged with terrorism-related crimes, the report's authors determined the "common pathways and characteristics among these otherwise different groups and plots" by using their conversations with police officers and academics as their main source of evidence (15). To verify its conclusions, the NYPD then applied its framework to three additional terrorism cases, which confirmed the department's understanding of the radicalization process and the telltale signs of an individual's progression in this process.

Unfortunately, the NYPD's study did not include a control group, even though "accepted social science methodology requires a comparison between behaviors and beliefs common to terrorists and a control group" (Patel and Koushik 2017, 14). In court, Sageman (2015) identified similar concerns, explaining, "Any attempt to assess the validity of indicators or factors that might lead an individual to commit political violence would require a study to include both (a) individuals who actually carried out acts of political violence, and (b) individuals (the control group) who are similar to the first set in all respects except that they did not engage in violence" (9). To accurately determine if a person might be a future terrorist, the "use of a control group is critically important because it is only by a comparison with this control group, in which the indicator of actual violence is *absent*, that one can make the argument that other indicators specific to the subject group are valid" (9). Instead, the NYPD report merely assumed that if certain behaviors, such as adhering to doctrinally mandated daily prayers, appeared in all five cases, they could serve as early warning signs of terrorist radicalization (Huq 2007). Given this methodological flaw, social scientist Arun Kundnani (2014) concludes that the NYPD study "offers weak evidence for any correlation between religious behaviors and terrorist activity, because its assertations linking religious behaviors and terrorist acts are generally impressionistic, arbitrary, and lacking any analytic rigor" (135).

Security professionals also have acknowledged the methodological limitations of these research studies and the racial profiling they authorize. One national security researcher admitted that "one of the biggest criticisms . . . of certain radicalization models has been from the social science perspective, the fact that there's a lack of a control group and that there's a reliance on the dependent variable" (interview, January 2017). Without a control group, "we don't necessarily have the evidence yet that can speak to causality. So, for instance, a lot of people at an individual level have said, 'Oh, extremist ideology causes people to engage in violent extremism.' And then the criticism has been reliance on the dependent variable. If that was really the case, then why is it that most people who hold extremist views don't engage in acts of violent extremism?" (interview, January 2017). This researcher recognized the methodological limitations of "radicalization models," noting that current studies could not identify the behaviors, beliefs, and social conditions that drive the turn to political violence.

Despite these well-documented methodological limitations, law enforcement agencies continue to use radicalization research to inform their daily work. In this way, terrorism scholars have "manufactured the 'suspicious Muslim' through knowledge production that emphasizes a link between terrorism and religiosity" (Alimahomed-Wilson 2019, 877). As Kundnani (2012) explains, "Radicalization discourse claims predictive power, but lacks explanatory power: scholars generally talk of 'factors' or 'indicators' that are statistically associated with radicalization and which intelligence agencies can put to use in their efforts to detect future threats, while tending to refrain from reflecting on the larger question of causality" (10–11). Through these new theories and associated policing practices, radicalization research has expanded criminal liability by treating radical beliefs, social networks, and speech acts as precursors to or indicators of terrorist activity (Chesney 2009; Love 2012).

Although law enforcement agencies eagerly have integrated radicalization research into their policing practices, the judicial system has questioned the rigor of these studies. We saw, for example, how Judge Scriven used the *Daubert* test to evaluate the reliability of terrorologist Evan Kohlmann's research in *United States v. Sami Osmakac* (2014). As a part of her assessment, Judge Scriven observed that Kohlmann's list of radicalization factors never underwent peer review, a standard academic practice to ensure rigorous, even if controversial or contested, research.[8] Like social scientists critical of radicalization research, Judge Scriven identified the methodological limitations of Kohlmann's work, concluding, "You can't just pick one factor that you identify in an individual and say, 'Ah-ha! This is a homegrown terrorist.'"[9] Given these issues, Judge Scriven found that Kohlmann's list of radicalization factors did not stand up to academic scrutiny and therefore could not provide the scientific backing to reliably identify homegrown terrorists. Despite this finding, Judge Scriven permitted Kohlmann to testify under specific parameters: Kohlmann could use his "phraseology" to identify certain behaviors that "groom" individuals for terrorist activity, such as reading *Inspire* or practicing "countersurveillance," but he could not describe the "factors of homegrown terrorism."[10] In other words, Kohlmann could discuss Osmakac's online activities by "testify[ing] as to the content of materials derived from the internet and what they mean in the context of terrorism, and associated motive of the conduct at issue."[11] Judge Scriven's concerns with Kohlmann's research did not prohibit his testimony at trial, illustrating the durability of radicalization theories in the courts.

Although security professionals understood the academic community's concerns with radicalization research, many insisted that these methodological limitations should not stall local antiterrorism efforts. One practitioner recognized that despite "*millions* of dollars in research to determine what causes radicalization, there is no such thing as a terrorist profile and there is no single factor that can predict who will become a terrorist." Yet she also argued that "what we *do know* from the empirical research on convicted terrorists and terrorist incidences are some common indicators that exist in many of those cases, which *may* make an individual more vulnerable to terrorist recruitment and radicalization." This practitioner suggested that "social alienation," "psychological conditions," "circumstances that erode a person's sense of self-worth," "trauma," "shame," "deviant religious tenets," and "*perceived* economic inequalities or political disenfranchisement" constituted the "warning signs" or "risk factors" of terrorist radicalization. Local antiterrorism initiatives therefore intended to "educate the stakeholders about the warning signs of radicalization so they have the ability to intervene" (participant observation, August 2016). This practitioner understood the limits of radicalization research while also using these studies to guide local antiterrorism initiatives.

Despite this practitioner's creative reinterpretation of radicalization research, other security professionals argued that these studies criminalized innocuous behaviors and treated Muslim communities as uniquely susceptible to terrorist radicalization and recruitment. One practitioner asked, "Can we even talk about [radicalization] without profiling? How do we know who's actually vulnerable? . . . I'm trying to think of an incident where there was a [Muslim] lady who asked [in a community town hall with national security experts] about her seven-year-old son, that he likes to watch a whole bunch of YouTube videos on car crashes. And should she worry?" In response, "the very helpful FBI counterterrorism agent told her that if someone reported that to the FBI, they would be forced—they *would* investigate to see if her son is potentially radicalizing" (interview, January 2017). The concept of radicalization codes innocuous behaviors like watching videos of car crashes or even "showing signs of withdrawing or isolation" as indicators of terrorist radicalization, rather than as "young people struggling to grow up" (interview, January 2017). Given her concerns about the relationship between radicalization research and racial profiling, this practitioner focused her antiterrorism initiatives on broader security campaigns, such as "teaching internet safety" to all children by addressing the "whole spectrum" of online threats, including "child predators," "pedophiles," "cyberbullies," and "people who might be trying to recruit young people online." Understanding how law enforcement agencies have racially profiled Muslim youth as uniquely susceptible to terrorist radicalization, this practitioner created security programming that targeted a wide range of public safety threats.

Given their concerns with racial profiling, some security professionals developed what they referred to as "ideologically ecumenical" antiterrorism initiatives that arguably targeted all forms of political violence. One practitioner criticized how radicalization research had directed "99.9%" of the federal government's antiterrorism efforts at "Muslim and Arab communities," ultimately "eviscerating trust" and "securitizing relationships between law enforcement and these minority communities" (interview, November 2016). Despite developing partnerships with specifically Muslim institutions, this practitioner insisted that he focused on a broader range of "targeted violence," including "white supremacists, neo-Nazi skinheads, and violent militias" (interview, November 2016). Rather than reject antiterrorism campaigns organized by the concept of radicalization, practitioners found ways to create alternative approaches still aimed at reducing the threat of homegrown terrorism. Even as community organizers have argued against "equal opportunity" antiterrorism initiatives (F. Ahmad 2018), law enforcement agencies have widened their aperture to include other forms of political violence, ultimately expanding policing powers and broadening surveillance practices. Local practitioners, however, have implemented federal initiatives unevenly, depending on their own personal and professional understandings of terrorist radicalization, illustrating how state security projects are far from totalizing processes as the operation of power unfolds in diffuse ways fraught with internal inconsistencies.

Because practitioners worried about public perceptions of their work, community organizers could make antiterrorism programs "politically untenable" for their architects, leading to programmatic changes or even outright abandonment (personal communication, May 2019). In this charged context, practitioners unevenly integrated radicalization theories into their daily work, with some strategically reinterpreting this research to continue their already existing programs and others actively remaking their antiterrorism initiatives to avoid overt racial profiling. Despite these inconsistencies in its application, radicalization research dominates the national security policy environment and therefore continues to legitimize "the widespread suspicion, collective blame, and mistrust of Muslims" and shape how policy makers and practitioners understand the problem of political violence (Shafi and Qureshi 2020, 17).

Forced to respond to academic, professional, and public critiques of their work, terrorism scholars began developing new radicalization models that could still support antiterrorism initiatives popular among security professionals and government officials. One researcher affirmed the methodological limitations of these studies, noting, "We, as social scientists, don't want to engage in those kinds of very strong *causal* claims, in large part, because, again, as . . . radicalization critics have rightly pointed out . . . there have been no comparison and control groups which we can begin to adequately isolate some of those variables and tease out causality." Instead, this researcher argued that "we can say there are certain factors that are *associated with* [radicalization] and that they may be necessary or near necessary conditions, but we can't say, for instance, that they directly cause these kinds of things. At most, we can say that they're associated to some degree, whether weakly, moderately, or strongly" (interview, January 2017). If this research could not demonstrate a causal connection between certain risk factors and terrorist radicalization, it could still provide insight into concerning behaviors law enforcement and communities could use to identify potential threats. Rather than concede that radicalization research could not offer scientific insight into political violence, practitioners simply reframed these findings to justify their work as "evidence-based" programming (participant observation, August 2016).

Other researchers similarly affirmed that "attempts to profile terrorists have failed resoundingly" and called on their colleagues to "trace not roots (either in terms of personality factors or root causes) but *routes*" to determine "more generalizable patterns of individual involvement" (Horgan 2008, 81, 82). Rather than rethink the concept of radicalization and the inherent analytical limitations in identifying the psychological, theological, and cultural drivers of terrorist violence, these researchers examined the different "terrorist pathways," not profiles, to violence (Horgan 2008). By understanding radicalization as a psychological process, antiterrorism programs could address the "pull" factors or "lures" that draw individuals into political violence, rather than the "push" factors like "the broad sociopolitical conditions" that "give rise to the increased likelihood of the emergence of terrorism" (Horgan 2008, 90). Rather than question the concept of radicalization, researchers have encouraged additional studies that examine terrorist pathways by arguing that "it is important to be able to detect the early signs of behavior associated with violent extremism," whether "the result of a severely dysfunctional home, psychological illness, or social alienation" (Williams, Horgan, and Evans 2016, 14). In other words, scholars recognized the significant limitations of early radicalization research and proposed alternative frameworks for conducting new studies while affirming this scholarship's original findings: that there are observable warning signs, risk factors, and/or concerning behaviors that can be used to identify individuals at risk of or in the process of terrorist radicalization.

Rather than focus primarily on religious and cultural practices, this next generation of radicalization research listed generic "concerning behaviors" police officers and community members could use to identify and report vulnerable individuals, such as "feelings of hopelessness" and a "sudden change in physical appearance" (Illinois Criminal Justice Information Authority et al. 2019, 24). Even though these new lists do not explicitly identify racial, religious, or cultural markers as signs of terrorist radicalization, such concerning behaviors typically only arouse suspicion when exhibited by Muslims and thus reinforce the anti-Muslim racism inherent in this behavioral model of terrorist radicalization (Alimahomed-Wilson 2019). Lacking explanatory power, such anticipatory risk assessments also assume that the general public can apply its suspicions evenly, despite the long-standing vigilante policing of Black, Muslim, and other communities of color for innocuous behaviors such as running, bird-watching, and barbecuing. Furthermore, security professionals themselves admit that such lists "do not predict or conclusively indicate that someone may use violence" (Illinois Criminal Justice Information Authority et al. 2019, 24). In this way, "U.S. policymakers, while acknowledging that there are no telltale signs of who is likely to be a terrorist, nonetheless promote an approach that maintains that likely terrorists come with visible flags" (Patel and Koushik 2017, 16). Like practitioners, these scholars have encouraged local communities to establish programs that educate law enforcement agents, community members, and social service providers on how to use these warning signs of terrorist radicalization in their everyday lives, transforming trusted adults into proxy national security agents who take on the work of law enforcement. Critics, however, continue to demand that terrorism experts "euthanize this erroneous and dangerous theory," which, "like a villain in a horror movie," is continuously "raised from the dead" to inform the domestic war on terror (German 2013).

Misunderstanding Political Violence: Pathologizing Violent Nonstate Actors

These academic interventions importantly highlight the methodological limitations of radicalization research and demonstrate that security professionals cannot scientifically identify individuals vulnerable to or in the process of terrorist radicalization. Despite these critical appraisals, law enforcement agencies "have adopted theories of radicalization that draw conclusions at odds with the social science research" and "attach significance" to the perceived markers of terrorist radicalization, leading them to "monitor a very large set of people without much likelihood of finding terrorists" (Patel 2011, 12, 16). Such methodological critiques, however, do not fully question the concept of radicalization as an object of study, which has led to the development of alternative frameworks that justify the same antiterrorism practices, such as relying on lists of risk factors that are "associated with" terrorist radicalization and that continuously "link Muslims and the practice of Islam to violence and terror" (Beydoun and Choudhury 2020, 8).

By understanding radicalization as "the *human* developments that precede [a] terrorist attack," terrorism experts typically treat politics and violence as separate spheres (McCauley and Moskalenko 2017, 205, emphasis added). The focus on individual psychology persists, even as terrorologists admit that "what nearly all suicide terrorist campaigns have in common is a specific secular and strategic goal: to compel liberal democracies to withdraw military forces from territory that the terrorists consider to be their homeland" (Pape 2003). In the elusive search for a "terrorist profile" or "terrorism pathway," radicalization theorists take the (pious) individual as their unit of analysis, irrespective of the intolerable social conditions in which people live and the armed campaigns they undertake in response. By reducing political violence to the pathologies of individual actors, radicalization research encourages law enforcement agencies to direct their efforts at identifying individuals who exhibit the perceived warning signs of terrorist radicalization and then initiating stings to ensnare them before the "real" terrorists do.

Challenging many of the underlying assumptions organizing radicalization research, social scientists have theorized alternative ways of understanding armed struggles by taking seriously the relationship between politics and violence. Historian Mohammad-Mahmoud Ould Mohamedou (2011) writes that although al-Qaeda "has made it clear that it is responding to American policies in the Middle East and has consistently linked three general political demands to cessation of hostilities, peripheral religious references and the group's leaders' religiosity have facilitated the persistence of the invisibilization of said *casus belli*" (3). Accounting for the social underpinnings of al-Qaeda's political violence demonstrates that the "issue is not Islamic fundamentalism, religious fanaticism, poverty, or the lack of democracy in the Arab world" (Ould Mohamedou 2011, 11). Instead, it is "justice and the yearning for it," especially given the United States' "unceasing and unflinching support for Israel's occupation of Palestinian territories, the continued assistance to authoritarian Arab regimes, and the expanded U.S. military presence in the Middle East" (Ould Mohamedou 2011, 11). Such an analysis insists on taking seriously the power relations, geopolitical contexts, and material conditions that incite armed transnational solidarity by militants seeking to create alternative governance regimes and, in some cases, destabilize the primacy of a world order rooted in the nation-state. Mueller and Stewart (2016) similarly report that nonstate soldiers often are driven by their "intense outrage at American and Israeli actions in the Middle East" and their desire to institute new forms of regional governance that protect their interests (36). Without considering these contexts, radicalization research cannot account for mujahids who have traveled to Afghanistan, Bosnia, Libya, Somalia, Syria, and elsewhere to counter anti-Muslim aggression, colonial incursions, and despotic regimes, even if we disagree with the politics animating their violence or their use of lethal force. Plotting the psychological, cultural, and theological pathologies that allegedly facilitate the turn to violence fixates on modifying the behaviors and beliefs of individual actors while absolving the United States of its role in the making of the violent conditions and multiscalar politics that give rise to armed resistance (Asad 2007; Bugnon 2002; Li 2020).

Understanding that armed resistance is intimately tied to politics means that law enforcement strategies targeting individual people exhibiting the so-called warning signs of terrorist radicalization is as untenable as it is ineffective. History, after all, "teaches us that engagement with terrorists invariably requires addressing the issues raised, namely acknowledging the collective grievances in which they anchor their acts of force, depicted as political actions in response to specific issues" (Ould Mohamedou 2007, 89). The current hunt for individual actors exhibiting cultural, psychological, or theological pathologies simply reasserts a racialized narrative that intensifies the role of U.S. empire in world affairs, ultimately deepening the very conditions contested by transnational fighters. The scale of this hunt—the bodies and psyches of Muslims— misses the power and politics inherent in terrorist violence, opting for a framework that justifies the use of brute force, whether through preemptive policing or through military operations. The continued incarceration of captured fighters alongside the mobilization of stings that manipulate ordinary people into contributing to a concocted terrorist plot do little to address the role of U.S. empire and its devastating impact on world affairs or to rethink the primacy of the nation-state in global, regional, and local governance regimes. Unfortunately, radicalization research continues to prevail, offering the interpretive frameworks used to understand and respond to the perceived terrorist threat, ultimately legitimizing antiterrorism tactics that refuse to acknowledge let alone reckon with the power relations and political conditions that give rise to violence.

By abstracting political violence from its formative conditions, radicalization research authorizes carceral solutions to the problem of political violence while absolving the United States of its role in making the un-livable conditions that incite armed resistance, such as repressive regimes and colonial occupations. In this context, the United States continues to rely on its criminal-legal system to incapacitate perceived terrorists, especially as judges and jurors reach for radicalization theories to make sense of the defendants before them. The durable prominence of radicalization research has material effects by facilitating preemptive policing, justifying sting operations, informing court proceedings, and nullifying the legal defenses available to terrorism defendants, such as the imperfect entrapment doctrine. By informing the judicial system and its responses to terrorism-related cases, radicalization research reinforces the use of policing and prisons to neutralize perceived terrorist threats.

Predisposition: How Radicalization Theories Thwart the Entrapment Defense

To prevent terrorist attacks before they occur, the FBI increasingly has used sting operations to ensnare potential threats. Relying on deception, the FBI deploys undercover agents and confidential human sources (informants) who often are "working off" their own criminal or immigration charges and/or compensated financially for helping the police (Norris and Grol-Prokopczyk 2017, 618). By infiltrating Muslim community spaces like mosques, undercover agents and informants collaborate to identify individuals perceived to be vulnerable to radicalization and then lure them into plotting an act of terrorism. These undercover operatives often furnish the ideas, money, and (inert) weapons central to planning and executing these plots; sometimes they "resort to extraordinary measures to persuade individuals to engage in terrorism," such as "repeatedly badgering them, offering them jobs, promising hundreds of thousands or even millions of dollars, actively attempting to radicalize them, and even threatening to kill the defendant or commit suicide if he backs out" (Norris and Grol-Prokopczyk 2017, 618). During these sting operations, "the authorities create or facilitate the very offense of which the defendant is convicted" by "having an undercover agent hold out some sort of bait, or opportunity, to commit a crime, and then punishing the person who takes the bait" (Hay 2005, 388). To support these efforts, the FBI has drawn on radicalization research to guide its identification of individuals believed to be vulnerable to or in the process of terrorist radicalization, and then devise elaborate undercover operations to ensnare its targets in fake plots. Ensnaring individuals with no history of criminal violence has generated resistance from targeted communities; security professionals, however, have celebrated this approach as a way to thwart terrorist threats "at the earliest stage possible and to respond with forward-leaning—preventative—prosecutions" (McNulty 2006).

The FBI argues that these deceptive undercover operations defuse national security threats by facilitating the arrest, prosecution, and incarceration of individuals predisposed to terrorism. Recognizing that "the number of al-Qaeda operatives actually in the country has held at zero or nearly so" and that intelligence agencies "have concluded that ISIS poses no immediate threat to the United States," critics contend that the FBI uses these covert stings to manufacture domestic "lone wolf" or "homegrown" terrorists to justify its ever-expanding antiterrorism operations, without enhancing national security (Mueller and Stewart 2016, 17, 46). In his investigative reporting on these stings, journalist Trevor Aaronson (2013) found that the "FBI currently spends $3 billion annually to hunt an enemy that is largely of its own creation" (234). In fact, "evidence in dozens of terrorism cases . . . suggests that today's terrorists in the United States are nothing more than FBI creations, impressionable men living on the edges of society who become bomb-triggering would-be killers only because of the actions of FBI informants," as in *Osmakac* (Aaronson 2013, 234). Given these statistics, prominent terrorism scholar Brian Michael Jenkins (2011) admits that these stings sometimes have served as a "psychological accelerant" to induce otherwise incapable and "half-hearted" individuals to commit a terrorist act concocted by the FBI.

Despite these critiques, FBI stings remain a key fixture of the United States' domestic war on terror strategy. Sensationalized in popular media, the ensuing court proceedings reaffirm the threat of homegrown terrorism and thus the need for expansive antiterrorism programs that identify, incapacitate, and incarcerate individuals allegedly predisposed to terrorist violence. Assistant Attorney General for National Security John P. Carlin celebrated the conviction of Mohmad Osman Mohamud, stating, "This case highlights how the use of undercover operations against would-be terrorists allows us to engage and disrupt those who wish to commit horrific acts of violence against the innocent public" (qtd. in Office of Public Affairs 2014). In this case, undercover operatives ensnared a Somali American college student, Mohamud, in a sting after he wrote three articles on physical fitness in *Jihad Recollections*. Mohamud was arrested after he attempted to detonate an inert bomb supplied by the undercover FBI agents. Given the police's preference for sting operations, former assistant U.S. attorney Christine Biederman reported that she could not "begin to describe the pressure prosecutors face to produce convictions to justify the massive expenditures in the 'war on terror'" (qtd. in Bergman and de Granados 2006). Such pressure demonstrates how domestic courts do not simply adjudicate criminal cases related to terrorism; as the last stop in sting operations, the courts also play a central role in justifying, legitimizing, and enhancing the global war on terror.

Although domestic laws do not prohibit the government from inciting an individual to commit a crime, the entrapment defense legally protects members of society from manipulative law enforcement tactics and provides relief to defendants facing charges as a result of these tactics. In 1932, the Supreme Court affirmatively recognized the entrapment defense by barring the prosecution of defendants for "a crime where the government officials are the instigators of [their] conduct."[12] The Supreme Court also determined that while "artifice and stratagem may be employed to catch those engaged in criminal enterprises," the government exceeds its police powers when it "implant[s] in the mind of an innocent person the disposition to commit the alleged offense and induce[s] its commission in order that [it] may prosecute."[13] In *Sherman v. United States,* the Court applied an even more restrictive standard, observing that government conduct rises to entrapment when it "plays on the weaknesses of an innocent party and beguiles him into committing crimes he otherwise would not have attempted."[14] Following this precedent, defense attorneys argued in *United States v. Mohamed Osman Mohamud* that cases "must result in acquittal as a matter of law where the government encouraged crime, even if the charged individuals demonstrated interest in the subject matter of the sting."[15]

Entrapment offers a complete defense of a criminal charge. According to the Department of Justice (2020), a "valid entrapment defense has two related elements: (1) government inducement of the crime and

(2) the defendant's lack of predisposition to engage in the criminal conduct." This follows the Supreme Court's ruling that "to determine whether entrapment has been established, a line must be drawn between the trap for the unwary innocent and the trap for the unwary criminal."[16] Defendants must prove that the police induced them to commit a crime that they were not predisposed to commit, although the government bears the burden in demonstrating predisposition.[17]

Given these two prongs, entrapment defenses examine the origin of criminal intent by assessing whether the government coerced the defendant to commit a crime or merely provided the opportunity to commit a crime. To determine the origins of criminal intent (coercion or opportunity), the courts rely on two tests, objective and subjective. The objective test focuses on police conduct by examining whether their tactics would induce a reasonable person to commit a crime. The subjective test assesses if the defendant was predisposed to commit the crime without law enforcement pressure. Even if inducement has been shown through the objective test, a finding of predisposition is "fatal to an entrapment defense" (Department of Justice 2020). Given these two tests, a successful entrapment defense demonstrates that law enforcement agents induced a nonpredisposed person to commit a crime.

Although some defendants charged with terrorism crimes have asserted an entrapment defense, this legal strategy has never resulted in an acquittal, and indeed has introduced evidence otherwise considered more prejudicial than probative to establish predisposition, such as inflammatory videos of terrorist propaganda. Legal scholar Dru Stevenson (2008) even argues that in terrorism-related cases, we "can infer predisposition merely by the fact that the person agreed to engage in such a horrible act, and that other evidence of predisposition is unnecessary" (144). This view assumes that participating in a plot concocted by coercive undercover agents demonstrates a predisposition to terrorism-related crimes, making the objective test, and its assessment of police conduct, unnecessary.

In considering entrapment defenses, the courts also have debated whether defendants can be convicted of terrorism-related crimes if they would have lacked the capacity to carry out the plot suggested by undercover operatives without their intervention. The Seventh Circuit found in *United States v. Hollingsworth* (1994) that although "all that must be shown to establish predisposition and thus defeat the defense of entrapment is willingness to violate the law without extraordinary inducements" as "ability can be presumed," "it is different when the defendant is not in a position without the government's help to become involved in illegal activity."[18] In this decision, Judge Posner interpreted the findings in *United States v. Jacobson* to determine that

> predisposition is not a purely mental state, the state of being willing to swallow the government's bait. It has positional as well as dispositional force . . . The defendant must be so situated by reason of previous training or experience or occupation or acquaintances that it is likely that if the government had not induced him to commit the crime some criminal would have done so; only then does a sting or other arranged crime take a dangerous person out of circulation.[19]

The U.S. Court of Appeals for the Ninth Circuit, however, ruled that *Jacobson* "does not require a 'positional' predisposition" such that it is unnecessary to prove "positional readiness" or ability to commit the crime at hand.[20] Jon Sherman (2009) argues that the "circuit split remains unresolved, but the weight of opinion seems to side with the rejection of a capacity or '*present means*' test" such that prosecutors do not need to prove that defendants had a "readiness" or "ability" to commit crimes without the assistance of the government (1482). Judges have relied on this understanding of entrapment, determining that defendants without the "readiness" or "ability" to commit an act of terrorism can still be found guilty.

The question of positional readiness surfaced in the case of Amer Alhaggagi, who was arrested after rebuffing a sting operation. Rejecting the present means test in *United States v. Amer Alhaggagi* (2018), Judge Breyer observed that the defendant's activities researching ways to conduct a mass attack, including "looking at car bombs, looking at the poisoning, looking at the fires, and looking at the backpack bombs," amounted to "four discrete and very serious criminal activities *if pursued.*"[21] Although an undercover agent tried to enlist Alhaggagi in a terrorist attack, Alhaggagi stopped communicating with the agent after he took Alhaggagi to a storage locker full of mock barrels of explosives. A month before the FBI arrested him on identity theft charges,

Alhaggagi opened three social media accounts for alleged ISIS supporters while resisting pressure to stage a domestic attack. Although Alhaggagi refused to cooperate with the undercover operatives, Judge Breyer viewed Alhaggagi's interactions with the agents as a "reverse sting," evidenced in the defendant's suggestions to conduct arson or use a backpack bomb.[22] For Judge Breyer, "the facts are that these proposed activities or contemplated activities, notwithstanding the fact that *the defendant would never go through with them,* emanated from the defendant and not the Government."[23] Judge Breyer viewed Alhaggagi's online discussions in ISIS-related forums as indicia of the defendant's predisposition to terrorism-related crimes, regardless of his ability to carry out the plans, and therefore irreducible to "trollish joking," as proffered by the defense.[24] Judge Breyer also determined that Alhaggagi's stated intention in opening social media accounts for three online users—to spread "battlefield news and generic exhortations in praise of ISIS"— was a "euphemism for battlefield propaganda" at a time when the "U.S.-backed Iraqi military" fought to "liberate the city of Mosul from ISIS."[25] In other words, Judge Breyer found that although Alhaggagi "would never go through with" the activities discussed with the undercover agents, his conduct constituted a federal crime of terrorism.

Although Judge Breyer only partially applied the terrorism enhancement by holding Alhaggagi's Total Offense Level at 36 while reducing his Criminal History Category from VI to I, Judge Breyer sentenced Alhaggagi to 188 months in prison, followed by ten years of supervised release. The defense argued that this constituted a "brutal" sentence, one that "has absolutely no consideration for the fact that [Alhaggagi] did not plant a bomb, he didn't get a gun, he didn't make any plans to do any of those things. What he did was talk."[26] Rejecting the present means test, Judge Breyer held Alhaggagi accountable for activities he was incapable of committing.[27]

Given the prominence of radicalization research in court proceedings and the government's targeting of hapless individuals, Judge Posner's finding in *Hollingsworth*—that a defendant must have the "present means" or capacity to become involved in illegal activity—is especially critical, as it offers potential relief to some defendants. *Jacobson,* however, continues to be the favored opinion where "readiness" is not considered a distinct factor in determining entrapment; in *Jacobson,* predisposition simply means that a defendant is "ready and willing" to commit an offense if presented with the opportunity, irrespective of their capacity to carry out that crime. In fact, most courts have rejected the "positional predisposition" inquiry, as in *United States v. James Cromitie* (2013), where the U.S. Court of Appeals for the Second Circuit determined that

> a person who has a pre-existing design to commit terrorist acts against United States interests or who promptly agrees to play a part in such activity should not escape punishment just because he was not in the position to obtain Stinger missiles and launch them at United States airplanes. The Government need not leave him at large until a real terrorist suggests such action and supplies real missiles.[28]

In this interpretation of the law, a defendant's "pre-existing design to commit terrorist acts" supersedes consideration of their capacity to carry out such plans. In this logic, sting operations ensnare individuals who could later be duped by "real" terrorists using similar methods, making their arrest, conviction, and incarceration necessary steps to enhance national security. These legal arguments dismiss the alternative options available to law enforcement, such as referring their targets to social services and community resources, rather than staging elaborate stings that ensnare otherwise disinterested individuals by introducing, incentivizing, and encouraging activities that constitute federal crimes of terrorism.

Given the centrality of a defendant's mental state in the adjudication of terrorism-related crimes, legal scholars have challenged the concept of predisposition. Jessica A. Roth (2014), for example, contends that "determining a defendant's mental state at a *prior* point in time in addition to the defendant's mental state at the time of the offense may be assigning the jury a task that is outside of its core competency," especially in "highly sensational cases like those involving terrorism" (1030–31). Sherman (2009) similarly argues that "revising entrapment in the context of inchoate terrorism-related offenses is particularly necessary to safeguard the freedoms of speech and association that American government officials swear to uphold, no matter how unpopular" (1510). Examples of such inchoate offenses include Alhaggagi's "profanity-laden set of real-time joking about his efforts in group chatrooms to find girls to talk to them" and stated desire to cause "millions of dollars' worth of damages and *Insha'Allah* 100's of bodies" by placing "a bomb in a gay club" in San Francisco.[29] Legal scholar Wadie E. Said (2015) also contends that in cases where defendants raised the entrapment defense, "the government proved their predisposition by playing both the recordings of the conversations with the informants as well as videotapes seized from the defendants that purported to show beheadings carried out by al-Qaeda"—evidence usually considered more prejudicial than probative under the Federal Rules of Evidence (37). Yet "in the absence of any other proof that the defendants were a threat . . . political discussions and inflammatory videos from terrorist groups [have] served the purpose of establishing predisposition," illustrating how "raising the entrapment defense comes with the real risk that it can open the door to introduce evidence that may well have been excluded had the defense not been asserted" (Said 2015, 37). However despicable jurors may find such comments, they do not indicate a propensity for or predisposition to terrorist violence, and as such, "prosecutors need to ensure that their charges of choice do not unconstitutionally infringe these protected outlets" (Sherman 2009, 1510). Unfortunately, in the current legal context, "demonstrating predisposition can transform a criminal prosecution into a referendum on a defendant's political or religious views" as the inquiry often "turns to the matter of how sympathetic the defendant is to terrorist objectives" (Said 2015, 33). In this way, radicalization research continues to shape legal outcomes, even as social scientists have shown how such sympathies have no predictive value in forecasting future dangerousness or in determining what a defendant would have done without the intervention of law enforcement.

Through these legal analyses, critical scholars encourage the courts to classify religious beliefs and political speech as prejudicial and not probative of a predisposition to commit a terrorism-related crime (Sherman 2009) and to establish a "tailored entrapment defense" specific to terrorism-related cases (Stevenson 2008, 215). Unfortunately, the courts continue to reach for radicalization research to determine defendants' predisposition to terrorism and to limit the scope of this predisposition to defendants' "mental state," irrespective of their positional readiness. In fact, some legal scholars argue that "the entrapment defense is the primary means by which we regulate sting operations in this country" (Stevenson 2008, 215). If, however, prosecutors easily can demonstrate predisposition through a defendant's noncriminal statements and therefore nullify an entrapment defense, then the courts do little to regulate terrorism stings because law enforcement agents can act with impunity while securing convictions.

Given these stark outcomes, radicalization research's prevailing assumption—that radical ideas drive political violence—precludes the possibility of an entrapment defense as prosecutors easily can demonstrate a "predisposition" to terrorism by showcasing a defendant's political or religious views. In fact, prosecutors have introduced speech acts and religious beliefs protected by the First Amendment to establish defendants' predisposition to terrorism-related crimes, despite the Supreme Court finding in *Brandenburg v. Ohio* (1969) that speech encouraging illegal conduct is protected unless it incites "imminent lawless action."[30] In *United States v. Matin Siraj* (2006), for example, "the evidence submitted by the prosecution to prove Siraj's predisposition included a range of political statements, including his empathy for Palestinian suicide bombers living under occupation and his fascination with Osama bin Laden"— inflammatory evidence that made it impossible for Siraj to mount a successful entrapment defense (Human Rights Watch 2014, 58). In *United States v. Hamid Hayat* (2006), the prosecution used Hayat's support of Daniel Pearl's beheading, possession of Jaish-e-Mohammed publications, and curation of a scrapbook with clippings praising the Taliban as evidence of his predisposition to terrorism. Prosecutors even referred to a scrap of paper with a message written in Arabic—"Oh Allah, we place you at their throats, and we seek refuge from their evil"—as a "jihadist note" that demonstrated Hayat's "requisite jihadist intent" when he allegedly traveled to Afghanistan for training. The admittance of such evidence reflects legal efforts to rebut entrapment defenses through the subjective test. Juries in both *Hayat* and *Siraj* returned guilty verdicts, although a judge later overturned Hayat's conviction after a juror recanted, saying in an affidavit, "I never once throughout the deliberation process and the reading of the verdict believed Hamid Hayat to be guilty" (qtd. in Waldman 2006). Peer jurors pressured each other to find Hayat guilty, vocalizing their anti-Muslim racism through the use of racial slurs and other racialized commentary, such as one juror who said that Muslims "all pretty much look alike . . . it's hard to distinguish within that race who is who" (qtd. in Waldman 2006). The recanting juror explained that she changed her vote to guilty during the deliberations "because the pressure began to take its toll on me," not because the evidence proved Hayat's guilt (qtd. in Waldman 2006). Although a judge vacated Hayat's conviction after he served fourteen years in prison—citing juror misconduct and other legal issues—this case demonstrates how the government has used political speech and religious beliefs to establish a predisposition to terrorism that secures convictions. Cases like *Hayat* and *Siraj* illustrate how, even under the subjective entrapment test, "prosecutors run a far higher risk of convicting the 'unwary innocent' whose conduct may well have been within the law, widely despised but not illegal" (Sherman 2009, 1489).

Despite these legal findings, terrorologists admit that "the overwhelming majority of people who hold radical beliefs do not engage in violence [and] there is increasing evidence that people who engage in terrorism don't necessarily hold radical beliefs" (John Horgan, qtd. in Knefel 2013). In fact, "many defendants in cases viewed as egregious examples of entrapment had radical sympathies," yet they "never showed any intention to perpetrate terrorism" (Norris 2020, 144). Even as terrorologists concede that "nobody watches YouTube or reads *Inspire* and becomes a terrorist," the courts have interpreted these activities as evidence of a predisposition to terrorism (John Horgan, qtd. in Knefel 2013).

Raising the Entrapment Defense: A Matter of Law and Due Process

Given the limited legal tools available to contest sting operations in terrorism-related cases, defendants continue to raise the entrapment defense. The routine dismissal of entrapment claims allows the court to abdicate its responsibility in regulating sting operations (Stevenson 2008); contributes to the continued "manufacturing" (Aaronson 2013) or "creating" (Mueller and Stewart 2016) of terrorist threats that recursively justifies the use of preemptive prosecutions; and reaffirms the scientifically disproven finding that we can identify future threats using lists of warning signs, risk factors, or indicators of terrorist radicalization. Law professor Bernard Harcourt (2020) argues that "the preemptive identification of foreign enemies abroad and of internal enemies on domestic soil" is central to U.S. governance, even as "the former raises problems of prediction" and "the latter compounds those problems given that, in the absence of an internal enemy, one has to be invented and sustained" (144). Harcourt therefore calls for the administration of "due process penal justice" by "restraining from predicting future behavior, but punishing past bad acts judiciously" (142). Yet "giving up on the prediction of who is going to become our next enemy" also requires alternative understandings of terrorism that locate political violence in its formative conditions and refuting radicalization research's currency in the judicial system (141).

Legal justice depends on an epistemic struggle to reimagine terrorism and terrorists by refusing the depoliticization and ahistoricization of violence through state-sponsored frameworks, such as the new terrorism thesis or radicalization theories. By locating political violence in the psychological, cultural, or theological pathologies of individual actors, "agents and prosecutors today use terrorism stings to demonstrate" that the United States is winning the war on terror, although "no data supports the assumption that a would-be terrorist would find the means to commit a terrorist act if not preempted by an FBI sting" or "through a chance meeting with someone able to provide the means for a terrorist attack" (Aaronson 2013, 206–7). By focusing on individual pathologies and motivations allegedly driving terrorist violence, radicalization research strategically erases the political conditions under which nonstate violence emerges and obfuscates the power asymmetries in governance regimes that narrow the political tools available to nonstate political actors to demand change in intolerable contexts and enact alternatives to the interventions offered by the international community. Because "the causes and the actions of insurgent sub-state political violence are presented as a technical problem, devoid of politics, motivated by irrationality, barbarism, and evil," the act of "'bringing politics back in' . . . entails a focus on both state and counter-state political violence, and indeed the connections between the two" (Poynting and Whyte 2012a, 235). With this analysis of political violence, terrorism stings are legally, geopolitically, and operationally untenable because such tactics individualize political violence and permit pursuit of "artificial terrorists" of the FBI's own making (S. Ahmad 2009). Rather than condemn or condone political violence, the retheorization of terrorism as political violence insists on understanding the use of lethal force by analyzing the power and politics animating that violence. This means that the concept of political violence does not morally evaluate or adjudicate which armed struggles or political positions are justified or justifiable. Instead, it merely offers a lens to critically understand the use of lethal force by employing a rubric that more seriously considers how certain power relations, geopolitical contexts, governance regimes, and material conditions participate in the making of violence.

In this section, I examine the case of Mohamed Osman Mohamud to investigate how sting operations criminalize radical beliefs, social networks, and political speech usually protected by the First Amendment. Drawing on radicalization research, prosecutors easily can frame these behaviors and beliefs as indicative of a predisposition to terrorism and therefore invalidate an entrapment defense. Although "repugnant religious and political beliefs do not equate to predisposition to commit the crime charged," terrorism scholars have primed the courts to evaluate defendants according to disproven radicalization theories.[31] Such logic functions recursively: radicalization research reinforces the necessity of terrorism stings to inoculate incipient terrorists, which leads to sensationalized prosecutions that frame innocuous behaviors like watching YouTube videos as evidence of a predisposition to terrorism. Such claims of predisposition invalidate entrapment defenses and return guilty verdicts, ultimately reaffirming radicalization research. Mohamud's case therefore illustrates how police officers and paid informants can coerce an otherwise law-abiding individual to commit a terrorism offense with impunity.

As a young child, Mohamud immigrated to the United States in 1993, amid the Somali civil war. Court filings described Mohamud as "an ordinary immigrant youngster" who "read Harry Potter books, attended local public schools, and quickly learned English."[32] Although Mohamud attended a local mosque, he spent part of his teenage years researching his religion online, where he "encountered pro-jihadi websites and became very familiar with the extremist language of that internet community."[33] In 2008, Mohamud met Amro al-Ali, a Saudi college student who came to study in the United States on a valid student visa. After al-Ali returned to Saudi Arabia at the end of the school year, Mohamud communicated with him sporadically over email about "religious subjects" and about an Islamic school, Dar al-Hadith, in Yemen.

In one exchange, Mohamud complained about being stopped and questioned at the airport while on a family trip to London, blaming the "evil Zionist-crusader lobbyists who control the world" and calling on Allah to bring his fighters against such unbelievers. Without evidence, prosecutors referred to al-Ali as a "known al-Qaeda terrorist" and "al-Qaeda recruiter," suggesting a more nefarious intent behind Mohamud's communications with his Saudi friend.[34]

In 2009, Mohamud also began corresponding with Samir Khan, a U.S. citizen who "openly administered an extremist jihadi website and published an online magazine, *Jihad Recollections,*" before traveling to Yemen to join al-Qaeda in the Arabian Peninsula.[35] In his emails, Mohamud asked Khan for advice on his personal relationships and on Islamic law. Soon after, in February 2009, Mohamud began writing for *Jihad Recollections* under the pen name Ibn al-Mubarak, a well-known poet. Mohamud's three articles offered advice on how to stay mentally and physically fit to prepare for jihad; praised al-Qaeda's media production house, As-Sahab; and assessed Europe's vulnerability to a jihadi attack.[36] According to the U.S. Court of Appeals for the Ninth Circuit, Mohamud's "more incendiary content" drafted for *Jihad Recollections* included praising the September 11 hijackers who "hit them so fast the Americans became dumbfounded" and fighters in Afghanistan who attacked U.S. helicopters and "finish[ed] off the wounded American soldiers."[37] During this time, Mohamud also wrote posts on the website Dawn of the Ummah, including a list of people he considered to have "offended Allah," similar to a police department's most wanted list.[38] Mohamud used *Jihad Recollections* and Dawn of the Ummah to publish articles on fitness, praise al-Qaeda, and criticize the United States.

Four days after Mohamud turned eighteen, he abruptly ended his communications with Khan. He also stopped writing for *Jihad Recollections,* ending his brief stint as a contributing author. In fact, on August 15, 2009, Mohamud wrote to Khan to report that he would not write for the upcoming edition. Mohamud desisted from activity law enforcement agents viewed as indicative of his predisposition to terrorist violence.

Despite Mohamud's contributions to *Jihad Recollections,* it was his own father—not his writings—that first placed him under police scrutiny. On August 31, 2009, al-Ali sent Mohamud information about a religious school in Yemen. Mohamud then called his father to say he was leaving the country. Panicked, Mohamud's father contacted the FBI, asking for assistance in stopping his son and sharing Mohamud's emails about the school in Yemen. Meanwhile, Mohamud's mother picked him up from a nearby playground and discovered he never obtained a visa or airplane ticket. Mohamud's threat to leave—for the purposes of attending school—was never real. The FBI, however, used Mohamud's emails to tie him to "an ongoing FBI investigation of Samir Khan."[39] The FBI never told Mohamud's parents about his "earlier online contacts with extremists," which later frustrated his father as "he would have contacted counselors and elders in the Muslim and Somali communities who could have steered [him] away from extremist viewpoints."[40] As in other cases, FBI agents pursued a sting operation instead of offering alternative interventions.[41]

That night, Mohamud expressed his desire to study Arabic and learn more about Islam by going to school in Yemen after hearing about it from al-Ali. His parents convinced him to stay in the United States and attend college before venturing farther from home. Mohamud obliged and enrolled in college at nearby Oregon State University in 2009. The FBI went with him, conducting undercover physical and electronic surveillance, including videotaping Mohamud and his friends in the school cafeteria. In reviewing the case, the FBI case agent determined that Mohamud's communications did not have "the same radical speak that he had espoused early on, when he was communicating with Samir Khan," concluding to his supervisors that "for the most part he has left behind his radical thinking."[42] A month later, the same case agent explained that while Mohamud's *Jihad Recollections* articles reflected a "hard ruling Islamic life," Mohamud no longer subscribed to this framework, although he remained a "pretty manipulable, conflicted kid."[43]

Mohamud's move to college meant relocating to a new town, Corvallis, which also led the FBI to transfer his case to another agent and field office. Soon after, the new case agent authorized an undercover operation against Mohamud, which was led by a special agent using the name Bill Smith. In an introductory email to Mohamud, Smith expressed a desire to "fight for the Ummah" and "fulfill my purpose and help with what is to come."[44] Mohamud irregularly replied to Smith's emails and never responded to his calls for violence. During this time, al-Ali also reconnected with Mohamud by email, offering to help him relocate to Yemen for school. Mohamud never successfully contacted al-Ali's reference to arrange his travel, instead making plans to begin the spring semester at Oregon State University.

Referring to unknown and unnamed sources, Interpol reported to the FBI that al-Ali "was known to be connected to a fugitive wanted by Saudi Arabian authorities who is an expert in manufacturing explosives and in facilitating the movement of extremists inside Saudi Arabia."[45] At trial, government agents testified that the Interpol notice affected their decision-making related to the surveillance of Mohamud. The FBI's suspicions intensified when Mohamud began communicating with a friend, Beau Stuart, the son of an FBI agent. Though their emails discussed benign topics such as traveling abroad, the FBI worried when Mohamud responded to Stuart's plans to travel to the holy city of Mecca by writing, "Oh, nice. Make lots of dua for me. Make dua that I will be [the] one to open Al Quds and make dua that I will be a martyr in the highest chambers of paradise."[46] The language of martyrdom triggered suspicion among FBI agents who interpreted the email as an expression of Mohamud's commitment to becoming a suicide bomber. At trial, expert and lay witnesses testified that Mohamud's response "was a common phrase that reflected a larger principle in Islam, namely that to die as a martyr for the sake of one's religion is the most noble death" and that "the phrase is like a greeting or salutation from a hadith or proverb and was not concerning."[47] The FBI, however, used Mohamud's emails with al-Ali and Stuart as a pretext to begin a sting operation led by an undercover agent going by the name Youssef.

Youssef's initial emails to Mohamud asked if he was "still able to help his brothers," alleging he was "on the move." Mohamud declined the invitation, stating he could no longer travel after learning that he had been barred from flying while on his way to Alaska for a summer job with his college roommate. Youssef then said Mohamud could find a way to contribute locally and requested an in-person meeting. Using the FBI's knowledge of the nineteen-year-old, Youssef pressured Mohamud to consent to the bombing of Pioneer Square. Another undercover agent, who used the name Hussein, joined the operation, and the trio discussed "U.S. losses in Afghanistan and how Muslim civilians were being killed."[48] Still, Mohamud also expressed a desire to study Islam and learn Arabic in Yemen.

Despite Mohamud's stated intentions to attend school in Yemen, the FBI worried that Mohamud might mobilize his own terrorist plot within the United States. The undercover agents intensified their pressure and eventually convinced Mohamud to park a truck bomb in Pioneer Square and then travel abroad to flee law enforcement. To operationalize this plan, Hussein gave Mohamud money to rent his own apartment, rather than live on campus with a roommate, and to purchase supplies for the attack. In late 2010, Mohamud accompanied Hussein to Pioneer Square, where he pushed a cellphone trigger twice in an attempt to detonate the inert bomb. FBI agents arrested Mohamud shortly after his failed effort.

At trial, expert witness Evan Kohlmann identified the six factors he used to "see whether or not someone is potentially a threat":

1. evidence of self-selecting plots or schemes by actively trying to come up with a terrorist plot to the point that they have details;
2. previous or existing ties to a known extremist or known representative of a terrorist organization or a known recruiter for a terrorist organization;
3. adopted a radical sectarian ideology that has put them at odds not only within the mainstream community inside the United States, but even within the Muslim community itself;
4. engaged in logistical subterfuge by trying to conceal their activities from law enforcement;
5. deliberately collecting and/or redistributing large amounts of terrorist propaganda; and
6. browsing websites or social networking forums which are explicitly run by or on behalf of terrorist groups or terrorist organizations.[49]

Although Judge Mary Scriven concluded in *Osmakac* that Kohlmann's factors did not meet *Daubert* standards, Judge Garr King relied on them to determine if Mohamud constituted a "potential violent threat."[50] At Mohamud's trial, Kohlmann testified that he "found evidence of at least one, if not two, serious efforts to travel to Yemen in order to join— *presumably* in order to join a violent jihadi group there, which at the time of this trip was supposed to take place, would have been al-Qaeda in the Arabian Peninsula."[51] Kohlmann inferred that Mohamud's efforts to travel to Yemen to enroll in seminary (Dar al-Hadith) constituted a concerted effort to "join a violent jihadi group." Without supporting evidence to tie Mohamud's educational aspirations to "jihad," Kohlmann argued that Dar al-Hadith's founder was "an avid supporter of jihad" and that "his seminary in Yemen gained a reputation among—particularly amongst English-speaking jihadists from the West—to be a good place to go to be a steppingstone to find either a violent jihadi group or a very, very jihadist cleric or some—somewhere in the jihadi community."[52] Using his scientifically specious six factors, Kohlmann infused Mohamud's behavior with meaning: traveling to Yemen for an Islamic education was indicative of his desire to join a "violent jihadi group," consuming online propaganda was symptomatic of his radicalization, and communicating with alleged terrorist operatives like Khan and al-Ali was demonstrative of his terrorist social networks.

On cross-examination, the defense challenged Kohlmann's reasoning, arguing that "there are hundreds of thousands or in excess of a million hits on some of the al-Qaeda videos or postings," while Kohlmann only had access to the hard drives of thirty to forty such viewers. Although thousands of people view propaganda videos for all kinds of reasons, Kohlmann assessed a mere fraction of them, concluding that such media consumption could serve as a reliable sign of a potential threat. Kohlmann also confirmed that "the fact that an individual acts at the direction of the FBI is irrelevant to [his] analysis."[53] Kohlmann's methodology and findings reflect dominant studies on radicalization, which unscientifically conclude that we can use these "hallmarks of radicalization to hone in on incipient terrorists" (Patel 2011, 8). Kohlmann's six factors provided jurors with a framework to interpret Mohamud's activities as signs of his predisposition to terrorism.

Understanding the power of Kohlmann's findings, the defense called its own expert witness, psychologist Fathali Moghaddam, who testified that the FBI's undercover operation, not an underlying predisposition, affected Mohamud's behavior. Expert witness Marc Sageman similarly determined that although Mohamud engaged in extremist dialogue common among Muslim youth, he did not pose a threat. As in other cases, terrorologists differentially interpreted the predictive value of certain behaviors in their court testimony, often drawing on radicalization research to demonstrate or refute the defendant's predisposition to terrorism-related crimes. Through this expert testimony, the defense argued that Mohamud never would have participated in a plot without the provocation of the undercover agents, whereas the prosecution—buoyed by Kohlmann's testimony—viewed the sting operation as an effective antiterrorism strategy that incapacitated a would-be terrorist.

In its closing arguments, the prosecution implored the jury to convict Mohamud, concluding that "an individual simply cannot be entrapped to commit an offense such as this."[54] In this view, a terrorism charge itself nullified an entrapment defense, especially because the defendant exhibited some of the behaviors Kohlmann alleged to be indicative of a homegrown terrorist. The jury ultimately rejected Mohamud's entrapment defense, finding him guilty of attempting to use a weapon of mass destruction. Judge King sentenced Mohamud to thirty years in prison, followed by a lifetime of supervised release.

As *Mohamud* illustrates, radicalization research offers an interpretive framework to demonstrate a defendant's predisposition to terrorism-related crimes, particularly in cases that stem from sting operations. By treating terrorism as the result of an individual's psychological, cultural, and/other theological pathologies, radicalization research directs law enforcement to identify individuals who are "manipulable," and then mobilize a sting operation to ensnare its targets and incapacitate them, all on the premise that certain religious beliefs, political ideologies, social networks, and concerning behaviors can serve as a proxy for a predisposition to terrorist violence.

Radicalization research also supports efforts to invalidate an entrapment defense by demonstrating the defendant's predisposition to engage in criminal conduct. This means that the prosecution can argue that the "routine, normal behavior of the defendants—dress, religious observances, Islamic financial transactions, literature, etc.—indicates a 'predisposition' to commit terrorism, based on the false stereotype that *all* Muslims are predisposed to commit terrorism. If they are sufficiently 'Muslim,' they are sufficiently 'predisposed'" (Downs 2012, 17). Given the long-standing racial formations that organize U.S. society, "anxieties about terrorism, or stereotypes about Muslim terrorists, may make it difficult for factfinders to conclude that defendants were not predisposed to commit the offense" (Norris and Grol-Prokopczyk 2017, 625). Far from a neutral institution, the law "serves not only to reflect but to solidify social prejudice, making law a prime instrument in the construction and reinforcement of racial subordination," evident in pre-emptive prosecutions explicitly targeting Muslim defendants (Lopez 1994, 3). In this legal context, radicalization research contributes to the wholesale nullification of the entrapment defense in terrorism-related cases by creating new "geographies of suspicion" that mark Muslim spaces, bodies, and psyches as terrorist incubators and identify the everyday behaviors of Muslims as indicative of a propensity for or vulnerability to terrorist violence (Akbar 2020, 188). In this racial context, the "sole possible defense—entrapment—has proven ineffectual; there has not been one successful instance of an entrapment defense for defendants charged with terrorist crimes in the decade-plus since September 11, 2001" (Said 2015, 42).

Imperfect Entrapment: Punishing Individuals Convicted of Terrorism-Related Crimes

With an affirmative entrapment defense unavailable to individuals charged with terrorism-related crimes, defendants have raised the imperfect entrapment doctrine. According to the Sentencing Guidelines, a convicted defendant should spend less time in prison because of "serious coercion, blackmail, or duress, under circumstances not amounting to a complete defense."[55] Applied to terrorism-related cases, defendants can assert imperfect entrapment to argue that they should spend less time in prison because undercover operatives coerced them to commit crimes to which they were predisposed. This means that the sentencing court could depart downward from the recommended range outlined in the Sentencing Guidelines. For example, in *Mohamud,* Judge King determined that "the jury found that [the] defendant was not entrapped, but imperfect entrapment is available as a defense," and "in this case, it weighs slightly in favor of the defendant in this case" (qtd. in Mora and Hayes 2015). Affirming that Youssef and Hussein imperfectly entrapped Mohamud, Judge King sentenced the defendant to thirty years, departing from the Sentencing Guidelines' call for a life sentence and the prosecution's recommendation of forty years. Although defense attorneys often demonstrated that their clients lacked a predisposition to terrorism and that undercover agents acted egregiously, they limited their legal claims to imperfect entrapment to fight for a shorter prison term. Even when judges agreed that undercover operatives imperfectly entrapped defendants, they still issued harsh prison terms, as in Mohamud's thirty-year sentence.

Because imperfect entrapment can be raised only when criminal predisposition exists (or is argued to exist), the courts focus their evaluation on the behavior of undercover operatives—a potentially mitigating or aggravating factor—in rendering sentencing decisions. Although "entrapment-like conduct" typically does not amount to a complete defense in terrorism-related cases, it can "provide partial grounds for departure from the Guidelines," especially when a judge is "uncomfortable with particular police conduct" (Meadows 2002, 347). In this view, "sentencing courts departing on imperfect entrapment grounds take remedial action according to the actions of the police, whether or not the defendant was predisposed" (Meadows 2002, 353). Unfortunately, the criminal-legal system offers little guidance on how to determine what kind of conduct constitutes imperfect entrapment, and in lieu of such assessments, the courts have turned to evaluating the defendants, rather than police conduct, in terrorism-related cases.

Two additional cases provide examples of defendants seeking downward departures on the grounds of imperfect entrapment: *United States v. Adel Daoud* (2018) and *United States v. James Cromitie* (2010). Like *Mohamud,* these cases illustrate how the courts have directed their focus on the mental state and behavior of defendants, rather than the conduct of undercover operatives, to evaluate claims of imperfect entrapment. Like the entrapment defense, the imperfect entrapment doctrine should offer some relief to defendants by assessing and responding to claims of police inducement if not outright abuse. Although these forms of relief may be available to defendants in ordinary criminal cases, judges rarely affirm that undercover operatives imperfectly entrapped defendants in terrorism-related cases, as the government effectively brings charges with statutory minimums that do not lend themselves to judicial discretion and/or redirects legal inquiries into how defendants exhibited the early warning signs of terrorist radicalization rather than into the conduct of undercover operatives. *Daoud* reveals how the government uses radicalization research to effectively nullify both the entrapment defense and imperfect entrapment doctrine, ultimately leading to a devastatingly harsh punishments. *Cromitie* showcases how sting operations often induce defendants to commit a spectacular terrorist plot that narrows judicial discretion; rather than induce defendants to minor offenses that could lead to their incapacitation, such as a scheme encouraging the targeted individual to send money to a designated foreign terrorist organization, FBI agents often choose a more serious offense that generates public outrage, like attempting to bomb a popular tourist site. Together, these cases demonstrate how the prosecution of terrorism-related cases rarely regulates police misconduct; instead, they justify the continued use of sting operations and broader antiterrorism strategies informed by radicalization research. In this legal context, defendants convicted of terrorism-related crimes have few legal options to contest police misconduct and to challenge their perceived predisposition to terrorism.

The Case against Adel Daoud: Predisposition, Coercion, and Imperfect Entrapment

In the case of teenager Adel Daoud, the FBI initiated an elaborate sting operation after Polish national Artur Letowski contacted Daoud in early 2012. Facing terrorism-related charges himself, Letowski first communicated with Daoud through internet forums, where he sent links to *anāshīd* (Islamic songs) and to al-Qaeda's *Inspire* magazine. The FBI used Daoud's conversations with Letowski as a pretext to launch a sting operation that lured Daoud to detonate an inert bomb in downtown Chicago even as Polish officials dismissed all charges against Letowski, given his psychiatric disabilities.

After a "rigorous undercover operation" that ended after Daoud pressed an inert detonator to bomb a popular Chicago restaurant, federal prosecutors charged Daoud with one count of attempting to use a weapon of mass destruction and one count of attempting to destroy a building by means of an explosive (U.S. Attorney's Office, Northern District of Illinois 2012).[56] While security professionals like FBI Special Agent in Charge Jeffrey Sallet celebrated Daoud's arrest as "evidence of the FBI's commitment to working vigilantly with our local, state, and federal law enforcement partners to prevent violent attacks before they occur," the defense argued that "in early May 2012, both Polish and U.S. intelligence agencies—including the FBI—knew full well or should have known that young and impressionable and likely mentally ill Daoud was talking online about 'jihad' with another mentally ill person, not a real jihadi associated with any organization."[57] Ableist language aside, the case against Daoud hinged on whether he was predisposed to commit a federal crime of terrorism.

Despite this "sensational headline-grabbing prosecution," Daoud expressed equivocation in his commitment to a terrorist attack and demonstrated an inability to execute such an attack throughout the sting operation.[58] For example, when asked to concoct his own terrorist plot, Daoud responded, "If you need ideas, I'm, I, I, I think about ideas, I don't have anything, like you know what I mean?"[59] The only plan Daoud suggested was buying a "flying car," although he never explained how such a car could contribute to a violent attack. In fact, Daoud questioned the terrorist plots suggested by the undercover agents. Daoud recognized that *Inspire* "encourage[d] attacks in America" by "attacking in Markets, crowded places, planes, etc." and therefore asked in an online forum if there was "a hadith or Quran verse that says kill the residents of the kuffar who are in war with you while they are traveling."[60] After talking with his imam about these issues, Daoud had "serious questions about going forward with the plot." Yet "the FBI decided to tell him *not* to talk to his imam or anyone else, like his father, for religious guidance."[61] Although case law asks the court to consider a defendant's reluctance to commit the criminal act in evaluating entrapment claims, the FBI continued its operation by "invent[ing] a fake imam that provided the religious instruction Daoud so desperately sought."[62]

Despite Daoud's equivocation in killing in the name of Islam and in the religious doctrines that allegedly supported such violence, the undercover agents continued pressuring Daoud. The agents intensified their operation even after they learned that Daoud's father might "encourage his son to cooperate with the FBI if he felt his son was in trouble with the law."[63] Rather than warn Daoud's father that his son was in trouble, undercover agents continued to coerce Daoud to commit to a terrorist plot, ultimately arresting him after he attempted to detonate an inert thousand-pound bomb supplied by the FBI. Given this course of events, the defense concluded that "the Government arguably induced Daoud to commit the charged crimes by isolating him, persuading him through pleas to his religion, by inflating his naïve perception of himself as a budding Islamic scholar, and providing all the necessary equipment that Daoud would not have been able to obtain if left to his own devices."[64]

The prosecution, however, argued that "the defendant's conduct resulted from a deeply held religious belief that he was born to kill somebody in the way of God," particularly "on behalf of al-Qaeda in order to strike fear in the hearts of the American people."[65] For the prosecution, Daoud's willingness to engage the FBI's concocted plot superseded any inducement or coercion by law enforcement.

The sensationalized terrorist plot devised by the FBI and the prosecution's dramatized retelling of the sting operation framed Daoud as a terrorist with a bloodthirsty "desire to kill" and therefore deserving of a forty-year prison sentence.[66] The defense, however, challenged the FBI's use of a sting operation to ensnare Daoud in a spectacular terrorist plot, arguing that the agents could have chosen a less serious offense or engaged in efforts to deter Daoud, as in the case of Shannon Conley, a white woman who allegedly attempted to travel to Syria to marry an ISIS fighter she met online. Unlike their interactions with Daoud, law enforcement agents met with Conley eight times in an "overt effort to dissuade Conley from violent criminal activity and give her the opportunity to turn away from her intention to participate in supporting terrorist activities."[67] Although Conley sought to join ISIS on her own accord—without police provocation—the FBI repeatedly warned her that "travel with intent to wage Jihad may be illegal and result in her arrest" and encouraged her to "support Muslim lands by getting involved in humanitarian efforts, such as the Red Crescent."[68] Conley, however, insisted that "she preferred to wage Jihad overseas so she could be with Jihadist fighters" rather than contribute to humanitarian work, which she viewed as an ineffective strategy to protect Muslims.[69] While the FBI worked to deter Conley from her plans, undercover operatives actively induced Daoud to contribute to a terrorist plot he was incapable of planning and executing without police intervention. After entering a plea agreement, Conley was sentenced to four years in prison—well below the average sentence of 11.2 years for defendants who pleaded guilty in ISIS-related cases (Center on National Security 2017).

Recognizing it could not challenge the FBI's deceptive strategies after Daoud entered an Alford plea—through which a defendant admits the government has enough evidence to convict while maintaining their innocence—the defense raised the imperfect entrapment theory at sentencing. In doing so, the defense did not "seek a final ruling on whether or not Daoud was 'imperfectly entrapped.'" Instead, it offered "the facts and analysis of 'imperfect entrapment'" to "counter the government's anticipated fear-driven sentencing arguments" proposing that Daoud is "too dangerous to be released—now or forever, one supposes."[70] In this view, "Daoud's immaturity, naiveté, and mental health issues made him susceptible to the suggestion and influence of the FBI."[71] Given this imperfect entrapment theory, the defense argued that "what both the public and Daoud need most to safeguard against any recidivist conduct is ongoing mental health treatment, group therapy, and pro-social interactions with peers rather than prisoners."[72] The defense therefore sought a downward departure from the recommended sentence under the imperfect entrapment doctrine.

In response, prosecutors argued that "imperfect entrapment involves interaction with the government and the defendant, coercion, that sort of thing," but "not predisposition, which is one of the factors of entrapment"—but not imperfect entrapment.[73] Despite this understanding of imperfect entrapment, prosecutors focused on Daoud's mental state and online activities to illustrate his predisposition to terrorism. To demonstrate that the police did not coerce Daoud, one prosecutor pointed to defense exhibits where "the defendant had stated on a web forum that he has read an article on bombmaking in *Inspire* magazine and would make the bomb if he can find the required materials." The prosecutor concluded, "I think that speaks volumes as to where his mind was at."[74] By citing Daoud's online comments expressing his "desire to engage in violent jihad in the name of Islam" and consumption of "material that supported his violent beliefs," prosecutors used Daoud's political and religious beliefs as a proxy for his predisposition to terrorist violence.[75] An undercover agent also testified that Daoud's laughter was a telltale sign of terrorist radicalization, explaining, "From my experience in other undercover operations with counterterrorism and subjects of the jihadi or radicalized mindset, they were all excited and happy about following through with their terrorist plan. It isn't an indication of mental instability, but rather joyful jubilation that they're getting to do what it is they want to do."[76] To clarify Daoud's perceived "mental state," prosecutors reminded the court that the defendant had "viewed a significant amount of material that was jihadist in nature, terrorism in nature"; "made comments publicly regarding a desire to become a

314 Prosecuting Lone Wolves

terrorist"; "expressed hatred against the United States"; and "distributed much of this material to friends of his and other third parties, including *Inspire* magazine, which was a magazine created by al-Qaeda, whose purpose is to inspire, as the title suggests, individuals to commit attacks in their homeland, if not travel abroad."[77] Informed by radicalization research, prosecutors imbued common behaviors with meaning: signs of a "jihadi or radicalized mindset" committed to violence.

Given this perceived predisposition to terrorist violence, prosecutors concluded that the undercover operatives "did not induce the defendant to try to kill hundreds of people in a terrorist attack," explicitly asking the court to "appreciate the level of unbridled enthusiasm the defendant expressed in his desire to kill."[78] By sensationalizing Daoud's actions, prosecutors directed attention away from the aggressive tactics of the FBI and onto the defendant's alleged "pursuit of a path to commit violence against innocent people."[79] In doing so, prosecutors concluded that "the defendant's case is a striking example of a predisposed defendant who was actively *discouraged* from engaging in the underlying criminal conduct," as "there was no encouragement of wrongdoing" by the undercover agents.[80] The court thus should not consider imperfect entrapment as a mitigating factor in sentencing Daoud. Even though FBI agents concocted the terrorist plot for Daoud, planted the inert bombs, and used a fake imam to encourage Daoud to carry out the attack, prosecutors argued that law enforcement never incited or induced Daoud to commit a crime. Judge Sharon Coleman therefore rejected the imperfect entrapment doctrine raised by the defense. In this view, Daoud's perceived predisposition to terrorism nullified the imperfect entrapment doctrine, even without considering the actions of the police.

Having accepted the defendant's Alford plea, Judge Coleman expressed equivocation in the threat Daoud posed, in his commitment to "violent Jihad," and in his capacity to devise and execute an act of mass violence on his own, despite the prosecution's contentions. As she explained:

> There is no dispute that Mr. Daoud was an awkward young man with few friends. . . . There is little doubt that objectively Daoud was an immature young man at eighteen—seventeen actually when the investigation started—who giggled constantly at a high pitch

at times and even when talking fast about serious matters. . . . He did not know how to build a bomb. He drove around looking like a Ninja Warrior.[81]

Even though the Sentencing Guidelines recommended lifetime imprisonment, Judge Coleman imposed a sixteen-year prison sentence, followed by forty-five years of supervised release. She explained that this sentence "address[ed] both the safety of individuals, the general public, and the future of a young man who has been in custody his entire adulthood."[82] Although the public views imperfect entrapment as an important mitigating factor to consider at sentencing (Robinson and Darley 1995), judges adjudicating terrorism-related cases rarely depart from the Sentencing Guidelines on these grounds; even when they do depart downward for other reasons, as in *Daoud,* judges still impose harsh sentences.

Viewing Judge Coleman's decision as "substantively unreasonable" given Daoud's "exceptionally serious" criminal conduct, the prosecution appealed her sentence. In its motion, the prosecution argued that in sentencing Daoud, Judge Coleman "did not adequately account for the defendant's staunch commitment to executing a deadly terrorist attack," especially because Daoud "consumed jihadi literature (videos and anāshīd celebrating terrorists), expressed a strong desire to participate in jihad, and sought out how-to publications like *Inspire,* a magazine tailor-made for individuals, such as the defendant, who had the desire but lacked the technical expertise to execute a terrorist attack."[83] In granting the prosecution's appeal, the U.S. Court of Appeals for the Seventh Circuit found that Judge Coleman "sterilized Daoud's offense conduct in ways that cannot be reconciled with the objective facts of these violent offenses," that she gave "short shrift" to the public safety threat Daoud posed, and that her sentence "fell outside the range of reasonable sentences."[84] The Seventh Circuit therefore vacated Daoud's sentence and remanded the case for resentencing.[85]

As *Daoud* illustrates, even when judges determine that a sting operation involved manipulation by law enforcement agents, they are reluctant to offer relief through the imperfect entrapment doctrine. The FBI's sensationalized tactics have intensified this reluctance, as terrorism-related stings often end in spectacular plots that narrow the perceived scope of judicial discretion. For example, in *United States v. James Cromitie* (2010), Judge Colleen McMahon affirmed the defense's claim of "sentencing manipulation" or "sentencing entrapment" (that is, imperfect entrapment) while also concluding that she "would be unable to fashion any meaningful remedy," given the role of mandatory minimums. If the entrapment defense and imperfect entrapment doctrine serve as the primary tools to "regulate undercover operations judicially" but individuals targeted by terrorism stings cannot effectively use these legal tools, then these undercover operations grant law enforcement agents unregulated and unchecked police powers (McAdams 2005, 110). *Cromitie* illustrates how undercover agents have protected such unfettered power by inducing their targets to commit offenses with harsh mandatory minimum sentences that preclude judicial discretion such that judges cannot consider imperfect entrapment as a mitigating factor at sentencing, even if they find that the agents engaged in "outrageous" conduct.[86]

The Case against James Cromitie: Judicial Discretion, Sensational Crimes, and Imperfect Entrapment

In 2008, a paid undercover informant known as Maqsood approached Walmart stocker James Cromitie in the parking lot of Masjid Al-Ikhals in Newburgh, New York. Known for driving luxury cars, Masqood indulged Cromitie's desire to "be rich" to build rapport and develop trust with his target.[87] As Cromitie described his dreams of owning a "big business," he explained, "I know Allah didn't bring me here to fight a war." Masqood, however, insisted, "Oh, Allah didn't bring you here to work for Walmart, too."[88] Cromitie disagreed, saying, "Just, ah, no, it didn't, he didn't bring me here to fight a war either. He also sent me here to make peace amongst the people as well."[89] However, a few seconds later, Cromitie agreed that "right now, it don't look like the peace is coming. I might as well stick to the war."[90] Hearing Cromitie's interest in war, Masqood explained that according to "the organization JEM that I belong to, Jaish-e-Mohammed . . . the wars come first, okay? There is no peace in Jaish-e-Mohammed."[91] Masqood began pressuring Cromitie to contribute to a terrorist plot on behalf of Jaish-e-Mohammed.

As a part of the sting operation, Masqood asked Cromitie to recruit potential fighters and do reconnaissance to identify viable targets for an attack. Masqood then went on a two-month hiatus. "Without the informant driving the action in Newburgh, the plot ran aground" as Cromitie simply "spent his time working at Walmart, hanging around Newburgh, and watching a lot of television" (Aaronson 2013, 144). Without Masqood's pressure, Cromitie returned to his daily life without completing the tasks to advance a violent attack.

When Masqood returned, he effectively exploited Cromitie's anti-Semitism and outrage over anti-Muslim racism to initiate a plan to design and execute a terrorist plot, with the help of three additional recruits. Understanding Cromitie's desire to "be rich," Masqood's "inducements included offers of $250,000, a barber shop at a cost of $70,000, a BMW, and an all-expense paid, two-week vacation to Puerto Rico for Cromitie and his family."[92] Lured by these financial incentives, Cromitie helped Masqood and the three additional recruits develop a plan to bomb synagogues in the Bronx and fire a Stinger missile at Stewart Air National Guard Base. The sting ended in the arrest of all four men when they placed the FBI's inert bombs in cars near the two synagogues and then fled to the getaway car.

At sentencing, Judge McMahon described Cromitie as "utterly inept" and concluded that "only the government could have made a 'terrorist' out of Mr. Cromitie, whose buffoonery is positively Shakespearean in its scope" (qtd. in Weiser 2011). Despite these conclusions about Cromitie's positional readiness, Judge McMahon sentenced Cromitie to the mandatory minimum, twenty-five years, admitting that "twenty-five years in the sort of conditions I anticipate you are facing is easily the equivalent of life in other conditions" (qtd. in Weiser 2011). In sentencing Cromitie to the statutory minimum, Judge McMahon refused the defense's appeals for a downward departure on the basis of imperfect entrapment, arguing that "the record affords no basis for concluding that the Government overcame any defendant's will in this manner," even while finding that "the FBI created acts of terrorism out of [Cromitie's] fantasies of bravado and bigotry, and then made those fantasies come true."[93] Judge McMahon aligned her decision with *United States v. Gomez*, which found that imperfect entrapment only applies when "outrageous official conduct . . . overcomes the defendant's will."[94] Although other sentencing decisions in terrorism-related cases evaluated official conduct, Judge McMahon focused her analysis on the extent to which undercover operatives overcame Cromitie's will.

In addition to this case precedent, the charges the government brought against Cromitie limited Judge McMahon's discretion. Although Judge McMahon determined that Cromitie and his coconspirators "were not engaged in any terrorist activity before they encountered the [confidential informant]" and that FBI agent Fuller "heard chilling expressions uttered by a bigoted human being and transformed that man's fantasies—fantasies the defendant, James Cromitie, had no way of bringing into being—into very real criminal activity, whose every movement was directed and dictated by the Government," she also concluded that she believed that she did not have "any discretion to sentence the defendant to less than 25 years in this case" because "no circuit has actually upheld a district court's decision not to impose a mandatory minimum because of manipulation."[95] In fact, Judge McMahon observed that "the Government devised the plot to fire a Stinger missile toward Stewart AFB—and even went so far as to create an inert Stinger—for the sole purposes of making sure that, in the event of a conviction, the court could not sentence the defendant[] to less than 25 years," as this planned attack carried with it a mandatory minimum sentence of twenty-five years' imprisonment.[96] In this determination, FBI agents crafted heinous plots specifically to incarcerate, and thus incapacitate, their targets for as long as legally possible, ultimately eliminating any possible avenues of relief. Although imperfect entrapment theory specifically allows judges to depart from the Sentencing Guidelines, the sensationalized nature of terrorism stings often narrows judicial discretion, either in legal doctrine or in its uneven application. In the end, Cromitie is serving a sentence "equivalent of life" for conduct he never would have engaged in without the provocation of the FBI. As *Cromitie* and *Daoud* illustrate, defendants convicted of terrorism-related crimes generally cannot invoke the imperfect entrapment doctrine as a mitigating factor at sentencing.

To ensure defendants face long prison terms, government officials ensnare their targets in sensationalized terrorism stings that narrow judicial discretion and emphasize defendants' perceived predisposition to terrorist violence, rather than assess the conduct of undercover operatives. For example, in *United States v. Yassin Aref and Mohammed Hossain*, the prosecution argued that "the Guidelines do not provide any reductions in sentencing—either through an adjustment or departure—for sting cases" and that "there is no 'sting exception' for the terrorism enhancement."[97] The prosecution therefore rejected "efforts to reduce sentences based upon allegations of 'sentencing entrapment,' 'imperfect entrapment,' or 'sentencing manipulation.'"[98] In other words, "a downward departure for sting cases is not available."[99] Furthermore, "the terrorism enhancement applies regardless of whether defendants had any real ability to carry out their planned attacks."[100] Although these legal matters are still open to interpretation as judges unevenly have applied the imperfect entrapment doctrine and considered positional readiness, such legal tools are generally unavailable to individuals charged with and convicted of terrorism-related crimes. Without the tools to regulate sting operations, "government officials have the ability to impose serious criminal sanctions on almost anyone they want," meaning that the FBI can continue its practice of "inducing otherwise law-abiding individuals to commit terrorist offenses" even though it "is virtually incapable of preventing real terrorist attacks" (Norris 2015, 1259). As legal scholar Jesse J. Norris (2015) concludes, "the FBI is wrong to place so many of its counterterrorism eggs in its entrapment-prone basket, and the courts are wrong to tolerate these tactics" (1261). If the entrapment defense and imperfect entrapment doctrine are the two legal tools defendants can use to challenge aggressive police practices that formulate the basis of terrorism stings, then the near-zero success rate indicates that undercover agents can operate with impunity because the law does little to regulate their conduct or manage their abuses.

Conclusion: Radicalization Research, Unregulated Sting Operations, and the Law

In the U.S. criminal-legal system, the entrapment defense and imperfect entrapment doctrine nominally protect its constituents from abusive police tactics unique to sting operations. Indeed, "the entrapment defense is the principal means by which state and federal courts regulate the government's use of undercover operations" (McAdams 2005, 108). In practice, however, these legal tools offer little relief to defendants because the courts almost always reject these defenses in terrorism-related cases.

In cases where terrorism defendants raised the entrapment defense or the imperfect entrapment doctrine, prosecutors often mobilized radicalization theories to demonstrate the defendant's predisposition to terrorist violence. This approach infuses political statements and religious beliefs with predictive value: engaging in "jihadi talk" or consuming "jihadi literature" signifies progression in the terrorist radicalization process and indicates a predisposition to terrorist violence. Radicalization research therefore offers the courts a conceptual framework that nullifies the entrapment defense, which must meet two fundamental elements: the inducement of a crime by government officials and the lack of predisposition to engage in the criminal conduct. This means that a finding of predisposition is "fatal" to an entrapment defense, even if the court determines that inducement occurred in terrorism-related cases (Department of Justice 2020). Although the imperfect entrapment doctrine qualifies defendants for a downward departure from the Sentencing Guidelines if criminal predisposition exists but government officials induced the defendant's criminal conduct, judges have been reluctant to reduce sentences given the sensationalized nature of sting operations, their interpretation of mandatory minimums, and the alleged threat the defendant poses given their perceived predisposition to terrorist violence.

As *Daoud, Alhaggagi,* and *Mohamud* demonstrate, radicalization research influences the outcomes of cases by precluding a complete defense of entrapment and invalidating the use of imperfect entrapment doctrine to reduce sentences. In fact, of the 135 defendants prosecuted in federal court in ISIS-related cases, none has been acquitted (Center on National Security 2017, 4). Furthermore, "the average sentence for those who went to trial is 32.2 years, while the average sentence for those who pleaded guilty is 11.2 years" (4). Radicalization research justifies the conviction and harsh sentencing of individuals charged with terrorism-related crimes by tying First Amendment–protected activities, like expressing support for designated foreign terrorist organizations or engaging in religious practices, to a predisposition to terrorist violence.

By reducing political violence to the perverse manifestation of cultural, psychological, and/or theological pathologies, radicalization research encourages the targeting of individual actors through aggressive sting operations. These efforts support the mobilization of the criminal-legal system to incapacitate so-called terrorists, regardless of the manipulative tactics used or the effectiveness of preemptive prosecutions as an antiterrorism strategy. This approach pursues individual actors while simultaneously ignoring how power and politics give rise to armed resistance.

Without competing theories with the legitimacy to contest these dominant frameworks, radicalization research will continue to shape the adjudication of terrorism-related cases, limit the regulation of terrorism stings, and authorize predictive policing practices that induce vulnerable Muslims to commit sensationalized terrorism-related crimes. Anchored by the new terrorism thesis, radicalization research portrays "a terrorist threat as a force that cannot be politically bargained with" and "an enemy that is both more apocalyptic and dangerous, and at the same time less amenable to traditional forms of control" (Poynting and Whyte 2012b, 5). By design, this conceptual framework "decontextualizes the formative conditions of violence and eradicates its socio-economic and political content," meaning "our capacity for understanding the political and historical context for this violence is lost" (6). In other words, "substate political violence in opposition to the state appears ideologically as irrational and driven by fanaticism," ultimately necessitating anti-terrorism strategies that identify and squelch such fanaticism before the "real" terrorists exploit such vulnerabilities (9). By theorizing political violence as an outcome of individual pathologies, radicalization research justifies the pursuit of individual actors exhibiting the perceived warning signs, risk factors, or indicators of terrorist radicalization, ultimately ignoring the political dimensions of violence and absolving the United States of its role in creating the conditions contested by armed struggles. Such theorizations have material effects by supporting the conviction of individuals targeted by aggressive terrorism stings, encouraging judges to sentence defendants to long prison terms, and narrowing the legal tools available to contest abusive police practices.

As these cases illustrate, struggles over domestic articulations of the global war on terror are intimately epistemic. How we come to understand political violence determines the strategies the state mobilizes to respond to such violence. Through this recursive process, terrorism research justifies the police pursuit of individual actors, whose prosecution, conviction, and sentencing reaffirm the threat of the fanatical yet lone-wolf terrorist. Such convictions reassert the necessity of sting operations to thwart the threat of homegrown terrorism. Unfortunately, the specters of terrorism and the terrorist continue to haunt domestic courts and promote a fear of menacing Islam, thereby reinforcing the role of the criminal-legal system in incapacitating individual political actors, irrespective of the broader geopolitical contexts, such as U.S. empire, that shape the making of political violence, or the criminalizing anti-Muslim practices that manufacture terrorist threats.

Without alternative epistemic frameworks to examine the relationship between power, politics, and violence, state-sponsored research on terrorism, radicalization, and extremism will continue to define the U.S. global war on terror, including the use of the courts to punish violent political actors and to preemptively incapacitate individuals exhibiting behaviors allegedly demonstrating a predisposition to terrorist violence. Rethinking terrorism requires an analysis of the political orientation rather than the individual motivations, driving militant groups, like al-Qaeda, engaged in "miniwars of rebellion" (Asad 2007, 55). Such an analysis denies the liberal democratic state its status as the sole defender of both liberty and life and its monopoly on the legal right to violent self-defense. To engage in the radical reimagining of a world without war and prisons, we cannot turn to state-sponsored concepts like terrorism and radicalization to inform our analyses. Depending on these decontextualizing and depoliticizing terms forecloses anti-imperial abolitionist responses to political violence and reinforces the racial formations that shape, and are shaped by, military, security, and carceral practices.

Conclusion

ABOLITIONIST FUTURES
RETHINKING POWER, POLITICS, AND VIOLENCE

"I DO JIHAD IN MEDIA." Prosecutor Melody Wells began her opening statement by provocatively (mis)translating defendant Thomas Osadzinski's Telegram message as "I do battle for ISIS in media." Her translation effectively marked the twenty-two-year-old college student as a terrorist operative using the internet to support ISIS, not as a victim of an elaborate sting operation.

Throughout this jury trial, such mistranslations transformed common Arabic words and Islamic concepts into evidence of Osadzinski's terrorist activity. An undercover FBI agent testified that *hijrah* referred to migration from non-Islamic lands to Islamic lands "for the purposes of jihad," thereby casting suspicion on Osadzinski's use of *hijrah* in Telegram messages about Syria. The agent also explained that the emoji showing a hand pointing upward with its index finger symbolized *tawhid*. While *tawhid* refers to the oneness of God, the agent viewed Osadzinski's use of the emoji as a commitment to "fighting for the Islamic State."[1] The agent also interpreted Osadzinski's frequent use of *akhi* (brother) in his messages as references to "ISIS members" despite Osadzinski never mentioning ISIS on Telegram. These essentializing inferences assumed that how Islamic State leaders understood and invoked these terms—which "revolve around the questions of: monotheism *(tawhid)*, rejection of innovation, emigration *(hijrah)*, and holy war *(jihad)*, subjection to the law of God, and congregation *(jama'ah)*"—represented the religious interpretations and political commitments of all Muslims, including Osadzinski (Saleh 2022). The undercover agent's cover story as an ISIS operative in Lebanon recruiting U.S. fighters to Syria, however, made little geopolitical sense given Hezbollah's role in Lebanon as a Shia political party and militant group and ISIS's status as a Sunni rebel group seeking to establish a caliphate across parts of Iraq and Syria. Would a hardened ISIS follower overlook these religious, geographic, and political contradictions? Could the undercover agent ascertain Osadzinski's intentions by studying his use of what the agent referred to as "Islamic talk"?[2]

The wholesale criminalization of such "Islamic talk" occludes how the Islamic State emerged "against the backdrop of the 2003 U.S. invasion and occupation of Iraq, the sectarian political system installed by the occupying powers, al-Qaeda's military infiltration into Iraq, the uprising in Syria, and regional politics" (Saleh 2022). A focus on the doctrinal statements of Islamic State leaders obscures the political orientation and colonial genealogy of the armed group—even if textured by religious idioms—and casts Islamic concepts as always already imbued with violent intentions, regardless of how the user understands and deploys such terms. The prosecution, for example, alleged that Osadzinski's use of common Arabic terms and Islamic referents illustrated his desire to "do battle for ISIS in the media" rather than his developing—and sometimes confused or facile—piety and politics, both expertly exploited by the undercover agents. Understanding race and racism as embedded in the law's "very structure and makeup" clarifies how prosecutors could easily, and credibly, interpret "I do jihad in media" as "I do battle for ISIS in media," use Arabic vocabularies as indicators of terrorist activity, and introduce testimony on a sting operation that misunderstood the region's geopolitical realities (Delgado and Farber 1998, 364).

Marked by religious, cultural, and political overtures, this terrorism trial asked the jury to discern whether Osadzinski was a hardened ISIS operative or, as the defense argued, a "fanboy of ISIS"—an impressionable college student lured by four undercover FBI agents to engage in speech acts usually protected by the First Amendment.[3] After a two-week trial, the jury convicted Osadzinski of conspiring to provide material support and resources to a designated foreign terrorist organization after the college student developed a computer script to more easily disseminate ISIS propaganda on Telegram. Osadzinski, however, merely reproduced many of the ISIS files the government's expert witness, Aaron Zelin, archived on his own personal website, Jihadology.net, which, at the time, made primary-source documents available to the public to facilitate research on armed groups.[4] Although the defense viewed Osadzinski as "scraping Zelin's site" for ISIS content to disseminate through Telegram chat rooms using the computer code he developed, the jury found that this conduct, while legal for Zelin, constituted a federal crime of terrorism.

As in the case against Osadzinski, terrorism trials amply demonstrate how the courts circulate, legitimize, and advance Islamophobia as a "lay ideology" that offers a "common sense" explanatory framework to make sense of terrorism defendants (Kundnani 2016, 1). By depoliticizing Muslim resistance to imperial formations and despotic regimes, this explanatory framework blames "'their' culture, not 'our' politics" for the rise of armed struggles and therefore connects ordinary Islamic practices, Arabic vocabularies, and radical beliefs to a predisposition to violence (Kundnani 2017, 35). Deepa Kumar (2012) similarly argues, "The logic underlying these cases is that Muslims are naturally 'predisposed' to commit violent acts and should therefore be put away" (147). FBI agents, for example, asked Osadzinski's acquaintances if he prayed five times a day and if he discussed his views on ISIS with them as a way to assess "his capabilities" for conducting a terrorist attack.[5] Such anti-Muslim logics and corresponding understandings of armed struggles make defendants like Osadzinski legible as irredeemable terrorists undeserving of the "First Amendment right to advocate on behalf of anyone, even if we dislike what they do."[6]

This means that the U.S. security state treats Arabic vocabularies and Islamic doctrines as terrorist etiologies that can inform preemptive national security strategies, reflective of enduring desires to "ascertain unseen and 'hostile' mental states" that "imperial formations have long tracked" (Stoler 2008a, 355). Yet such epistemic politics also occlude the imperial histories, interpretive categories, and explanatory frameworks that draw judges and jurors into the "force field of colonialism's conceptual web" by foreclosing alternative ways of understanding political propaganda, cultural difference, and armed resistance (Stoler 2016, 9). In other words, the concepts the courts have called on to make sense of terrorism-related cases typically prefigure Islamic doctrine, Arab culture, and political dissidence as security threats and therefore narrow their understanding of terrorism defendants. In this way, the figure of the terrorist gestures to how colonial pasts "persist, reactivate, and recur in transfigured forms" (Stoler 2016, 33). By depoliticizing armed resistance used by (sometimes pious) nonstate actors, radicalization research and antiterrorism initiatives—legitimized in and through the courts—refuse to reckon with how such colonial histories contribute to the conditions that incite political violence.

Uneven legal outcomes in terrorism-related cases, however, illustrate both the moments when ready-made narratives no longer worked— demonstrative of how the practices and sites of governance have become "ever more dispersed, diversified, and fraught with internal inconsistencies and contradictions" (Hansen and Stepputat 2001, 16)—and the persistent role of the courts in reproducing racial hierarchies through their day-to-day operations, despite their internal incoherence. Given these epistemic struggles, the field of terrorism studies has continued to refashion its theoretical, methodological, and conceptual approaches to assuage the epistemic anxieties of legal actors worried about "what they could know and how they could know it" (Stoler 2009, 3).

Affirming racism as the law's "genetic flaw" (Delgado and Farber 1998), legal scholar Ian Haney Lopez (1994) writes, "Judges and legislators, in their role as arbiters and violent creators of the social order, continue to concentrate and magnify the power of race in the field of law" (3–4). Some judges presiding over terrorism-related cases, however, questioned prevailing racial logics in their decision-making processes. In the case against Babar Ahmad, Judge Hall refused to equate jihad with terrorism or reduce armed resistance in the context of ethnic cleansing to expressions of Islamic fanaticism. Although Judge Hall credited Ahmad's time served, his sentence still amounted to 150 months in prison. In the case against Asher Khan, Judge Hughes declined to apply the terrorism enhancement at sentencing, a ruling that was overturned twice and resulted in another judge imposing a twelve-year sentence. In the case against Muhamed Mubayyid, Judge Saylor observed that the role of the court was "not to help or hinder" U.S. foreign policy or law enforcement priorities, handing down a sentence of eleven months in this "ordinary tax case" celebrated by prosecutors as a global war on terror victory. In the case against Adnan Farah, however, Judge Davis identified what he viewed as a "terrorist cell" in Minnesota that, "left unchecked, could have caused immense destruction and the loss of many lives, both here and abroad," necessitating the punishment of "terrorists and their supporters." Judge Davis sentenced Farah to ten years in prison and twenty years of supervised release, even though Farah never stepped foot in Syria and never committed an act of violence. Although legal actors have debated, challenged, and reformed epistemic regimes that are always already "provisional and subject to change," the courts have continued to serve as counterterrorism tools, as referendums on violent extremism, and as technologies of control that reflect and reinforce prevailing racial hierarchies (Stoler 2009, 43). The role of the courts as a counterterrorism tool is evident in judicial rulings that challenged anti-Muslim logics while still imposing harsh sentences, as in the case of Babar Ahmad, or overturning seemingly lenient sentences for terrorism offenses, as in the case of Asher Khan.

Some view the near-perfect prosecution rate in terrorism-related cases as evidence that federal courts and lawyers have weakened the rule of law and protected excesses of state violence. To be sure, powerful legal actors have shaped the execution of the global war on terror: the assistant attorney general for the Office of Legal Counsel, Jay Bybee, wrote a series of memos that provided the legal foundation for the use of torture in 2002. Congress passed 2015 legislation that prohibited the Department of Justice from bringing Guantánamo detainees onto U.S. soil for prosecution or incarceration. A 2002 Foreign Intelligence Surveillance Court Review ruling legalized warrantless surveillance. District Judge John D. Bates dismissed a complaint filed by Nasser al-Awlaki—whose son, Anwar al-Awlaki, was executed in a drone strike ordered by President Obama—ruling that Nasser lacked legal standing, such that only victims of extrajudicial killings—the dead—could challenge the government's "targeted assassinations" in court. These otherwise banal decisions certainly reflect the "distortion" of law to expand U.S. security regimes (Greenberg 2016, 8; Said 2015, 4).

Yet focusing on how powerful actors have weaponized the law during the global war on terror misses how the courts always have served as a racial and racializing institution, such that the challenges raised by defense attorneys and decisions made by judges do little to disrupt the social forces set to work in and through the courts. Sociologist Nicole

Gonzalez Van Cleve (2016) studied the largest unified criminal court system in the United States—Cook County, Chicago—and found that racism "serves as an essential function" of criminal courts, particularly as "racial meanings [have] become ingrained within the administration of justice despite procedural protections" (xiii, 2). Legal actors therefore "inherit a culture of racism that has existed 'a priori' (before) their participation. The *a priori racism* that defines the courthouse culture and the legal habitus existed long before they arrived at the courthouse, and it will sustain itself long after they retire," ultimately driving "all of the taken-for-granted assumptions that define discretion in the criminal courts" (4). Although some defense attorneys and their clients sought to unsettle these sedimented assumptions, and some judges observed how dominant explanatory frameworks failed to account for the material conditions in which defendants lived or the police excesses they endured, the courts largely have affirmed the racial logics underwriting contemporary security regimes. This means that individual legal actors can do little in their professional roles to undo the structural functions of the criminal-legal system in its pursuit, prosecution, and punishment of Muslim defendants targeted as potential or actual terrorists, even in ordinary criminal cases.

In this legal context, antiracist reforms to the criminal-legal system, such as proposing new domestic terrorism statutes targeting white supremacist violence or establishing specialized national security courts, can forestall abolitionist futures invested in "a messy breakup with the state—rending, not reparation" (Shange 2019, 4). As legal scholars Matthew Clair and Amanda Woog (2022) explain, while "short term, non-reformist reforms could make criminal courts a venue to unmask, and therefore aid in dismantling, the carceral state," such efforts should not eclipse the larger project to "abolish criminal courts as systems of coercion, violence, and exploitation," "replace them with other social institutions," and "invest in the robust provision of social, political, and economic resources in marginalized communities" (4). The epistemic frictions and legal hesitancies that have defined terrorism prosecutions signal both the imminent political potentialities and the persistent institutional impossibilities of mobilizing the courts as a site of abolitionist struggle.

Through my study of terrorism trials, I came to see how the figure of the terrorist expands abolitionist frameworks beyond "undoing our dependence on punishment and violence to watch over and judge individual behavior and social structures to create a new society" within the United States (Critical Resistance 2004, 19). Given the centrality of terrorism prosecutions in U.S. security regimes, the figure of the terrorist demands a transnational abolitionist approach that integrates an anti-imperial framework and that recognizes violence as a form of political action, even if we disagree with the politics animating violence or the use of lethal force. Thinking transnationally encourages us to ask: Do abolitionist demands to #FreeThemAll equally include Thomas Osadzinski, who was ensnared in a sting operation; Khalid Sheikh Mohammed, who served as the principal architect of the September 11 attacks; Aws al-Jayab, who traveled to Syria to depose the Assad regime; and U.S. Army Major Nidal Hassan, who fatally shot thirteen people in his Fort Hood military base attack? How do we broaden our conceptual understanding of abolitionist practices to stretch beyond restorative justice programs to address the underwriting geopolitical contexts and material conditions that incite armed resistance, such as colonial occupation, military aggression, authoritarian rule, racist governance, and repressive security regimes? In Iraq, for example, Iraqis viewed Baghdad's checkpoints as sites of fear and uncertainty—affective responses that also cultivated "a desire for better, more reliable security infrastructures" in the context of a "total breakdown of state security," which itself was a crisis created in part by occupying forces that institutionalized a sectarian political system and gutted civil society (Martínez and Sirri 2020, 851). If abolitionist thinking recognizes the structural conditions that engineer conflict in the United States (Stovall 2020), how might a transnational abolitionist framework capture the formative contexts in which political violence circulates; respond to the material realities driving affective desires for "more reliable" security infrastructures; and challenge the normative distinction between routinized structural violence waged by state militaries and occupying forces, and criminalized episodic violence enacted by political militants and armed militias? How might we nourish an anti-imperial abolitionist imaginary that takes seriously the figure of the terrorist and the use of lethal force as violent political action? In this way, *Terrorism on Trial* attempts to take up the provocation that "engaging in the work of undoing carcerality necessarily beckons the work of undoing a social landscape productive of empire, for carcerality is derivative of and co-constituted by empire" (Rojas and Naber 2022, 18).

The figure of the terrorist also demands a reckoning with the violence mobilized by political militants, as offered by reframings of terrorism as "counterviolence" (Singh 1976, 60), "decolonization gone global" (Kawash 1999, 240), "hostile dialectics" between state and nonstate actors (Thorup 2010, 2), "divine violence" capable of instituting "a new historical epoch" (Benjamin 1978), "revolutionary violence" that "opposes the violence of the sovereign" (Munif 2020, 19), and "social warfare" (Hyams 1975, 175). To initiate this nascent conversation on transnational abolitionist approaches responsive to the use of violence by (sometimes pious) nonstate militants in contexts wrought by colonial occupation, military intervention, and repressive regimes, I explore how part of the work of abolition requires unlearning dominant understandings of terrorism, employing a transnational analysis of policing and security regimes, and taking armed resistance seriously as violent political action challenging the material conditions in which people live. In doing so, I gesture to possible abolitionist imaginaries capacious enough to center the figure of the terrorist, and its transnational entanglements, as we work to radically transform society in the context of engineered conflict.

Rethinking Terrorism: On Questions of Violence, Politics, and Empire

My immersion in terrorism trials clarified how prevailing conceptual frameworks furnished by the government, such as terrorism and radicalization, have circumscribed how I, and legal actors, have come to understand political violence. One lawyer, for example, explained that terrorism experts strategically organized their testimony around the racialized narratives judges and jurors have heard in popular media. Rather than offer a more nuanced understanding of political violence, these experts reaffirmed popular understandings of terrorism as an irrational, unscrupulous, and incorrigible campaign of lethal violence waged by

"Islamic extremists" seeking to install a new world order. In this way, terrorism experts "who are employed by the state, or would like to offer their services to it, propose that the definition of terrorism is an easy matter having nothing to do with politics" (Asad 2007, 27). Expert witness Charles Lister, for example, testified that the "core reason for why [ISIS] wanted to operate in Syria all along" was to "bring about the end of days" and "obtain a high place in paradise alongside God."[7] Obscuring the geopolitical contexts in which such violence emerges "precludes the possibility of developing interventions that deal with root causes, located in many cases in historical or ongoing U.S. state violence" (Hilal 2021a, 24). Expert witnesses make terrorism knowable in legally strategic ways, ultimately erasing the material conditions that give rise to armed resistance, occluding the politics animating the use of lethal force, and justifying brutal security regimes and military campaigns that exacerbate, not mitigate, the root causes of violent political action.

As a consumer of popular media coverage of ISIS's highly publicized beheadings, kidnappings, and suicide bombings, I also struggled to understand ISIS's violence and its political aims. To make sense of the rise of ISIS and its transnational appeal, I needed to better understand the geopolitical conditions across the region and reckon with the racialized lens I used to interpret the legitimacy, morality, and utility of such violence. In doing so, I did not seek to condone such violence, or its underwriting politics, but to understand the contexts in which violence circulates to further develop abolition as a theory of change that makes sense in Iraq, Syria, and elsewhere. As Rami G. Khouri (2014) explains, "When citizens suffer both police state-style governments with stagnant economies that mostly favor a small number of families close to ruling regimes, we end up with situations like the ones in Syria and Iraq. Citizens who have grown frustrated because of their mistreatment by their own governments desperately turn to groups such as ISIS to give them an alternative lifestyle." Shadi Hamid (2019) similarly argues, "In Syria, civilians routinely suffered atrocities under Bashar al-Assad's dictatorship, which, in terms of the sheer human toll, was more brutal and destructive than ISIS ever could have hoped to be." Although ISIS "didn't practice good governance so much as less bad governance," it offered a "somewhat better alternative to absolute chaos or sectarian repression," allowing the militant organization to "hold on to power—not necessarily in spite of its brutality but because of it." Anthropologist Zainab Saleh (2020) also assesses that the "U.S. occupation of Iraq and the sectarian politics of successive Iraqi governments eventually led to the rise of the Islamic State" (10). These analyses challenge simple conclusions that ISIS's "siren song" duped Syrians and transnational fighters to participate in its armed struggles by offering a deeper understanding of the brutality of the Assad regime, the failure of the international community to hold Assad accountable, and the demand for new forms of governance that reject colonial incursions and authoritarian rulers.[8]

Although ISIS's political platform certainly appeals to transnational fighters, journalists and academics also have documented how rebel groups across Syria have enacted "state-like" functions, such as "establishing checkpoints that control the movement of people and goods, taxing local businesses, founding courts to resolve local disputes, coordinating agricultural production, and organizing schooling" (Martínez and Eng 2018, 237). Such state performances can "foster legitimacy and demonstrate an ability to govern proficiently while making explicit the contingent nature of the incumbent's rule" (237). In other words, the singular focus on ISIS's brutality misses the rise of such rebel groups as a possible "state-like" alternative to the Assad regime and its systematic death dealing. The exclusive attention on ISIS's atrocities misses how such nonstate countercampaigns demand different forms of governance that do not capitulate to colonial powers or despotic regimes. If abolition is a theory of change to destroy and then rebuild structures and societies in liberatory ways (Gilmore 2022), then what does this new world order look like in Iraq and Syria, particularly if, as Fanon (1963) contends, revolutionary violence is part of the work of decolonization?[9] What is the relationship between force and freedom (Jackson 2019), and how do we reckon with the necessity of anti-imperial violence given the current world order defined by U.S. empire?

Understanding the geopolitical contexts and material conditions in which people live can help us understand the appeal of ISIS, even if we disagree with its political orientation and death dealing. As Yasser Munif (2020) writes:

> Death worlds operate in uneven ways depending on the exposure they get and the type of witnesses that inhabit them. . . . When

ISIS tortures its prisoners to death and films them with high-quality equipment for the world to see, its goal is to create a death world where the inside and outside are indistinguishable. The difference between ISIS and the Syrian state is not about the level of cruelty, but rather the degree of visibility. When pro-regime militias kill more than 100 Aleppans and throw them in the river, knowing that the water will drag their bodies to east Aleppo, which is controlled by the opposition, their purpose is that inhabitants of these neighborhoods see the massacre. The violence of such an act is mostly invisible to the outside, especially when media and images are easily manipulated, but is unmistakably visible to the inside. (36)

Munif (2020) does not seek to condone one form of violence and not another; instead, he troubles the normative assumption that what distinguishes ISIS from legitimate states is its cruelty. This assumption ignores the brutality of Assad's regime, the statelike functions ISIS enacts, and the alternative forms of governance that everyday people seek, all of which contribute to the appeal of the rebel group. It also glosses over how the Syrian uprising cultivated an "emergent popular nationalism" challenging Assad's despotism and ISIS's extremism and working toward a "parallel structure to the state that could ultimately undermine the existence of colonial and neocolonial states" (Munif 2020, 99, 101). As a counter to state-sponsored nationalism, the 2011 uprisings demonstrate the possibility of a polyvalent popular nationalism that is "grassroots, praxis-oriented, bottom-up, and liberatory" without seeking to capture or mimic state power—a political horizon suppressed by the resurgence of ISIS and other rebel groups across Syria (Munif 2020, 99). In studying the violence Iraqis endured at Baghdad's checkpoints by Iraqi security forces after the temporary U.S. withdrawal in 2011, José Ciro Martínez and Omar Sirri (2020) found that the everyday desire for "better checkpoints" derived from the intersections of the fears felt passing through them as well as the "oft-expressed desperation over urban disorder and precarity after more than a generation of war and sanctions, violence and instability" (862). By engaging a transnational analysis, abolitionists must refuse reductive narratives that extract the politics from the use of violence and that categorically criminalize violence waged by armed militants while attending to the social, geopolitical, and material conditions that demand more than improved security checkpoints.

Refusing the "territorial trap" that views the territorial state as a container of society and a fixed unit of secure sovereign space (Agnew 1994, 77), ISIS has sought to "recreate the Islamic caliphate dissolved in 1924" to "eliminate the corrupt legacy of Western colonialism, the nation-state—or, rather, the state—introduced into the region by the Sykes-Picot Agreement of 1916" (Joffé 2018, 505). This agreement partitioned the Ottoman Empire into modern Middle East states by dividing territories that were held under French and British rule, generating a "bitter reaction" evident in "the most politically powerful ideologies to emerge—Nasserism, in Egypt, and Baathism, in Iraq and Syria—based on a single nationalism covering the entire Arab world" (Wright 2016). ISIS, Kurdish political parties, and other armed groups have sought to undo the borders imposed by the Sykes-Picot Agreement. In 2014, for example, Abu Bakr al-Baghdadi celebrated ISIS's territorial gains, declaring, "We have now trespassed the borders that were drawn by malicious hands in lands of Islam in order to limit our movements and confine us inside them. And we are working, Allah permitting, to eliminate them [the borders]. And this blessed advance will not stop until we hit the last nail in the coffin of the Sykes-Picot conspiracy" (qtd. in Poplin and Bissell 2014). Even as we condemn al-Baghdadi's violence, we must be careful not to reduce ISIS's brutality to a problem of religious fanaticism; it is only through an understanding of the haunting legacies of colonial rule and anticolonial struggle that we can begin to make sense of its transnational war making and death dealing (Fanon 1963; Stoler 2008b, 2016; Gordon 1997).

Against this backdrop, we can see the limits of using the courts to punish and deter young people like Aws al-Jayab for traveling to Syria to join Ansar al-Sham in a concerted effort to depose the Assad regime and install a new form of governance in the region. Like other transnational fighters, al-Jayab's childhood experiences with war in Iraq and Syria informed his decision to take up arms and reach toward a new political horizon. In fact, al-Jayab's story resonates with European "war volunteers" celebrated for joining the "International Legion," made up of transnational fighters defending Ukraine after Russia's 2022 invasion. These transnational fighters cited personal experiences under Soviet occupation and Europe's future as the motivating factors behind their participation in this military conflict as nonstate soldiers (Abend 2022).

Taking seriously while not condoning this use of violence, what abolitionist alternatives can we conjure for al-Jayab and other war volunteers? How do we build a world less violent than our current one in a way that accounts for U.S. empire and its war-making enterprises? Many of the conceptual frameworks we may use to inform our analyses, such as terrorism and radicalization, locate the problem of political violence in the cultural, psychological, and/or theological pathologies of individual actors like al-Jayab, often ignoring the broader geopolitical contexts, regimes of war, and power asymmetries that shape what Muslim nonstate soldiers are fighting for and why. Human rights expert Cristián Correa (2021), for example, advocates for a "transitional justice approach to foreign fighters" that both "addresses the serious human rights violations committed in violent conflicts where significant numbers of foreign fighters are present" and "develops justice responses to the causes and consequences of those violations" (1). Rather than focus on punitive responses to political violence, a transitional justice approach "promotes accountability, truth, reparation, rehabilitation, reintegration, memorialization, and reform," while creating the conditions for a less violent world order (2).

Interrupting the carceral punishment of armed militants like al-Jayab requires attending to the "ruins of empire" through which imperial formations "persist in their material debris, in ruined landscapes, and through the social ruination of people's lives" (Stoler 2008b, 194). Terrorism prosecutions, as in the case against al-Jayab, demonstrate that these carceral entanglements stretch across histories, continents, and contexts, such that U.S.-based demands to defund the police must connect to a wider decolonial project that recognizes the haunting excesses of empire that continue to bear on global, regional, local, and embodied politics, which, like the Sykes-Picot Agreement, create the material conditions that incite armed resistance of all stripes. As Muslim Abolitionist Futures (2021) writes, anti-Muslim racism anchors the global war on terror; articulates with "broader structures of anti-Black racism, white supremacy, settler colonialism, and imperialism"; and intensifies policing regimes targeting "Black people, including Black Muslims and immigrants, Indigenous communities, and other people of color" such that "there can be no real distinction between domestic and foreign policy" (4). To attend to these material conditions, we must cultivate a transnational abolitionism steeped in a geographical imagination that conjures a more associative politics by recognizing the relations of force that connect distinct places and, in doing so, nourishes coalitionary formations that challenge the structures that depend on and sustain military-carceral modalities, such as racial capitalism, settler colonialism, and state power.

Centering al-Jayab, including his use of violence, can sharpen how we build toward what Julia Oparah referred to as *un outro mundo* (a different world); what Black political protestors declared in U.S. streets—Black Lives Matter; what Egyptians chanted in Tahrir Square—*aish, horria, adala igtimaiya* (bread, freedom, social justice); and what the Arab uprisings demanded across the region—*isqat al-nizam* (topple the regime).

NOTES

Introduction

1. These actions were in violation of 50 U.S.C. § 1705(b), 18 U.S.C. § 2, 31 C.F.R. §§ 545.204 and 545.206(a), and 18 U.S.C. § 844(h)(2).

2. United States v. Meskini, 319 F.3d, 92 (2nd Cir. 2003).

3. As Erik Love (2017) writes, "The racial lens through which Americans see the world distorts and conceals the obvious truth that it is basically impossible to accurately determine someone's religion based solely on their physical appearance. That racial lens is why it is possible to 'look Muslim' in America" (2). Given the racialization of Muslims, any person who "looks Muslim" can experience anti-Muslim racism, such as Hindus, Sikhs, and Christian Arabs. Such racial formations necessarily articulate with antiblackness, such that Black Muslims, and Black African Muslims in particular, face additional state-sanctioned scrutiny, harm, and violence in the United States.

4. Sentencing at 12, United States v. Asher Abid Khan, No. 15-CR-263 (S.D. Tex. Jul. 10, 2018).

5. Memorandum and Order at 4, United States v. Mubayyid, No. 05-CR-40026 (D. Mass. Aug. 1, 2008).

6. Proceedings at 16, United States v. Mohammed Hamza Khan, No. 14-CR-564 (N.D. Ill. Dec. 12, 2016).

7. Sentencing at 49, United States v. Mohamed Farah, No. 15-CR-49 (D. Minn. Jun. 28, 2017).

8. Sentencing at 47, *M. Farah,* No. 15-CR-49.

9. *Mubayyid,* No. 05-CR-40026, Daubert hearing at 91.

10. The statistics of the 892 state criminal cases are as follows: dismissed, 392; acquitted at trial, 42; pretrial diversion, 185; plea agreement, 146; convicted at trial, 26; inactive/warrant status, 45 (Water Protector Legal Collective 2019).

11. Montoya and Reznicek pleaded guilty to conspiracy to damage an energy facility, a violation of 18 U.S.C. § 1366(a).

12. Memorandum and Order at 3; 4, United States v. Mubayyid, No. 05-CR-40026 (D. Mass. Jul. 24, 2008).

13. Throughout, I use Sudbury's (2004) term "globalized punishment" to denote the ever-expanding transnational web of policing, war making, and empire building that confine, enclose, and kill racialized communities. Studying terrorism prosecutions taught me to view the U.S. judicial system as one node in a larger "global circuit of carcerality and torture" whereby colonial feedback loops continuously circulate carceral technologies and colonize both the United States' "racialized interior" and its "racialized populations overseas" (Heiner 2007, 97). For example, Chicago Police Department detective Richard Zuley used violent interrogation sessions that included shackling Black suspects to police precinct walls for hours and threatening to harm family members in a coercive effort to elicit murder confessions from innocent Black Chicagoans. Zuley "supercharged" these torture techniques in his violent interrogation of Mohamedou Ould Slahi, a global war on terror detainee held, without charge or trial, at Guantánamo Bay for fourteen years (Ackerman 2015).

14. Sentencing at 21; 25, United States v. Abdurahman, No. 15-CR-49 (D. Minn. Aug. 25, 2017).

15. Evidentiary Hearing at 80, United States v. Abdurahman, No. 15-CR-49 (D. Minn. Sep. 26, 2016).

16. Evidentiary Hearing at 80, *Abdurahman*, No. 15-CR-49.

17. Sentencing at 21, *Abdurahman*, No. 15-CR-49.

18. Sixteenth-century historian Zainuddin Makhdoom (1583) described the ongoing struggles between Mappila Muslims of Malabar and Portuguese colonial forces in *Tuhfat al-Mujāhidīn fī ba'd a wāl al-Burtuġāliyyīn* (A gift to the holy warriors in respect to some deeds of the Portuguese), writing that Portuguese authorities "forbade the Muslims to trade in pepper and ginger, and then later cinnamon, cloves, and other commodities which yielded the largest profits" (67). The Portuguese also engaged in "vile and disgusting acts," such as burning mosques, in an effort Makhdoom viewed as reflective of Portuguese ambitions to "force Muslims to abjure Islam and accept Christianity" (46). Given these "evils which the Portuguese inflicted upon the Muslims of Malabar," Makhdoom encouraged Muslims to "undertake a jihad against the worshippers of the cross" (5). Dale (1988) draws on Makhdoom to argue that ensuing

Muslim suicide attacks on European commercial settlements in the 1700s cannot be viewed as fanatical attacks but instead as an enduring struggle over the spice trade. Although Makhdoom (1583) evoked religious idioms to condemn Portuguese colonists and encourage Muslim resistance, his analysis fundamentally centers the struggle for economic justice. Dale (1980), however, insists on mapping the "influence of ideology [and] religion among the Mappilas during the British period," arguing that throughout the 1800s, "Mappilas mobilized around Islamic ideology and sometimes attacked Hindus for solely doctrinal purposes" (225).

1. Offensive Lawfare

1. 66 Fed. Reg. 57831 (November 13, 2001).

2. Military Order of November 13, 2001—Detention, Treatment, and Trial of Certain Non-citizens in the War against Terrorism, 66 Fed. Reg. 57831 (November 16, 2001).

3. In March 2006, the Defense Department released Military Commission Instruction No. 10. Citing Article 15 of the Convention Against Torture and Other Cruel, Inhuman, or Degrading Treatment, the Defense Department clarified that prosecutors could not submit, nor could military commissions admit, evidence gathered through torture. The Defense Department, however, also denied that U.S. interrogators used torture, reaffirming the interpretation of such practices as "enhanced interrogation techniques."

4. Office of Legal Counsel deputy John Yoo drafted this "torture memo," which Bybee signed.

5. Francis Lieber and Board of Officers, *General Orders Number 100: Adjutant-General's Office, Instructions for the Government of Armies of the United States, in the Field* (D Van Nostrand, 1863), also known as the Lieber Code.

6. Convention for the Amelioration of the Condition of the Wounded in Armies in the Field, Geneva, August 22, 1864, https://web.archive.org/web/20230204195600/https://ihl-databases.icrc.org/assets/treaties/120-IHL-GC1864-EN.pdf.

7. U.N. General Assembly, *Convention on the Prevention and Punishment of the Crime of Genocide,* December 9, 1948, United Nations, Treaty Series, vol. 78, p. 277, https://web.archive.org/web/20230204200244/https://www.un.org/en/genocideprevention/documents/atrocity-crimes/Doc.1_Convention%20on%20the%20Prevention%20and%20Punishment%20of%20the%20Crime%20of%20Genocide.pdf, accessed February 4, 2023.

8. Protocol Additional to the Geneva Conventions of 12 August 1949, and relating to the Protection of Victims of International Armed Conflicts;

Adopted on 8 June 1977 by the Diplomatic Conference on the Reaffirmation and Development of International Humanitarian Law Applicable in Armed Conflicts Entry into force: 7 December 1979, in accordance with Article 95, https://web.archive.org/web/20230204200631/https://www.ohchr.org/en/instruments-mechanisms/instruments/protocol-additional-geneva-conventions-12-august-1949-and.

9. The International Committee of the Red Cross (2015) explains that *jus ad bellum* "refers to the conditions under which States may resort to war or to the use of armed force in general," while *jus in bello* "regulates the conduct of parties engaged in an armed conflict." International humanitarian law primarily concerns itself with *jus in bello*—justice in war—to minimize suffering.

10. Documents obtained by the *Intercept* revealed that drone strikes between January 2012 and February 2013 killed more than two hundred people. Only thirty-five were intended targets. This means that almost 90 percent of the people killed in these air strikes were civilians (Scahill 2015). The thirty-five targets were assassinated without charge or trial.

11. Although international law historically has operated as a "regime and discourse of domination and subordination, not resistance and liberation" (Mutua 2000, 31), government lawyers shaping the global war on terror also have objected to the normative assumptions organizing these international agreements and their perceived infringement on state sovereignty by binding the United States to "international rules to which the nation's political leaders had not consented" (Goldsmith 2009, 21). Military strategist and legal scholar Kevin Rousseau (2017) similarly argues, "Greater deference to humanitarian law principles conflicts with the principle of sovereignty, and the evolving relationship between these two principles exerts an increasing influence on strategy" (3). In this view, the judicialization of international politics abrogates state sovereignty and shapes military strategy, leading powerful states to reinterpret international law.

12. Organized by the logic of preemption, the Bush Doctrine initiated a kind of "defensive imperialism" that "derives its power and resonance in part through its invocation of a very old set of ideas, those of the 'civilizing missions'" (Anghie 2004, 292). Historically, empires have justified the abrogation of state sovereignty and the principle of nonintervention through the essentialist rhetoric of the "civilizing mission." Under the Bush Doctrine, "it is precisely by invoking the primordial, imperial structures latent within international law that this supposedly new initiative seeks to disrupt and transform existing international law" (Anghie 2004, 309). In the context of the global war on terror, preemptive military interventions rely on the colonial assumption that "the transformation of the 'other' is essential for the defense, the very survival of the

Western self" (Anghie 2004, 309). Through the integration of liberal doctrines such as human rights and women's empowerment, the Bush administration quietly invoked the imperial logics of the civilizing mission as the foundation of its preemptive global war on terror. Yet as political theorist Richard Tuck (1999) explains, "the imperial annexation of remote corners of the globe was often justified in terms of the hazard which the indigenous inhabitants represented to the imperial power and its citizens" (18). Hardly an objective science, "the fear which the aggressor feels may be of very remote or indirect harm" (18).

13. President Roosevelt eventually commuted two of the men's sentences to life in prison because they backed out of the mission after landing onshore.

14. Ex parte Quirin, 317 U.S. 1 (1942). According to the Legal Information Institute at Cornell Law School, "a writ of habeas corpus is used to bring a prisoner or other detainee (e.g. institutionalized mental patient) before the court to determine if the person's imprisonment or detention is lawful. A *habeas* petition proceeds as a civil action against the State agent (usually a warden) who holds the defendant in custody" (Kim 2022).

15. Opinion at 7, In re Yamashita, 327 U.S. 1, 66 Supreme Court 340 (Feb. 4, 1946).

16. Ex parte Milligan, 71 U.S. 2 (1866).

17. In the years leading up to the global war on terror, the Antiterrorism and Death Penalty Act of 1996 further limited the substantive and procedural scope of the writ of habeas corpus. Responding to complaints that defendants abused the writ by challenging their convictions on frivolous grounds, the act imposes a one-year statute of limitations and prohibits petitioners from filing "a second or successive habeas corpus application."

18. Public Law 107-40, 115 Stat. 224.

19. Public Law 107-40, 115 Stat. 224.

20. Hamdan v. Rumsfeld, 548 U.S. 557 (2006).

21. Rasul v. Bush, 542 U.S. 466 (2004).

22. Hamdi v. Rumsfeld, 542 U.S. 507 (2004).

23. Padilla v. Rumsfeld, 352 F.3d 695 (2d Cir. 2003), *rev'd,* 542 U.S. 426 (2004).

24. *Hamdi,* 542 U.S. 507 at 29.

25. On October 5, 2005, Senator McCain issued a statement from the floor of the Senate. A version of that statement was published in a 2006 volume of *Human Rights* and cited here (McCain 2006).

26. Detainee Treatment Act of 2005.

27. Military Commissions Act of 2006.

28. Boumediene v. Bush, 553 U.S. 723 (2008).

29. Al Maqaleh v. Gates, 604 F. Supp. 2d 205 (D.D.C. 2009), *rev'd*, 605 F.3d 84 (D.C. Cir. 2010).

30. Johnson v. Eisentrager, 339 U.S. 763 (1950).

31. *Boumediene*, 553 U.S. at 766.

32. *Al-Maqaleh*, 604 F. Supp. 2d at 206.

33. *Al-Maqaleh*, 605 F.3d 84 (D.C. Cir. 2010).

34. 3 C.F.R. 13492 (Jan. 22, 2009).

35. The term "Article III courts" refers to the courts authorized through Article III, Section 1, of the U.S. Constitution. Article III courts include the Supreme Court of the United States, U.S. courts of appeals, U.S. district courts, and the U.S. Court of International Trade. Article III courts constitute the judicial branch of the federal government.

36. President Obama's federal court strategy aligned with his use of drone strikes to kill, rather than detain, suspected terrorists. Guantánamo detainee Moazzam Begg explained, "I often say that Bush was the president of extrajudicial detention and Obama was the president of extrajudicial killing. They realized they could avoid being called human rights violators by prisoners giving testimony about what was done to them if they just killed people instead. . . . That's why the drone program has become so widespread" (qtd. in Manzoor-Khan 2022, 37).

37. United States v. Warsame, 537 F. Supp. 2d 1005 (D. Minn. 2008).

38. Judgment at 4, United States v. Abood, No. 15-CR-256 (N.D. Tex. May 25, 2016).

39. Judgment at 4, United States v. Naji, No. 16-CR-653 (E.D. N.Y. Jun. 27, 2019).

40. This also means that if the original offense level is 4 and is terrorism enhanced to 16, then the recommendation is to double that to 32, because the "resulting [terrorism-enhanced] offense level is less than 32."

41. United States v. Booker, 543 U.S. 220 (2005).

42. Corrected Transcript of Sentencing Hearing at 23, United States v. Omar, No. 15-CR-49 (D. Minn. May 17, 2017).

43. Government's Position on Sentencing at 50, United States v. Omar, No. 15-CR-49 (D. Minn. Nov. 3, 2016).

44. See, e.g., Hassoun v. Searls, 524 F. Supp. 3d 101 (W.D. N.Y. 2021).

2. Defining the Bad Guys

1. The Afghanistan Papers comprise two sets of materials. The first set includes notes and transcripts of interviews with more than four hundred people conducted by the Special Inspector General for Afghanistan Reconstruction

between 2014 and 2018. The second set includes 2001–4 memos written by Secretary of Defense Donald Rumsfeld.

2. September 8, 2003, memo, National Security Archive, https://nsar chive.gwu.edu/document/24553-office-secretary-defense-donald-rumsfeld -snowflake-steve-cambone-no-subject.

3. With a deadlocked jury, the first trial ended in a mistrial. The second trial led to the conviction of all five defendants, even as prosecutors admitted that the defendants' financial donations intended to support humanitarian projects. The trial effectively criminalized humanitarian donations to Hamas—both the official elected administrative authority of Palestine and a designated foreign terrorist organization. U.S. District Judge Jorge Solis sentenced Shukri Abu Baker and Ghassan Elashi to sixty-five years in prison, Mohammed El-Mezain and Abdulrahman Odeh to fifteen years, and Mufid Abdulqader to ten years.

4. United States v. El-Mezain, 664 F.3d 467, 501 (5th Cir. 2011).

5. Transcript of Sentencing Hearing at 40, United States v. Adnan Farah, No. 15-CR-49 (D. Minn. Dec. 5, 2016).

6. Defendant's Sentencing Position at 11, United States v. Adnan Farah, No. 15-CR-49 (D. Minn. Nov. 3, 2016).

7. Sentencing Memorandum and Opinion at 14, United States v. Adnan Farah, No. 15-CR-49 (D. Minn. Dec. 2, 2016).

8. Sentencing Memorandum and Opinion at 15, *A. Farah,* No. 15-CR-49.

9. Transcript re: Sentencing at 40; 8, United States v. Khan, No. 15-CR-263 (S.D. Tex. Jul. 10, 2018).

10. Transcript re: Sentencing at 16, *Khan,* No. 15-CR-263.

11. Although most terrorism-related cases end in plea deals, even defendants who went to trial often waited until sentencing to raise these contextualizing arguments because this strategy "can work at trial only if you have a way to get in evidence, which judges don't necessarily like to make the political opportunity for the defense" (interview, October 2020). Defendants also worried that these arguments could introduce damaging evidence, such as terrorist propaganda they read or watched.

12. Defendant's Sentencing Memorandum at 1, United States v. Al-Jayab, No. 16-CR-181 (N.D. Ill. Jul. 26, 2019).

13. 18 U.S. Code § 3553.

14. Defendant's Sentencing Memorandum at 12, *Al-Jayab,* No. 16-CR-181.

15. Defendant's Sentencing Memorandum at 45, *Al-Jayab,* No. 16-CR-181.

16. Defendant's Sentencing Memorandum at 16, *Al-Jayab,* No. 16-CR-181.

17. Qtd. in Defendant's Sentencing Memorandum at 19, *Al-Jayab,* No. 16-CR-181.

18. Defendant's Sentencing Memorandum at 21, *Al-Jayab,* No. 16-CR-181.

19. Defendant's Sentencing Memorandum at 22, *Al-Jayab*, No. 16-CR-181.

20. Defendant's Sentencing Memorandum at 22, *Al-Jayab*, No. 16-CR-181.

21. Defendant's Sentencing Memorandum at 24, *Al-Jayab*, No. 16-CR-181.

22. Palestinians in Iraq documented al-Jayab's kidnapping online (http://www.paliraq.com/news.aspx?id=5445).

23. Defendant's Sentencing Memorandum at 29, *Al-Jayab*, No. 16-CR-181.

24. Defendant's Sentencing Memorandum at 29, *Al-Jayab*, No. 16-CR-181.

25. Defendant's Sentencing Memorandum at 31, *Al-Jayab*, No. 16-CR-181.

26. Defendant's Sentencing Memorandum at 31, *Al-Jayab*, No. 16-CR-181.

27. Defendant's Sentencing Memorandum at 32, *Al-Jayab*, No. 16-CR-181.

28. Defendant's Sentencing Memorandum at 33, *Al-Jayab*, No. 16-CR-181.

29. Defendant's Sentencing Memorandum at 33, *Al-Jayab*, No. 16-CR-181.

30. Defendant's Sentencing Memorandum at 12, *Al-Jayab*, No. 16-CR-181.

31. Defendant's Sentencing Memorandum at 35, *Al-Jayab*, No. 16-CR-181.

32. Defendant's Sentencing Memorandum at 34, *Al-Jayab*, No. 16-CR-181.

33. Defendant's Sentencing Memorandum at 40, *Al-Jayab*, No. 16-CR-181.

34. Defendant's Sentencing Memorandum at 7 n.5, *Al-Jayab*, No. 16-CR-181.

35. Defendant's Sentencing Memorandum at 15, *Al-Jayab*, No. 16-CR-181.

36. Defendant's Sentencing Memorandum at 51, *Al-Jayab*, No. 16-CR-181.

37. Government Sentencing Memorandum at 1, United States v. Al-Jayab, No. 16-CR-181 (N.D. Ill. Aug. 19, 2019).

38. Government Sentencing Memorandum at 1–2, *Al-Jayab*, No. 16-CR-181.

39. Government Sentencing Memorandum at 4, *Al-Jayab*, No. 16-CR-181.

40. Government Sentencing Memorandum at 32, *Al-Jayab*, No. 16-CR-181, emphasis added.

41. Although philosopher Thomas Hobbes (1484) agreed that the state serves as the sole arbiter of the use of force, he also argued that the failure of the state to protect its citizens and ensure their security could justify self-defense: "a covenant not to defend myself from force by force is always void" (70).

42. 18 U.S.C. § 2331(5).

43. The Convention of Montevideo on the Rights and Duties of States lists territory, population, governmental authority, and capacity to enter into international relations as the defining features of a state.

44. United States v. Lindh, 227 F. Supp. 2d 565, 567 (E.D. Va. 2002).

45. *Lindh,* 227 F. Supp. 2d at 568.

46. Sentencing Memorandum at 4, *United States v. John Walker Lindh,* No. 02-CR-37A (E.D. Va. Oct. 4, 2002).

47. United States v. Lindh, 212 F. Supp. 2d 541, 557 (E.D. Va. 2002).

48. *Lindh,* 212 F. Supp. 2d at 558.

49. *Lindh,* 212 F. Supp. 2d at 556.

50. President Bush reversed his position after military and public objections, announcing that he would "apply the principles of the Third Geneva Convention" but would not consider suspected Taliban or al-Qaeda fighters as "prisoners of war" (qtd. in Human Rights Watch 2004, 6). Denied prisoner of war status, suspected fighters are categorically unentitled to combatant immunity.

51. Johnson v. Eisentrager, 339 U.S. 763, 793 (1950).

52. Defendant's Reply in Support of Motion to Dismiss at 2, United States v. Al-Jayab, No. 16-CR-181 (N.D. Ill. May 21, 2018).

53. Defendant's Memorandum of Law in Support of Motion to Dismiss at 35, United States v. Al-Jayab, No. 16-CR-181 (N.D. Ill. Jan. 16, 2018).

54. Defendant's Memorandum of Law in Support of Motion to Dismiss at 38, *Al-Jayab,* No. 16-CR-181.

55. Defendant's Memorandum of Law in Support of Motion to Dismiss at 48, *Al-Jayab,* No. 16-CR-181.

56. Defendant's Memorandum of Law in Support of Motion to Dismiss at 25, *Al-Jayab,* No. 16-CR-181.

57. Defendant's Memorandum of Law in Support of Motion to Dismiss at 30; 31, *Al-Jayab,* No. 16-CR-181.

58. Defendant's Memorandum of Law in Support of Motion to Dismiss at 36, *Al-Jayab,* No. 16-CR-181.

59. Defendant's Memorandum of Law in Support of Motion to Dismiss at 41, *Al-Jayab,* No. 16-CR-181.

60. Defendant's Memorandum of Law in Support of Motion to Dismiss at 50, *Al-Jayab,* No. 16-CR-181.

61. Government's Response to Defendant's Motion to Dismiss at 1, United States v. Al-Jayab, No. 16-CR-181 (N.D. Ill. Apr. 20, 2018).

62. Government's Response to Defendant's Motion to Dismiss at 33, *Al-Jayab,* No. 16-CR-181.

63. Government's Response to Defendant's Motion to Dismiss at 14, *Al-Jayab,* No. 16-CR-181.

64. Defendant's Reply in Support of Motion to Dismiss at 6, *Al-Jayab,* No. 16-CR-181.

65. Qtd. in Government's Response to Defendant's Motion to Dismiss at 6, *Al-Jayab,* No. 16-CR-181.

66. Qtd. in Government's Response to Defendant's Motion to Dismiss at 6, *Al-Jayab,* No. 16-CR-181.

67. Government's Response to Defendant's Motion to Dismiss at 7, *Al-Jayab,* No. 16-CR-181.

346 Notes to Chapter 2

68. Government's Response to Defendant's Motion to Dismiss at 1, *Al-Jayab*, No. 16-CR-181.

69. Government Sentencing Memorandum at 4, *Al-Jayab*, No. 16-CR-181.

70. Government's Response to Defendant's Motion to Dismiss at 6 n.9, *Al-Jayab*, No. 16-CR-181.

71. Government Sentencing Memorandum at 4; 3, *Al-Jayab*, No. 16-CR-181.

72. Government Sentencing Memorandum at 6; 3, *Al-Jayab*, No. 16-CR-181.

73. Government's Response to Defendant's Motion to Dismiss at 33, *Al-Jayab*, No. 16-CR-181.

74. Government's Response to Defendant's Motion to Dismiss at 27, *Al-Jayab*, No. 16-CR-181.

75. Government's Response to Defendant's Motion to Dismiss at 27 n.25, *Al-Jayab*, No. 16-CR-181.

76. Government's Response to Defendant's Motion to Dismiss at 8, *Al-Jayab*, No. 16-CR-181.

77. For more cases in which defendants claimed combatant immunity, see *United States v. Hamza Ahmed* (2016), *United States v. Mohamed Farah* (2016), *United States v. Adnan Farah* (2016), *United States v. Abdirahman Daud* (2016), and *United States v. Guled Omar* (2016).

78. Complaint at 4, United States v. Abood, No. 15-MJ-316 (N.D. Tex. May 13, 2015).

79. Transcript of Sentencing at 39; 37, United States v. Abood, No. 15-CR-256 (N.D. Tex. Jun. 2, 2017).

80. Transcript of Sentencing at 37, *Abood*, No. 15-CR-256.

81. Transcript of Sentencing at 83, *Abood*, No. 15-CR-256.

82. Transcript of Sentencing at 88, *Abood*, No. 15-CR-256.

83. Transcript of Sentencing at 93, *Abood*, No. 15-CR-256.

84. Transcript of Sentencing at 30, *Abood*, No. 15-CR-256.

85. Transcript of Sentencing at 46, *Abood*, No. 15-CR-256.

86. Transcript of Sentencing at 87, *Abood*, No. 15-CR-256.

87. Transcript of Sentencing at 23, *Abood*, No. 15-CR-256.

88. Transcript of Sentencing at 42, *Abood*, No. 15-CR-256.

89. Transcript of Sentencing at 52–53, *Abood*, No. 15-CR-256.

90. Transcript of Sentencing at 53, *Abood*, No. 15-CR-256.

91. Transcript of Sentencing at 71, *Abood*, No. 15-CR-256.

92. Transcript of Sentencing at 45, *Abood*, No. 15-CR-256.

93. Transcript of Sentencing at 70, *Abood*, No. 15-CR-256.

94. Transcript of Sentencing at 94, *Abood*, No. 15-CR-256.

95. Qtd. in Transcript of Sentencing at 84, *Abood,* No. 15-CR-256, emphasis added.

96. Transcript of Sentencing at 93, *Abood,* No. 15-CR-256.

97. Transcript of Sentencing at 53, *Abood,* No. 15-CR-256.

98. Brief in Support of Motion for Recusal at 3, United States v. Odeh, No. 13-CR-20772 (E.D. Mich. Jul. 14, 2014).

99. Transcript of Sentencing Hearing at 53, United States v. Ali, No. 10-CR-187 (D. Minn. May 30, 2013).

100. Qtd. in Government's Position on Sentencing at 6, United States v. Ali, No. 10-CR-187 (D. Minn. Apr. 19, 2013).

101. Transcript of Sentencing Hearing at 73, *Ali,* No. 10-CR-187.

102. Transcript of Sentencing Hearing at 13, *Ali,* No. 10-CR-187.

103. Transcript of Sentencing Hearing at 13, *Ali,* No. 10-CR-187.

104. 18 U.S.C. § 2331.

105. Transcript of Sentencing Hearing at 18, *Ali,* No. 10-CR-187.

106. Transcript of Sentencing Hearing at 21, *Ali,* No. 10-CR-187.

107. Transcript of Sentencing Hearing at 71, *Ali,* No. 10-CR-187.

108. Transcript of Sentencing Hearing at 18, *Ali,* No. 10-CR-187.

109. Transcript of Sentencing Hearing at 25, *Ali,* No. 10-CR-187.

110. Transcript of Sentencing Hearing at 25, *Ali,* No. 10-CR-187.

111. Qtd. in Opinion at 8, United States v. Ali, No. 13-2208 (8th Cir. Aug. 25, 2015).

112. Opinion at 8, *Ali,* No. 13-2208.

113. Opinion at 9, *Ali,* No. 13-2208.

114. Opinion at 10, *Ali,* No. 13-2208.

115. Opinion at 10, *Ali,* No. 13-2208.

116. Opinion at 18, United States v. Hassan, No. 13-2209 (8th Cir. Aug. 25, 2015).

117. Transcript of Sentencing Hearing at 74, *Ali,* No. 10-CR-187.

118. Government's Position on Sentencing at 50, United States v. Omar, No. 15-CR-49 (D. Minn. Nov. 3, 2016).

3. The Racialization of Legal Categories

1. During the first wave of Arab immigration in the late nineteenth and early twentieth centuries, most immigrants were poor and working-class Christians (Beydoun 2018). Before the collapse of the Ottoman Empire, Syria referred to present-day Syria, Lebanon, Israel, and Jordan. Court rulings therefore describe petitioners as Syrian.

2. Ex parte Shahid, 205 F.812 (E.D.S.C. 1913).

3. In 1913, Moses Gandur challenged the judicial classification of Syrians as "Colored Asiatics" before the Supreme Court of South Africa. Gandur argued that although Syrians lived in Asia, they were still white and therefore not subject to restrictive immigration and citizenship laws. Through this and other court decisions, Arabs today are considered white. Using "a modern Syrian of Asiatic birth and descent" as a pretext to deny Shahid naturalization in the United States, however, portended ensuing legislation further restricting immigration, such as the Immigration Act of 1917, which expanded the legal restrictions and racial logics organizing the Chinese Exclusion Act of 1882 to prohibit migration from a newly established "Asiatic barred zone."

4. Ex parte Dow, 211 F.486 (E.D.S.C. 1914).

5. In re Najour, 174 F.735 (N.D. Ga. 1909).

6. Ross v. McIntyre, 140 U.S. 453 (1891).

7. *Ross,* 140 U.S. at 472.

8. *Ross,* 140 U.S. at 480.

9. Sentencing at 20, United States v. Adnan Farah, No. 15-CR-49 (D. Minn. Dec. 2, 2016).

10. Sentencing at 29, *A. Farah,* No. 15-CR-49.

11. 18 U.S.C. § 2331.

12. 18 U.S.C. § 2331.

13. Sentencing at 8; 12, United States v. Khan, No. 15-CR-263 (S.D. Tex. Jul. 2, 2018).

14. Sentencing at 20, *Khan,* No. 15-CR-263.

15. Sentencing at 4, *Khan,* No. 15-CR-263.

16. Sentencing at 6–7, *Khan,* No. 15-CR-263.

17. Sentencing at 7, *Khan,* No. 15-CR-263.

18. Sentencing at 8, *Khan,* No. 15-CR-263.

19. Sentencing at 12, *Khan,* No. 15-CR-263.

20. Sentencing at 12, *Khan,* No. 15-CR-263.

21. Sentencing at 13, *Khan,* No. 15-CR-263.

22. See, e.g., United States v. Alhaggagi, No. 17-CR-387 (N.D. Calif. Apr. 18, 2019).

23. Sentencing at 17–18, *Khan,* No. 15-CR-263.

24. Sentencing at 23, *Khan,* No. 15-CR-263.

25. Sentencing at 37, *Khan,* No. 15-CR-263.

26. Sentencing at 13–14, *Khan,* No. 15-CR-263.

27. Sentencing at 2, *Khan,* No. 15-CR-263.

28. Sentencing at 38–39, *Khan,* No. 15-CR-263, emphasis added.

29. Opinion at 5, United States v. Khan, No. 18-20519 (5th Cir. Sep. 16, 2019).

30. In its appeal, the government also argued that the court did not need to determine the legitimacy of Assad's regime because "supporting ISIS . . . is some evidence that Khan's conduct was calculated to influence or affect the conduct of the United States because ISIS's terrorist acts are intended to intimidate or coerce the United States" (opinion at 10, *Khan,* No. 18-20519). If the judge affirmed Khan's desire to depose Assad and considered the regime to be illegitimate and thus not constitutive of a formal government that could be influenced through violence, Khan's actions still amounted to a federal crime of terrorism as ISIS has sought to influence the conduct of the United States. Although the government's theory of the crime was that Khan wanted to join ISIS to depose Assad using brutal violence, the prosecution also argued that ISIS's distant desire to influence the United States meant that Khan also sought to intimidate or coerce the United States, even in the absence of evidence to support such a derivative claim.

31. Opinion at 10, *Khan,* No. 18-20519.

32. Opinion at 1–2, United States v. Khan, No. 20-20030 (5th Cir. May 6, 2021).

33. Sentencing at 24–25, United States v. Al Hardan, No. 16-CR-3 (S.D. Tex. Feb. 20, 2018).

34. Sentencing at 25, *Al Hardan,* No. 16-CR-3.

35. Sentencing at 26, *Al Hardan,* No. 16-CR-3.

36. Sentencing at 26, *Al Hardan,* No. 16-CR-3.

37. Sentencing at 27, *Al Hardan,* No. 16-CR-3.

38. Qtd. in Unpublished Per Curiam Opinion at 16, United States v. Chandia, No. 08-4529 (4th Cir. Sep. 14, 2010).

39. Unpublished Per Curiam Opinion at 16, *Chandia,* No. 08-4529.

40. By 2013, the number of cases in which judges applied the terrorism enhancement rose to forty-four, with only three instances of a court of appeals "upholding a district court's refusal to apply it or to issue a much lower sentence than prescribed by the enhancement in clear and final terms; in all other cases, the court ruled in favor of applying it" (Said 2015, 124). This means that once a court applies the enhancement, this ruling is "likely to be upheld on appeal" (124).

41. United States v. Parr, 545 F.3d at 491 (7th Cir. 2008).

42. Government's Sentencing Memorandum at 9, United States v. Hassoun, No. 04-CR-60001 (S.D. Fla. Nov. 29, 2007).

43. Government's Sentencing Memorandum at 27, *Hassoun,* No. 04-CR-60001.

44. Government's Sentencing Memorandum at 16, *Hassoun,* No. 04-CR-60001.

45. Defendant's Objection to Presentence Investigation Report at 3, United States v. Hassoun, No. 04-CR-60001 (S.D. Fla. Nov. 14, 2007).

46. Defendant's Objection to Presentence Investigation Report at 3–4, *Hassoun,* No. 04-CR-60001.

47. Defendant's Objection to Presentence Investigation Report at 6–7, *Hassoun,* No. 04-CR-60001.

48. Defendant's Objection to Presentence Investigation Report at 7, *Hassoun,* No. 04-CR-60001.

49. Qtd. in Defendant's Objection to Presentence Investigation Report at 10; 11, *Hassoun,* No. 04-CR-60001.

50. Defendant's Objection to Revised Presentence Investigation Report at 18, United States v. Hassoun, No. 04-CR-60001 (S.D. Fla. Dec. 3, 2007).

51. Defendant's Objection to Revised Presentence Investigation Report at 18–19, *Hassoun,* No. 04-CR-60001.

52. Defendant's Objection to Revised Presentence Investigation Report at 18–19, *Hassoun,* No. 04-CR-60001.

53. Qtd. in Brief for United States at 9; 22, Jayyousi v. United States, No. 11-1194, Hassoun v. United States, No. 11-1198, and Padilla v. United States, No. 11-9672 (U.S. Jun. 1, 2012).

54. Decision and Order, Hassoun v. Searls, No. 19-CV-370 (W.D. N.Y. Jun. 29, 2020).

55. Sentencing at 9, *Khan,* No. 15-CR-263.

56. Government's Sentencing Memorandum at 1, *Hassoun,* No. 04-CR-60001.

57. Day 32 Jury Trial Proceedings at 136, *Hassoun,* No. 04-CR-60001.

58. Transcript of Proceedings at 113, United States v. Alhaggagi, No. 17-CR-387 (N.D. Calif. Dec. 20, 2018).

59. Transcript of Proceedings at 113, *Alhaggagi,* No. 17-CR-387.

60. Transcript of Proceedings at 25–26, United States v. Mohammed Hamza Khan, No. 14-CR-564 (N.D. Ill. Dec. 12, 2016).

61. Government Sentencing Memorandum at 4, United States v. Al-Jayab, No. 16-CR-181 (N.D. Ill. Aug. 19, 2019).

62. Defendant's Objection to Revised Presentence Investigation Report at 7, *Hassoun,* No. 04-CR-60001; Government's Sentencing Memorandum at 45, *Hassoun,* No. 04-CR-60001.

63. Government Sentencing Memorandum at 4, *Al-Jayab,* No. 16-CR-181.

64. Transcript of Proceedings for Jun. 9, 2014, at 163, United States v. Osmakac, No. 12-CR-45 (M.D. Fla. Jun. 16, 2015).

65. Transcript of Proceedings for Jun. 9, 2014, at 163; 59, *Osmakac,* No. 12-CR-45.

66. Transcript of Daubert Proceedings at 22, *Osmakac,* No. 12-CR-45.
67. Transcript of Proceedings for Jun. 9, 2014, at 102, *Osmakac,* No. 12-CR-45.
68. Transcript of Proceedings for Jun. 4, 2014, at 159, United States v. Osmakac, No. 12-CR-45 (M.D. Fla. Jun. 16, 2015).
69. Transcript of Proceedings for Jun. 4, 2014, at 159, *Osmakac,* No. 12-CR-45.
70. Transcript of Proceedings for Jun. 4, 2014, at 160, *Osmakac,* No. 12-CR-45.
71. Transcript of Proceedings for Jun. 4, 2014, at 179, *Osmakac,* No. 12-CR-45.
72. Transcript of Proceedings for Jun. 9, 2014, at 108, *Osmakac,* No. 12-CR-45.
73. Expert Report I: U.S. v. Sami Osmakac at 6; 37, United States v. Osmakac, No. 12-CR-45 (M.D. Fla. Mar. 13, 2014).
74. Expert Report I: U.S. v. Sami Osmakac at 36, *Osmakac,* No. 12-CR-45.
75. Expert Report I: U.S. v. Sami Osmakac at 11, *Osmakac,* No. 12-CR-45.
76. Transcript of Sentencing Proceedings at 73; 37, *Osmakac,* No. 12-CR-45.
77. Transcript of Proceedings for Jun. 9, 2014, at 134, United States v. Osmakac, No. 12-CR-45 (M.D. Fla. Jun. 16, 2015).
78. Transcript of Proceedings for Jun. 3, 2014, at 270, United States v. Osmakac, No. 12-CR-45 (M.D. Fla. Jun. 16, 2015).
79. Sentencing Hearing at 40–41, United States v. Ahmad, No. 04-CR-301 (D. Conn. Jul. 16, 2014).
80. Sentencing Hearing at 49, *Ahmad,* No. 04-CR-301.
81. Sentencing Hearing at 40, *Ahmad,* No. 04-CR-301.
82. Sentencing Hearing at 35–36, *Ahmad,* No. 04-CR-301.
83. Sentencing Hearing at 39, *Ahmad,* No. 04-CR-301.
84. Sentencing Hearing at 49, *Ahmad,* No. 04-CR-301.
85. Sentencing Hearing at 56, *Ahmad,* No. 04-CR-301.
86. Sentencing Hearing at 105, *Ahmad,* No. 04-CR-301.
87. Ahmad received credit for time served while in U.K. and U.S. custody between 2003 and 2014, which is why he served only six more months after his sentencing hearing.
88. Sentencing Hearing at 107, *Ahmad,* No. 04-CR-301.
89. Sentencing Hearing at 108, *Ahmad,* No. 04-CR-301.
90. Sentencing Hearing at 54; 21, United States v. Mohamed Farah, No. 15-CR-49 (D. Minn. Dec. 2, 2016), qtd. in Yuen and Xaykaothao (2016).

91. Memorandum in Support of Motion to Vacate, United States v. Omar, No. 15-CR-49 (D. Minn. Dec. 23, 2019).

92. Evidentiary Hearing at 11, United States v. Mohamed Farah, No. 15-CR-49 (D. Minn. Sep. 26, 2016); see also chapter 4. Because not all of the nine young men charged in this alleged conspiracy went to trial, this joint evidentiary hearing involved only four defendants: Hamza Ahmed, Adnan Farah, Zacharia Abdurahman, and Hanad Musse.

93. Evidentiary Hearing at 36, *M. Farah,* No. 15-CR-49.

94. Evidentiary Hearing at 52, *M. Farah,* No. 15-CR-49.

95. Evidentiary Hearing at 36–37, *M. Farah,* No. 15-CR-49.

96. Evidentiary Hearing at 45, *M. Farah,* No. 15-CR-49.

97. Evidentiary Hearing at 38, *M. Farah,* No. 15-CR-49.

98. Evidentiary Hearing at 39–40, *M. Farah,* No. 15-CR-49.

99. Evidentiary Hearing at 39–40, *M. Farah,* No. 15-CR-49.

100. Evidentiary Hearing at 40, *M. Farah,* No. 15-CR-49.

101. Evidentiary Hearing at 42, *M. Farah,* No. 15-CR-49.

102. Evidentiary Hearing at 44–45, *M. Farah,* No. 15-CR-49.

103. Evidentiary Hearing at 45, *M. Farah,* No. 15-CR-49.

104. Evidentiary Hearing at 45, *M. Farah,* No. 15-CR-49.

105. Evidentiary Hearing at 43, *M. Farah,* No. 15-CR-49.

106. Government's Position on Sentencing at 3, United States v. Daud, No. 15-CR-49 (D. Minn. Nov. 3, 2016).

107. Government's Position on Sentencing at 2, United States v. Omar, No. 15-CR-49 (D. Minn. Nov. 3, 2016).

108. Government's Position on Sentencing at 2, *Omar,* No. 15-CR-49.

109. Sentencing Hearing at 33; 49, *M. Farah,* No. 15-CR-49.

110. Defendant's Position on Sentencing at 3, United States v. Mohamed Farah, No. 15-CR-49 (D. Minn. Nov. 3, 2016).

111. Defendant's Position on Sentencing at 4–5, *M. Farah,* No. 15-CR-49.

112. Government's Position on Sentencing at 30, United States v. Mohamed Farah, No. 15-CR-49 (D. Minn. Nov. 3, 2016).

113. Government's Position on Sentencing at 49, *M. Farah,* No. 15-CR-49.

114. Sentencing Hearing at 54, *M. Farah,* No. 15-CR-49.

115. Sentencing Hearing at 21, United States v. Yusuf, No. 15-CR-46 (D. Minn. Nov. 23, 2016).

116. Sentencing Hearing at 25, United States v. Abdurahman, No. 15-CR-49 (D. Minn. Aug. 25, 2017).

117. Such an analysis does not endorse the politics animating ISIS's violence or condone the use of lethal force; it merely takes seriously the geopolitical contexts that give rise to armed groups and that incite armed resistance.

118. Sentencing Hearing at 20–22, *Abdurahman,* No. 15-CR-49.

119. Sentencing Hearing at 24–25, *Abdurahman,* No. 15-CR-49.

120. Memorandum in Support of Motion to Vacate at 4, United States v. Omar, No. 15-CR-49 (D. Minn. Dec. 23, 2019).

121. Sentencing Hearing at 31, United States v. Omar, No. 15-CR-49 (D. Minn. May 17, 2017).

122. In clarifying what constitutes "material support" under 18 U.S. Code § 2339B, some courts have determined a person could provide "medicine" to a designated foreign terrorist organization but not "medical supplies" or "medical support." The court defined Warsame's English-language lessons as "medical supplies." The U.S. Court of Appeals for the Second Circuit concluded in *United States v. Farhane* that the medicine exception to the material support statute "shields only those who provide substances qualifying as medicine to terrorist organizations," while the U.S. Court of Appeals for the Seventh Circuit held in *Boim v. Holy Land Foundation* that "medicine" should be broadly construed to include the provision of medical services.

123. Referring to the U.S.S.G. § 5G1.2(d), which provides guidance on sentences for multiple counts of conviction, the U.S. Court of Appeals for the Second Circuit held that "where the Guidelines-recommended sentence exceeds the statutory maximum on some counts but not others, the court should impose no more than the statutory maximum on any one count but should impose the sentences consecutively to the extent necessary to reach the recommended Guidelines range." U.S.A. v. Reifler, 446 F.3d 65, 113 (2d Cir. 2006). Text of the U.S. Sentencing Commission's *Guidelines Manual* (U.S.S.G.) is available online (https://guidelines.ussc.gov/).

124. Transcript of Sentencing at 36, United States v. Aref, No. 04-CR-402 (N.D. N.Y. Mar. 8, 2007).

4. Terrorologists

1. Transcript of Daubert Proceedings at 47, United States v. Osmakac, No. 12-CR-45 (M.D. Fla. Jun. 16, 2015).

2. Transcript of Daubert Proceedings at 24; 134, *Osmakac,* No. 12-CR-45.

3. Transcript of Daubert Proceedings at 134, *Osmakac,* No. 12-CR-45.

4. Transcript of Daubert Proceedings at 137, *Osmakac,* No. 12-CR-45.

5. Transcript of Daubert Proceedings at 138, *Osmakac,* No. 12-CR-45.

6. Sentencing Hearing at 16, United States v. Musse, No. 15-CR-49 (D. Minn. Nov. 23, 2016).

7. This critique should not be read as an endorsement of academic credentialing practices that often deny nondominant scholars, such as women of color, access to the university despite their robust credentials. This critique merely communicates that self-styled experts and their research undergo little vetting, even though they play a significant role within the national security industry.

8. U.S.S.G. § 3A1.4, Terrorism.

9. U.S. v. Meskini, 319 F.3d 88, 92 (2d Cir. 2003).

10. *Meskini,* 319 F.3d at 92.

11. Transcript of Daubert Proceedings at 142, *Osmakac,* No. 12-CR-45.

12. Transcript of Daubert Proceedings at 106, *Osmakac,* No. 12-CR-45.

13. Daubert v. Merrell Dow Pharmaceuticals, Inc., 509 U.S. 579 (1993); see also Kuhmo Tire Co. v. Carmichael, 526 U.S. 137 (1999).

14. Brief Amici Curiae of Nicolaas Bloembergen et al. at 22, *Daubert,* 509 U.S. 579.

15. Like Adham Amin Hassoun (chapter 3), Majid Khan continued to be detained at Guantánamo Bay after he served his ten-year sentence. The Center for Constitutional Rights (2022) reports that Khan was first captured in Pakistan in 2003 and then "disappeared into the CIA torture program" before being sent to Guantánamo in 2006. In 2012, Khan pleaded guilty to serious offenses before a military commission, which sentenced him to ten years in prison. In June 2022, Khan's lawyers filed a habeas petition challenging their client's continued imprisonment despite completing his sentence. In February 2023, Khan was released from custody. After a deal brokered by the United States, Khan resettled in Belize.

16. United States v. Paracha, No. 03-CR-1197 (S.D. N.Y. Mar. 16, 2020).

17. As cited in Stein's Opinion and Order at 14, United States v. Paracha, No. 03-CR-1197 (S.D. N.Y. Jul. 3, 2018).

18. Opinion and Order at 14, *Paracha,* No. 03-CR-1197.

19. Opinion and Order at 6, *Paracha,* No. 03-CR-1197.

20. Opinion and Order at 24, *Paracha,* No. 03-CR-1197.

21. Transcript of Daubert Hearing at 215, United States v. Paracha, No. 03-CR-1197 (S.D. N.Y. Nov. 2, 2015).

22. Transcript of Daubert Hearing at 215, *Paracha,* No. 03-CR-1197.

23. Transcript of Daubert Hearing at 215, *Paracha,* No. 03-CR-1197.

24. Transcript of Daubert Hearing at 195, *Paracha,* No. 03-CR-1197.

25. Transcript of Daubert Hearing at 197; 198, *Paracha,* No. 03-CR-1197.

26. Transcript of Daubert Hearing at 198, *Paracha,* No. 03-CR-1197.

27. Transcript of Daubert Hearing at 212, *Paracha,* No. 03-CR-1197.

28. Transcript of Daubert Hearing at 214, *Paracha,* No. 03-CR-1197.

29. Opinion at 19, United States v. Paracha, No. 03-CR-1197 (S.D. N.Y. Jan. 3, 2006).

30. Opinion at 19–20, *Paracha,* No. 03-CR-1197.

31. Opinion at 20, *Paracha,* No. 03-CR-1197.

32. Opinion at 24, *Paracha,* No. 03-CR-1197.

33. Opinion at 25, *Paracha,* No. 03-CR-1197.

34. Opinion at 26, *Paracha,* No. 03-CR-1197.

35. Opinion at 27, *Paracha,* No. 03-CR-1197.

36. Opinion at 27, *Paracha,* No. 03-CR-1197.

37. Opinion at 27, *Paracha,* No. 03-CR-1197.

38. Federal Rules of Evidence, Rule 609, "Impeachment by Evidence of a Criminal Conviction."

39. United States v. Amaral, 488 F.2d 1152 (9th Cir. 1973).

40. Brief Amicus Curiae at 5, George v. Intl. Society for Krishna Consciousness, No. D007153 (4th Dist. Ct. App. Calif. Jan. 30, 1992).

41. In delivering these instructions, Judge Stein erroneously confirmed that Khan and al-Baluchi were "two al-Qaeda operatives"—facts prosecutors had yet to prove. Opinion at 32, *Paracha,* No. 03-CR-1197.

42. Opinion at 35, *Paracha,* No. 03-CR-1197.

43. Opinion at 35–36, *Paracha,* No. 03-CR-1197.

44. Opinion at 36, *Paracha,* No. 03-CR-1197.

45. Opinion at 36, *Paracha,* No. 03-CR-1197.

46. Transcript of Daubert Hearing at 19, *Paracha,* No. 03-CR-1197.

47. Opinion and Order at 24–25, *Paracha,* No. 03-CR-1197.

48. Opinion and Order at 24, *Paracha,* No. 03-CR-1197.

49. It is important to note that Fricker (2008) does not use the term "testimonial injustice" to narrow her analysis to court testimony. Rather, Fricker refers to all forms of testimonial transactions; testimony in this sense "can be spoken or written, or for that matter signed or sung; it can be direct, when someone tells us face to face what the time is; or indirect, as when we learn about world events from newspapers" (69).

50. Opinion and Order at 17, United States v. Kassir, No. 04-CR-356 (S.D. N.Y. Apr. 2, 2009).

51. Memorandum and Order at 1, United States v. Abu Ghayth, No. 98-CR-1023 (S.D. N.Y. Feb. 28, 2014).

52. Motion in Limine at 4–6, United States v. Salman, No. 17-CR-18 (M.D. Fla. Oct. 2, 2017).

53. Response in Opposition at 6–7, United States v. Salman, No. 17-CR-18 (M.D. Fla. Oct. 16, 2017).

54. These experts included Maxine Goodman, professor of law, South Texas College of Law Houston; Jeff Goodwin, professor of sociology, New York University; Arun Kundnani, visiting assistant professor of media, culture, and communication, New York University; David Miller, professor of sociology, University of Bath; and Lisa Stampnitzky, lecturer in politics, University of Sheffield. See Brief of Terrorism and Evidence Experts at 2, Sudan v. Owens, No. 17-1236 (U.S. May 26, 2020).

55. Opinion and Order at 2, United States v. Mohamud, No. 10-CR-475 (D. Ore. Jan. 3, 2014).

56. Opinion and Order at 12, *Mohamud,* No. 10-CR-475.

57. Opinion and Order at 12, *Mohamud,* No. 10-CR-475.

58. Opinion and Order at 12, *Mohamud,* No. 10-CR-475.

59. Opinion and Order at 12, *Mohamud,* No. 10-CR-475.

60. United States v. Mehanna, No. 09-CR-10017 (D. Mass. Apr. 13, 2012).

61. Response in Opposition at 27, United States v. Hausa, No. 12-CR-134 (E.D. N.Y. Jan. 5, 2017).

62. Response in Opposition at 27, *Hausa,* No. 12-CR-134. Rule 403 allows courts to "exclude relevant evidence if its probative value is substantially outweighed by a danger of one or more of the following: unfair prejudice, confusing the issues, misleading the jury, undue delay, wasting time, or needlessly presenting cumulative evidence."

63. Response in Opposition at 29, *Hausa,* No. 12-CR-134.

64. Response in Opposition at 29, *Hausa,* No. 12-CR-134.

65. Response in Opposition at 21, *Hausa,* No. 12-CR-134.

66. Endorsed Letter from Jeremy Schneider at 1, United States v. Mustafa, No. 04-CR-356 (S.D. N.Y. May 8, 2014).

67. Memorandum Decision and Order at 8, United States v. Mustafa, No. 04-CR-356 (S.D. N.Y. Apr. 23, 2014).

68. Letter Motion re: Memorandum in Support of Motion to Preclude at 3, United States v. Mustafa, No. 04-CR-356 (S.D. N.Y. Apr. 20, 2014).

69. Letter Motion re: Memorandum in Support of Motion to Preclude at 3, *Mustafa,* No. 04-CR-356.

70. Letter Motion re: Memorandum in Support of Motion to Preclude at 3, *Mustafa,* No. 04-CR-356.

71. Letter Motion re: Memorandum in Support of Motion to Preclude at 12, *Mustafa,* No. 04-CR-356.

72. Motion in Limine at 3, United States v. Mubayyid, No. 05-CR-40026 (D. Mass. Oct. 19, 2007).

73. Memorandum and Order on Defendant's Motions at 8, United States v. Mubayyid, No. 05-CR-40026 (D. Mass. Jul. 24, 2008).

74. Qtd. in Memorandum and Order on Defendant's Motions at 24, *Mubayyid,* 05-CR-40026.

75. Government's Opposition to Defendant's Motion at 3, United States v. Mubayyid, No. 05-CR-40026 (D. Mass. Nov. 5, 2007).

76. Memorandum and Order on Defendant's Motions at 4, *Mubayyid,* 05-CR-40026.

77. Transcript of Daubert Hearing at 91, *Mubayyid,* No. 05-CR-40026.

78. Transcript of Jury Trial Day 14, *Mubayyid,* No. 05-CR-40026.

79. Memorandum and Order on Defendant's Motions at 6, *Mubayyid,* 05-CR-40026.

80. Transcript of Daubert Hearing at 86, United States v. Mubayyid, No. 05-CR-40026 (D. Mass. Feb. 6, 2008).

81. Memorandum of Law in Support of Defendant's Motion at 2, United States v. Mubayyid, No. 05-CR-40026 (D. Mass. Oct. 19, 2007).

82. Memorandum of Law in Support of Defendant's Motion at 2, *Mubayyid,* No. 05-CR-40026.

83. Defendant's Omnibus Response to Government's Motions in Limine at 14, *Mubayyid,* No. 05-CR-40026.

84. Memorandum of Law in Support of Defendant's Motion at 2; 11, *Mubayyid,* No. 05-CR-40026.

85. Memorandum of Law in Support of Defendant's Motion at 20–21, *Mubayyid,* No. 05-CR-40026.

86. Memorandum of Law in Support of Defendant's Motion at 126, *Mubayyid,* No. 05-CR-40026.

87. Memorandum of Law in Support of Defendant's Motion at 89, *Mubayyid,* No. 05-CR-40026.

88. Memorandum of Law in Support of Defendant's Motion at 89, *Mubayyid,* No. 05-CR-40026.

89. Memorandum of Law in Support of Defendant's Motion at 92, *Mubayyid,* No. 05-CR-40026.

90. Defendant's Omnibus Response to Government's Motions in Limine at 13, United States v. Mubayyid, No. 05-CR-40026 (D. Mass. Nov. 2, 2007).

91. Expert Testimony of Dr. Matthew Levitt at 21–22, United States v. Mubayyid, No. 05-CR-40026 (D. Mass. Oct. 19, 2007).

92. Expert Testimony of Dr. Matthew Levitt at 21–22, *Mubayyid,* No. 05-CR-40026.

93. Transcript of Daubert Hearing at 94, *Mubayyid,* No. 05-CR-40026.

94. Transcript of Jury Trial Day 14 at 61–62, United States v. Mubayyid, No. 05-CR-40026 (D. Mass. Feb. 6, 2008).

95. Transcript of Jury Trial Day 14 at 157, *Mubayyid,* No. 05-CR-40026.

96. Transcript of Jury Trial Day 14 at 51, *Mubayyid,* No. 05-CR-40026.

97. Transcript of Jury Trial Day 14 at 51, *Mubayyid,* No. 05-CR-40026.

98. Transcript of Jury Trial Day 14 at 51–52, *Mubayyid,* No. 05-CR-40026.

99. Transcript of Jury Trial Day 14 at 140, *Mubayyid,* No. 05-CR-40026.

100. Defendant's Omnibus Response to Government's Motions in Limine at 14, *Mubayyid,* No. 05-CR-40026.

101. Defendant's Omnibus Response to Government's Motions in Limine at 14, *Mubayyid,* No. 05-CR-40026.

102. Transcript of Jury Trial Day 14 at 145, *Mubayyid,* No. 05-CR-40026.

103. Defendant's Omnibus Response to Government's Motions in Limine at 16–17, *Mubayyid,* No. 05-CR-40026.

104. Defendant's Omnibus Response to Government's Motions in Limine at 17, *Mubayyid,* No. 05-CR-40026.

105. Transcript of Daubert Hearing at 84, *Mubayyid,* No. 05-CR-40026.

106. Government's Motion in Limine at 1, United States v. Mubayyid, No. 05-CR-40026 (D. Mass. Oct. 19, 2007).

107. Government's Motion in Limine at 2, *Mubayyid,* No. 05-CR-40026.

108. Government's Motion in Limine at 2, *Mubayyid,* No. 05-CR-40026, emphasis added.

109. Government's Motion in Limine at 2, *Mubayyid,* No. 05-CR-40026.

110. Government's Motion in Limine at 2, *Mubayyid,* No. 05-CR-40026.

111. Government's Motion in Limine at 2, *Mubayyid,* No. 05-CR-40026.

112. Government's Motion in Limine at 4, *Mubayyid,* No. 05-CR-40026.

113. Transcript of Jury Trial Day 14 at 157, *Mubayyid,* No. 05-CR-40026.

114. Transcript of Jury Trial Day 14 at 146, *Mubayyid,* No. 05-CR-40026.

115. Transcript of Jury Trial Day 14 at 145–46, *Mubayyid,* No. 05-CR-40026.

116. Transcript of Jury Trial Day 14 at 153, *Mubayyid,* No. 05-CR-40026.

117. Transcript of Jury Trial Day 14 at 157, *Mubayyid,* No. 05-CR-40026, emphasis added.

118. Transcript of Jury Trial Day 14 at 159, *Mubayyid,* No. 05-CR-40026.

119. Transcript of Jury Trial Day 14 at 38, *Mubayyid,* No. 05-CR-40026.

120. Transcript of Jury Trial Day 14 at 40, *Mubayyid,* No. 05-CR-40026.

121. Transcript of Jury Trial Day 15 at 115, United States v. Mubayyid, No. 05-CR-40026 (D. Mass. Feb. 6, 2008).

122. Transcript of Jury Trial Day 15 at 117, *Mubayyid,* No. 05-CR-40026.

123. As cited in Memorandum and Order on Defendant's Motions at 11, *Mubayyid,* No. 05-CR-40026.

124. Transcript of Continued Motions for Judgment at 81, United States v. Mubayyid, No. 05-CR-40026 (D. Mass. May 21, 2008).

125. Transcript of Continued Motions for Judgment at 81, *Mubayyid*, No. 05-CR-40026.

126. Transcript of Continued Motions for Judgment at 81, *Mubayyid*, No. 05-CR-40026.

127. United States v. Shah, 474 F. Supp. 2d 492 (S.D. N.Y. 2007).

128. United States v. Warsame, No. 04-CR-29 (D. Minn. Jul. 17, 2009).

5. Prosecuting Lone Wolves

1. I explored these cases at length in chapter 3. The defendants included Hamza Ahmed, Adnan Farah, Zacharia Abdurahman, Hanad Musse, Abdullahi Yusuf, and Abdirizak Warsame. All six young men pleaded guilty and filed both joint and individual sentencing position papers. Coconspirators Guled Omar, Mohamed Farah, and Abdirahman Daud were sentenced in different proceedings after their individual cases went to jury trials.

2. Court Order at 2, United States v. Yusuf, No. 15-CR-46 (D. Minn. Mar. 2, 2016).

3. Sentencing Memorandum and Opinion at 17, United States v. Yusuf, No. 15-CR-46 (D. Minn. Dec. 1, 2016).

4. Sentencing Memorandum and Opinion at 18, United States v. Adnan Farah, No. 15-CR-49 (D. Minn. Dec. 2, 2016).

5. Sentencing Memorandum and Opinion at 18, *A. Farah*, No. 15-CR-49.

6. Transcript of Evidentiary Hearing at 143, United States v. Ahmed et al., No. 15-CR-49 (D. Minn. Sep. 26, 2016).

7. Defendant's Reply Memorandum at 7, United States v. Warsame, No. 16-CR-37 (D. Minn. Nov. 7, 2016).

8. Transcript of Daubert Proceedings at 57, United States v. Osmakac, No. 12-CR-45 (M.D. Fla. Jun. 16, 2015).

9. Transcript of Daubert Proceedings at 58, *Osmakac*, No. 12-CR-45.

10. Transcript of Daubert Proceedings at 143, *Osmakac*, No. 12-CR-45.

11. Transcript of Daubert Proceedings at 142, *Osmakac*, No. 12-CR-45.

12. Sorrells v. United States, 287 U.S. 435, 452 (1932).

13. *Sorrells*, 287 U.S. at 441–42.

14. Sherman v. United States, 356 U.S. 369, 376 (1958).

15. Opening Brief of Appellant at 74, United States v. Mohamud, No. 14-30217 (9th Cir. Sep. 4, 2015).

16. *Sherman*, 356 U.S. at 385.

17. United States v. Jacobson, 916 F.2d 467 (8th Cir. 1990), *rev'd*, 503 U.S. 540 (1992).

18. United States v. Hollingsworth, 27 F.3d 1196, 1200 (7th Cir. 1993).

19. *Hollingsworth*, 27 F.3d at 1205–6.

20. United States v. Thickstun, 110 F.3d 1394, 1398 (9th Cir. 1997).

21. Transcript of Proceedings at 152, United States v. Alhaggagi, No. 17-CR-387 (N.D. Calif. Dec. 20, 2018), emphasis added.

22. Transcript of Proceedings at 153, *Alhaggagi*, No. 17-CR-387.

23. Transcript of Proceedings at 153, *Alhaggagi*, No. 17-CR-387, emphasis added.

24. Defendant's Sentencing Memorandum at 10–11, United States v. Alhaggagi, No. 17-CR-387 (N.D. Calif. Dec. 4, 2018).

25. Order re: Terrorism Enhancement at 7, United States v. Alhaggagi, No. 17-CR-387 (N.D. Calif. Mar. 8, 2019).

26. Transcript of Proceedings at 185, United States v. Alhaggagi, No. 17-CR-387 (N.D. Calif. May 2, 2019).

27. In 2020, the U.S. Court of Appeals for the Ninth Circuit found that Judge Breyer failed to establish that Alhaggagi intended to influence or retaliate against a government and therefore incorrectly applied the terrorism enhancement. The Ninth Circuit vacated Alhaggagi's sentence and remanded the case for resentencing; Judge Breyer resentenced Alhaggagi to eighty-one months.

28. United States v. Cromitie, 727 F.3d 217, 227 (2d Cir. 2013).

29. Defendant's Sentencing Memorandum at 23, 16, *Alhaggagi*, No. 17-CR-387.

30. Brandenburg v. Ohio, 395 U.S. 444, 447 (1969).

31. Opening Brief of Appellant at 65, *Mohamud*, No. 14-30217.

32. Opening Brief of Appellant at 31, *Mohamud*, No. 14-30217.

33. Opening Brief of Appellant at 32, *Mohamud*, No. 14-30217.

34. Opening Brief of Appellant at 33, *Mohamud*, No. 14-30217.

35. Although the government referred to Samir Khan as a "terrorist," the defense noted that Khan "was living openly in the United States during the entire period of their communication, and the government presented no evidence that he had been accused of any terrorist activities or done anything more than exercise his First Amendment right to publish controversial political expressions." Opening Brief of Appellant at 35, *Mohamud*, No. 14-30217.

36. Opening Brief of Appellant at 34, *Mohamud*, No. 14-30217.

37. Samir Khan edited Mohamud's writings, eventually removing this "incendiary" content. United States v. Mohamud, 843 F.3d 420, 423–24 (9th Cir. 2016).

38. Opening Brief of Appellant at 36, *Mohamud*, No. 14-30217.

39. Opening Brief of Appellant at 37, *Mohamud,* No. 14-30217.

40. Opening Brief of Appellant at 38, *Mohamud,* No. 14-30217.

41. See, e.g., United States v. Adel Daoud, No. 12-CR-723 (N.D. Ill. May 20, 2019).

42. Opening Brief of Appellant at 40, *Mohamud,* No. 14-30217.

43. Opening Brief of Appellant at 40, *Mohamud,* No. 14-30217.

44. Opening Brief of Appellant at 42, 43, *Mohamud,* No. 14-30217.

45. As cited in Opening Brief of Appellant at 45, *Mohamud,* No. 14-30217.

46. Opening Brief of Appellant at 46, *Mohamud,* No. 14-30217.

47. Opening Brief of Appellant at 47, *Mohamud,* No. 14-30217.

48. Opening Brief of Appellant at 58–59, *Mohamud,* No. 14-30217.

49. Transcript of Proceedings: Trial Day 10, Afternoon Session, at 80, United States v. Mohamud, No. 10-CR-475 (D. Ore. Mar. 20, 2013).

50. Transcript of Proceedings: Trial Day 10, Afternoon Session, at 80, *Mohamud,* No. 10-CR-475.

51. Transcript of Proceedings: Trial Day 10, Afternoon Session, at 94, *Mohamud,* No. 10-CR-475, emphasis added.

52. Transcript of Proceedings: Trial Day 10, Afternoon Session, at 95, *Mohamud,* No. 10-CR-475.

53. Transcript of Proceedings: Trial Day 11, Morning Session, at 60, United States v. Mohamud, No. 10-CR-475 (D. Ore. Mar. 20, 2013).

54. Opening Brief of Appellant at 68, *Mohamud,* No. 14-30217.

55. U.S.S.G. § 5K2.12, Coercion and Duress.

56. These actions were in violation of 18 U.S.C. § 2332(a)(2)(D) and 18 U.S.C. § 844(i).

57. Defendant's Sentencing Memorandum at 63, United States v. Daoud, No. 12-CR-723 (N.D. Ill. Apr. 26, 2019).

58. Defendant's Sentencing Memorandum at 13, *Daoud,* No. 12-CR-723.

59. Qtd. in Defendant's Sentencing Memorandum at 69, *Daoud,* No. 12-CR-723.

60. Qtd. in Defendant's Sentencing Memorandum at 77, *Daoud,* No. 12-CR-723.

61. Defendant's Sentencing Memorandum at 14, *Daoud,* No. 12-CR-723.

62. Defendant's Sentencing Memorandum at 14, *Daoud,* No. 12-CR-723.

63. Qtd. in Defendant's Sentencing Memorandum at 64, *Daoud,* No. 12-CR-723.

64. Defendant's Sentencing Memorandum at 88, *Daoud,* No. 12-CR-723.

65. Qtd. in Government's Sentencing Memorandum at 10, *Daoud,* No. 12-CR-723.

66. Government's Sentencing Memorandum at 11, *Daoud,* No. 12-CR-723.

67. Criminal Complaint Affidavit at 6, United States v. Conley, No. 14-MJ-1045 (D. Colo. Apr. 9, 2014).

68. Criminal Complaint Affidavit at 4, *Conley,* No. 14-MJ-1045.

69. Criminal Complaint Affidavit at 6, *Conley,* No. 14-MJ-1045.

70. Defendant's Sentencing Memorandum at 21, *Daoud,* No. 12-CR-723.

71. Defendant's Sentencing Memorandum at 21, *Daoud,* No. 12-CR-723.

72. Defendant's Sentencing Memorandum at 21, *Daoud,* No. 12-CR-723.

73. Transcript of Proceedings: Volume 3 at 32, United States v. Daoud, No. 12-CR-723 (N.D. Ill. Jun. 10, 2019).

74. Transcript of Proceedings: Volume 3 at 32, *Daoud,* No. 12-CR-723.

75. Government's Sentencing Memorandum at 14, United States v. Daoud, No. 12-CR-723 (N.D. Ill. Apr. 26, 2019).

76. Transcript of Proceedings: Volume 2 at 120, United States v. Daoud, No. 12-CR-723 (N.D. Ill. Jun. 10, 2019).

77. Transcript of Proceedings: Guilty Plea at 49, United States v. Daoud, No. 12-CR-723 (N.D. Ill. Jan. 29, 2019).

78. Government's Sentencing Memorandum at 16, *Daoud,* No. 12-CR-723.

79. Government's Sentencing Memorandum at 35, *Daoud,* No. 12-CR-723.

80. Government's Sentencing Memorandum at 43, *Daoud,* No. 12-CR-723.

81. Transcript of Proceedings: Continued Sentencing Hearing at 7–8, United States v. Daoud, No. 12-CR-723 (N.D. Ill. Jun. 10, 2019).

82. Transcript of Proceedings: Continued Sentencing Hearing at 5, *Daoud,* No. 12-CR-723.

83. Brief and Appendix of the United States at 39; 44, United States v. Daoud, No. 19-2174 (7th Cir. Jan. 8, 2020).

84. Decision at 19; 21; 15, United States v. Daoud, No. 19-2174 (7th Cir. Nov. 17, 2020).

85. At the time of this writing, Daoud is awaiting resentencing.

86. United States v. Bala, 236 F.3d 87, 90, 92 (2d Cir. 2000).

87. Exhibit 107-E1-T at 1, United States v. Cromitie, No. 09-CR-558 (S.D. N.Y. Jul. 6, 2010).

88. Exhibit 107-E1-T at 2, *Cromitie,* No. 09-CR-558.

89. Exhibit 107-E1-T at 2, *Cromitie,* No. 09-CR-558.

90. Exhibit 107-E1-T at 3, *Cromitie,* No. 09-CR-558.

91. Exhibit 107-E1-T at 3, *Cromitie*, No. 09-CR-558.

92. United States v. Cromitie, 727 F.3d 194, 211 (2d Cir. 2013).

93. Decision on Sentencing Entrapment/Manipulation at 1, United States v. Cromitie, No. 09-CR-558 (S.D. N.Y. Jun. 29, 2011).

94. United States v. Gomez, 103 F.3d 249, 256 (2d Cir. 1997).

95. Decision on Sentencing Entrapment/Manipulation at 4–5, *Cromitie*, No. 09-CR-558.

96. Decision on Sentencing Entrapment/Manipulation at 2, *Cromitie*, No. 09-CR-558. Under 18 U.S.C. § 2332g, the unlawful possession or use of antiaircraft missiles is punishable by imprisonment of not less than twenty-five years.

97. Government's Sentencing Memorandum at 12, United States v. Aref, No. 04-CR-402 (N.D. N.Y. Jan. 29, 2007).

98. Government's Sentencing Memorandum at 13, *Aref*, No. 04-CR-402.

99. Government's Sentencing Memorandum at 11, *Aref*, No. 04-CR-402.

100. Government's Sentencing Memorandum at 15, *Aref*, No. 04-CR-402.

Conclusion

1. In the case against Mohamed Farah, a prosecutor complained to the court that after the sentencing hearing, Farah "turned to the gallery of the courtroom and raised his left hand with the index finger extended straight upwards, the symbol of *tawhid* that we have seen in a number of exhibits of this case, most notably I believe by ISIS commander Omar Al-Shishani in a photograph. . . . There was a reply, exuberant would be my characterization of the tone, from the gallery, it was in the Somali language which I recognize but do not speak so I do not know what was said." Farah's defense attorney refused to reduce this common Islamic doctrine to the "exuberant" support for ISIS, explaining, "My understanding, according to my client, is that he was simply acknowledging the people [who] came to see him today." Sentencing Hearing at 57–58, United States v. Mohamed Farah, No. 15-CR-49 (D. Minn. Jun. 28, 2017). The prosecutor's desire to "simply make a record" of Farah's gesture after the court proceeding adjourned reflects how legal actors have implicated Islam and Islamic practices in the making of terrorism; if ISIS invoked any Islamic doctrines, as with *tawhid,* their use by Muslims triggered suspicion.

2. Participant observation, October 2021.

3. Participant observation, October 2021.

4. As noted on Jihadology.net, the website "is widely regarded as an essential source for those conducting research on jihadi groups, thanks to its collation of extensive amounts of primary source material produced by such groups.

However, there have been concerns that the site is used by jihadis who exploit the fact that material on the site is publicly available. As such, Jihadology wanted to find a way to password protect the most sensitive material. In order to make the site more secure whilst ensuring that the site can remain open and continue to increase understanding of jihadism, we have updated the site with the aim of denying jihadists and those vulnerable to recruitment easy access to the most sensitive content hosted on the site." More information about the security practices undertaken is available at the site's FAQ (https://jihadology.net/about/faq/).

5. Participant observation, October 2021.

6. Participant observation, October 2021.

7. Qtd. in Common Appendix A at 9, United States v. Ahmed, No. 15-CR-49 (D. Minn. Nov. 30, 2016).

8. Joint Sentencing Memorandum at 4, United States v. Ahmed, No. 15-CR-49 (D. Minn. Nov. 3, 2016).

9. As Kelli Jackson (2019) reminds us, moral suasion and nonviolence during the transatlantic slave trade "offered no practical benefits" and was "irrational in light of the African American experience," so "Black abolitionists were prepared to accept any force, including violence, that could provide and institute real change in their political and socioeconomic status" (33–35).

BIBLIOGRAPHY

Aaronson, Trevor. 2013. *The Terror Factory: Inside the FBI's Manufactured War on Terrorism.* New York: Ig.

Abend, Lisa. 2022. "Meet the Foreign Volunteers Risking Their Lives to Defend Ukraine—And Europe." *Time,* March 7, 2022. https://time.com/61556 70/foreign-fighters-ukraine-europe/.

Abraham, Santhosh. 2014. "Constructing the 'Extraordinary Criminals': Mappila Muslims and Legal Encounters in Early British Colonial Malabar." *Journal of World History* 25 (2–3): 373–95. https://doi.org/10.1353/jwh .2014.0022.

Ackerman, Spencer. 2015. "Bad Lieutenant: American Police Brutality, Exported from Chicago to Guantánamo." *Guardian,* February 18, 2015. https:// www.theguardian.com/us-news/2015/feb/18/american-police-brutality -chicago-guantanamo.

Aggelen, Johannes van. 2009. "The Consequences of Unlawful Preemption and the Legal Duty to Protect the Human Rights of Its Victims." *Case Western Reserve Journal of International Law* 42 (1): 21–89.

Agnew, John. 1994. "The Territorial Trap: The Geographical Assumptions of International Relations Theory." *Review of International Political Economy* 1 (1): 53–80.

Ahmad, Aisha. 2009. "Taliban and Islamic Courts Union: How They Changed the Game in Afghanistan and Somalia?" *Policy Perspectives* 6 (2): 55–72.

Ahmad, Fatema. 2018. "Why 'Countering Violent Extremism' Programs Won't Stop White Supremacists." *Truthout,* November 15, 2018. https://truth

out.org/articles/why-countering-violent-extremism-programs-wont-stop
-white-supremacists/.

Ahmad, Muneer. 2004. "A Rage Shared by Law: Post–September 11 Racial Violence as Crimes of Passion." *California Law Review* 92 (5): 1259–1330.

Ahmad, Shamshad. 2009. *Rounded Up: Artificial Terrorists and Muslim Entrapment after 9/11*. London: Troy.

Ahmed, Sameer. 2017. "Is History Repeating Itself? Sentencing Young American Muslims in the War on Terror." *Yale Law Journal* 126 (5): 1520–76.

Ahmed, Sara. 2004. *The Cultural Politics of Emotion*. Edinburgh: Edinburgh University Press.

Akbar, Amna A. 2020. "National Security's Broken Windows." In *Islamophobia and the Law*, edited by Cyra Akila Choudhury and Khaled A. Beydoun, 170–92. Cambridge: Cambridge University Press.

Akram, Susan M., and Kevin R. Johnson. 2002. "Race, Civil Rights, and Immigration Law after September 11, 2001: The Targeting of Arabs and Muslims." *NYU Annual Survey of American Law* 58 (3): 295–356.

al-Haj Saleh, Yassin. 2017. *The Impossible Revolution: Making Sense of the Syrian Tragedy*. Chicago, Ill.: Haymarket.

Al-Kassimi, Khaled. 2019. "Critical Terrorism Studies (CTS): (State) (Sponsored) Terrorism Identified in the (Militarized) Pedagogy of (U.S.) Law Enforcement Agencies." *Cogent Social Sciences* 5 (1): 1–27. https://doi.org/10.1080/23311886.2019.1586813.

Alimahomed-Wilson, Sabrina. 2019. "When the FBI Knocks: Racialized State Surveillance of Muslims." *Critical Sociology* 45 (6): 871–87. https://doi.org/10.1177/0896920517750742.

Alouni, Tayseer. 2005. "Osama Bin Laden Interview with Tayseer Alouni." In *Al Qaeda Now—Understanding Today's Terrorists*, edited by Karen J. Greenberg, 192–206. Cambridge: Cambridge University Press.

Alsultany, Evelyn. 2008. "The Prime-Time Plight of the Arab Muslim American after 9/11: Configurations of Race and Nation in TV Dramas." In *Race and Arab Americans before and after 9/11: From Invisible Citizens to Visible Subjects*, edited by Amaney Jamal and Nadine Naber, 204–28. Syracuse, N.Y.: Syracuse University Press.

American Civil Liberties Union. 2006. "Military Commissions Act of 2006." https://web.archive.org/web/20230218184428/https://www.aclu.org/other/military-commissions-act-2006. Accessed February 10, 2023.

American Red Cross. 2011. "Summary of the Geneva Conventions of 1949 and Their Additional Protocols." *International Humanitarian Law*, April 2011. https://www.redcross.org/content/dam/redcross/atg/PDF_s/International

_Services/International_Humanitarian_Law/IHL_SummaryGenevaConv
.pdf.

Amoore, Louise. 2013. *The Politics of Possibility: Risk and Security beyond Probability.* Durham, N.C.: Duke University Press.

Anghie, Antony. 2004. *Imperialism, Sovereignty, and the Making of International Law.* Cambridge: Cambridge University Press.

Arendt, Hannah. 1951. *The Origins of Totalitarianism.* Cleveland, Ohio: Meridian.

Arielli, Nir. 2012. "In Search of Meaning: Foreign Volunteers in the Croatian Armed Forces, 1991–95." *Contemporary European History* 21 (1): 1–17.

Arik, Doran G. 2009. "The Tug of War: Combatant Status Review Tribunals and the Struggle to Balance National Security and Constitutional Values during the War on Terror." *Journal of Law and Policy* 16 (2): 657–716.

Asad, Talal. 2007. *On Suicide Bombing.* New York: Columbia University Press.

Ashcroft, John. 2003. "Prepared Remarks of Attorney General John Ashcroft." Remarks delivered to the Council on Foreign Relations, February 10, 2003. Department of Justice Archive. https://www.justice.gov/archive/ag/speech es/2003/021003agcouncilonforeignrelation.htm.

Ashcroft, John. 2004. "Prepared Remarks of Attorney General John Ashcroft." Remarks regarding the Holy Land Foundation indictment, July 27, 2004. Department of Justice Archive. https://www.justice.gov/archive/ag/speech es/2004/72704ag.htm.

Badalič, Vasja. 2021. "The War against Vague Threats: The Redefinitions of Imminent Threat and Anticipatory Use of Force." *Security Dialogue* 52 (2): 174–91.

Bail, Christopher. 2015. *Terrified: How Anti-Muslim Fringe Organizations Became Mainstream.* Princeton, N.J.: Princeton University Press.

Balanche, Fabrice. 2017. "The End of the CIA Program in Syria: Washington Cedes the Field." *Foreign Affairs,* August 2, 2017. https://www.foreignaf fairs.com/articles/syria/2017-08-02/end-cia-program-syria.

Baltes, Joanna, Karen J. Greenberg, Gerald Bruce Lee, Robert Timothy Reagan, and Stephen I. Vladeck. 2016. "Convicted Terrorists: Sentencing Considerations and Their Policy Implications." *Journal of National Security Law and Policy* 8:347–76.

Banks, Gabrielle. 2019. "Federal Judge Lynn Hughes Resists Adding More Time for Man Who Got 18 Months in ISIS Case." *Microsoft News,* December 13, 2019. https://web.archive.org/web/20191214011541/https://www .msn.com/en-us/news/crime/federal-judge-lynn-hughes-resists-adding -more-time-for-man-who-got-18-months-in-isis-case/ar-AAK6EWM.

Barker, Joanne. 2021. *Red Scare: The State's Indigenous Terrorist.* Berkeley: University of California Press.

Barron, David J. 2010. "Applicability of Federal Criminal Laws and the Constitution to Contemplated Lethal Operations against Shaykh Anwar Al-Aulaqi." Washington, D.C.: Department of Justice.

Bartosiewicz, Petra. 2008. "Experts in Terror." *Nation,* January 17, 2008. https://www.thenation.com/article/archive/experts-terror/.

Battye, Greg, and Meredith Rossner. 2017. "How Juries Talked about Visual Evidence." In *Juries, Science, and Popular Culture in the Age of Terror: The Case of the Sydney Bomber,* edited by David Tait and Jane Goodman-Delahunty, 193–215. London: Palgrave Macmillan.

Baxi, Upendra. 1993. *Marx, Law, and Justice.* Bombay: N. M. Tripathi.

Begg, Moazzam. 2007. *Enemy Combatant: My Imprisonment at Guantánamo, Bagram, and Kandahar.* New York: New Press.

Belcher, Oliver, Lauren Martin, Anna Secor, Stephanie Simon, and Tommy Wilson. 2008. "Everywhere and Nowhere: The Exception and the Topological Challenge to Geography." *Antipode* 40 (4): 499–503.

Belknap, Michal R. 2002. "A Putrid Pedigree: The Bush Administration's Military Tribunals in Historical Perspective." *California Western Law Review* 38 (2): 433–80.

Bell, Colleen. 2015. "The Police Power in Counterinsurgencies: Discretion, Patrolling, and Evidence." In *War, Police, and Assemblages of Intervention,* edited by Jan Bachman, Colleen Bell, and Caroline Holmqvist, 17–35. London: Routledge.

Bell, Derrick. 1991. "The Law of Racial Standing." *Yale Journal of Law and Liberation* 2 (1): 117–21.

Benjamin, Walter. 1978. *Reflections: Essays, Aphorisms, Autobiographical Writings.* New York: Schocken.

Bennis, Phyllis. 2015. *Understanding ISIS and the New Global War on Terror: A Primer.* Northampton, Mass.: Olive Branch.

Bergman, Lowell, and Oriana Zill de Granados. 2006. "The Enemy Within." Public Broadcasting Service (PBS), October 10, 2006. https://www.pbs.org/wgbh/pages/frontline/enemywithin/.

Beydoun, Khaled A. 2013. "Between Muslim and White: The Legal Construction of Arab American Identity." *New York University Annual Survey of American Law* 69 (1): 29–76.

Beydoun, Khaled A. 2015. "Viewpoint: Islamophobia Has a Long History in the U.S." *BBC News,* September 29, 2015. https://www.bbc.com/news/magazine-34385051.

Beydoun, Khaled A. 2018. *American Islamophobia: Understanding the Roots and Rise of Fear*. Berkeley: University of California Press.

Beydoun, Khaled A., and Cyra Akila Choudhury. 2020. Introduction to *Islamophobia and the Law*, edited by Cyra Akila Choudhury and Khaled A. Beydoun, 1–15. Cambridge: Cambridge University Press.

Bialke, Joseph P. 2004. "Al-Qaeda and Taliban Unlawful Combatant Detainees, Unlawful Belligerency, and the International Laws of Armed Conflict." *Air Force Law Review* 55:1–85.

bin Laden, Osama. 1996. "Declaration of Jihad against the Americans Occupying the Land of the Two Holiest Sites." August 23, 1996. https://web.archive.org/web/20220918125725/https://ctc.usma.edu/wp-content/uploads/2013/10/Declaration-of-Jihad-against-the-Americans-Occupying-the-Land-of-the-Two-Holiest-Sites-Translation.pdf.

bin Laden, Osama. 1998. "Jihad Against Jews and Crusaders." February 23, 1998. https://web.archive.org/web/20230205225650/https://irp.fas.org/world/para/docs/980223-fatwa.htm.

Borum, Randy. 2011. "Radicalization into Violent Extremism I: A Review of Social Science Theories." *Journal of Strategic Security* 4 (4): 7–36. https://doi.org/10.5038/1944-0472.4.4.1.

Brännström, Leila. 2008. "How I Learned to Stop Worrying and Use the Legal Argument: A Critique of Giorgio Agamben's Conception of Law." *No Foundations* 5:22–49.

Breen, Damian. 2018. "Critical Race Theory, Policy Rhetoric, and Outcomes: The Case of Muslim Schools in Britain." *Race, Ethnicity, and Education* 21 (1): 30–44.

Brennan Center for Justice. 2019. "Why Countering Violent Extremism Programs Are Bad Policy." September 9, 2019. https://www.brennancenter.org/our-work/research-reports/why-countering-violent-extremism-programs-are-bad-policy.

Brennan, John. 2011. "Strengthening Our Security by Adhering to Our Values and Laws." Press release, White House Office of the Press Secretary, Barack Obama White House Archives, September 16, 2011. https://obamawhitehouse.archives.gov/the-press-office/2011/09/16/remarks-john-o-brennan-strengthening-our-security-adhering-our-values-an.

Brickell, Katherine, and Dana Cuomo. 2019. "Feminist Geolegality." *Progress in Human Geography* 43 (1): 104–22. https://doi.org/10.1177/0309132517735706.

Bromberg, Walter, and Franck Simon. 1968. "The Protest Psychosis: A Special Type of Reactive Psychosis." *Archives of General Psychiatry* 19 (2): 155–60.

Brown, George D. 2012. "Notes on a Terrorism Trial: Preventative Prosecution, 'Material Support' and the Role of the Judge after *United States v. Mehanna*." *Harvard Law School National Security Journal* 4 (1): 1–57.

Brown, George D. 2014. "Punishing Terrorists: Congress, the Sentencing Commission, the Guidelines, and the Courts." *Cornell Journal of Law* 23 (3): 517–51. https://doi.org/10.3366/ajicl.2011.0005.

Brown, Katherine E. 2018. "Violence and Gender Politics in the Proto-state 'Islamic State.'" In *Revisiting Gendered States: Feminist Imaginings of the State in International Relations,* edited by Swati Parashar, J. Ann Tickner, and Jacqui True, 174–90. Oxford: Oxford University Press.

Buerger, Michael E., and Lorraine Green Mazerolle. 1998. "Third-Party Policing: A Theoretical Analysis of an Emerging Trend." *Justice Quarterly* 15 (2): 301- 27.

Bugnon, François. 2002. "Just Wars, Wars of Aggression and International Humanitarian Law." *International Review of the Red Cross* 84 (847): 523–46.

Bunglawala, Shenaz. 2017. "The 'War on Terror' and the Attack on Muslim Civil Society." In *What Is Islamophobia? Racism, Social Movements, and the State,* edited by Narzanin Massoumi, Tom Mills, and David Miller, 97–119. London: Pluto.

Burnett, Jonny, and Dave Whyte. 2005. "Embedded Expertise and the New Terrorism." *Journal for Crime, Conflict, and the Media* 1 (4): 1–18.

Bush, George W. 2001a. "An Address to a Joint Session of Congress and the American People." *Washington Post,* September 20, 2011. https://www.washingtonpost.com/wp-srv/nation/specials/attacked/transcripts/bush address_092001.html.

Bush, George W. 2001b. "Address to the Nation on the September 11 Attacks." Delivered September 11, 2001. George Bush White House Archives, Office of the White House. https://georgewbush-whitehouse.archives.gov/infocus/bushrecord/documents/Selected_Speeches_George_W_Bush .pdf, 57–58.

Bush, George W. 2001c. "Presidential Address to the Nation." George Bush White House Archives, Office of the White House, October 2001. https://georgewbush-whitehouse.archives.gov/news/releases/2001/10/200110 07-8.html.

Bush, George W. 2002. "The National Security Strategy of the United States." White House, September 17, 2002. https://2009-2017.state.gov/docu ments/organization/63562.pdf.

Bush, George W. 2003. "President Bush Addresses the Nation." George Bush White House Archives, Office of the White House, March 19, 2003.

https://georgewbush-whitehouse.archives.gov/news/releases/2003/03/20
030319-17.html.

Butler, Judith. 2002. "Guantanamo Limbo." *Nation,* March 14, 2002. https://
www.thenation.com/article/archive/guantanamo-limbo/.

Butler, Judith. 2004. *Precarious Life: The Power and Mourning of Violence.* New
York: Verso.

Bybee, Jay. 2002. "Memorandum for William J. Haynes, II, General Counsel,
Department Defense." Office of the Assistant Attorney General, Office of
Legal Counsel, Department of Justice, March 13, 2002. https://www.jus
tice.gov/sites/default/files/olc/legacy/2009/08/24/memorandum031320
02.pdf.

Cacho, Lisa Marie. 2012. *Social Death: Racialized Rightlessness and the Criminalization of the Unprotected.* New York: New York University Press.

Cainkar, Louise A. 2009. *Homeland Insecurity: The Arab American and Muslim
American Experience after 9/11.* New York: Russell Sage Foundation.

Cainkar, Louise A. 2019. "Fluid Terror Threat." *Amerasia Journal* 44 (1): 27–
59. https://doi.org/10.17953/aj.44.1.27-59.

Cainkar, Louise A., and Saher Selod. 2018. "Review of Race Scholarship and
the War on Terror." *American Sociological Association* 4 (2): 165–77.

Candiotti, Susan. 2002. "Walker Lindh Sentenced to 20 Years." CNN, October 4, 2002. https://www.cnn.com/2002/LAW/10/04/lindh.statement/.

Carr, Caleb. 2007. "'Terrorism': Why the Definition Must Be Broad." *World
Policy Journal* 24 (1): 47–50.

Center for Constitutional Rights. 2022. "Majid Khan Challenges Imprisonment at Guantánamo beyond Completion of Sentence." Last modified
June 8, 2022. https://web.archive.org/web/20230210205417/https://ccr
justice.org/home/press-center/press-releases/majid-khan-challenges
-imprisonment-guant-namo-beyond-completion.

Center on Law and Security. 2011. "Terrorist Trial Report Card: September
11, 2001–September 11, 2011." New York University School of Law.
https://www.lawandsecurity.org/wp-content/uploads/2011/09/TTRC
-Ten-Year-Issue.pdf.

Center on National Security. 2017. "The American Exception: Terrorism Prosecutions in the United States—The ISIS Cases, March 2014–August 2017."
Center on National Security at Fordham Law. https://news.law.fordham
.edu/wp-content/uploads/2017/09/TheAmericanException9-17.pdf.

Center on National Security. 2022. "Terrorism Prosecution Database." Center
on National Security at Fordham Law. https://web.archive.org/web/2023
0218184518/https://www.centeronnationalsecurity.org/terrorism-data
base. Accessed February 10, 2023.

Charles, Mark. 2017. "The Hanging of the Dakota 38 and the Troubling Legacy of President Lincoln." *Native News Online,* December 26, 2017. https://web.archive.org/web/20230210205632/https://nativenewsonline.net/opinion/the-hanging-of-the-dakota-38-and-the-troubling-legacy-of-president-lincoln.

Chesney, Robert M. 2007. "Beyond Conspiracy? Anticipatory Prosecution and the Challenge of Unaffiliated Terrorism." *Southern California Law Review* 80 (3): 425–502.

Chesney, Robert M. 2009. "Optimizing Criminal Prosecution as a Counterterrorism Tool." In *Legislating the War on Terror: An Agenda for Reform,* edited by Benjamin Wittes, 98–141. Washington, D.C.: Brookings Institution.

Chew, Pat K., and Robert E. Kelley. 2009. "Myth of the Color-Blind Judge: An Empirical Analysis of Racial Harassment Cases." *Washington University Law Review* 86 (5): 1117–66.

Chomsky, Carol. 1990. "The United States–Dakota War Trials: A Study in Military Injustice." *Stanford Law Review* 43 (1): 13–98. https://doi.org/10.2307/1228993.

Christodoulou, Eleni. 2018. "Deconstructing Resistance towards Textbook Revisions: The Securitization of History Textbooks and the Cyprus Conflict." *Global Change, Peace and Security* 30 (3): 373–93. https://doi.org/10.1080/14781158.2018.1453492.

CISAC (Center for International Security and Cooperation, Stanford University). 2019. "Mapping Militant Organizations: Islamic Courts Union." Last updated February 2019. https://cisac.fsi.stanford.edu/mappingmilitants/profiles/islamic-courts-union.

Clair, Matthew, and Amanda Woog. 2022. "Courts and the Abolition Movement." *California Law Review* 110 (1): 1–30.

Clancy, Timothy. 2018. "Theory of an Emerging-State Actor: The Islamic State of Iraq and Syria (ISIS) Case." *Systems* 6 (2): 16. https://doi.org/10.3390/systems6020016.

Clark, Karis. 2021. "Abolition Is." *Michigan Daily,* April 19, 2021. https://web.archive.org/web/20230210205722/https://www.michigandaily.com/michigan-in-color/abolition-is/.

Coates, Rodney D. 2003. "Law and the Cultural Production of Race and Racialized Systems of Oppression: Early American Court Cases." *American Behavioral Scientist* 47 (3): 329–51.

Cole, David. 2013. "Military Commissions and the Paradigm of Prevention." In *Guantánamo and Beyond: Exceptional Courts and Military Commissions in Comparative Perspective,* edited by Fionnuala Ni Aoláin and Oren Gross, 95–116. Cambridge: Cambridge University Press.

Comerford, Brian P. 2005. "Preventing Terrorism by Prosecuting Material Support." *Notre Dame Law Review* 80 (2): 723–57.

Conboye, Janina. 2017. "Why Geopolitics Is Finding a Place on the Business School Map." *Financial Times,* December 3, 2017. https://www.ft.com/content/3aa439a8-cbc1-11e7-8536-d321d0d897a3.

Corn, Geoffrey. 2011. "Thinking the Unthinkable: Has the Time Come to Offer Combatant Immunity to Non-state Actors?" *Stanford Law and Policy Review* 22 (1): 253–94.

Corn, Geoffrey. 2012. "Self-Defense Targeting: Blurring the Line between the Jus ad Bellum and the Jus in Bello." *International Law Studies* 88 (1): 57–92. https://doi.org/10.2139/ssrn.1947838.

Correa, Cristián. 2021. "A Transitional Justice Approach to Foreign Fighters." International Center for Transitional Justice, December 2021. https://www.ictj.org/sites/default/files/2022-03/ICTJ_Report_Foreign-Fighters_EN_0.pdf.

Cox, Robert. 1981. "Social Forces, States and World Orders: Beyond International Relations Theory." *Millennium* 10 (2): 126–55.

Crace, John. 2008. "Just How Expert Are the Expert Witnesses?" *Guardian,* May 12, 2008. https://www.theguardian.com/education/2008/may/13/highereducation.academicexperts.

Crenshaw, Kimberlé. 1989. "Mapping the Margins: Intersectionality, Identity Politics, and Violence against Women of Color." *Stanford Law Review* 43:1241–99.

Crenshaw, Martha. 2000. "The Psychology of Terrorism: An Agenda for the 21st Century." *Political Psychology* 21 (2): 405–20.

Critical Resistance. 2004. "The CR Abolition Organizing Toolkit." http://criticalresistance.org/wp-content/uploads/2012/06/CR-Abolitionist-Toolkit-online.pdf.

Dale, Stephen Frederic. 1980. *Islamic Society on the South Asian Frontier: The Mappilas of Malabar, 1498–1922.* Oxford: Oxford University Press.

Dale, Stephen Frederic. 1988. "Religious Suicide in Islamic Asia: Anticolonial Terrorism in India, Indonesia, and the Philippines." *Journal of Conflict Resolution* 32 (1): 37–60.

Daulatzai, Sohail. 2007. "Protect Ya Neck: Muslims and the Carceral Imagination in the Age of Guantánamo." *Souls* 9 (5): 132–47.

Daulatzai, Sohail. 2012. *Black Star, Crescent Moon: The Muslim International and Black Freedom beyond American.* Minneapolis: University of Minnesota Press.

Dayan, Colin. 2005. "Legal Terrors." *Representations* 92 (1): 42–80. https://doi.org/10.1017/CBO9781107415324.004.

Dayan, Colin. 2011. *The Law Is a White Dog: How Legal Rituals Make and Unmake Persons.* Princeton, N.J.: Princeton University Press.

Deeb, Lara. 2006. *An Enchanted Modern: Gender and Public Piety in Shi'i Lebanon.* Princeton, N.J.: Princeton University Press.

Delaney, David. 2015. "Legal Geography I: Constitutivities, Complexities, and Contingencies." *Progress in Human Geography* 39 (1): 96–102. https://doi.org/10.1177/0309132514527035.

Delgado, Richard, and Daniel A. Farber. 1998. "Is American Law Inherently Racist?" *Thomas M. Cooley Law Review* 15 (361): 361–90.

Delgado, Richard, and Jean Stefancic. 2012. *Critical Race Theory: An Introduction.* 2nd ed. New York: New York University Press.

Department of Defense. 2015. *Law of War Manual.* Washington, D.C.: Department of Defense.

Department of Defense and Department of Justice. 2009. "Determination of Guantanamo Cases Referred for Prosecution." Department of Justice Archive. https://www.justice.gov/archive/opa/documents/taba-prel-rpt-dptf-072009.pdf.

Department of Justice. 2006. "Pakistani Man Convicted of Providing Material Support to Al-Qaeda Sentenced to Thirty Years." Press release, United States Attorney, Southern District of New York, July 20, 2006. Department of Justice Archive. https://www.justice.gov/archive/usao/nys/press releases/July06/parachasentencingpr.pdf.

Department of Justice. 2008. "Former Officers of a Muslim Charity, Care International, Inc., Convicted." Press release, January 11, 2008. Department of Justice Archive. https://www.justice.gov/archive/opa/pr/2008/January/08_nsd_021.html.

Department of Justice. 2020. "645. Entrapment." In *Criminal Resource Manual 601-699.* Department of Justice Archive. https://www.justice.gov/archives/jm/criminal-resource-manual-645-entrapment-elements.

DiIulio, John J. 1995. "The Coming of the Super-predators." *Washington Examiner,* November 27, 1995. https://www.washingtonexaminer.com/weekly-standard/the-coming-of-the-super-predators.

DiIulio, John J. 1996. "My Black Crime Problem, and Ours." *City Journal* 32. https://www.city-journal.org/html/my-black-crime-problem-and-ours-11773.html.

Donohue, Laura K. 2007. "Terrorism and Trial by Jury: The Vices and Virtues of British and American Criminal Law." *Stanford Law Review* 59:1321–64.

Dorf, Michael C. 2007. "The Detention and Trial of Enemy Combatants: A Drama in Three Branches." *Political Science Quarterly* 122 (1): 47–58. https://doi.org/10.1002/j.1538-165X.2007.tb00591.x.

Downs, Stephen. 2012. "Victims of America's Dirty Wars: Tactics and Reasons from COINTELPRO to the War on Terror." Project SALAM, revised February 2012. http://www.projectsalam.org/downloads/Victims_of_Ameri cas_Dirty_Wars.pdf.

Dratel, Joshua L. 2011. "The Literal Third Way in Approaching 'Material Support for Terrorism': Whatever Happened to U.S.C. § 2339B(C) and the Civil Injunction Option." *Wayne Law Review* 57 (1): 11–97.

Dunlap, Charles J., Jr. 2001. "Law and Military Interventions: Preserving Humanitarian Values in 21st Century Conflicts." Prepared for the Humanitarian Challenges in Military Intervention Conference, Carr Center for Human Rights Policy, Kennedy School of Government, Harvard University, November 29, 2001. https://people.duke.edu/~pfeaver/dunlap .pdf.

Dunlap, Charles J., Jr. 2017. "Lawfare 101: A Primer." *Military Review* 97 (May/ June): 8–17.

Edwards, Erica. 2021. *The Other Side of Terror: Black Women and the Culture of U.S. Empire.* New York: New York University Press.

El-Ibiary, Rasha. 2011. "New Media, Geopolitics, and Terror: Discursive Analysis of Bush and Bin Laden's Rhetoric." *Arab World Geographer* 14 (3): 215–34.

Ellis, T. S. 2013. "The National Security Trials: A Judge's Perspective." *Virginia Law Review* 99 (7): 1607–33.

Energy Transfer. 2017. "Energy Transfer Files Federal Lawsuit against Greenpeace International, Greenpeace Inc., Greenpeace Fund, Inc., BankTrack and Earth First! for Violation of Federal and State Racketeering Statutes." August 22, 2017. https://ir.energytransfer.com/node/14226/pdf.

Engle, Karen. 2004. "Constructing Good Aliens and Good Citizens: Legitimizing the War on Terror(ism)." *University of Colorado Law Review* 75 (1): 59–114.

Erlenbusch, Verena. 2010. "Notes on Violence: Walter Benjamin's Relevance for the Study of Terrorism." *Journal of Global Ethics* 6 (2): 167–78. https:// doi.org/10.1080/17449626.2010.494363.

Erlenbusch-Anderson, Verena. 2018. *Genealogies of Terrorism: Revolution, State Violence, Empire.* New York: Columbia University Press.

Esmeir, Samera. 2012. *Juridical Humanity: A Colonial History.* Palo Alto, Calif.: Stanford University Press.

Euben, Roxanne L. 2002. "Killing (for) Politics: Jihad, Martyrdom, and Political Action." *Political Theory* 30 (1): 4–35. https://doi.org/10.1177/0090 591702030001002.

Fanon, Frantz. 1963. *The Wretched of the Earth.* New York: Grove.

FBI (Federal Bureau of Investigation). n.d. "Nazi Saboteurs and George Dasch." FBI, History, Famous Cases and Criminals. https://web.archive.org/web/20230218184600/https://www.fbi.gov/history/famous-cases/nazi-sabo teurs-and-george-dasch. Accessed February 10, 2023.

FBI (Federal Bureau of Investigation). 2006. "The Radicalization Process: From Conversion to Jihad." FBI Intelligence Assessment prepared by the FBI Counterterrorism Division, May 10, 2006. https://cryptome.org/fbi -jihad.pdf.

FBI (Federal Bureau of Investigation). 2017. "Black Identity Extremists Likely Motivated to Target Law Enforcement Officers." FBI Intelligence Assess- ment, August 3, 2017. https://www.documentcloud.org/documents/406 7711-BIE-Redacted.html.

FBI (Federal Bureau of Investigation). 2018. "FBI Strategy Guide FY2018–20 and Threat Guidance for Racial Extremists." Uploaded to Scribd by Ken Klippenstein. https://www.scribd.com/document/421166393/FBI-Strat egy-Guide-FY2018-20-and-Threat-Guidance-for-Racial-Extremists.

Fernandez, Ronald. 2008. *America beyond Black and White: How Immigrants and Fusions Are Helping Us Overcome the Racial Divide.* Ann Arbor: Uni- versity of Michigan Press.

Fitzgerald, David. 2017. "The History of Racialized Citizenship." In *The Oxford Handbook of Citizenship,* edited by Ayelet Shachar, Rainer Baubock, Irene Bloemraad, and Maarten Vink, 129–52. Oxford: Oxford University Press.

Floyd, Stephen. 2021. "Irredeemably Violent and Undeterrable: How Flawed Assumptions Justify a Broad Application of the Terrorism Enhancement, Contradict Sentencing Policy, and Diminish U.S. National Security." *Georgetown Law Journal Online* 109:142–72.

Foucault, Michel. 1972. *"The Archaeology of Knowledge" and "The Discourse on Language."* New York: Pantheon.

Fricker, Miranda. 2007. *Epistemic Injustice: Power and the Ethics of Knowing.* Oxford: Oxford University Press.

Fricker, Miranda. 2008. "Précis: Forum on Miranda Fricker's Epistemic Injus- tice: Power and the Ethics of Knowing." *Theoria* 23 (61): 69–71.

Galton, Francis. 1909. *Essays in Eugenics.* London: Eugenics Education Society. https://galton.org/books/essays-on-eugenics/galton-1909-essays-eugen ics-1up.pdf.

Galtung, Johan. 1969. "Violence, Peace, and Peace Research." *Journal of Peace Research* 6 (3): 167–91.

Gartenstein-Ross, Daveed, and Laura Grossman. 2009. *Homegrown Terrorists in the U.S. and U.K.: An Empirical Examination of the Radicalization Pro- cess.* Washington, D.C.: FDD.

German, Michael. 2013. "Debunked NYPD Radicalization Report Just Won't Die." American Civil Liberties Union (ACLU), February 11, 2013. https://www.aclu.org/news/national-security/debunked-nypd-radicalization-report-just-wont-die.

German, Michael. 2021. "Written Testimony of Michael German." Hearing before the House of Representatives Committee on the Judiciary Subcommittee on Crime, Terrorism, and Homeland Security, February 24, 2021. https://www.brennancenter.org/sites/default/files/2021-02/Michael%20German%20House%20Judiciary%20Testimony%20Final.pdf.

Gershman, Bennett. 2005. "How Juries Get It Wrong—Anatomy of the Detroit Terror Case." Washburn Law Journal 44 (2): 327–54.

Gerstein, Josh. 2022. "Why DOJ Is Avoiding Domestic Terrorism Sentences for Jan. 6 Defendants." Politico, January 4, 2022. https://www.politico.com/news/2022/01/04/doj-domestic-terrorism-sentences-jan-6-526407.

Ghosh, Durba. 2017. Gentlemanly Terrorists: Political Violence and the Colonial State in India, 1919–1947. Cambridge: Cambridge University Press.

Gillan, Audrey. 2002. "Pakistani Intelligence and Americans 'Abduct' Briton." Guardian, March 8, 2002. https://www.theguardian.com/world/2002/mar/09/september11.pakistan.

Gilmore, Ruth Wilson. 2022. Change Everything: Racial Capitalism and the Case for Abolition. Chicago, Ill.: Haymarket.

Giraldi, Philip. 2011. "Terrorism Experts on Parade." Antiwar.com, July 28, 2011. https://original.antiwar.com/giraldi/2011/07/27/terrorism-experts-on-parade/.

Goede, Marieke de. 2012. Speculative Security: The Politics of Pursuing Terrorist Monies. Minneapolis: University of Minnesota Press.

Goldsmith, Jack. 2009. The Terror Presidency: Law and Judgment inside the Bush Administration. New York: Norton.

Gonzales, Alberto R. 2002. "Memorandum from Alberto R. Gonzales to the President." Department of Justice. http://hrlibrary.umn.edu/OathBetrayed/Gonzales%201-25-02.pdf.

Good, Anthony. 2008. "Cultural Evidence in Courts of Law." Journal of the Royal Anthropological Institute 14 (suppl. 1): s47–60. https://doi.org/10.1111/j.1467-9655.2008.00492.x.

Goodman, Maxine D. 2010a. "A Hedgehog on the Witness Stand—What's the Big Idea? The Challenges of Using Daubert to Assess Social Science and Nonscientific Testimony." American University Law Review 59 (3): 635–84.

Goodman, Maxine D. 2010b. "Slipping through the Gate: Trusting Daubert and Trial Procedures to Reveal the 'Pseudo-Historian' Expert Witness and

Enable the Reliable Historian Expert Witness—Troubling Lessons from Holocaust-Related Trials." *Baylor Law Review* 60 (3): 824–79.

Gordon, Avery. 1997. *Ghostly Matters: Haunting and the Sociological Imagination.* Minneapolis: University of Minnesota Press.

Gramsci, Antonio. 1971. *Selections from the Prison Notebooks.* Edited by Quintin Hoare and Geoffrey Nowell Smith. New York: International.

Greenberg, Karen J. 2011. "Executive Director's Introduction: The Ten-Year Record: Terrorism and the U.S. Courts." In *Terrorist Trial Report Card: September 11, 2001–September 11, 2011,* 2–5. New York: New York University School of Law. https://www.lawandsecurity.org/wp-content/uploads/2011/09/TTRC-Ten-Year-Issue.pdf.

Greenberg, Karen J. 2016. *Rogue Justice: The Making of the Security State.* New York: Broadway.

Greenberg, Karen J., Collin Beck, Chantene Berger, et al. 2011. *Terrorist Trial Report Card: September 11, 2001–September 11, 2011.* New York: New York University School of Law. https://www.lawandsecurity.org/wp-content/uploads/2011/09/TTRC-Ten-Year-Issue.pdf.

Gregory, Derek. 2004. *The Colonial Present: Afghanistan, Palestine, Iraq.* Hoboken, N.J.: Wiley.

Gregory, Derek. 2006. "The Black Flag: Guantánamo Bay and the Space of Exception." *Geografiska Annaler: Series B, Human Geography* 88 (4): 405–27.

Grewal, Zareena. 2014. *Islam Is a Foreign Country: American Muslims and the Global Crisis of Authority.* New York: New York University Press.

Gudavarthy, Ajay. 2017. "Introduction: Is Violence Necessary for Revolutionary Change Today?" In *Revolutionary Violence versus Democracy: Narratives from India,* edited by Ajay Gudavarthy, 1–32. Los Angeles, Calif.: Sage.

Gunaratna, Rohan. 2013. "Terrorist Rehabilitation and Community Engagement: New Frontiers in Combating Terrorism." *Counter Terrorist Trends and Analyses* 5 (4): 2–4.

Gunning, Jeroen. 2007. "A Case for Critical Terrorism Studies?" *Government and Opposition* 42 (3): 363–93.

Hafetz, Jonathan. 2008. "Supreme Court Deals Death Blow to Gitmo." *Nation,* June 12, 2008. https://www.thenation.com/article/archive/supreme-court-deals-death-blow-gitmo/.

Hajjar, Lisa. 2005. *Courting Conflict: The Israeli Military Court System in the West Bank and Gaza.* Berkeley: University of California Press.

Hall, Stuart, Chas Critcher, Tony Jefferson, John Clarke, and Brian Roberts. 1978. *Policing the Crisis: Mugging, the State, and Law and Order.* London: Macmillan.

Hamdar, Abir. 2009. "Jihad of Words: Gender and Contemporary Karbala Narratives." *Yearbook of English Studies* 39 (1/2): 84–100.

Hamid, Shadi. 2019. "What America Never Understood about ISIS." *Atlantic,* October 2019. https://www.theatlantic.com/ideas/archive/2019/10/what -america-never-understood-about-isis/601156/.

Hammond, Laura. 2014. "Somali Refugee Displacements in the Near Region: Analysis and Recommendation." U.N. Refugee Agency USA (UNHCR). https://www.unhcr.org/55152c699.pdf.

Hansen, Thomas Blom, and Finn Stedputat. 2001. "Introduction: States of Imagination." In *States of Imagination: Ethnographic Explorations of the Postcolonial State,* edited by Thomas Blom Hansen and Finn Stepputat, 1–38. Durham, N.C.: Duke University Press.

Harcourt, Bernard. 2020. "Beyond the Counterinsurgency Paradigm of Governing: Letting Go of Prediction and the Illusion of an Internal Enemy." In *Reimagining the National Security State: Liberalism on the Brink,* edited by Karen J. Greenberg, 141–53. Cambridge: Cambridge University Press.

Hashemi, Nader. 2016. "Toward a Political Theory of Sectarianism in the Middle East: The Salience of Authoritarianism over Theology." *Journal of Islamic and Muslim Studies* 1 (1): 65–76. https://doi.org/10.2979/jims.1.1.05.

Hay, Bruce. 2005. "Sting Operations, Undercover Agents, and Entrapment." *Missouri Law Review* 70 (2): 387–431.

Heiner, Brady Thomas. 2007. "The American Archipelago: The Global Circuit of Carcerality and Torture." In *Colonial and Global Interfacings: Imperial Hegemonies and Democratizing Resistance,* edited by Gary Backhaus and John Murungi, 84–117. Newcastle upon Tyne, U.K.: Cambridge Scholars.

Henry, Stuart. 2017. "What Is School Violence? An Integrated Definition." *Annals of the American Academy of Political and Social Science* 567 (1): 16–29.

Hilal, Maha. 2021a. *Innocent until Proven Muslim: Islamophobia, the War on Terror, and the Muslim Experience since 9/11.* Minneapolis, Minn.: Broadleaf.

Hilal, Maha. 2021b. "We Can't Just Close Guantanamo Bay Prison, We Also Have to Abolish the Injustice that Allowed It to Exist." *Business Insider,* February 3, 2021. https://www.businessinsider.com/guantanamo-bay -prison-abolish-biden-bush-administration-war-terror-2021-2.

Hobbes, Thomas. 1484. *Leviathan, or The Matter, Form, and Power of a Commonwealth, Ecclesiastical, and Civil.* 4th ed. London: George Routledge and Sons.

Hoffman, Bruce. 1998. *Inside Terrorism.* London: Indigo.

Hogle, Charlie, and Courteney Leinonen. 2019. "The Trump Administration Is Unlawfully Detaining a U.S. Resident without Charge." American Civil Liberties Union (ACLU), November 25, 2019. https://www.aclu.org/

news/immigrants-rights/the-trump-administration-is-unlawfully-detaining-a-u-s-resident-without-charge.

Holder, Eric. 2009. "Attorney General Announces Forum Decisions for Ten Guantanamo Bay Detainees." Video, Department of Justice, November 13, 2009. https://www.justice.gov/opa/video/attorney-general-announces-forum-decisions-ten-guantanamo-bay-detainees.

Holder, Eric. 2011. "Statement of the Attorney General on the Prosecution of the 9/11 Conspirators." Department of Justice, Office of Public Affairs, Justice News, April 4, 2011. https://www.justice.gov/opa/speech/statement-attorney-general-prosecution-911-conspirators.

Hollander, Nancy. 2013. "The Holy Land Foundation Case: The Collapse of American Justice." *Washington and Lee Journal of Civil Rights and Social Justice* 20 (1): 45–61.

Holzer, Mark W. 2012. "Offensive Lawfare and the Current Conflict." *Harvard Law School National Security Journal,* April 10, 2012. https://harvardnsj.org/2012/04/offensive-lawfare-and-the-current-conflict/#_ftn31.

Hong, Sun Ha, and Piotr M. Szpunar. 2019. "The Futures of Anticipatory Reason: Contingency and Speculation in the Sting Operation." *Security Dialogue* 50 (4): 314–30. https://doi.org/10.1177/0967010619850332.

Hoover, J. Edgar. 1967. "Counterintelligence Program." Washington, D.C.: FBI.

Horgan, John. 2003. "The Case for Firsthand Research." In *Research on Terrorism: Trends, Achievements and Failures,* edited by Andrew Silke, 30–56. London: Routledge. https://doi.org/10.4324/9780203500972.

Horgan, John. 2008. "From Profiles to Pathways and Roots to Routes: Perspectives from Psychology on Radicalization into Terrorism." *Annals of the American Academy of Political and Social Science* 618 (1): 80–94.

Horton, Alex, Razzan Nakhlawi, and Souad Mekhennet. 2022. "Ukraine War Volunteers Are Coming Home, Reckoning with Difficult Fight." *Washington Post,* May 28, 2022. https://www.washingtonpost.com/national-security/2022/05/28/americans-fighting-in-ukraine/.

Horwitz, Sari. 2014. "Terror Trial Tests How Federal Courts Handle Such Cases." *Washington Post,* April 2, 2014.

Human Rights Watch. 2004. "The Road to Abu Ghraib." June 2004. https://www.hrw.org/reports/2004/usa0604/usa0604.pdf.

Human Rights Watch. 2014. "Illusion of Justice: Human Rights Abuses in U.S. Terrorism Prosecutions." July 21, 2014. http://www.hrw.org/node/126101.

Huntington, Samuel P. 1993. "The Clash of Civilizations?" *Foreign Affairs* 72 (3): 22–49.

Huntington, Samuel P. 1996. *The Clash of Civilizations and the Remaking of World Order.* New York: Touchstone.

Huq, Aziz. 2007. "Concerns with Mitchell D. Silber and Arvin Bhatt, N.Y. Police Department, Radicalization in the West: The Homegrown Threat (August 2007)." Brennan Center for Justice, August 30, 2007. https://www.brennancenter.org/sites/default/files/legacy/Justice/Aziz%20Memo%20NYPD.pdf.

Huq, Maimuna. 2009. "Talking Jihad and Piety: Reformist Exertions among Islamist Women in Bangladesh." *Journal of the Royal Anthropological Institute* 15:S163–82. https://doi.org/10.1002/9781444324402.ch10.

Husain, Atiya. 2020. "Terror and Abolition." *Boston Review,* June 11, 2020. https://bostonreview.net/race/atiya-husain-terror-and-abolition.

Husain, Atiya. 2021. "Deracialization, Dissent, and Terrorism in the FBI's Most Wanted Program." *Sociology of Race and Ethnicity* 7 (2): 208–25. https://doi.org/10.1177/2332649220921898.

Hussain, Nasser. 2007. "Beyond the Norm and Exception: Guantánamo." *Critical Inquiry* 33 (4): 734–53.

Hyams, Edward. 1975. *Terrorists and Terrorism.* London: J. M. Dent & Sons.

Ide, Tobias. 2016. "Critical Geopolitics and School Textbooks: The Case of Environment–Conflict Links in Germany." *Political Geography* 55 (1): 60–71.

Illinois Criminal Justice Information Authority. 2016. "Engaged Bystander-Gatekeeper Training for Ideologically Inspired Targeted Violence Grant Proposal." Chicago: Illinois Criminal Justice Information Authority.

Illinois Criminal Justice Information Authority, Stevan Weine, Linda Langford, and Nancy Zarse. 2019. "Communities Acting to Refer and Engage (CARE) Curriculum Contents." Illinois Criminal Justice Information Authority.

Imwinkelried, Edward J. 1994. "The Next Step after Daubert: Developing Similarly Epistemological Approach to Ensuring the Reliability of Non-scientific Expert Testimony." *Cardozo Law Review* 15 (6): 2271–94.

International Committee of the Red Cross. 2015. "What Are Jus ad Bellum and Jus in Bello?" Extract from ICRC publication "International Humanitarian Law: Answers to Your Questions," January 22, 2015. https://www.icrc.org/en/document/what-are-jus-ad-bellum-and-jus-bello-0.

Islam, Jaan. 2021. "'Salafi-Jihadism': Frightening Menace or Scapegoat for the War on Terror?" *Cage,* July 15, 2021. https://www.cage.ngo/salafi-jihadism-frightening-menace-or-scapegoat-for-the-war-on-terror.

Jackson, Kellie Carter. 2019. *Force and Freedom: Black Abolitionists and the Politics of Violence.* Philadelphia: University of Pennsylvania Press.

Jackson, Richard, Jeroen Gunning, and Marie Breen Smyth. 2007. "The Case for a Critical Terrorism Studies." Paper presented at the annual meeting of the American Political Science Association, August 30–September 2, 2007. https://www.aber.ac.uk/en/media/departmental/interpol/csrv/case-for-a-critical-terrorism-studies-richard-7.pdf.

Jackson, Richard, Marie Breen Smyth, and Jeroen Gunning. 2009. "Introduction: The Case for Critical Terrorism Studies." In *Critical Terrorism Studies: A New Research Agenda,* edited by Richard Jackson, Marie Breen Smyth, and Jeroen Gunning, 1–10. London: Routledge.

Jamal, Amaney. 2008. "Civil Liberties and the Otherization of Arab and Muslim Americans." In *Race and Arab Americans before and after 9/11: From Invisible Citizens to Visible Subjects,* edited by Amaney Jamal and Nadine Naber, 114–30. Syracuse, N.Y.: Syracuse University Press.

Jamshidi, Maryam. 2020. "Bringing Abolition to National Security." *Just Security,* August 27, 2020. https://www.justsecurity.org/72160/bringing-abolition-to-national-security/.

Jenkins, Brian Michael. 1974. "International Terrorism: A New Kind of Warfare." Santa Monica, Calif.: Rand. https://www.rand.org/pubs/papers/P5261.html.

Jenkins, Brian Michael. 2010. "Would-Be Warriors: Incidents of Jihadist Terrorist Radicalization in the United States since September 11, 2001." Santa Monica, Calif.: Rand. https://www.rand.org/pubs/occasional_papers/OP292.html.

Jenkins, Brian Michael. 2011. "Stray Dogs and Virtual Enemies." Santa Monica, Calif.: Rand. https://www.rand.org/pubs/occasional_papers/OP343.html.

Joffé, George. 2018. "States and Caliphates." *Geopolitics* 23 (3): 505–24. https://doi.org/10.1080/14650045.2017.1349111.

Johns, Fleur. 2005. "Guantánamo Bay and the Annihilation of the Exception." *European Journal of International Law* 16 (4): 613–35. https://doi.org/10.1093/ejil/chi135.

Jones, Craig A. 2016. "Lawfare and the Juridification of Late Modern War." *Progress in Human Geography* 40 (2): 221–39. https://doi.org/10.1177/0309132515572270.

Kaeble, Danielle. 2018. "Time Served in State Prison, 2016." Department of Justice, Office of Justice Programs, Bureau of Justice Statistics, NCJ 252205, November 2018. https://bjs.ojp.gov/content/pub/pdf/tssp16.pdf.

Kahn, E. J., Jr. 1978. "How Do We Explain Them?" *New Yorker,* June 4, 1978. https://www.newyorker.com/magazine/1978/06/12/how-do-we-explain-them.

Kaiser, Joshua, and John Hagan. 2018. "Crimes of Terror, Counterterrorism, and the Unanticipated Consequences of a Militarized Incapacitation Strategy in Iraq." *Social Forces* 97 (1): 309–46. https://doi.org/10.1093/SF/SOY059.

Kaneva, Nadia, and Andrea Stanton. 2020. "An Alternative Vision of Statehood: Islamic State's Ideological Challenge to the Nation-State." *Studies in Conflict and Terrorism.* https://doi.org/10.1080/1057610X.2020.178 0030.

Kaplan, Amy. 2005. "Where Is Guantánamo?" *American Quarterly* 57 (3): 831–59.

Kapoor, Nisha. 2018. *Deport, Deprive, Extradite: 21st Century State Extremism.* London: Verso.

Kassem, Ramzi, and Diala Shamas. 2017. "Rebellious Lawyering in the Security State." *Clinical Law Review* 23 (2): 671–705.

Katz, Cindi. 2001a. "On the Grounds of Globalization: A Topography for Feminist Political Engagement." *Signs* 26 (4): 1213–34. https://doi.org/10.1086/495653.

Katz, Cindi. 2001b. "Vagabond Capitalism and the Necessity of Social Reproduction." *Antipode* 33 (4): 709–28. https://doi.org/10.1111/1467-8330 .00207.

Kawash, Samira. 1999. "Terrorists and Vampires: Fanon's Spectral Violence of Decolonization." In *Frantz Fanon: Critical Perspectives,* edited by Anthony C. Alessandrini, 237–59. London: Routledge.

Kazi, Nazia. 2019. *Islamophobia, Race, and Global Politics.* Lanham, Md.: Rowman & Littlefield.

Kellenberger, Jakob. 2008. Foreword to "Increasing Respect for International Humanitarian Law in Non-international Armed Conflicts," edited by Michelle Mack, 4. International Committee of the Red Cross (ICRC), February 2008. https://www.icrc.org/sites/default/files/topic/file_plus_list/0923-increasing_respect_for_international_humanitarian_law_in_non -international_armed_conflicts.pdf.

Kelly, Lidia, and Ron Popeski. 2022. "Two Detained Americans Endangered Russian Servicemen, Kremlin Says." Reuters, June 20, 2022. https://www .reuters.com/world/kremlin-says-american-basketball-player-griner-broke -law-faces-prosecution-ria-2022-06-20/.

Khalili, Laleh. 2013. *Time in the Shadows: Confinement in Counterinsurgencies.* Palo Alto: Stanford University Press.

Khouri, Rami G. 2014. "The ISIS Peril Clarifies What Arabs Need." *Daily Star,* June 14, 2014. https://www.belfercenter.org/publication/isis-peril -clarifies-what-arabs-need.

Kiernat, Kourtney. 2015. "Minneapolis Public School CVE Program." Video, February 18, 2015. https://www.c-span.org/video/?c4530677/user-clip-minneapolis-public-school-cve-program.

Kim, Jonathan. 2022. "Habeas Corpus." Legal Information Institute. Updated March 2022. https://www.law.cornell.edu/wex/habeas_corpus.

Knefel, John. 2013. "Everything You've Been Told about Radicalization Is Wrong." *Rolling Stone,* May 6, 2013. https://www.rollingstone.com/politics/politics-news/everything-youve-been-told-about-radicalization-is-wrong-80445/.

Koprowski, Agatha. 2011. "Islamophobia, Neo-Orientalism, and the Specter of Jihad: Problems Facing Muslim Litigants in U.S. Courts." *University of Pennsylvania Journal of Law and Social Change* 14 (1): 183–200.

Kraychik, Robert. 2019. "Rep. Bradley Byrne: We Have Terrorists 'Stacked Up Behind' John Walker Lindh 'Trying to Get Off Early for Good Behavior.'" *Breitbart,* May 24, 2019. https://www.breitbart.com/radio/2019/05/24/bradley-byrne-we-have-terrorists-stacked-up-behind-john-walker-lindh-trying-get-off-early-good-behavior/.

Kris, David S. 2011. "Law Enforcement as a Counterterrorism Tool." *Journal of National Security Law and Policy* 5 (1): 1–104.

Kroenig, Matthew, and Barry Pavel. 2012. "How to Deter Terrorism." *Washington Quarterly* 35 (2): 21–36. https://doi.org/10.1080/0163660X.2012.665339.

Kruglanski, Arie W., and Shira Fishman. 2006. "The Psychology of Terrorism: 'Syndrome' versus 'Tool' Perspectives." *Terrorism and Political Violence* 18 (2): 193–215.

Kumar, Deepa. 2012. *Islamophobia and the Politics of Empire.* Chicago, Ill.: Haymarket.

Kundnani, Arun. 2012. "Radicalization: The Journey of a Concept." *Race and Class* 54 (2): 3–25. https://doi.org/10.1177/0306396812454984.

Kundnani, Arun. 2014. *The Muslims Are Coming! Islamophobia, Extremism, and the Domestic War on Terror.* London: Verso.

Kundnani, Arun. 2016. "Islamophobia: Lay Ideology of U.S.-Led Empire." Kundnani.org (blog). https://kundnani.org/wp-content/uploads/Kundnani-Islamophobia-as-lay-ideology-of-US-empire.pdf.

Kundnani, Arun. 2017. "Islamophobia as Ideology of U.S. Empire." In *What Is Islamophobia? Racism, Social Movements, and the State,* edited by Narzanin Massoumi, Tom Mills, and David Miller, 35–48. London: Pluto.

Landler, Mark, Michael R. Gordon, and Anne Barnard. 2012. "U.S. Will Grant Recognition to Syrian Rebels, Obama Says." *New York Times,* December 11,

2012. https://www.nytimes.com/2012/12/12/world/middleeast/united
-states-involvement-in-syria.html.

Laqueur, Walter. 1996. "Postmodern Terrorism." *Foreign Affairs* 75 (5): 24–36.

Laqueur, Walter. 1999. *The New Terrorism: Fanaticism and the Arms of Mass Destruction.* Oxford: Oxford University Press.

Laqueur, Walter. 2004. "The Terrorism to Come." Hoover Institution, August 1, 2004. https://www.hoover.org/research/terrorism-come.

Laqueur, Walter. 2006. "Terror's New Face." *Harvard International Review* 20 (4): 48–51.

"A Lawless Enclave?" 2004. *Economist* 371 (8372): 32–33.

Lawrence, Bruce. 1998. *Shattering the Myth: Islam beyond Violence.* Princeton, N.J.: Princeton University Press.

Lean, Nathan. 2012. *The Islamophobia Industry: How the Right Manufactures Fear of Muslims.* London: Pluto.

Levitt, Matthew. 2008. "Prosecuting Terrorism beyond 'Material Support.'" Washington Institute for Near East Policy, January 14, 2008. https://www.washingtoninstitute.org/policy-analysis/view/prosecuting-terrorism-beyond-material-support.

Lewis, Bernard. 1990. "The Roots of Muslim Rage." *Atlantic,* September 1990. https://www.theatlantic.com/magazine/archive/1990/09/the-roots-of-muslim-rage/304643/.

Li, Darryl. 2011. "Lies, Damned Lies and Plagiarizing 'Experts.'" *Middle East Report* 41 (260): 9–10. https://doi.org/10.2307/41408014.

Li, Darryl. 2015. "A Jihadism Anti-primer." *Middle East Research and Information Project* 276:12–17. https://merip.org/2015/12/a-jihadism-anti-primer/.

Li, Darryl. 2016. "Jihad in a World of Sovereigns: Law, Violence, and Islam in the Bosnia Crisis." *Law and Social Inquiry* 41 (2): 371–401. https://doi.org/10.1111/lsi.12152.

Li, Darryl. 2020. *The Universal Enemy: Jihad, Empire, and the Challenge of Solidarity.* Palo Alto, Calif.: Stanford University Press.

Loewen, James. 1994. *Lies My Teacher Told Me: Everything Your American History Textbook Got Wrong.* New York: Touchstone.

Lokaneeta, Jinee. 2011. *Transnational Torture: Law, Violence, and State Power in the United States and India.* New York: New York University Press.

Lopez, Ian F. Haney. 1994. "The Social Construction of Race: Some Observations on Illusion, Fabrication, and Choice." *Harvard Civil Rights–Civil Liberties Law Review* 29:1–62.

Love, Erik. 2012. "What to Do about Islamophobia: Why the Election Counts." Institute for Social Policy and Understanding, November 2012.

https://www.ispu.org/wp-content/uploads/2016/08/ISPU_Brief_Islama phobia.pdf.

Love, Erik. 2017. *Islamophobia and Racism in America.* New York: New York University Press.

Mabon, Simon. 2017. "Nationalist Jāhiliyyah and the Flag of the Two Crusaders, or ISIS, Sovereignty, and the 'Owl of Minerva.'" *Studies in Conflict and Terrorism* 40 (11): 966–85. https://doi.org/10.1080/1057610X.20 16.1258863.

Makdisi, Ussama. 2017. "The Mythology of the Sectarian Middle East." Rice University's James A. Baker III Institute for Public Policy, February 2017. https://www.bakerinstitute.org/sites/default/files/2017-02/import/CME -pub-Sectarianism-021317.pdf.

Makhdoom, Zainuddin. 1583. *Tuhfat Al-Mujāhidīn Fī Baʿd a Wāl Al-Burtuġāliyyīn.* Edited by S. Muhammad Husayn Nainar. Madras: University of Madras.

Mamdani, Mahmood. 2004. *Good Muslim, Bad Muslim: America, the Cold War, and the Roots of Terror.* New York: Three Leaves.

Manzoor-Khan, Suhaiymah. 2022. *Tangled in Terror: Uprooting Islamophobia.* London: Pluto.

Margulies, Joseph. 2006. *Guantánamo and the Abuse of Presidential Power.* New York: Simon and Schuster.

Martínez, José Ciro, and Brent Eng. 2018. "Stifling Stateness: The Assad Regime's Campaign against Rebel Governance." *Security Dialogue* 49 (4): 235–53. https://doi.org/10.1177/0967010618768622.

Martínez, José Ciro, and Omar Sirri. 2020. "Of Bakeries and Checkpoints: Stately Affects in Amman and Baghdad." *Environment and Planning D: Society and Space* 38 (5): 849–66.

May, Vivian M. 2014. "'Speaking into the Void'? Intersectionality Critiques and Epistemic Backlash." *Hypatia* 29 (1): 94–112. https://doi.org/10.11 11/hypa.12060.

McAdams, Richard H. 2005. "The Political Economy of Entrapment." *Journal of Criminal Law and Criminology* 96 (1): 107–85.

McCain, John. 2006. "It's about Us." *Human Rights* 33 (1): 20–22.

McCauley, Clark, and Sophia Moskalenko. 2017. "Understanding Political Radicalization: The Two-Pyramids Model." *American Psychologist* 72 (3): 205–16. https://doi.org/10.1037/amp0000062.

McCord, Mary B. 2017. "Federal Prosecution Is a Viable Option for Enemy Combatants." *Lawfare,* July 24, 2017. https://www.lawfareblog.com/fed eral-prosecution-viable-option-enemy-combatants.

McEnroe, Paul. 2015. "A Heartbroken Minneapolis Mother Agonizes over Son's Arrest." *Star Tribune,* April 21, 2015. https://www.startribune.com/ heartbroken-minneapolis-mother-puzzles-over-son-s-arrest/300740951/.

McEvoy, Kieran, and Brian Gormally. 1997. "'Seeing' Is Believing: Positivist Terrorology, Peacemaking Criminology, and the Northern Ireland Peace Process." *Critical Criminology* 8 (1): 9–30.

McGhee, Derek. 2008. *The End of Multiculturalism? Terrorism, Integration and Human Rights.* Maidenhead, U.K.: Open University Press.

McKelvey, Tara. 2019. "John Walker Lindh: Anger as 'American Taliban' Freed." *BBC News,* May 23, 2019. https://www.bbc.com/news/world-us -canada-48386000.

McMahon, James. 1986. "Prior Convictions Offered for Impeachment in Civil Trials: The Interaction of Federal Rules of Evidence 609(a) and 403." *Fordham Law Review* 54 (6): 1063–79.

McNulty, Paul J. 2006. "Prepared Remarks of Deputy Attorney General Paul J. McNulty at the American Enterprise Institute." Remarks delivered at the American Enterprise Institute, Washington, D.C., May 24, 2006. Department of Justice Archive. https://www.justice.gov/archive/dag/speeches/ 2006/dag_speech_060524.html.

McQuade, Joseph. 2021. *A Genealogy of Terrorism: Colonial Law and the Origins of an Idea.* Cambridge: Cambridge University Press.

Meadows, Joseph M. 2002. "The Koon Trap: Why Imperfect Entrapment Fails to Justify Departure from the Federal Sentencing Guidelines." *Indiana Law Journal* 77 (2): 341–62.

Meek, James. 2003. "People the Law Forgot." *Guardian,* December 2, 2003. https://www.theguardian.com/world/2003/dec/03/guantanamo.usa1.

Meer, Nasar. 2007. "Muslim Schools in Britain: Challenging Mobilizations or Logical Developments." *Asia Pacific Journal of Education* 27 (1): 55–71.

Menon, Dilip M. 1999. "Houses by the Sea State-Formation Experiments in Malabar, 1760–1800." *Economic and Political Weekly* 34 (29): 1995–2003.

Miller, Banks, Linda Camp Keith, and Jennifer S. Holmes. 2015. *Immigration Judges and U.S. Asylum Policy.* Philadelphia: University of Pennsylvania Press.

Miller, David, and Tom Mills. 2009. "The Terror Experts and the Mainstream Media: The Expert Nexus and Its Dominance in the News Media." *Critical Studies on Terrorism* 2 (3): 414–37. https://doi.org/10.1080/17539 150903306113.

Miller, John. 1999. "Greetings, America. My Name Is Osama Bin Laden." *Esquire,* February 1999. https://www.esquire.com/news-politics/a1813/ osama-bin-laden-interview/.

Mills, Charles. 2015. "Global White Ignorance." In *Routledge International Handbook of Ignorance Studies*, edited by Matthias Gross and Linsey McGoey, 217–27. London: Routledge.

Moeckli, Daniel. 2008–9. "The Emergence of Terrorism as a Distinct Category of International Law." *Texas International Law Journal* 44 (2): 157–84. https://heinonline.org/HOL/LandingPage?handle=hein.journals/tilj44&div=11&id=&page=.

Mofidi, Manooher, and Amy E. Eckert. 2003. "Unlawful Combatants or Prisoners of War: The Law and Politics of Labels." *Cornell International Law Journal* 36 (3): 59–92.

Moghaddam, Fathali. 2005. "The Staircase to Terrorism: A Psychological Exploration." *American Psychologist* 60 (2): 161–69.

Monaghan, Jeffrey. 2014. "Security Traps and Discourses of Radicalization: Examining Surveillance Practices Targeting Muslims in Canada." *Surveillance and Society* 12 (4): 485–501.

Montanaro, David. 2019. "Release of 'American Taliban' John Walker Lindh from Prison Is Unconscionable, Says Pompeo." *Fox News,* May 23, 2019. https://www.foxnews.com/us/mike-pompeo-release-of-american-taliban-john-walker-lindh.

Mora, Nicolás Medina, and Mike Hayes. 2015. "Did the FBI Transform This Teenager into a Terrorist after Reading His Emails?" *BuzzFeed,* November 15, 2015. https://www.buzzfeednews.com/article/nicolasmedinamora/did-the-fbi-transform-this-teenager-into-a-terrorist.

Mountz, Alison. 2004. "Embodying the Nation-State: Canada's Response to Human Smuggling." *Political Geography* 23 (3): 323–45. https://doi.org/10.1016/j.polgeo.2003.12.017.

Mountz, Alison. 2010. *Seeking Asylum: Human Smuggling and Bureaucracy at the Border.* Minneapolis: University of Minnesota Press.

Mueller, John, and Mark G. Stewart. 2016. *Chasing Ghosts: The Policing of Terrorism.* Oxford: Oxford University Press.

Muna, Afrida Arinal. 2002. "Religious Expression of Hijrah Celebrities: Accommodating Protest and the Political Economy of Public Piety." *Islam Realitas* 6 (1): 90–99.

Munif, Yasser. 2020. *The Syrian Revolution: Between the Politics of Life and the Geopolitics of Death.* London: Pluto.

Munkler, Herfried. 2003. "The Wars of the 21st Century." *International Review of the Red Cross* 85 (849): 7–22.

Murakawa, Naomi, and Katherine Beckett. 2010. "The Penology of Racial Innocence: The Erasure of Racism in the Study and Practice of Punishment." *Law and Society Review* 44 (3/4): 695–730.

Muslim Abolitionist Futures. 2021. "Abolishing the War on Terror, Building Communities of Care: A Grassroots Policy Agenda." https://static1.square spacc.com/static/6117f102ff217d11f9a70b8d/t/613cd2ea37254528345 fa95d/1631376107957/Abolishing+the+War+on+Terror%2C+Building+ Communities+of+Care.pdf.

Mutua, Makau. 2000. "What Is TWAIL." *American Society of International Law* 94:31–40.

Myre, Greg. 2017. "What Is the U.S. Goal in Syria?" National Public Radio (NPR), April 8, 2017. https://www.npr.org/sections/parallels/2017/04/ 08/523016523/what-is-the-u-s-goal-in-syria.

Naber, Nadine. 2006. "The Rules of Forced Engagement: Race, Gender, and the Culture of Fear among Arab Immigrants in San Francisco Post-9/11." *Cultural Dynamics* 18 (3): 235–67.

Naber, Nadine, Eman Desouky, and Lina Baroudi. 2016. "The Forgotten '-Ism': An Arab American Woman's Perspective on Zionism, Racism, and Sexism." In *Color of Violence: The INCITE! Anthology,* edited by INCITE! Women of Color against Violence, 97–112. Durham, N.C.: Duke University Press.

Naber, Nadine, and Clarissa Rojas. 2021. "To Abolish Prisons and Militarism, We Need Anti-imperialist Abolition Feminism." *Truthout,* July 16, 2021. https://truthout.org/articles/to-abolish-prisons-and-militarism-we-need -anti-imperialist-abolition-feminism/.

Nasir, M. Bilal. 2019. "Mad Kids, Good City: Counterterrorism, Mental Health, and the Resilient Muslim Subject." *Anthropological Quarterly* 92 (3): 817–44. https://doi.org/10.1353/anq.2019.0053.

National Counterterrorism Center. 2014. *Countering Violent Extremism: A Guide for Practitioners and Analysts.* Washington, D.C.: National Counterterrorism Center. https://www.dcjs.virginia.gov/sites/dcjs.virginia.gov/ files/cve_guide_for_practitioners_and_analysts.pdf.

National Counterterrorism Center. 2017. "U.S. Homegrown Violent Extremism Recidivism Likely." *NCTC Current,* January 24, 2017. https://s3.doc umentcloud.org/documents/3873025/NCTC-Report.pdf.

Nawwab, Nimah Ismail. 2021. "History of Hijrah: Migration for Peace and Justice." IslamiCity. 2021. https://www.islamicity.org/6327/history-of -hijrah-migration-for-peace-and-justice/.

Newsweek. 1999. "Bin Laden Speaks." January 1999.

Nguyen, Nicole. 2014. "Education as Warfare? Mapping Securitized Education Interventions as War on Terror Strategy." *Geopolitics* 19 (1): 109–39. https://doi.org/10.1080/14650045.2013.789866.

Nguyen, Nicole. 2019. *Suspect Communities: Anti-Muslim Racism and the Domestic War on Terror.* Minneapolis: University of Minnesota Press.

Noormega, Rayi. 2019. "Hijrah: The Pursuit of Identity for Millennials." IDN Research Institute, October 7, 2019. https://medium.com/idn-research -institute/hijrah-the-pursuit-of-identity-for-millennials-7de449d86ed0.

Norris, Jesse J. 2015. "Why the FBI and the Courts Are Wrong about Entrapment and Terrorism." *Mississippi Law Journal* 84 (5): 1257–327.

Norris, Jesse J. 2020. "How Entrapment Still Matters: Partial Success of Entrapment Claims in Terrorism Prosecutions." In *Studies in Law, Politics, and Society,* vol. 82, edited by Austin Sarat, 141–66. Bingley, U.K.: Emerald.

Norris, Jesse J., and Hanna Grol-Prokopczyk. 2017. "Estimating the Prevalence of Entrapment in Post-9/11 Terrorism Cases." *Journal of Criminal Law and Criminology* 105 (3): 609–78.

Norris, Jesse J., and Hanna Grol Prokopczyk. 2018. "Temporal Trends in U.S. Counterterrorism Sting Operations, 1989–2014." *Critical Studies on Terrorism* 11 (2): 243–71. https://doi.org/10.1080/17539153.2017.1400421.

Norris, Jesse J., and Hanna Grol-Prokopczyk. 2019. "Racial and Other Sociodemographic Disparities in Terrorism Sting Operations." *Sociology of Race and Ethnicity* 5 (3): 416–31. https://doi.org/10.1177/23326492 18756136.

Novogrodsky, Noah. 2018. "Is ISIS a State? The Status of Statehood in the Age of Terror." *Berkeley Journal of International Law* 36 (1): 2.

O'Leary, Brendan, and Andrew Silke. 2007. "Understanding and Ending Persistent Conflicts: Bridging Research and Policy." In *Terror, Insurgency, and the State: Ending Protracted Conflicts,* edited by Marianne Heiberg, Brendan O'Leary, and John Tirman, 387–426. Philadelphia: University of Pennsylvania Press.

Obama, Barack. 2009a. "Remarks by the President on National Security, 5-21-09." Press release, Barack Obama White House Archives, Office of the White House, May 21, 2009. https://obamawhitehouse.archives.gov/the -press-office/remarks-president-national-security-5-21-09.

Obama, Barack. 2009b. "Statement of President Barack Obama on Military Commissions." Press release, Barack Obama White House Archives, Office of the White House, May 15, 2009. https://obamawhitehouse.archives .gov/the-press-office/statement-president-barack-obama-military-com missions.

Office of Public Affairs. 2010. "The Criminal Justice System as a Counterterrorism Tool: A Fact Sheet." Office of Public Affairs, January 6, 2010. Department of Justice Archive. https://www.justice.gov/archives/opa/blog/ criminal-justice-system-counterterrorism-tool-fact-sheet.

Office of Public Affairs. 2014. "Convicted Bomb Plotter Sentenced to 30 Years." Press release, Office of Public Affairs, Department of Justice, October 1, 2014. https://www.justice.gov/nsd/pr/convicted-bomb-plotter-sen tenced-30-years.

Office of Public Affairs. 2016. "Federal Jury Convicts Three Minnesota Men for Conspiring to Join ISIL and Commit Murder in Syria." Press release, Office of Public Affairs, Department of Justice, June 3, 2016. https:// www.justice.gov/opa/pr/federal-jury-convicts-three-minnesota-men-con spiring-join-isil-and-commit-murder-syria.

Office of the Director of National Intelligence. 2021. "Domestic Violent Extremism Poses Heightened Threat in 2021." Office of the Director of National Intelligence, March 1, 2021. https://www.dni.gov/files/ODNI/ documents/assessments/UnclassSummaryofDVEAssessment-17MAR21 .pdf.

Oorschot, Irene van. 2020. "Culture, Milieu, Phenotype: Articulating Race in Judicial Sense-Making Practices." *Social and Legal Studies* 29 (6): 790–811.

Ould Mohamedou, Mohammad-Mahmoud. 2007. *Understanding Al Qaeda: The Transformation of War.* London: Pluto.

Ould Mohamedou, Mohammad-Mahmoud. 2011. *Understanding Al-Qaeda: Changing War and Global Politics.* 2nd ed. London: Pluto.

Özpek, Burak Bilgehan, and Yavuz Yağiş. 2019. "Competitive Jihadism: Understanding the Survival Strategies of Jihadist de Facto States." *All Azimuth* 8 (1): 23–36. https://doi.org/10.20991/allazimuth.376259.

Painter, Joe. 2006. "Prosaic Geographies of Stateness." *Political Geography* 25 (7): 752–74.

Panikkar, K. N. 1989. *Against Lord and State: Religion and Peasant Uprisings in Malabar, 1836–1921.* Oxford: Oxford University Press.

Pape, Robert A. 2003. "Dying to Kill Us." *New York Times,* September 22, 2003. https://www.nytimes.com/2003/09/22/opinion/dying-to-kill-us.html.

Patai, Raphael. 1973. *The Arab Mind.* New York: Charles Scribner's Sons.

Patel, Faiza. 2011. "Rethinking Radicalization." Brennan Center for Justice at New York University School of Law, March 8, 2011. https://www.brennan center.org/our-work/research-reports/rethinking-radicalization.

Patel, Faiza, and Meghan Koushik. 2017. "Countering Violent Extremism." Brennan Center for Justice at New York University School of Law, March 16, 2017. https://www.brennancenter.org/our-work/research-reports/coun tering-violent-extremism.

Patel, Tina G. 2017. "It's Not about Security, It's about Racism: Counter-terror Strategies, Civilizing Processes and the Post-race Fiction." *Palgrave Communications* 3:1–8. https://www.nature.com/articles/palcomms201731.pdf.

Perdue, William D. 1989. *Terrorism and the State: A Critique of Domination through Fear.* New York: Praeger.

Petras, James. 2004. "Meet the Mandarins of Abu Ghraib." *Counter Punch,* August 7, 2004. https://www.counterpunch.org/2004/08/07/meet-the -mandarins-of-abu-ghraib/.

Petras, James. 2006. *The Power of Israel in the United States.* Atlanta, Ga.: Clarity.

Pfanner, Toni. 2005. *Asymmetrical Warfare from the Perspective of Humanitarian Law and Humanitarian Action.* Cambridge: Cambridge University Press.

Platt, Tony, and Gregory Shank. 2004. "Introduction: Imprisonment, Immigration Control, and Drug Enforcement." *Social Justice* 31 (1/2): 1–6.

Poplin, Cody M., and Benjamin Bissell. 2014. "Throwback Thursday: The Sykes-Picot Agreement." *Lawfare,* November 13, 2014. https://www.law fareblog.com/throwback-thursday-sykes-picot-agreement.

Porges, Marisa L. 2010. "The Saudi Deradicalization Experiment." Expert brief. Council on Foreign Relations, January 22, 2010. https://www.cfr .org/expert-brief/saudi-deradicalization-experiment.

Porras, Ileana. 1994. "On Terrorism: Reflections on Violence and the Outlaw." *Utah Law Review* 1994 (1): 119–46.

Porter, John. 2016. "DAPL SITREP 004, 14 September 2016." *Intercept,* posted May 27, 2017. https://theintercept.com/document/2017/05/27/ internal-tigerswan-situation-report-2016-09-14/.

Porter, John. 2017. "DAPL SITREP 168, February 27, 2017." *Intercept,* posted June 21, 2017. https://theintercept.com/document/2017/06/21/internal -tigerswan-situation-report-2017-02-27/.

Post, Jerrold M. 2009. "Forward: Understanding the Radical Mind." In *Walking Away from Terrorism: Accounts of Disengagement from Radical and Extremist Movements,* xi–xiv. New York: Routledge.

Poynting, Scott, and David Whyte. 2012a. "Conclusion: Reconnecting the Asymmetries of Political Violence." In *Counter-terrorism and State Political Violence: The "War on Terror" as Terror,* edited by Scott Poynting and David Whyte, 235–41. London: Routledge.

Poynting, Scott, and David Whyte. 2012b. "Introduction: Counter-terrorism and the Terrorist State." In *Counter-terrorism and State Political Violence: The "War on Terror" as Terror,* 1–11. London: Routledge.

Price, Ned. 2022. "Department Press Briefing—June 21, 2022." Video and transcript, Department of State. https://www.state.gov/briefings/depart ment-press-briefing-june-21-2022/.

Prozorov, Sergei. 2014. *Agamben and Politics: A Critical Introduction.* Edinburgh: Edinburgh University Press.

Puar, Jasbir K., and Amit S. Rai. 2002. "Monster, Terrorist, Fag: The War on Terrorism and the Production of Docile Patriots." *Social Text* 20 (3 [72]): 118–48. https://doi.org/10.1215/01642472-20-3_72-117.

Pugliese, Joseph. 2013. *State Violence and the Execution of Law: Biopolitical Caesurae of Torture, Black Sites, Drones.* London: Routledge.

Qureshi, Asim. 2017. "Fight the Power: How CAGE Resists from within a 'Suspect Community.'" *Palgrave Communications* 3:17090. https://doi.org/10.1057/palcomms.2017.90.

Ramahi, Zainab. 2020. "The Muslim Ban Cases: A Lost Opportunity for the Court and a Lesson for the Future." *California Law Review* 108 (2): 557–86.

Rana, Junaid. 2011. *Terrifying Muslims: Race and Labor in the South Asian Diaspora.* Durham, N.C.: Duke University Press.

Rana, Junaid. 2017. "The Globality of AfPak: U.S. Empire and the Muslim Problem." In *The Routledge Handbook of Asian American Studies,* edited by Cindy I-Fen Cheng, 260–73. New York: Routledge.

Ranstorp, Magnus. 2009. "Mapping Terrorism Studies after 9/11." In *Critical Terrorism Studies: A New Research Agenda,* edited by Richard Jackson, Marie Breen Smyth, and Jeroen Gunning, 13–33. London: Routledge.

Rascoff, Samuel J. 2014. "Counterterrorism and New Deterrence." *New York University Law Review* 89 (3): 830–84.

Ray, Larry. 2011. *Violence and Society.* London: Sage.

Razack, Sherene H. 2008. *Casting Out: The Eviction of Muslims from Western Law and Politics.* Toronto: University of Toronto Press.

Razak, Muneerah Ab. 2018. "Can Violence Be Moral? Revisiting Fanon on Violence in *The Wretched of the Earth.*" LSE (London School of Economics and Political Science) Middle East Centre blog, January 8, 2018. https://blogs.lse.ac.uk/mec/2018/01/08/can-violence-be-moral-revisiting-fanon-on-violence-in-the-wretched-of-the-earth/.

Reid, Edna O. F. 1997. "Evolution of a Body of Knowledge: An Analysis of Terrorism Research." *Information Processing and Management* 33 (1): 91–106. https://doi.org/10.1016/S0306-4573(96)00052-0.

Robinson, Paul H., and John M. Darley. 1995. *Justice, Liability, and Blame: Community Views and the Criminal Law.* Boulder, Colo.: Westview.

Rojas, Clarissa, and Nadine Naber. 2022. "Genocide and 'U.S.' Domination ≠ Liberation, Only We Can Liberate Ourselves: Toward an Anti-imperialist Abolition Feminism." In *Abolition Feminisms: Organizing, Survival, and Transformative Practice,* edited by Alisa Bierria, Jakeya Caruthers, and Brooke Lober, 11–57. Chicago, Ill.: Haymarket.

Roth, Jessica A. 2014. "The Anomaly of Entrapment." *Washington University Law Review* 91 (4): 979–1034. https://journals.library.wustl.edu/lawre view/article/id/5518/.

Rousseau, Kevin. 2017. "International Law and Military Strategy: Changes in the Strategic Operating Environment." *Journal of National Security Law and Policy* 9 (1): 1–28.

Rovner, Laura, and Jeanne Theoharis. 2012. "Preferring Order to Justice Preferring Order to Justice." *American University Law Review* 61 (5): 1331–415.

Rubin, Barnett R. 2002. *The Fragmentation of Afghanistan: State Formation and the Collapse of the International System.* 2nd ed. New Haven, Conn.: Yale University Press.

Rumsfeld, Donald H. 2002. "Counter-resistance Techniques." Memos, Department of Defense, November 27, 2002. http://library.rumsfeld .com/doclib/sp/380/2002-11-27%20from%20Haynes%20re%20Coun ter-Resistance%20Techniques.pdf.

Sabir, Rizwaan. 2022. *The Suspect: Counterterrorism, Islam, and the Security State.* London: Pluto.

Sadequee, Sharmin. 2018. "Surveillance, Secular Law, and the Reconstruction of Islam in the United States." *Surveillance and Society* 16 (4): 473–87.

Sageman, Marc. 2008. *Leaderless Jihad: Terror Networks in the Twenty-First Century.* Philadelphia: University of Pennsylvania Press.

Sageman, Marc. 2014a. "Re.: U.S. v. Babar Ahmad, U.S.D.C., District of Connecticut, No. 3:04-CR-00301-JCH U.S. v. Syed Talha Ahsan, U.S.D.C., District of Connecticut, No. 3:06-CR-00194-JCH." Rockville, Md.

Sageman, Marc. 2014b. "The Stagnation in Terrorism Research." *Terrorism and Political Violence* 26 (4): 565–80.

Sageman, Marc. 2015. "Declaration of Marc Sageman in Opposition to Defendants' Cross-Motion for Summary Judgment, Latif v. U.S. Department of Justice et al., No. 3:100-Cv-00750." United States District Court, District of Oregon, filed August 7, 2015. https://www.aclu.org/sites/de fault/files/field_document/268._declaration_of_marc_sageman_8.7.15 .pdf.

Said, Edward. 1997. *Covering Islam: How the Media and the Experts Determine How We See the Rest of the World.* New York: Vintage.

Said, Wadie E. 2014. "Sentencing Terrorist Crimes." *Ohio State Law Journal* 75 (3): 477–528.

Said, Wadie E. 2015. *Crimes of Terror: The Legal and Political Implications of Federal Terrorism Prosecutions.* Oxford: Oxford University Press.

Salaita, Steven. 2006. *Anti-Arab Racism in the USA: Where It Comes from and What It Means for Politics Today.* Ann Arbor, Mich.: Pluto.

Saleh, Zainab. 2020. "The Human Cost of U.S. Interventions in Iraq: A History from the 1960s through the Post-9/11 Wars." Watson Institute at Brown University, October 13, 2020. https://watson.brown.edu/costsof war/papers/2020/IraqHistory.

Saleh, Zainab. 2022. "Islamic State in Iraq and Greater Syria." Oxford Islamic Studies Online. http://www.oxfordislamicstudies.com/article/opr/t343/e0 179

Savage, Charlie. 2010. "Terror Verdict Tests Obama's Strategy on Trials." *New York Times,* November 18, 2010. https://www.nytimes.com/2010/11/19/ nyregion/19detainees.html.

Scahill, Jeremy. 2015. "The Assassination Complex." *Intercept,* October 15, 2015. https://theintercept.com/drone-papers/the-assassination-complex/.

Schmid, Alex P., and A. J. Jongman. 1988. *Political Terrorism: A New Guide to Actors, Authors, Concepts, Data Bases, Theories, and Literature.* Amsterdam: Transaction.

Schwabauer, Barbara A. 2010. "The Emmett Till Unsolved Civil Rights Crime Act: The Cold Case of Racism in the Criminal Justice System." *Ohio State Law Journal* 71 (3): 653–98.

Scott, Eugene. 2019. "At a Hearing, an Expert Said the FBI Should Focus on White Nationalism, Not 'Black Identity Extremists.'" *Washington Post,* April 10, 2019. https://www.washingtonpost.com/politics/2019/04/10/ hearing-an-expert-said-fbi-should-focus-rise-white-nationalism-not-black -identity-extremists/.

Scott, Winfield. 1847. *General Headquarters of the Army, General Orders Number 20, February 19, 1847, Tampico, Mexico.* Translated by Gauthereau-Bryson, Lorena. Tampico, Mexico: Imprenta de la calle de la Carniceria, 1847. From Woodson Research Center, Rice University, Americas Collection, 1811–1920, MS 518. https://hdl.handle.net/1911/27562.

Secor, Anna. 2007. "Between Longing and Despair: State, Space and Subjectivity in Turkey." *Environment and Planning D: Society and Space* 25 (1): 33–52.

Selod, Saher. 2015. "Citizenship Denied: The Racialization of Muslim American Men and Women Post-9/11." *Critical Sociology* 41 (1): 77–95. https:// doi.org/10.1177/0896920513516022.

Selod, Saher. 2018. *Forever Suspect: Racialized Surveillance of Muslim Americans in the War on Terror.* New Brunswick, N.J.: Rutgers University Press.

Sen, Maya. 2015. "Is Justice Really Blind? Race and Reversal in U.S. Courts." *Journal of Legal Studies* 44 (S1): s187–229.

Setty, Sudha. 2010. "Comparative Perspectives on Specialized Trials for Terrorism." *Maine Law Review* 63 (1): 131–74.

Shafi, Azfar, and Asim Qureshi. 2020. "Stranger than Fiction: How 'Pre-crime' Approaches to 'Countering Violent Extremism' Institutionalise Islamophobia—A European Comparative Study." Amsterdam: Transnational Institute, January 2020. https://www.tni.org/files/publication-downloads/web_strangerthanfiction.pdf.

Shange, Savannah. 2019. *Progressive Dystopia: Abolition, Antiblackness, and Schooling in San Francisco.* Durham, N.C.: Duke University Press.

Shannon, Elaine. 2003. "Al-Qaeda Moneyman Caught." *Time,* May 2003. http://content.time.com/time/nation/article/0,8599,448922,00.html.

Sharma, Sanjay, and Jasbinder Nijjar. 2018. "The Racialized Surveillant Assemblage: Islam and the Fear of Terrorism." *Popular Communication* 16 (1): 72–85. https://doi.org/10.1080/15405702.2017.1412441.

Sheikh, Jakob. 2016. "'I Just Said It. The State': Examining the Motivations for Danish Foreign Fighting in Syria." *Perspectives on Terrorism* 10 (6): 59–67.

Sherman, Jon. 2009. "'A Person Otherwise Innocent': Policing Entrapment in Preventative, Undercover Counterterrorism Investigations." *University of Pennsylvania Journal of Constitutional Law* 11 (5): 1475–510.

Silber, Mitchell D., and Arvin Bhatt. 2007. *Radicalization in the West: The Homegrown Threat.* Office of Justice Programs, Department of Justice. https://www.ojp.gov/ncjrs/virtual-library/abstracts/radicalization-west-homegrown-threat.

Silke, Andrew. 2004. "An Introduction to Terrorism Research." In *Research on Terrorism: Trends, Achievements and Failures,* edited by Andrew Silke, 1–29. London: Routledge.

Silva, Kumarini. 2016. *Brown Threat: Identification in the Security State.* Minneapolis: University of Minnesota Press.

Silverblatt, Irene M. 2005. *Modern Inquisition: Peru and the Colonial Origins of the Civilized World.* Durham, N.C.: Duke University Press.

Singh, Gopal. 1976. "Politics and Violence." *Social Scientist* 4 (11): 58–66.

Skinner, Christina Parajon. 2013. "Punishing Crimes of Terror in Article III Courts." *Yale Law and Policy Review* 31 (2): 309–76.

Solow, Sara A. 2011. "Prosecuting Terrorists as Criminals and the Limits of Extraterritorial Jurisdiction." *St. John's Law Review* 85 (4): 1484–556. http://scholarship.law.stjohns.edu/cgi/viewcontent.cgi?article=5595&context=lawreview.

Somoza-Rodríguez, Miguel. 2011. "Education, Elite Formation, and Geopolitics: Americanism and the Regeneration of Spain." *Paedagogica Historica* 47 (5): 619–38. https://doi.org/10.1080/00309230.2011.607172.

Stampnitzky, Lisa. 2011. "Disciplining an Unruly Field: Terrorism Experts and Theories of Scientific/Intellectual Production." *Qualitative Sociology* 34 (1): 1–19. https://doi.org/10.1007/s11133-010-9187-4.

Stampnitzky, Lisa. 2013. *Disciplining Terror: How Experts Invented "Terrorism."* Cambridge: Cambridge University Press.

Stein, Jeff. 2011. "Rumsfeld Complained of 'Low Level' GTMO Prisoners, Memo Reveals." *Washington Post,* March 3, 2011. http://voices.washingtonpost.com/spy-talk/2011/03/rumsfeld_complained_of_low_lev.html.

Stevenson, Dru. 2008. "Entrapment and Terrorism." *Boston College Law Review* 49 (1): 125–215. https://doi.org/10.1525/sp.2007.54.1.23.

Steyn, Johan. 2004. "Guantanamo Bay: The Legal Black Hole." *International and Comparative Law Quarterly* 53 (1): 1–15.

Stoler, Ann Laura. 2008a. "Epistemic Politics: Ontologies of Colonial Common Sense." *Philosophical Forum Inc.* 39 (3): 349–61.

Stoler, Ann Laura. 2008b. "Imperial Debris: Reflections on Ruins and Ruination." *Cultural Anthropology* 23 (2): 191–219. https://doi.org/10.1525/can.2008.23.2.191.C.

Stoler, Ann Laura. 2009. *Along the Archival Grain: Epistemic Anxieties and Colonial Common Sense.* Princeton, N.J.: Princeton University Press.

Stoler, Ann Laura. 2016. *Duress: Imperial Durabilities in Our Times.* Durham, N.C.: Duke University Press.

Stovall, David. 2020. "Chicago's Population Loss and the Engineering of Conflict." In *Between the Great Migration and the Growing Exodus: The Future of Black Chicago?,* edited by William Scarborough, Iván Arenas, and Amanda E. Lewis, 47–51. Institute for Research on Race and Public Policy, University of Illinois Chicago, January 2020. https://news.wttw.com/sites/default/files/article/file-attachments/Black%20Exodus%20IRRPP_StateOfRacialJustice_FutureOfBlackChicago.pdf.

Stremlau, Nicole. 2018. "Governance without Government in Somali Territories." *Journal of International Affairs* 71 (2): 73–89.

Sudbury, Julia. 2004. "A World without Prisons: Resisting Militarism, Globalized Punishment, and Empire." *Social Justice* 31 (1/2): 9–30.

Sulmasy, Glenn. 2009. "The Need for a National Security Court System." *Journal of Civil Rights and Economic Development* 23 (4): 1007–16.

Sulmasy, Glenn, and Andrea K. Logman. 2009. "A Hybrid Court for a Hybrid War." *Case Western Reserve Journal of International Law* 42 (1): 299–320.

Suskind, Ron. 2006. *The One Percent Doctrine: Deep inside America's Pursuit of Its Enemies since 9/11.* New York: Simon and Schuster.

Sutton, Jane. 2007. "Ban Word 'Terrorist' from U.S. Trial, Lawyer Asks." Reuters, March 16, 2007. https://www.reuters.com/article/us-usa-padilla/ban-word -terrorist-from-u-s-trial-lawyer-asks-idUSN1624043020070317.

Szpunar, Piotr M. 2017. "Premediating Predisposition: Informants, Entrapment, and Connectivity in Counterterrorism." *Critical Studies in Media Communication* 34 (4): 371–85. https://doi.org/10.1080/15295036.201 7.1319966.

Tait, David, and Jane Goodman-Delahunty. 2017. "Conclusions." In *Juries, Science, and Popular Culture in the Age of Terror: The Case of the Sydney Bomber,* edited by David Tait and Jane Goodman-Delahunty, 273–85. London: Palgrave Macmillan.

Teltumbde, Anand. 2017. "Examining the Logic of Revolutionary Violence." In *Revolutionary Violence versus Democracy: Narratives from India,* edited by Ajay Gudavarthy, 48–73. Los Angeles, Calif.: Sage.

Thorup, Mikkel. 2010. *An Intellectual History of Terror: War, Violence and the State.* London: Routledge.

Toal, Gerard. 1996. *Critical Geopolitics.* Minneapolis: University of Minnesota Press.

Tomuschat, Christian. 2015. "The Status of the 'Islamic State' under International Law." *Die Friedens-Warte* 90 (3/4): 223–44.

Tuck, Richard. 1999. *Rights of War and Peace: Political Thought and the International Order from Grotius to Kant.* Oxford: Oxford University Press.

Uberman, Matan, and Shaul Shay. 2016. "Hijrah According to the Islamic State: An Analysis of Dabiq." *Counter Terrorist Trends and Analyses* 8 (9): 16–20.

U.S. Attorney's Office, Northern District of Illinois. 2012. "Hillside Man Arrested after FBI Undercover Investigation on Federal Charges for Attempting to Bomb Downtown Chicago Bar." Press release, FBI, Chicago Division, Department of Justice, September 15, 2012. https://archives .fbi.gov/archives/chicago/press-releases/2012/hillside-man-arrested-after -fbi-undercover-investigation-on-federal-charges-for-attempting-to-bomb -downtown-chicago-bar.

U.S. Attorney's Office, Northern District of Illinois. 2018. "Chicago Man Charged with Conspiring to Support ISIS." Press release, Department of Justice, October 19, 2018. https://www.justice.gov/usao-ndil/pr/chicago -man-charged-conspiring-support-isis.

U.S. Attorney's Office, Southern District of Iowa. 2021. "Des Moines Woman Sentenced to Eight Years in Prison for Conspiracy to Damage the Dakota Access Pipeline." Press release, Department of Justice, June 30, 2021.

https://www.justice.gov/usao-sdia/pr/des-moines-woman-sentenced
-eight-years-prison-conspiracy-damage-dakota-access-pipeline.

Valdes, Francisco, Jerome McCristal Culp, and Angela P. Harris. 2002. "Introduction: Battles Waged, Won, and Lost: Critical Race Theory at the Turn
of the Millennium." In *Crossroads, Directions, and a New Critical Race
Theory,* edited by Francisco Valdes, Jerome McCristal Culp, and Angela P.
Harris, 1–6. Philadelphia, Pa.: Temple University Press.

Valensi, Carmit. 2015. "Non-state Actors: A Theoretical Limitation in a Changing Middle East." *Military and Strategic Affairs* 7 (1): 59–78.

Van Cleve, Nicole Gonzalez. 2016. *Crook County: Racism and Injustice in America's Largest Criminal Court.* Stanford, Calif.: Stanford University Press.

Verhoeven, Harry. 2009. "The Self-Fulfilling Prophecy of Failed States: Somalia, State Collapse and the Global War on Terror." *Journal of Eastern African Studies* 3 (3): 405–25. https://doi.org/10.1080/17531050903273719.

Vladeck, Steve. 2014. "The Supreme Court Goes to War: Hamdi, Padilla, and
Rasul at 10." *Just Security,* June 27, 2014. https://www.justsecurity.org/
12260/supreme-court-war/.

Volpp, Leti. 2002. "The Citizen and the Terrorist." *UCLA Law Review*
49:1575–1600.

Wagner, Rob. 2010. "Rehabilitation and Deradicalization: Saudi Arabi's Counterterrorism Successes and Failures." https://www.ideasforpeace.org/con
tent/rehabilitation-and-deradicalization-saudi-arabias-counterterrorism
-successes-and-failures/.

Walcott, John. 2017. "Trump Ends CIA Arms Support for Anti-Assad Syria
Rebels: U.S. Officials." Reuters, July 19, 2017. https://www.reuters.com/
article/us-mideast-crisis-usa-syria/trump-ends-cia-arms-support-for-anti
-assad-syria-rebels-u-s-officials-idUSKBN1A42KC.

Waldman, Amy. 2006. "Prophetic Justice." *Atlantic,* October 2006. https://
www.theatlantic.com/magazine/archive/2006/10/prophetic-justice/3052
34/.

Walia, Harsha. 2021. *Border and Rule: Global Migration, Capitalism, and the
Rise of Racist Nationalism.* Chicago, Ill.: Haymarket.

Walker, Rob Faure. 2021. *The Emergence of "Extremism": Exposing the Violent Discourse and Language of "Radicalization."* New York: Bloomsbury
Academic.

Wassenberg, Pinky. 2017. "U.S. Circuit Courts and the Application of the Terrorism Enhancement Provision." *Southern Illinois University Law Journal*
42 (1): 85–98.

Water Protector Legal Collective. 2019. "WPLC Concludes NoDAPL Criminal
Defense Program in North Dakota." Press release, Water Protector Legal

Collective, February 5, 2019. https://www.waterprotectorlegal.org/post/
wplc-concludes-nodapl-criminal-defense-program-in-north-dakota.

Weber, Max. 1946. "Politics as a Vocation." In *From Max Weber: Essays in Sociology*, edited by H. H. Gerth and C. Wright Mills, 77–128. Oxford: Oxford
University Press.

Weiser, Benjamin. 2011. "3 Men Draw 25-Year Terms in Synagogue Bomb
Plot." *New York Times,* June 29, 2011. https://www.nytimes.com/2011/06/
30/nyregion/3-men-get-25-years-in-plot-to-bomb-bronx-synagogues.html.

Weiser, Benjamin. 2014. "Jurors Convict Abu Ghaith, Bin Laden Son-in-Law,
in Terror Case." *New York Times,* March 26, 2014. https://www.nytimes
.com/2014/03/27/nyregion/bin-ladens-son-in-law-is-convicted-in-terror
-trial.html.

Whitlock, Craig. 2019. "At War with the Truth." *Washington Post,* December
9, 2019. https://www.washingtonpost.com/graphics/2019/investigations/
afghanistan-papers/afghanistan-war-confidential-documents/.

Wiktorowicz, Quintan. 2005. *Radical Islam Rising: Muslim Extremism in the
West.* Lanham, Md.: Rowman & Littlefield.

Wilkinson, Paul. 2007. "The Threat from the Al-Qaeda Network." In *Homeland Security in the U.K.: Future Preparedness for Terrorist Attack since 9/11,*
edited by Paul Wilkinson, 25–36. London: Routledge.

Williams, Michael J., John G. Horgan, and William P. Evans. 2016. "Evaluation
of a Multi-faceted, U.S. Community-Based, Muslim-Led CVE Program."
Office of Justice Programs, Department of Justice, June 2016. https://
www.ojp.gov/ncjrs/virtual-library/abstracts/evaluation-multi-faceted-us
-community-based-muslim-led-cve-program.

Wise, Rob. 2008. "Al Shabaab." Center for Strategic and International Studies
(CSIS), July 2011. https://csis-website-prod.s3.amazonaws.com/s3fs-pub
lic/legacy_files/files/publication/110715_Wise_AlShabaab_AQAM%20
Futures%20Case%20Study_WEB.pdf.

Witt, John Fabian. 2012. *Lincoln's Code: The Laws of War in American History.*
New York: Free Press.

Wood, Graeme. 2019. "I Wrote to John Walker Lindh. He Wrote Back."
Atlantic, May 23, 2019. https://www.theatlantic.com/ideas/archive/2019/
05/my-letters-john-walker-lindh-american-jidahist/590071/.

World Organization for Resource Development and Education. 2014. "COPS
Application." Montgomery Village, Md.: World Organization for Resource
Development and Education.

Wright, Robin. 2016. "How the Curse of Sykes-Picot Still Haunts the Middle
East." *New Yorker,* April 30, 2016. https://www.newyorker.com/news/
news-desk/how-the-curse-of-sykes-picot-still-haunts-the-middle-east.

Yang, Wesley. 2010. "The Terrorist Search Engine." *New York Magazine,* December 2010. https://nymag.com/news/features/69920/.

Yoo, John. 2006. "Courts at War." *Cornell Law Review* 91 (2): 573–601.

Yoo, John. 2010. "The Ghailani Verdict and the War on Terror." *Wall Street Journal,* November 20, 2010. https://www.wsj.com/articles/SB10001424 052748704170404575624301340456756.

Yoo, John, and Robert J. Delahunty. 2002. "Re: Application of Treaties and Laws to al Qaeda and Taliban Detainees." Office of Legal Counsel, Department of Justice, January 22, 2002. https://www.justice.gov/sites/default/files/ olc/legacy/2009/08/24/memo-laws-taliban-detainees.pdf.

Yuen, Laura, and Doualy Xaykaothao. 2016. "Judge Sentences Three Men to Decades in Prison in ISIS Trial." *MPR (Minnesota Public Radio) News,* November 16, 2016. https://www.mprnews.org/story/2016/11/16/third -day-of-isis-trial.

Zabel, Richard B., and James J. Benjamin Jr. 2008. "In Pursuit of Justice: Prosecuting Terrorism Cases in the Federal Courts." White paper, Human Rights First, May 2008. https://www.akingump.com/a/web/22428/0805 21-USLS-pursuit-justice.pdf.

Zedner, Lucia. 2007. "Pre-crime and Post-criminology?" *Theoretical Criminology* 11 (2): 261–81. https://doi.org/10.1177/1362480607075851.

Zulaika, Joseba, and William Douglass. 1996. *Terror and Taboo: The Follies, Fables, and Faces of Terrorism.* New York: Routledge.

INDEX

Daoud and, 310, 314; deceptive strategies by, 312; influence of, 313; informants for, 291; Khan and, 303; Mohamud and, 303, 305; Osadzinski and, 323; Osmakac and, 177; radicalization and, 272–73, 279, 290–91; terrorism protection and, 10, 290, 319; undercover operations and, 291, 292

federal courts, 88; global war on terror and, 75, 89, 90; military commission failures and, 74–86; prosecution in, 80, 196; rule of law and, 75. *See also* Article III courts

Federal Rules of Evidence, 40, 220, 221, 297

Federal Rules of Evidence 401, 237

Federal Rules of Evidence 402, 237

Federal Rules of Evidence 403, 237, 239, 352n62

Federal Rules of Evidence 609, 231

Federal Rules of Evidence 701, 237

Federal Rules of Evidence 702, 220, 236

First Amendment, 133, 167, 298, 301, 320, 324, 325, 360n35

First Geneva Convention for the Amelioration of the Condition of the Wounded and Sick Armed Forces in the Field (1864), 47

Foreign Intelligence Surveillance Act (FISA), 134

Foreign Intelligence Surveillance Court Review, 327

foreign policy, 89, 93, 253, 326; imperialist, 34; violent responses to, 264

foreign terrorist organizations (FTOs), 79, 84, 85, 86, 95, 97,

100, 102, 103, 106, 107, 121, 137, 198, 310

Forrest, Katherine, 232, 242

Fort Hood, 329

Fort Sumter, 62

Foucault, Michel, 72

Free Syrian Army, 107, 121, 122, 128, 129, 132; Assad and, 130–31; ISIS and, 132

Fricker, Miranda, 235, 262, 355n49

FTOs. *See* foreign terrorist organizations

fundamentalism, 215, 288; terrorism and, 71, 134–41

Galton, Francis, 17

Gandur, Moses, 348n3

Garcia, Michael, 226

gender equity, 178

General Orders Number 20, 44, 46

Geneva Convention, 47, 48, 49, 114, 120, 142; POW protections and, 60; Protocol I and, 109. *See also* Third Geneva Convention

Geneva Convention III Relative to the Treatment of Prisoners of War, 48, 64, 114

Geneva Convention III Treatment of Prisoners of War (GPW), 116, 117

genocide: Muslim, 252; war and, 48, 166

geopolitical conflicts, 123, 187, 200; adjudicating, 102–8

geopolitical imagination, 100, 102, 171

geopolitical knowledge, 113; levels of, 127; sentencing and, 125–34

geopolitics, 12, 20, 36, 74, 92, 93, 97, 101, 143, 154, 188, 190;

328; global war on terror and,
335; a priori, 328; structural, 201;
terrorism and, 151
radicalization, 59, 185, 267, 280–81,
298, 306, 335; attempting, 290;
concept of, 268, 270, 278, 284,
286, 287; cycle, 272; models, 276,
281, 282, 286; prisons and, 268;
state-sponsored, 322; terrorist,
142, 184, 268, 271, 273, 275,
281, 284, 285, 287, 288; warning
signs of, 278, 287, 289
Radicalization in the West (Silber and
Bhatt), 273
radicalization process, 273, 275,
278, 280, 286, 287, 288;
behaviors/trajectory of, 274;
centrality of, 274; working
models of, 272
radicalization research, 37, 269, 271,
274, 278, 289–90, 295, 297, 300,
301, 307, 308, 314, 319–22;
assumptions of, 288; concerns
with, 280, 283; examination of,
270; FBI and, 290–91; law
enforcement and, 307; legal life
of, 37; methodological limitations
of, 280–87; racial profiling and,
284; rejecting, 279; scientific
insight and, 285
radicalization theories, 265, 269–70,
271–78, 283, 285, 288, 301;
entrapment defense and, 290–99;
national security and, 279; state-
sponsored, 268–69
Rand Corporation, 206–7, 211
Ranstorp, Magnus, 240
Rascoff, Samuel J., 80
Rasul, Shafiq, 66
Rasul v. Bush (2004), 65–66, 71

Razack, Sherene H., 151
recidivism, 2, 198, 199, 313
Red Crescent, 312
refugee camps, 104, 135, 137, 174
rehabilitation, 2, 80, 164, 184, 199,
267; capacity for, 200; custodial/
community, 81
religion, 151, 152–53, 297, 307,
339n18; physical experience and,
337n3
Reznicek, Jessica, 10, 338n11
risk assessments, 185, 267, 268, 286
Roosevelt, Franklin D., 61, 341n13
Ross, John, 148, 149, 150
Ross v. McIntyre (1891), 148, 150
Roth, Jessica A., 296
Rousseau, Kevin, 340n11
rule of law, 75, 136, 327; global war
on terror and, 2–3; upholding, 3,
62
Rumsfeld, Donald, 39, 114, 142,
207, 270, 343n1; Guantánamo
detainees and, 230; memos by,
93–94

Sack, Gerald, 249
Sageman, Marc, 173, 218, 223, 233,
238, 280, 306; Kohlmann and,
239, 240; on political violence,
281; on radicalization process,
274, 275
Said, Edward, 169
Said, Wadie E., 150, 167, 218, 224,
297; terrorism and, 4; on violent/
nonviolent crimes, 83
Salafi-jihad, invention of, 164–72
Salafis, 165, 168, 175, 184, 186,
273, 274; classification of, 185
Salafism, 171, 185, 200, 279;
philosophy/theology of, 165,

239, 243–44; defining, 7, 74,
154, 155, 156, 158, 159, 171,
184, 212, 250, 331; degrees of, 8,
155–61, 197; emergence of, 84,
206, 286; engaging in, 190, 275,
299; federal crime of, 8, 82, 135,
137, 138, 154, 156, 161, 163,
177, 217, 295, 296, 311, 325;
fighting, 89, 130, 182, 257;
homegrown, 7, 10, 83, 154, 175,
176, 216, 271–78, 282, 291, 321,
328; incapacitation of, 85, 100,
290; orthodox, 20, 31, 34, 37,
205, 208, 213, 217, 237, 243,
244, 246, 249, 258, 259, 261,
264, 265; political, 20, 21, 26–35;
potential, 5, 153, 287; preventing,
40, 84, 85; rethinking, 210, 300,
330–36; as social/political process,
210; sociological interpretations
of, 155; state-sponsored, 207,
322; status of, 72, 73, 219–20;
understanding, 8, 21, 34, 88, 153,
155, 161, 164, 171, 210, 212,
225, 237, 244, 260, 261. *See also*
new terrorism thesis
terrorism charges: changes in, 102;
criminal cases and, 244–47, 258
terrorism enhancement, 8, 10, 82,
83, 90, 133, 138, 141, 153,
318–19; applying, 104, 154, 155,
156–57, 159, 161–67, 177, 200,
349n40; legal struggles over,
155–61
terrorism expertise, 218–20, 222;
legal challenges to, 247–49;
questioning, 239, 240–41. *See
also* terrorologists
terrorism prosecutions, 3, 6, 72,
74–86, 89, 140, 143, 152,

182–83, 219, 329, 335; aftermath
of, 13–26; alternatives to, 14, 38,
102; concept-work and, 172; epistemic injustice and, 244, 258–65;
exploring, 35–38, 90, 102; immersion in, 14–15, 330; personhood
and, 153; strategies for, 257
terrorism-related cases, 5, 77, 102,
118, 128, 133, 183, 184, 203,
219, 221, 244, 254, 260, 262;
adjudication of, 3, 6, 12–13, 14,
37, 38, 86, 87–88, 90, 100, 101,
134, 205, 212, 220, 223, 237,
246, 310; combatant immunity
and, 123; complications of, 127,
232; contextualizing, 97; expert
witnesses and, 220, 225; factual
evidence in, 21, 37; genre of, 94;
gradations of, 170; outcomes in,
103, 161, 326; politics and, 3,
280; radicalization and, 280–81;
scientific methodology in, 222
terrorism-related crimes, 2, 8, 9, 74,
78–79, 88, 97, 112, 119, 125,
153, 182, 196, 198, 216–17, 245,
260; committing, 155, 297, 319;
conviction for, 82, 85, 319;
punishment for, 308–10; terrorologists and, 212
terrorism studies, 32, 151, 214,
225, 237, 258, 261, 271–72, 326;
academic knowledge and, 240;
critiques of, 21, 223, 241; establishing, 205, 206–12; funding for,
207, 222; impact of, 240, 243;
integrity of, 220; prioritization of,
208; scientific method and, 211;
status of, 259
terrorist acts, 27, 174, 181, 207,
217, 311, 315, 319; committing,

managerial approach to, 35; neo-
imperial, 35; new grammar of,
51–57; regulating, 44, 46, 48, 54;
rules of, 46, 119; symmetric, 52.
See also civil war; global war on
terror; holy war
war crimes, 47, 61–62, 80, 85, 87
Warsame, Abdirizak, 182, 268,
353n122, 359n1
wartime powers, constraints on,
65–71
Washington Post, 93
water protectors, 9, 10, 11, 15
weapons of mass destruction, 52,
214, 215, 216, 217
Weber, Max, 109
Wells, Melody, 323
whiteness, 145, 146, 148, 238
white supremacy, 11, 284, 335
Whitlock, Craig, 92

Wilkinson, Paul, 216
Wise, Rob, 137
witnesses: credibility of, 231;
impeachment of, 231; treatment
of, 227. *See also* expert witnesses
Woog, Amanda, 142, 328
World Food Programme, 137
World War II, 47, 65, 70
Wray, Christopher, 11

Yamashita, Tomoyuki, 61–62
Yoo, John, 75, 339n4
Youssef (undercover agent), 304,
308
Yugoslav wars, 251
Yusuf, Abdullahi, 182, 267, 359n1

Zabel, Richard B., 3
Zelin, Aaron, 325
Zuley, Richard, 338n13

Nicole Nguyen is associate professor of criminology, law, and justice at the University of Illinois Chicago. She is author of *A Curriculum of Fear: Homeland Security in U.S. Public Schools* (Minnesota, 2016) and *Suspect Communities: Anti-Muslim Racism and the Domestic War on Terror* (Minnesota, 2019).